Cisco Certified Support T[...]
Cybersecurity 100-160 O[...]

T0073904

Companion Website and Pearson [...]de

Access interactive study tools on this book's companion website, including practice test software, review exercises, Key Term flash card application, a study planner, and more!

To access the companion website, simply follow these steps:

1. Go to www.ciscopress.com/register.

2. Enter the **print book ISBN**: 9780138203924.

3. Answer the security question to validate your purchase.

4. Go to your account page.

5. Click on the **Registered Products** tab.

6. Under the book listing, click on the **Access Bonus Content** link.

When you register your book, your Pearson Test Prep practice test access code will automatically be populated with the book listing under the Registered Products tab. You will need this code to access the practice test that comes with this book. You can redeem the code at **PearsonTestPrep.com**. Simply choose Pearson IT Certification as your product group and log into the site with the same credentials you used to register your book. Click the **Activate New Product** button and enter the access code. More detailed instructions on how to redeem your access code for both the online and desktop versions can be found on the companion website.

If you have any issues accessing the companion website or obtaining your Pearson Test Prep practice test access code, you can contact our support team by going to **pearsonitp.echelp.org**.

Cisco Certified Support Technician (CCST) Cybersecurity

100-160

Official Cert Guide

SHANE SEXTON

RAYMOND LACOSTE

Cisco Press

Cisco Certified Support Technician (CCST) Cybersecurity 100-160 Official Cert Guide

Shane Sexton and Raymond Lacoste

Copyright © 2024 Pearson Education, Inc.

Published by Cisco Press

Hoboken, New Jersey

1 2024

Library of Congress Control Number: 2023951714

ISBN-13: 978-0-13-820392-4

ISBN-10: 0-13-820392-X

Warning and Disclaimer

This book is designed to provide information about the Cisco Certified Support Technician (CCST) Cybersecurity 100-160 exam. Every effort has been made to make this book as complete and as accurate as possible, but no warranty or fitness is implied.

The information is provided on an "as is" basis. The authors, Cisco Press, and Cisco Systems, Inc. shall have neither liability nor responsibility to any person or entity with respect to any loss or damages arising from the information contained in this book or from the use of the discs or programs that may accompany it.

The opinions expressed in this book belong to the author and are not necessarily those of Cisco Systems, Inc.

Trademark Acknowledgments

All terms mentioned in this book that are known to be trademarks or service marks have been appropriately capitalized. Cisco Press or Cisco Systems, Inc., cannot attest to the accuracy of this information. Use of a term in this book should not be regarded as affecting the validity of any trademark or service mark.

All terms mentioned in this book that are known to be trademarks or service marks have been appropriately capitalized. Pearson IT Certification cannot attest to the accuracy of this information. Use of a term in this book should not be regarded as affecting the validity of any trademark or service mark.

Microsoft and/or its respective suppliers make no representations about the suitability of the information contained in the documents and related graphics published as part of the services for any purpose. All such documents and related graphics are provided "as is" without warranty of any kind. Microsoft and/or its respective suppliers hereby disclaim all warranties and conditions with regard to this information, including all warranties and conditions of merchantability, whether express, implied or statutory, fitness for a particular purpose, title and non-infringement. In no event shall Microsoft and/or its respective suppliers be liable for any special, indirect or consequential damages or any damages whatsoever resulting from loss of use, data or profits, whether in an action of contract, negligence or other tortious action, arising out of or in connection with the use or performance of information available from the services.

The documents and related graphics contained herein could include technical inaccuracies or typographical errors. Changes are periodically added to the information herein. Microsoft and/or its respective suppliers may make improvements and/or changes in the product(s) and/or the program(s) described herein at any time. Partial screenshots may be viewed in full within the software version specified.

Microsoft® and Windows® are registered trademarks of the Microsoft Corporation in the U.S.A. and other countries. Screenshots and icons reprinted with permission from the Microsoft Corporation. This book is not sponsored or endorsed by or affiliated with the Microsoft Corporation.

Special Sales

For information about buying this title in bulk quantities, or for special sales opportunities (which may include electronic versions; custom cover designs; and content particular to your business, training goals, marketing focus, or branding interests), please contact our corporate sales department at corpsales@pearsoned.com or (800) 382-3419.

For government sales inquiries, please contact governmentsales@pearsoned.com.

For questions about sales outside the U.S., please contact intlcs@pearson.com.

Feedback Information

At Cisco Press, our goal is to create in-depth technical books of the highest quality and value. Each book is crafted with care and precision, undergoing rigorous development that involves the unique expertise of members from the professional technical community.

Readers' feedback is a natural continuation of this process. If you have any comments regarding how we could improve the quality of this book, or otherwise alter it to better suit your needs, you can contact us through email at feedback@ciscopress.com. Please make sure to include the book title and ISBN in your message.

We greatly appreciate your assistance.

Vice President, IT Professional: Mark Taub	**Copy Editor:** Kitty Wilson
Alliances Manager, Cisco Press: Caroline Antonio	**Technical Editor:** Russell Long
Director, ITP Product Management: Brett Bartow	**Editorial Assistant:** Cindy Teeters
Executive Editor: James Manly	**Cover Designer:** Chuti Prasertsith
Managing Editor: Sandra Schroeder	**Composition:** codeMantra
Development Editor: Ellie Bru	**Indexer:** Timothy Wright
Senior Project Editor: Tonya Simpson	**Proofreader:** Barbara Mack

Please contact us with concerns about any potential bias at www.pearson.com/report-bias.html.

Americas Headquarters
Cisco Systems, Inc.
San Jose, CA

Asia Pacific Headquarters
Cisco Systems (USA) Pte. Ltd.
Singapore

Europe Headquarters
Cisco Systems International BV Amsterdam,
The Netherlands

Cisco has more than 200 offices worldwide. Addresses, phone numbers, and fax numbers are listed on the Cisco Website at **www.cisco.com/go**

Cisco and the Cisco logo are trademarks or registered trademarks of Cisco and/or its affiliates in the U.S. and other countries. To view a list of Cisco trad
to this URL: www.cisco.com/go/trademarks. Third party trademarks mentioned are the property of their respective owners. The use of the word partner
a partnership relationship between Cisco and any other company. (1110R)

About the Authors

Shane Sexton has spent years learning and teaching all things IT. He holds CCNP Security, CND, CySA+, CCNA CyberOps, and numerous other certifications and has prepared thousands of students to take these exams. Shane earned bachelor's degrees in technology management and liberal studies (and wishes he'd taken fewer philosophy classes). He currently works as a network and system administrator at an MSP, where every day brings new learning opportunities. When he's not tackling IT emergencies, Shane practices piano, reads anything nonfiction, and expertly avoids family members with printer issues. He currently resides in Phoenix, Arizona, with three cats who have no respect for his property or the rule of law.

Raymond Lacoste has dedicated his career to developing the skills of those interested in IT. In 2001, he began to mentor hundreds of IT professionals pursuing their Cisco certification dreams. This role led to teaching Cisco courses full time. Raymond is currently a master instructor for Cisco Enterprise Routing and Switching, AWS, ITIL, and Cybersecurity at Stormwind Studios. Raymond treats all technologies as an escape room, working to uncover every mystery in the protocols he works with. Along this journey, Raymond has passed more than 120 exams, and his office wall includes certificates from Microsoft, Cisco, ISC2, ITIL, AWS, and CompTIA. If you were visualizing Raymond's office, you'd probably expect the usual network equipment, certifications, and awards. Those certainly take up space, but they aren't his pride and joy. Most impressive, at least to Raymond, is his gemstone and mineral collection; once he starts talking about it, he just can't stop. Who doesn't get excited by a wondrous barite specimen in a pyrite matrix? Raymond presently resides with his wife and two children in eastern Canada, where they experience many adventures together.

About the Technical Reviewer

The first time **Russell Long** opened a computer in the late 1980s was to install the latest and greatest technology of the time: a sound card. That interest later turned into a profession. Since then, he's held 13 different IT certifications in addition to a CCSI. All these years later, he still finds himself digging into computer technologies and doing his best to optimize them. He's on the tail end of his second decade of working in IT and working toward his second decade of instructing and teaching IT. Russell's favorite IT disciplines include networking (wireless included), security, and virtualization. He hopes to pass on the information he has learned to those looking to make a career in IT.

Dedications

Shane Sexton:

I'd like to dedicate this book to everyone who has supported and mentored me over the years. Dan Young and the entire Stormwind Studios crew have fostered a fun and supportive environment where I nerded out for a living. I also dedicate this book to my mom, who's been in my corner during life's ups and downs and has always been my cheerleader. And to Ashley, for the many times she's held me up, for learning to "adult" together, and for all the good memories we've made on the way. Thank you all!

Raymond Lacoste:

To my beloved daughter Rylie,

Your presence in my life has enriched it in countless ways, and I'm eternally thankful for the love, joy, and inspiration you bring to our entire family. You have an infectious personality that is filled with compassion, thoughtfulness, and caring that will continue to light up the lives of those fortunate enough to know you.

Rylie, this book is dedicated to you as a symbol of my hopes and dreams for your future. Your presence in my life has inspired me to reach for the stars. May this book be a source of empowerment as you continue to grow and conquer new horizons. Always remember that you are capable of achieving greatness, and my love and support will be with you every step of the way.

Love,

Daddy

Acknowledgments

Shane Sexton:

Thanks to James, Ellie, Brett, and everyone else at Cisco Press. It has been an absolute pleasure to work with you, and I appreciate your patience and help while I learned the ropes. A giant thank you to Raymond Lacoste, who mentored me as a new instructor and now as a new author. Finally, an extra-giant thanks to Russ Long, for opening this unexpected door for me, for your excellent technical review, and for being a solid friend.

Raymond Lacoste:

A huge thank you to Shane for bringing me along on this writing adventure. Combining our skills and knowledge for this book was the right decision. Shane, keep on being amazing!

Thanks to James, Ellie, Brett, Tonya, Kitty, and everyone else who made this book come to life. Without the amazing team behind the scenes, this book would be a bunch of virtual crumpled-up pieces of paper on the floor surrounding a wastepaper basket. So, THANK YOU for taking our garbage and making it useful! :)

To Russ Long, a great trusted friend who has been by my side for 10+ years on many projects. Russ, you are an amazing person. Thank you for always being there for me.

And finally, a big thank you to my family, who supported me through the ups and downs. Without you, this book would not have happened.

Contents at a Glance

Online Elements

Contents

Icons Used in This Book

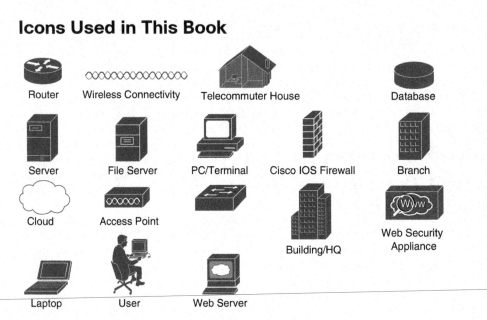

Command Syntax Conventions

The conventions used to present command syntax in this book are the same conventions used in the IOS Command Reference. The Command Reference describes these conventions as follows:

- **Boldface** indicates commands and keywords that are entered literally as shown. In actual configuration examples and output (not general command syntax), boldface indicates commands that are manually input by the user (such as a **show** command).

- *Italic* indicates arguments for which you supply actual values.

- Vertical bars (|) separate alternative, mutually exclusive elements.

- Square brackets ([ ]) indicate an optional element.

- Braces ({ }) indicate a required choice.

- Braces within brackets ([{ }]) indicate a required choice within an optional element.

Introduction

Congratulations! If you are reading this introduction, then you have probably decided that security is an important part of your future success and that obtaining security certifications will prove that you have a solid understanding of security related topics and concepts.

Professional certifications have been an important part of the computing industry for many years and will continue to be important for years to come. Many reasons exist for these certifications, but the most popularly cited reason is credibility. All other qualifications being equal, a certified employee/consultant/job candidate is considered more valuable than one who is not certified.

So, this book was written to help anyone from up-and-coming IT professionals to veterans of the IT industry build a solid foundational understanding of cybersecurity. This book is structured specifically to prepare candidates for the CCST Cybersecurity (100-160) exam but aims to equip you with knowledge that will remain useful long after you earn the certification.

Goals and Methods

The most important and somewhat obvious goal of this book is to help you pass the CCST Cybersecurity (100-160) exam. In fact, if the primary objective of this book were different, then the book's title would be misleading; however, the methods used in this book to help you pass the CCST Cybersecurity exam are designed to also make you much more knowledgeable about how to do your job. While this book has more than enough questions to help you prepare for the actual exam, the goal isn't to have you simply memorize as many questions and answers as you possibly can.

In this book, we help you discover the exam topics that you need to review in more depth, help you fully understand and remember those details, and help you prove to yourself that you have retained your knowledge of those topics. So, this book does not try to help you pass by memorization but helps you truly learn and understand the topics.

The knowledge the CCST Cybersecurity exam covers is vital for any cybersecurity professional. This book would do you a disservice if it didn't attempt to help you learn the material. To that end, this book helps you pass the CCST Cybersecurity exam by using the following methods:

- Helping you discover which test topics you have not mastered

- Providing explanations and information to fill in your knowledge gaps

- Supplying exercises and scenarios that enhance your ability to recall and deduce the answers to test questions

- Providing practice exercises on the topics and the testing process

Who Should Read This Book?

This book is geared toward new IT professionals and those with an interest in learning about cybersecurity; however, veteran IT professionals just getting into security or needing to obtain the certification will benefit as well. Although other objectives can be achieved from using this book, the book is written with one goal in mind: to help you pass the exam.

So why should you want to pass the CCST Cybersecurity exam? Earning the certification validates your understanding of core cybersecurity concepts and techniques. Furthermore, the CCST Cybersecurity certification serves as a springboard to more advanced certifications down the road. Many of the concepts and themes we introduce here are practically universal in cybersecurity exams.

Strategies for Exam Preparation

The strategy you use to prepare for the CCST Cybersecurity exam might be slightly different from the strategies used by other readers, mainly depending on the skills, knowledge, and experience you have already obtained. For instance, if you are already familiar with security concepts and techniques, your approach will likely differ from that of a person who is brand new to cybersecurity.

Regardless of the strategy you use or the background you have, this book is designed to help you get to the point where you can pass the exam with the least amount of time required. For instance, there is no need for you to practice or read about access management if you fully understand it already. However, many people like to make sure that they truly know a topic and thus read over material that they already know. Several book features will help you gain the confidence you need to be convinced that you know some material already and to also help you know what topics you need to study more.

The Companion Website for Online Content Review

All the electronic review elements, as well as other electronic components of the book, exist on this book's companion website.

How to Access the Companion Website

To access the companion website, which gives you access to the electronic content for this book, start by establishing a login at ciscopress.com and register your book. To do so, simply go to ciscopress.com/register and enter the ISBN of the print book: 9780138203924. After you have registered your book, go to your account page and click the Registered Products tab. From there, click the Access Bonus Content link to get access to the book's companion website.

Note that if you buy the Premium Edition eBook and Practice Test version of this book from Cisco Press, your book will automatically be registered on your account page.

Simply go to your account page, click the Registered Products tab, and select Access Bonus Content to access the book's companion website.

How to Access the Pearson Test Prep (PTP) App

You have two options for installing and using the Pearson Test Prep application: a web app and a desktop app. To use the Pearson Test Prep application, start by finding the registration code that comes with the book. You can find the code in these ways:

- **Print book or bookseller eBook versions:** You can get your access code by registering the print ISBN 9780138203924 on ciscopress.com/register. Make sure to use the print book ISBN regardless of whether you purchased an eBook or the print book. Once you register the book, your access code will be populated on your account page under the Registered Products tab. Instructions for how to redeem the code are available on the book's companion website by clicking the Access Bonus Content link.

- **Premium Edition:** If you purchase the Premium Edition eBook and Practice Test directly from the Cisco Press website, the code will be populated on your account page after purchase. Just log in at www.ciscopress.com, click Account to see details of your account, and click the digital purchases tab.

NOTE Do not lose the activation code because it is the only means with which you can access the QA content with the book.

When you have the access code, to find instructions about both the PTP web app and the desktop app, follow these steps:

Step 1. Open this book's companion website, as shown earlier in this Introduction under the heading "How to Access the Companion Website.

Step 2. Click the **Practice Exams** button.

Step 3. Follow the instructions listed there both for installing the desktop app and for using the web app.

Note that if you want to use the web app only at this point, just navigate to www.pearsontestprep.com, establish a free login if you do not already have one, and register this book's practice tests using the registration code you just found. The process should take only a couple of minutes.

How This Book Is Organized

Although this book could be read cover to cover, it is designed to be flexible and allow you to easily move between chapters and sections of chapters to cover just the material that you need more work with. Chapters 1 through 15 are the core chapters and can be covered in any order. If you do intend to read them all, the order in the book is an excellent sequence to use.

The core chapters, Chapters 1 through 15, cover the following topics:

- **Chapter 1, "Security Principles":** This chapter introduces core security concepts such as the CIA triad, vulnerabilities, threats, and risk. It also covers different types of attackers and common defensive measures.

- **Chapter 2, "Common Threats, Attacks, and Vulnerabilities":** This chapter discusses vulnerabilities and attacks that target hosts and networks. It also addresses the most common social engineering attacks, which target people.

- **Chapter 3, "Access Management":** This chapter covers authentication, authorization, and accounting (AAA). It describes various authentication mechanisms that can be used with AAA and concludes with an introduction to a common AAA protocol called RADIUS.

- **Chapter 4, "Cryptography":** This chapter introduces the basics of cryptography: its vocabulary, symmetric and asymmetric algorithms, and common applications of each.

- **Chapter 5, "Introduction to Networking, Addressing, and TCP/IP Protocols":** This chapter provides a crash course in networking. It introduces you to the OSI model and the TCP/IP stack. In addition, it provides you with an understanding of common TCP/IP protocols and their vulnerabilities. To wrap up, the chapter discusses network addressing and its impact on security.

- **Chapter 6, "Network Infrastructure":** This chapter discusses architectural concepts and commonly used network appliances. It introduces demilitarized zones (DMZs) and their uses and considerations for virtualized and cloud environments. It also describes common network appliances, such as proxies, honeypots, and intrusion detection systems (IDSs) and intrusion prevention systems (IPSs).

- **Chapter 7, "Controlling Network Access":** This chapter describes how network traffic can be shielded and controlled. It begins with a description of virtual private networks (VPNs) and their use cases. Next, it explains firewalls and access control lists (ACLs). The chapter concludes with a description of network access control (NAC), which grants extensive control over the devices allowed on your networks.

- **Chapter 8, "Wireless SOHO Security":** This chapter introduces how small office/home office (SOHO) wireless devices are secured. It describes the administrative interface, wireless encryption standards, and authentication mechanisms. Other considerations, such as the SSID, MAC address filtering, and firmware updates, are also covered. The chapter concludes by describing common attacks against wireless networks.

- **Chapter 9, "Operating Systems and Tools":** This chapter introduces common operating systems, such as Windows, macOS, and Linux. For each operating system, this chapter describes integrated security features. The chapter concludes by covering common security tools used on endpoints.

- **Chapter 10, "Endpoint Policies and Standards":** This chapter discusses various management considerations for endpoint devices. It begins with an introduction to asset inventories and their importance. Then it covers ubiquitous management tasks such as program deployment and data backups. The chapter concludes by describing bring your own device (BYOD) and regulatory considerations.

- **Chapter 11, "Network and Endpoint Malware Detection and Remediation":** This chapter introduces antimalware technologies. It describes how malware signatures work, different approaches to scanning, and Cisco's Advanced Malware Protection (AMP) technology. The chapter finishes with some best practices for malware remediation.

- **Chapter 12, "Risk and Vulnerability Management":** This chapter covers vulnerabilities and risk in more detail. It begins with a description of vulnerability management processes, tools, and techniques. Then it explains the broader topics of risk prioritization and management.

- **Chapter 13, "Threat Intelligence":** This chapter discusses threat intelligence, its sources, and its benefits. It describes intelligence sources such as vulnerability feeds, reports, and news articles. Then it covers collective and automated approaches to threat intelligence and the basics of Structured Threat Information Expression (STIX) and Trusted Automated Exchange of Intelligence Information (TAXII). The chapter concludes with a look at why sharing threat intelligence is beneficial.

- **Chapter 14, "Disaster Recovery and Business Continuity":** This chapter looks at how businesses plan for, survive, and recover from catastrophic events. It describes disaster recovery plans (DRPs), business impact analyses (BIAs), and business continuity plans (BCPs) and explores their similarities, differences, and relationships.

- **Chapter 15, "Incident Handling":** This chapter introduces what incidents are and discusses NIST's four phases of incident response. It also describes several attack frameworks (ways of thinking about attacks) and basic forensic concepts such as data volatility and chain of custody. The chapter ends with a discussion of how regulations impact the incident response process.

Certification Exam Topics and This Book

The questions for each certification exam are a closely guarded secret; however, we do know which topics you must know to *successfully* complete this exam. Cisco publishes them as an exam blueprint for Implementing CCST Cybersecurity (100-160). Table I-1 lists each exam topic listed in the blueprint along with a reference to the book chapter that covers the topic.

Table I-1   CCST Cybersecurity (100-160) Topics and Chapter References

CCST Cybersecurity	Chapter(s) in Which Topic Is Covered
1. Essential Security Principles	
1.1. Define essential security principles	1
1.2. Explain common threats and vulnerabilities	2
1.3. Explain access management principles	3
1.4. Explain encryption methods and applications	4
2. Basic Network Security Concepts	
2.1. Describe TCP/IP protocol vulnerabilities	5
2.2. Explain how network addresses impact network security	5

CCST Cybersecurity	Chapter(s) in Which Topic Is Covered
2.3. Describe network infrastructure and technologies	6
2.4. Set up a secure wireless SoHo network	8
2.5. Implement secure access technologies	7
3. Endpoint Security Concepts	
3.1. Describe operating system security concepts	9
3.2. Demonstrate familiarity with appropriate endpoint tools that gather security assessment information	9
3.3. Verify that endpoint systems meet security policies and standards	10
3.4. Implement software and hardware updates	9
3.5. Interpret system logs	9
3.6. Demonstrate familiarity with malware removal	11
4. Vulnerability Assessment and Risk Management	
4.1. Explain vulnerability management	12
4.2. Use threat intelligence techniques to identify potential network vulnerabilities	13
4.3. Explain risk management	12
4.4. Explain the importance of disaster recovery and business continuity planning	14
5. Incident Handling	
5.1. Monitor security events and know when escalation is required	15
5.2. Explain digital forensics and attack attribution processes	15
5.3. Explain the impact of compliance frameworks on incident handling	15
5.4. Describe the elements of cybersecurity incident response	15

The goal of this book is to provide the most comprehensive coverage to ensure that you are well prepared for the exam. Although some chapters might not address specific exam topics, they provide a foundation that is necessary for a clear understanding of important topics. Your short-term goal might be to pass this exam, but your long-term goal should be to become a qualified cybersecurity professional.

It is also important to understand that this book is a "static" reference, whereas the exam topics are dynamic. Cisco can and does change the topics covered on certification exams often.

This exam guide should not be your only reference when preparing for the certification exam. You can find a wealth of information available at Cisco.com that covers each topic in great detail. If you think you need more detailed information on a specific topic, read the Cisco documentation that focuses on that topic.

Note that as cybersecurity technologies continue to develop, Cisco reserves the right to change the exam topics without notice. Although you can refer to the list of exam topics in Table I-1, always check Cisco.com to verify the actual list of topics to ensure that you are prepared before taking the exam. You can view the current exam topics on any current Cisco certification exam by visiting the Cisco.com website, hovering over Training & Events, and selecting from the Certifications list. Note also that, if needed, Cisco Press might post additional preparatory content on the web page associated with this book at http://www.ciscopress.com/title/9780138203924. It's a good idea to check the website a couple of weeks before taking your exam to be sure that you have up-to-date content.

Taking the CCST Cybersecurity Certification Exam

As with any Cisco certification exam, you should strive to be thoroughly prepared before taking the exam. There is no way to determine exactly what questions are on the exam, so the best way to prepare is to have a good working knowledge of all subjects covered on it. Schedule the exam and be sure to be rested and ready to focus when taking it.

The best place to find out the latest available Cisco training and certifications is under the Training & Events section at Cisco.com.

Tracking Your Status

You can track your certification progress by checking http://www.cisco.com/go/certifications/login. You must create an account the first time you log in to the site.

How to Prepare for an Exam

The best way to prepare for any certification exam is to use a combination of the preparation resources, labs, and practice tests. This guide has integrated some practice questions and example scenarios to help you better prepare. If possible, get some hands-on experience with Cisco Cybersecurity equipment. There is no substitute for real-world experience.

Assessing Exam Readiness

Exam candidates never really know whether they are adequately prepared for the exam until they have completed about 30 percent of the questions. At that point, if you are not prepared, it is too late. The best way to determine your readiness is to work through the "Do I Know This Already?" quizzes at the beginning of each chapter and review the foundation and key topics presented in each chapter. It is best to work your way through the entire book unless you can complete each subject without having to do any research or look up any answers.

Cisco Cybersecurity Certifications in the Real World

Cisco has one of the most recognized names on the Internet. People with a Cisco Certified Support Technician (CCST) Cybersecurity certification can bring quite a bit of knowledge to the table because of their deep understanding of cybersecurity technologies and standards. This is why the Cisco certification carries such high respect in the marketplace. Cisco certifications demonstrate to potential employers and contract holders a certain professionalism, expertise, and dedication required to complete a difficult goal. If Cisco certifications were easy to obtain, everyone would have them.

Exam Registration

The Cisco Certified Support Technician (CCST) Cybersecurity 100-160 exam is a computer-based exam, with around 50 to 70 multiple-choice, fill-in-the-blank, list-in-order, and simulation-based questions. You can take the exam at any Pearson VUE (http://www.pearsonvue.com) testing center. According to Cisco, the exam should last about 50 minutes. Be aware that when you register for the exam, you might be told to allow a certain amount of time to take the exam that is longer than the testing time indicated by the testing software when you begin. This discrepancy is because the testing center will want you to allow for some time to get settled and take the tutorial about the test engine.

Book Content Updates

Because Cisco occasionally updates exam topics without notice, Cisco Press might post additional preparatory content on the web page associated with this book at http://www.ciscopress.com/title/9780138203924. It is a good idea to check the website a couple of weeks before taking your exam, to review any updated content that might be posted online. We also recommend that you periodically check back to this page on the Cisco Press website to view any errata or supporting book files that might be available.

Figure Credits

Figures 4.1, 4.7, 9.1–9.8: Microsoft Corporation

Figures 9.9, 9.12, 9.15: Red Hat, Inc

Figure 9.10: Canonical Ltd

Figures 9. 13, 9.14, 11.2: Apple Inc

Figure 9.16: Wireshark

Figure 11.3: Sophos Ltd

Figure 12.3: Tenable, Inc

Figure 12.4: Nmap Software LLC

Figure 13.1: The National Institute of Standards and Technology

CHAPTER 1

Security Principles

This chapter covers the following topics:

- **The CIA Triad:** This section discusses the need for confidentiality, integrity, and availability.

- **Common Security Terms:** This section focuses on a multitude of security terms that are foundational security knowledge.

- **Types of Attackers and Their Reasons for Attacks:** This section explores the various types of attackers and what primarily motivates them to attack.

- **Code of Ethics:** This section briefly discusses the importance of a code of ethics to a cybersecurity professional.

Everything that stands today stands because of a solid foundation. Foundations are not exciting, and they definitely do not stand out. But everything else in all its glory and beauty that stands above a foundation exists because of that foundation. To become a cybersecurity professional and protect all your data and all your resources, you need to have a solid foundation, and that foundation begins with learning and memorizing various terms and definitions.

This chapter begins with the CIA triad and explores the importance of confidentiality, integrity, and availability. It also covers a multitude of common security terms, including vulnerability, exploit, and threat. It also explores the different types of attackers and what motivates them. To wrap up, the chapter includes a brief discussion on what a code of ethics is and why it is important for cybersecurity.

This chapter covers information related to the following Cisco Certified Support Technician (CCST) Cybersecurity exam objective:

1.1. Define essential security principles.

"Do I Know This Already?" Quiz

The "Do I Know This Already?" quiz allows you to assess whether you should read this entire chapter thoroughly or jump to the "Exam Preparation Tasks" section. If you are in doubt about your answers to these questions or your own assessment of your knowledge of the topics, read the entire chapter. Table 1-1 lists the major headings in this chapter and their corresponding "Do I Know This Already?" quiz questions. You can find the answers in Appendix A, "Answers to the 'Do I Know This Already?' Quizzes and Review Questions."

Table 1-1 "Do I Know This Already?" Section-to-Question Mapping

Foundation Topics Section	Questions
The CIA Triad	1
Common Security Terms	2
Types of Attackers and Their Reasons for Attacks	3
Code of Ethics	4

CAUTION The goal of self-assessment is to gauge your mastery of the topics in this chapter. If you do not know the answer to a question or are only partially sure of the answer, you should mark that question incorrect for purposes of self-assessment. Giving yourself credit for an answer you correctly guess skews your self-assessment results and might provide you with a false sense of security.

1. Which of the following correctly describes the purpose of confidentiality in relation to the CIA triad?
   a. It is all about making sure that data is accurate and authentic.
   b. It is all about making sure that data is accessible when and where it needs to be.
   c. It is all about making sure that data is hashed and encrypted at rest and in transit.
   d. It is all about making sure that data is accessible and viewable only by those who need it.

2. Which of the following correctly identifies what unpatched software would be?
   a. Threat
   b. Exploit
   c. Vulnerability
   d. Hardening

3. Which of the following type of attackers typically attacks for financial gain?
   a. Recreational
   b. Script kiddie
   c. Cybercriminal
   d. Hacktivist
   e. Insider
   f. Cyberterrorist

4. What is a code of ethics?
   a. A set of policies that outline how firewalls are implemented.
   b. Rules you follow when you are a cybersecurity professional.
   c. A legal document outlining who to contact when a cybercriminal has been discovered.
   d. A U.S. government department tasked with protecting America.

Foundation Topics

The CIA Triad

The **CIA triad**, as shown in Figure 1-1, is a model that represents the foundational principles behind security. The *C* stands for *confidentiality*, the *I* stands for *integrity*, and the *A* stands for *availability*. Adhering to the CIA triad ensures that you are on the correct path for creating secured systems, data, and environments.

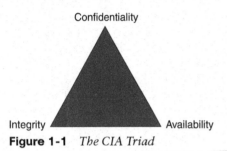

Confidentiality

Integrity   Availability

Figure 1-1   *The CIA Triad*

Confidentiality is all about privacy. It's about making sure that only those individuals who should be able to access systems and view data are able to do so. All others should be prevented. For example, having strict access control measures so only authenticated users can access systems and data helps enforce confidentiality. Implementing encryption for data at rest, in transit, and in use is another great example of how to enforce confidentiality as only those with the means to decrypt it can view the data.

Integrity is all about accuracy and authenticity of data. It's about making sure that our systems and data are exactly in the state they are supposed to be, and they have not been modified in any way that would jeopardize their accuracy and authenticity. For example, using configuration management systems and tools to track any modifications to our systems (by accident or on purpose) can help enforce integrity because any modification (authorized or unauthorized) is tracked, and any unauthorized change can be rolled back to ensure that integrity is upheld. Another example is hashing data as it is in transit and at rest. This involves generating a hash of the data and attaching it to the data before transmission so that the receiving device can generate a hash based on the received data; if the hashes before and after match, you know the data has not been modified, but if the hash computed on reception is different, you know the data has been modified in transit and should not be trusted. A similar process occurs with data at rest. If you store a hash of your data at rest with the data, then any time you hash that data again, you can compare the new hash to the stored hash. If the hash is the same as the original stored hash, you know the data has not been modified, but if the hash generated is different than the stored hash, you know the data has been modified. Figure 1-2 shows an example of a Cisco IOS image that has an MD5 hash and an SHA-512 hash. Once you download the IOS image, you can run the image through an MD5 hashing algorithm or SHA-512 hashing algorithm, and if the result is the same as the hash displayed on the website, you know the file has not been modified at rest or in transit since Cisco uploaded it.

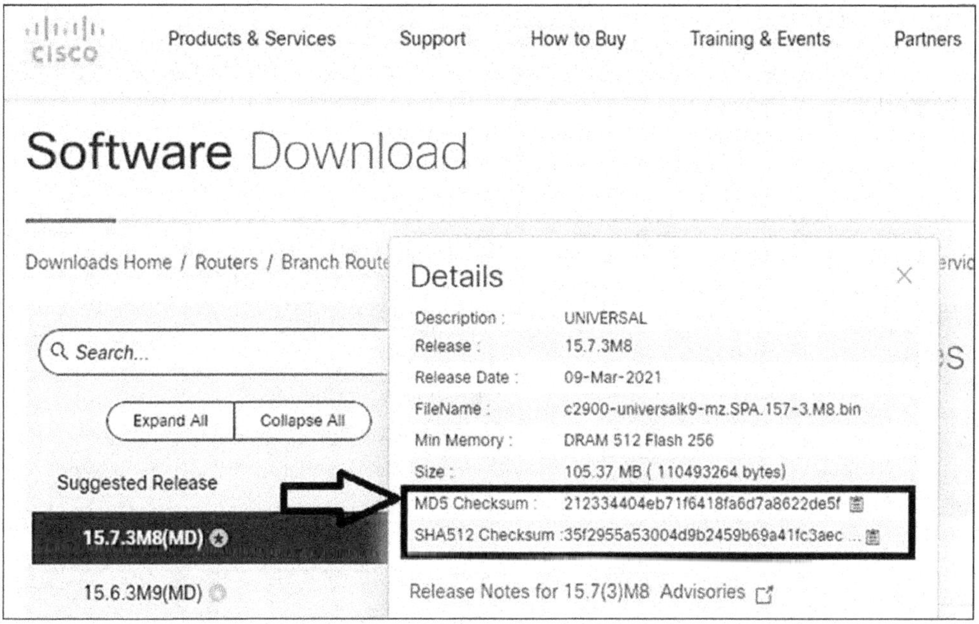

Figure 1-2 *Example of Hashes Used for Verifying the Integrity of a Cisco IOS Image*

Availability is all about warranty. It is about the systems functioning as they should when they should so that the data is available when and where it is needed. Availability requires systems to be resilient. For example, by having backup servers and databases, you can ensure that if the primary servers fail, the backup servers can take over, and everything will still be available. Another example is redundant paths throughout the network. If a path fails for any reason, another path is still available for the traffic to flow on. What about electricity? Well, if the electrical grid fails or a power supply fails, you need to have a backup solution like a secondary power supply, an uninterruptible power supply (UPS) or a generator to ensure availability.

Before you move on, take a moment to come to terms with the fact that everything security related is about one or more of the elements of the CIA triad. As a cybersecurity professional, you need to do everything in your power to uphold the CIA of everything from a software patch, to an ACL, to a firewall, to an acceptable use policy.

Common Security Terms

Every security professional needs to have a sound foundational vocabulary. Words such as *vulnerability*, *exploit*, *threat*, *risk*, *hardening*, *defense-in-depth*, and *attack vector* are going to be a part of your everyday conversations. Regardless of whether you are a seasoned cybersecurity professional or just beginning your cybersecurity journey with the CCST Cybersecurity certification, it is imperative that you are clear on what various terms in Table 1-2 mean.

Key Topic

Table 1-2   Common Terms and Definitions You Need to Know

Term	Definition	Examples
Vulnerability	A weakness in any part of an enterprise that, if exploited, could jeopardize the confidentiality, integrity, or availability of the systems and the data.	Unpatched software Use of superuser or admin account privileges Open ports and protocols that are not needed Unknown security bugs in software or programming interfaces Unencrypted data on the network Zero-day vulnerability
Exploit	Anything that can take advantage of a vulnerability.	SQL injection attack Cross-site scripting (XSS) Buffer overflow Memory safety violation Input validation error Remote code execution Privilege escalation Zero-day exploit Cross-site request forgery
Threat	Anyone or anything that could exploit vulnerabilities in an environment.	Malware and ransomware Viruses, worms, and spyware Insider threats Outsider threats Botnets
Risk	The probability or chance that anyone or anything could exploit a vulnerability in an environment.	Quantitative risk assessment Qualitative risk assessment
Hardening	The act of fixing vulnerabilities in an environment to eliminate or reduce the risk associated with a threat that could exploit a vulnerability.	Operating system (OS) hardening Server hardening Endpoint hardening Network hardening Database hardening Application hardening Password protection hardening Restricted network and physical access Using antivirus, malware, and spyware protection applications

Term	Definition	Examples
Defense-in-depth	A strategy that uses a multitude of layered measures to defend against various threats.	The Internet connection goes to a router with an ACL that filters traffic based on address, ports, and protocols. Whatever makes it though the router then goes to a firewall that provides deeper packet/application inspection. Whatever passes through the firewall then goes to an intrusion prevention system (IPS) for anomaly detection. Then whatever makes it through the IPS still has to be inspected by the host-based firewall, IPS, and antivirus and antimalware software.
Attack vector	The method a cybercriminal uses for an attack to exploit vulnerabilities.	Distributed denial of service (DDoS) Zero-day vulnerability Phishing Social engineering Active or passive scanning

Types of Attackers and Their Reasons for Attacks

What makes someone a criminal? There is no single, simple answer to this question. Only a deep psychological analysis of a criminal will get you to the truth about that person. As humans, we are all motivated to act for different reasons. Regardless of the reason and what motivated us, we do what we do as humans for some type of personal, group, or communal gain. A cybercriminal may do what they do for money or fame or career enhancement. We often categorize cybercriminals based on what motivates them and their level of sophistication. This gives us a better idea of what and who we are up against and why they are doing what they are doing. The more we know our adversaries, the better we will be able to protect ourselves from them. For the CCST Cybersecurity exam, you are encouraged to have an understanding of the following types of attackers so you can pick the right one out of a lineup:

Key Topic

■ **Recreational attacker:** A **recreational cybersecurity attacker** is someone who attacks computer systems or networks for fun or curiosity rather than for financial gain or malice. These attackers are often motivated by a desire to learn more about computer systems and networks, to test their own skills, or to prove to themselves and close friends that they can break into a system.

■ **Script kiddie:** A **script kiddie** is someone who takes advantage of already existing tools and scripts that are available on the Internet and Dark Web and is dedicated to becoming a more sophisticated cybersecurity attacker over time. Script kiddies are typically classified as amateurs, or "noobs," as they have limited knowledge or skills to create their own tools or scripts and are only as good as the tools and scripts they obtain. If the attack they are launching deviates from the purpose of the tool or script, they are unable to pivot as they lack the knowledge to do so. They are motivated by the excitement and thrill that comes with doing something illegal and the potential rewards that could result from their efforts. However, you can't underestimate script kiddies because over time, they may gain the knowledge and experience they need to become professional cybercriminals. In addition, this is one of the largest groups of cybercriminals. There are more script kiddies than any other category of cybercriminals because everyone must start somewhere. (Similarly, there are more Security+ certified people than CISSP certified people in the world.) In addition, since professional cybercriminals create the tools and scripts, they are essentially using the script kiddies for their low-level, initial grunt work. Protecting yourself from the script kiddie activity is a great way to protect yourself from the more sophisticated cyber activity you may encounter.

■ **Cybercriminal/organized crime:** A **cybercriminal** is a person or group that attacks for financial gain. Regardless of how they are attacking or what they are attacking, they are motivated by the money they will receive in the end. For example, they may illegally gain access to your system and encrypt all your data and ask you to pay a ransom for the decryption key (ransomware), or they may gain illegal access to your system, download data from your system, and threaten to post it on the Dark Web unless you pay them not to. Maybe they send you a phishing email, pretending to be someone you know and trust and asking for money in the form of gift cards. Regardless of what or how they are doing it, if they are motivated by money, this type of attacker is classified as a cybercriminal. As I am writing this, the top five cybercriminal organizations are DarkSide, REvil, Clop, Syrian Electronic Army, and FIN7.

■ **Hacktivist:** A **hacktivist** is a person or group that attacks for social or political purposes. They have some type of social or political agenda—a cause—and they attack to achieve that cause. A hacktivist fights for justice and uses digital disobedience to do so. They tend to use tools or scripts that are already available to help drive their agenda forward and will even work with professional hackers when the existing tools and scripts are not enough. However, in many cases, they will convince and team up with insiders so they can easily get their hands on the sensitive data they need to be successful. Anonymous is currently the most famous activist/hacktivist collective.

■ **Insider:** An **insider** is a person or group within an organization that poses a threat to the CIA of that environment. Note that an insider is not always a "bad" person. For example, someone who accidentally deletes a mission-critical file on a server would jeopardize the availability of the service that needs that file. This is still an insider, even though the deletion was an accident. On the flip side, a disgruntled employee might want to get even with the company they work for, so they team up with a hacktivist and leak highly classified information to them, which jeopardizes confidentiality. This is a malicious insider. Maybe you have an employee who accidentally enters $10000 in a database instead of $100.00. Even though it's an accident, this person is still considered an insider who has jeopardized the integrity of the data. So regardless of whether an insider's actions are malicious, accidental, or negligent, they present threats to CIA.

■ **State-sponsored attacker/nation-state attacker/cyberterrorist:** A **state-sponsored attacker** or **nation-state attacker**, also known as a **cyberterrorist**, is a person or group that works for their country to attack other countries. They typically have access to unlimited resources and can launch highly sophisticated attacks. Theft and leaking of state secrets, industrial espionage, cyberwars, and advanced persistent threats (APTs) are usually associated with state-sponsored attacks. Some examples of cyberterrorists as of this writing include Double Dragon "APT41" (China), Fancy Bear "APT28" (Russia), and Lazarus Group "APT38" (North Korea).

- **Terrorist:** A terrorist is a person or a group that is motivated by political or religious beliefs and whose primary goal is to cause harm. They will do whatever it takes to destroy, damage, or shut down their targets to achieve their political or religious beliefs.

- **Hacker:** A **hacker** is anyone who has the skills needed to breach systems and steal data by exploiting any number of vulnerabilities that exist in an environment.

- **White hat, or ethical, hacker:** An **ethical hacker** is a hacker who uses their skills for good. They use their skills in a just and lawful manner. This type of hacker is usually employed full time, part time, or contracted by an organization to find the vulnerabilities in the organization's systems and, ultimately, fix them.

- **Black hat, or unethical, hacker:** An **unethical hacker** is a hacker who uses their skills for bad. They use their skills in an unlawful and unjust manner. This type of hacker is usually a lone wolf, hacking for personal gain or working for a cybercrime organization or a nation-state to advance their agendas.

- **Gray hat hacker:** A **gray hat hacker** is a hacker who uses their skills for good and/ or bad, depending on how you look at it. They use their skills in a potentially unlawful way but don't cause any harm or damage and do not steal anything. They typically report and disclose any weakness they find, and they may even recommend potential fixes. However, because they typically do not have permission to attack the systems they are attacking, they are walking a very fine line between good and bad, and if they are ever caught in the act, they could be treated no differently than a black hat/unethical hacker.

Code of Ethics

A **code of ethics** is a set of rules a cybersecurity professional follows. Security practices deal with protecting private, confidential, mission-critical information, and without a code of ethics, cybersecurity professionals might not know how to conduct themselves inside and outside their organization. As a cybersecurity professional, you have great power, and with this great power, you have many responsibilities. Therefore, it is imperative that you follow strong ethical guidelines to protect yourself and everyone else in the organization you work for. For example, how do you deal with the personal information on BYOD devices? Is it subject to decryption as it passes through the firewall—or not? What traffic will you monitor and not monitor, and what happens if you come across questionable content? How do you deal with those who are not in alignment with or who break security policies that have been put in place? How do you deal with the vocal and written opposition you will face every day when it comes to security practices? Without a code of ethics, it is very difficult to make the consistent, repeatable decisions that need to be made every day to uphold the CIA in your organization.

Many frameworks exist, such as the Security Incident Management Maturity Model (SIM3); the CSIRT maturity assessment model, which is part of the European Union Agency for

Cybersecurity (ENISA); and the Global Forum on Cyber Expertise (GFCE) Maturity Initiative—all of which include sections on the conduct of humans in relation to cybersecurity.

Establishing your own code of ethics that will meet the needs of your organization and the organizations you interface with is critical for your security success. The TI CSIRT Code of Practice (CCoP v2.4 as of this writing), which is accessible at https://www.trusted-introducer.org/TI-CCoP.pdf, is a great example of what you are trying to accomplish with a code of ethics. Although this particular code is geared toward CSIRTs, it gives you a good idea of what a code of ethics is all about. The following are two examples directly from this document that help you understand the components of a code of ethics:

3.1 *MUST* The team and its members are expected to comply with the legal requirements of their individual countries at all times whilst dealing with incident management matters. Where there is any conflict, this article always takes precedence over other principles stated in this document.

6.1 *MUST* The team receiving or holding information, regardless of the subject matter, that may affect either another CSIRT team's constituency, a community of CSIRTs, or indeed the security of the Internet or user communities thereof, will handle this information responsibly and protect it against inadvertent disclosure to unauthorized parties.

Here is a list of potential high-level items you might consider for your code of ethics:

- Any legal standards and how everyone will comply with them
- How human rights will be respected
- How society will be protected
- Plans for disclosing any vulnerabilities
- How privacy will be upheld based on a need-to-know approach
- The acceptable use of computers and related systems and how they should never be used for harm

Once you have a code of ethics, it is important to adhere to it and enforce it. Having a code of ethics and not enforcing it or adhering to it could result in catastrophic consequences for you and everyone else in your organization. Making sure everyone reads it and signs a statement indicating that they have read it and understand it is imperative. But consistently monitoring and reviewing the day-to-day application of the code of ethics is even more important so that you can catch any violations early and deal with them as needed to reduce the potential damage caused by any violation.

Summary

IT security is a lifetime commitment, and your commitment begins with having an understanding of security principles, which include the following:

- The **CIA triad** is a model that represents the foundational principles behind security.
  - **Confidentiality** is all about privacy.

- **Integrity** is all about accuracy and authenticity of data.

- **Availability** is all about warranty.

- Understanding **common security terms** will provide you with a security foundation that you can build on.

  - A **vulnerability** is a weakness in any part of an enterprise that, if exploited, could jeopardize the confidentiality, availability, or integrity of systems and data.

  - An **exploit** is anything that can take advantage of a vulnerability.

  - A **threat** is anyone or anything that could exploit vulnerabilities in an environment.

  - A **risk** is the probability or chance that anyone or anything could exploit a vulnerability in an environment.

  - **Hardening** is the act of fixing vulnerabilities in an environment to eliminate or reduce the risk associated with a threat that could exploit a vulnerability.

  - **Defense-in-depth** is a strategy that uses a multitude of layered measures to defend against various threats.

  - An **attack vector** is the method a cybercriminal uses for an attack to exploit vulnerabilities.

- **Understanding types of attackers and their reasons for attacks** helps you understand the motives of attackers so you can better equip yourself to defend against them.

  - A **script kiddie** is someone who takes advantage of already existing tools and scripts that are available on the Internet and Dark Web.

  - A **cybercriminal** is a person or a group that attacks for financial gain.

  - A **hacktivist** is a person or group that attacks for social or political purposes.

  - An **insider** is a person or group within their own organization that poses a threat to the CIA of the environment.

  - A **state-sponsored/nation-state/cyberterrorist** is a person or group that works for their country to attack other countries.

  - A **terrorist** is a person or group that is motivated by political or religious beliefs and whose primary goal is to cause harm.

  - A **hacker** is anyone who has the skills needed to breach systems and steal data by exploiting the vulnerabilities that exist in an environment.

- A **code of ethics** is a set of rules a cybersecurity professional follows.

Exam Preparation Tasks

As mentioned in the Introduction, you can customize your strategy for exam preparation. Suggested tasks include the exercises here, Chapter 16, "Final Preparation," and the exam simulation questions on the companion website.

Review All Key Topics

Review the most important topics in this chapter, noted with the Key Topics icon in the outer margin of the page. Table 1-3 lists these key topics and the page number on which each is found.

Table 1-3 Key Topics for Chapter 1

Key Topic Element	Description	Page Number
Paragraph	Confidentiality	4
Paragraph	Integrity	4
Paragraph	Availability	5
Table 1-2	Common Terms and Definitions You Need to Know	6
List	Various types of attackers	7
Paragraph	Codes of ethics	9

Define Key Terms

Define the following key terms from this chapter and check your answers in the glossary:

CIA triad, confidentiality, integrity, availability, vulnerability, exploit, threat, risk, hardening, defense-in-depth, attack vector, recreational attacker, script kiddie, cybercriminal, hacktivist, insider, state-sponsored attacker, nation-state attacker, cyberterrorist, hacker, ethical hacker, unethical hacker, gray hat hacker, code of ethics

Complete Tables and Lists from Memory

Print a copy of Appendix B, "Memory Tables," found on the companion website, or at least the section for this chapter, and complete the tables and lists from memory. Appendix C, "Memory Tables Answer Key," includes completed tables and lists you can use to check your work.

Review Questions

1. Which of the following is an example of the integrity component of the CIA triad?

    a. Hashing data at rest

    b. Encrypting data at rest

    c. Encrypting data in transit

    d. Storing data in redundant locations

2. Which of the following best describes the act of fixing vulnerabilities in an environment to eliminate or reduce the risk associated with a threat that could exploit a vulnerability?

    a. Attack vector

    b. Defense-in-depth

    c. Hardening

    d. Risk

3. Which of the following types of attackers has some type of social or political agenda behind their attacks?

   a. Recreational

   b. Script kiddie

   c. Cybercriminal

   d. Hacktivist

   e. Insider

   f. Cyberterrorist

4. As a cybersecurity professional, why is it necessary for you to develop and follow a code of ethics for security?

   a. So you can implement confidentiality features efficiently and effectively

   b. So you can eliminate insider threats

   c. So you can build a defense-in-depth solution

   d. So you can make the consistent, repeatable decisions that need to be made every day to uphold the CIA in your organization

CHAPTER 2

Common Threats, Attacks, and Vulnerabilities

This chapter covers the following topics:

- **Malware Variants:** This section explores the most common types of malware that you need to be aware of.

- **IoT Vulnerabilities:** This section familiarizes you with some of the most common vulnerabilities associated with IoT devices.

- **Distributed Denial of Service:** This section introduces a very common worldwide threat known as DDoS.

- **On-Path Attacks:** This section explains what an on-path attack is and provides a few examples.

- **Insider Threats:** This section explores what an insider threat is and what motivates insiders to act the way they do.

- **Social Engineering Tactics:** This section dives into the multitude of social engineering attacks that exist.

- **Physical Attacks:** This section dives into the multitude of physical attacks that exist.

- **Advanced Persistent Threats (APTs):** This section explains what APTs are and why you need to be worried about them.

The only way you can secure your data, network, and systems is if you are aware of the threats, attacks, and vulnerabilities that you will face. Always remember that it is impossible to protect yourself from what you do not know. Therefore, it is imperative that from this day forward, you constantly stay up to speed on the latest threats, attacks, and vulnerabilities that you will face.

This chapter covers current common threats, attacks, and vulnerabilities related to various malware variants, IoT vulnerabilities, DoS and DDoS attacks, on-path attacks, insider threats, social engineering attacks, physical threats, as well as APTs.

This chapter covers information related to the following Cisco Certified Support Technician (CCST) Cybersecurity exam objective:

1.2. Explain common threats and vulnerabilities.

"Do I Know This Already?" Quiz

The "Do I Know This Already?" quiz allows you to assess whether you should read this entire chapter thoroughly or jump to the "Exam Preparation Tasks" section. If you are in doubt about your answers to these questions or your own assessment of your knowledge of the topics, read the entire chapter. Table 2-1 lists the major headings in this chapter and their corresponding "Do I Know This Already?" quiz questions. You can find the answers in Appendix A, "Answers to the 'Do I Know This Already?' Quizzes and Review Questions."

Table 2-1 "Do I Know This Already?" Section-to-Question Mapping

Foundation Topics Section	Questions
Malware Variants	1
IoT Vulnerabilities	2
Distributed Denial of Service	3
On-Path Attacks	4
Insider Threats	5
Social Engineering Tactics	6
Physical Attacks	7
Advanced Persistent Threats (APTs)	8

CAUTION The goal of self-assessment is to gauge your mastery of the topics in this chapter. If you do not know the answer to a question or are only partially sure of the answer, you should mark that question incorrect for purposes of self-assessment. Giving yourself credit for an answer you correctly guess skews your self-assessment results and might provide you with a false sense of security.

1. Which of the following BEST describes a virus?

   a. Malicious software that inserts its code into a system's programs and files and lives dormant until some type of human interaction causes it to execute

   b. Malicious standalone software that is self-replicating and does not need to be injected into other programs or files or rely on human interaction to spread

   c. Malicious software disguised as a legitimate program or file that executes when the user attempts to access the software

   d. Malicious software that is designed to allow an attacker to remotely access and control the system it has been installed on

2. Of the provided options, which is the greatest vulnerability associated with IoT devices?

   a. The use of Wi-Fi connections

   b. Lack of encryption or weak encryption

   c. Lack of regular patches, updates, and fixes

   d. Poor physical security

3. What is the purpose of a DoS attack?
   a. To compromise confidentiality
   b. To compromise integrity
   c. To compromise availability
   d. To compromise authentication

4. What type of attack is occurring when the attacker intercepts communications by placing themselves between two communicating devices?
   a. Phishing
   b. Downloader
   c. On-path
   d. DoS

5. Which of the following correctly defines *insider threat*?
   a. Any threat that originates inside an application or a service
   b. Any threat that originates from someone outside an organization
   c. Any threat that originates from a trusted person within the organization
   d. Any threat that originates from a cybercriminal organization against an organization

6. Which of the following BEST defines *social engineering attack*?
   a. Any attack that goes after the human element of an organization
   b. Any attack that installs malware on a system
   c. Any attack that exfiltrates data from a network
   d. Any attack that renders a system unavailable

7. Which of the following are examples of physical attacks? (Choose two.)
   a. Vehicle ramming
   b. Vishing
   c. On-path
   d. Dumpster diving

8. What is an APT?
   a. Any newly undiscovered zero-day software vulnerability
   b. A global phishing campaign that targets as many people as possible around the world
   c. A persistent threat that remains inside an organization, undetected, for a prolonged period of time
   d. A specific type of vehicle ramming attack that targets military facilities

Foundation Topics

Malware Variants

Malware is a fancy name that has been created to describe *mal*icious soft*ware*. So, technically speaking, any software that has malicious intent is considered malware. As a CCST

Cybersecurity candidate, you need to know different types of malware. This section provides a sort of "who's who" of malware. These are the most common types of malware:

■ **Virus:** A virus is malicious software that is designed to cause harm, such as deleting files, stealing information, corrupting information, or making a system or data unstable, unusable, or downright unavailable. It does all of this by inserting its code (payload) into a system's programs and files. It lives within a document or an executable file and remains dormant until some type of human interaction occurs to launch its attack and cause it to spread to other systems.

■ **Worm:** Like a virus, a worm is malicious software that is designed to cause harm, such as deleting files, stealing information, corrupting information, or making a system or data unstable, unusable, or downright unavailable. However, worms don't inject their code into other programs or files as viruses do, and they do not require human interaction to spread. They are standalone, self-replicating, malicious software that wreaks havoc. Typically, they spread through vulnerabilities in other software. Therefore, many worms also have the ability to scan a network and detect other devices that contain the same vulnerability and infect them. As a result, a worm can easily jump from device to device without human involvement.

■ **Trojan horse:** Like viruses and other malware, a Trojan horse is malicious software that is designed to cause harm, such as deleting files, stealing information, corrupting information, or making a system or data unstable, unusable, or downright unavailable. So, what makes a Trojan a Trojan? It is typically a program or file disguised as a legitimate program or file. Therefore, the victim is tricked into executing the Trojan, thinking it is legitimate. Also, Trojans typically do not replicate like viruses and worms do. A special form of Trojan is a **remote access Trojan (RAT)**, which is a type of backdoor (described next).

■ **Backdoor:** A backdoor is any type of malicious software that allows an attacker to remotely access and control the system it has been installed on. Backdoors can be as simple as opening ports and enabling services on a system so the system can be remotely accessed by an attacker at some point in time. However, the attacker in this case would be initiating a connection to the victim, which is difficult because most firewalls are designed to prevent inbound-initiated connections to devices. A more sophisticated backdoor might be designed to "beacon," which means it has a victim's machine make a dynamic call to the attacker's system so it can connect remotely through a connection initiated by the victim's system; this type of attack tricks a firewall because the connection is started by the client and not the attacker.

■ **Logic bomb:** This malicious software is designed to cause harm such as deleting files, stealing information, corrupting information, or making a system or data unstable, unusable, or downright unavailable. It sounds like a worm, a virus, or a Trojan horse, doesn't it? What distinguishes a logic bomb is a timing component or associated conditions that cause it to go off. For example, a logic bomb could be designed to trigger automatically on a certain day at a certain time and delete certain files. If the files are restored from a backup, the logic bomb deletes them again the next time it runs. Another example would be malicious software designed to round down to the nearest nickel any money being deposited into an account and to deposit the difference into a different account. Why would that be a logic bomb? Because there is a specific condition that is met (depositing money) that triggers the malicious software to execute. Without that specific action, it would not be executed.

- **Downloader:** This malicious software is designed to download other malicious software. For example, you accidentally click on an attachment in an email, and nothing happens. You figure that the attachment is corrupt and forget about it. But you might have executed a downloader that is now running in the background, downloading the real malicious software that the cybercriminals need on and in your system.

- **Spammer:** This type of malicious software is designed to send unsolicited messages to as many people as it can by using tools like email, instant messaging, and newsgroups. Usually, the messages have attachments with malware or links to websites designed to capture the user's credentials.

- **Key logger:** This malicious software is designed to capture the user's keystrokes. Once installed on a system, it captures everything the victim types on their keyboard. Emails, instant messages, passwords, PINs, any personally identifiable information (PII), credit card numbers, and a whole lot more.

- **Rootkit:** This malicious software is designed to provide an attacker with administrative-level access to a system. It is designed to give the attacker the highest level of privileges possible and even give the attacker the ability to access parts of the system and gain control of those parts that would normally not be accessible by people but only by the operating system. Therefore, a rootkit could modify and manipulate anything that an administrator can. A rootkit could be used to eavesdrop on the user and invade their privacy, gain remote access and create a permanent backdoor, steal sensitive data, tamper with or deactivate installed security programs, and even conceal malware so it is harder to detect and remove.

- **Ransomware:** This is malicious software that is designed to hold systems and data for ransom. For example, one form of ransomware gains access to a user's files and folders and encrypts them until the user pays the requested ransom. Upon payment, the user gets the decryption key that will decrypt their data. Another form of ransomware gains access to a user's files and folders and steals them. The user is notified that the data has been exfiltrated, and if they don't want it exposed to the world via the Internet or Dark Web, the user needs to pay a ransom. In both cases, there is no real guarantee that the attackers will provide the decryption key or not leak the data. Today, ransomware is the most popular type of attack, as it generates a very large amount of money for cybercriminals. The following are real-world examples of ransomware as of 2023:

  - **Ryuk:** Spread mainly via malicious emails or phishing emails that contain dangerous links and attachments.

  - **WannaCry:** Spread through an exploit in Microsoft Windows.

  - **Petya:** Spread through a malicious email attachment.

  - **TeslaCrypt:** Spread through exploit kits and phishing emails.

  - **CryptoLocker:** Spread through malicious email attachments.

IoT Vulnerabilities

Internet of Things (IoT) is the fancy name that has been given to all the Internet-enabled devices—smart fridges, thermostats, televisions, cameras, watches, sensors, trackers, tractors, and more. Each year, more and more devices are Internet enabled and join the IoT family. However, as cool and amazing as these products and services are, they are swimming in vulnerabilities because IoT manufacturers have a tendency to put functionality and coolness ahead of security. Therefore, before you adopt IoT devices, you need to understand the risks and how you can mitigate them or flat-out avoid them.

So, let's look at some of the most common vulnerabilities associated with IoT devices.

One very common vulnerability is default accounts with passwords that are weak, guessable, posted to the Internet, or hardcoded in the device. If you don't change the passwords or create different accounts with stronger passwords, you will be at risk.

In addition to weak, guessable passwords, updates are some of the greatest vulnerabilities for IoT devices at the moment. For one thing, updates are almost nonexistent for many IoT devices. It seems like manufacturers build an IoT device but forget about or ignore the need to support it. Therefore, the longer you use an IoT device with a lack of updates, the riskier it becomes as more vulnerabilities are uncovered and no patches exist to fix them. So, it is important that you choose your IoT devices wisely and stick to manufacturers that update their IoT devices. Second, IoT devices that do get updates do not necessarily get updated in a safe and secure way, making the updates themselves risky.

Poorly developed applications or web interfaces that are used to manage, monitor, and maintain IoT devices are also vulnerabilities. These applications and interfaces may have unpatched bugs, no or weak encryption when communicating with the IoT devices, and poorly implemented authentication and authorization factors.

Backend systems that support IoT devices are also vulnerabilities. Whether a system is in a public cloud provider's network or in an on-premises data center built by the IoT manufacturer, it is possible that the network is insecure, the ecosystem is insecure, the components are unpatched and outdated, there is weak or no encryption between the IoT devices and the backend, data at rest is not encrypted, and more. So, as you can see, not only are the IoT devices vulnerable, their entire infrastructure may be vulnerable as well.

IoT devices are here to stay, and more and more of them will be released in the marketplace. It is up to you as a cybersecurity professional to make sure that you fully vet all the IoT devices, their update policies, their management applications, and their backend infrastructure and systems before you implement them in your network. You need to eliminate as many vulnerabilities as you can in your environment, and the only way you can do so is by picking IoT devices that put security first.

Distributed Denial of Service

A **denial of service (DoS)** attack is an attack against availability. The goal of this type of attack is to make a service unavailable. There are a number of ways to make a service unavailable:

- A common way is to flood a server with useless traffic that overwhelms the server's resources and crashes it, making it unavailable.

- Another common way is to flood a server with a bunch of TCP SYN packets and then not complete the TCP three-way handshake, leaving the server with thousands of half-opened TCP sessions and preventing it from forming TCP sessions with other devices until the half-open sessions expire. This is known as a TCP SYN flood attack.

- Another way might be to overwhelm a network device so that it crashes and multiple resources on the network behind that device become unavailable.

- A poorly developed application that is susceptible to a buffer overflow attack may become unavailable, resulting in DoS.

- Malware installed on a system that shuts down the system would also be a DoS because the system is no longer available.

- A user who accidentally trips on a cable in the server room and inadvertently unplugs it and cuts power to multiple systems is not malicious but still creates denial of service.

- An excavator might accidentally sever the Internet cable while digging a hole. Again, this is not malicious, but it is still a denial of service.

So, technically speaking, does ransomware cause a DoS? Sure. Why? Well, the data is encrypted and unusable, and the services and systems that rely on that data are now unavailable.

Something to keep in mind is that DoS typically refers to a single or a few attacker systems causing the DoS attack, as shown in Figure 2-1, which shows a TCP SYN flood attack.

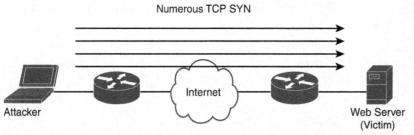

Figure 2-1   *A Type of DoS Attack Known as a TCP SYN Flood Attack*

However, with modern servers and network devices, a few attacker systems are not enough to bring down the victims' servers or networks, especially with a flooding-based DoS attack. Today, DoS attacks are being perpetrated by botnets (large groups of computers under the control of an attacker), as shown in Figure 2-2. The amalgamation of all the resources in the botnet flooding the servers and/or networks are guaranteed to grind the servers and networks to a halt and make them unavailable. This is referred to as a **distributed denial of service (DDoS)** attack because the sources of the attack are distributed in nature.

A **botnet** is a large group of computers under the control of an attacker. Each computer is classified as a **bot** because it is a system (computer/server) under the control of a C2 server. This is possible because a bot typically has a backdoor installed on it. So a botnet is a group of previously compromised systems (bots) in a network or networks that now have malware installed on them to allow the attacker to control them from a **command and control (C2 or CnC or C&C) server**. Bots within a botnet usually beacon to the C2 server to establish connections to get their commands.

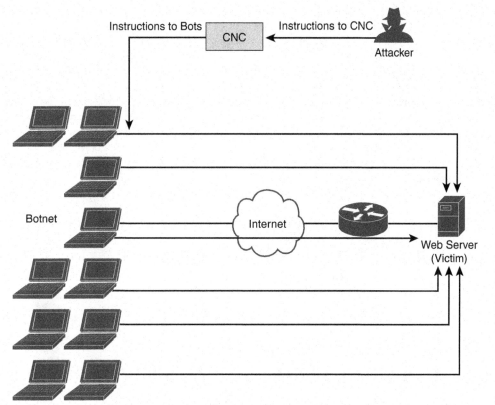

Figure 2-2 *An Example of DDoS Attack Using Bots Controlled by a CNC Server*

On-Path Attacks

An **on-path attack** (formerly known as a man-in-the-middle attack) occurs when an attacker intercepts communications by placing themself between two communicating devices, as shown in Figure 2-3. Basically, they are eavesdropping—either physically or virtually (by rerouting communications). An attacker does this to either capture data or manipulate data or both. An on-path attack can compromise confidentiality as the attacker has access to data they should not have access to and also integrity if the attacker manipulates the data.

Figure 2-3 *An On-Path Attack Where the Attacker Is Intercepting Traffic Between the Source and Destination*

A simple Layer 2 (L2) on-path attack happens when an attacker spoofs the L2 MAC address of the default gateway for a subnet/VLAN/broadcast domain (see Figure 2-4). By spoofing the MAC address of the default gateway, they can convince other devices in the subnet/ VLAN/broadcast domain that the MAC address of the default gateway is actually the MAC address of a system that has the ability to capture packets with a tool like Wireshark. Once the victims have poisoned ARP caches, when they need to send packets out of their subnet/VLAN/broadcast domain, they will encapsulate a packet into a frame with the destination MAC address set to the default gateway, which is the MAC address of the attacker device with Wireshark on it. The frame goes to the attacker device, and the attacker device copies the frame and keeps a copy of the frame and forwards the original to the real default gateway—and no one knows this is happening. To prevent this, you need to consider implementing a feature called Dynamic ARP (Address Resolution Protocol) Inspection (DAI) on your access layer switches. Note that encryption will not stop this type of attack, it will only prevent the attacker from being able to read your data.

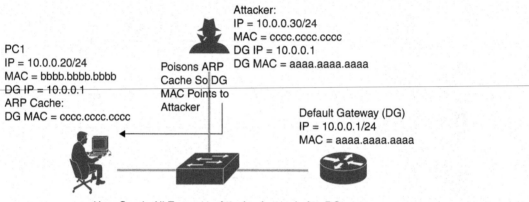

User Sends All Frames to Attacker Instead of to DG

Figure 2-4   *An ARP Cache Poisoning Attack That Results in an On-Path Attack*

The same thing can be accomplished with a rogue/fake DHCP server, as shown in Figure 2-5. If the attacker can set up a rogue DHCP server, they will be able to respond to DHCP requests before the real DHCP server can. The rogue DHCP server will be set up to hand out legitimate IP addresses, subnet masks, and DNS information for the subnet/ VLAN/broadcast domain the victim is in—but with one catch: The default gateway's IP address will be set to the IP address of an attacker device that has the ability to capture packets using a tool like Wireshark.

So now when the victim needs to access anything outside the subnet/VLAN/broadcast domain, they will use ARP for the MAC address of their default gateway, which is the Wireshark device. Once they get the MAC address, they will build the frame with a destination MAC address set to the Wireshark device. The frame then goes to the attacker device, and the attacker device copies the frame and keeps a copy of the frame and forwards the original to the real default gateway, and no one knows this is happening. To prevent this, you need to consider implementing a feature called DHCP snooping on your access layer switches. Again, encryption will not stop this type of attack, but strong encryption will prevent the attacker from being able to read your data.

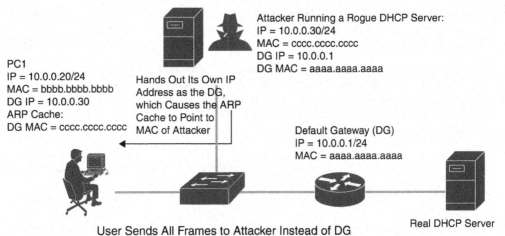

PC1
IP = 10.0.0.20/24
MAC = bbbb.bbbb.bbbb
DG IP = 10.0.0.30
ARP Cache:
DG MAC = cccc.cccc.cccc

Hands Out Its Own IP
Address as the DG,
which Causes the ARP
Cache to Point to
MAC of Attacker

Attacker Running a Rogue DHCP Server:
IP = 10.0.0.30/24
MAC = cccc.cccc.cccc
DG IP = 10.0.0.1
DG MAC = aaaa.aaaa.aaaa

Default Gateway (DG)
IP = 10.0.0.1/24
MAC = aaaa.aaaa.aaaa

Real DHCP Server

User Sends All Frames to Attacker Instead of DG

Figure 2-5 *A DHCP Spoofing Attack That Results in an On-Path Attack*

In the routed part of your network, a rogue router could cause an on-path attack as well.
If an attacker can set up a physical or virtual router in your environment that is running the
same dynamic routing protocol as your environment, then they could share false routing
information with your routers, making your routers believe that the rogue router is the preferred path for sending traffic, as shown in Figure 2-6. The attacker would also enable packet
captures on the router so that they can make a copy of all traffic before routing it to the
correct destination. Once again, encryption will not stop this type of attack but can prevent
the attacker from being able to read the data.

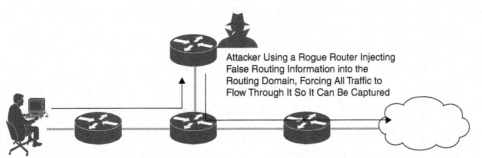

Attacker Using a Rogue Router Injecting
False Routing Information into the
Routing Domain, Forcing All Traffic to
Flow Through It So It Can Be Captured

Figure 2-6 *An Attacker Using a Rogue Router to Manipulate Traffic Flow So It Can
Be Captured*

Malware that can intercept packets before they leave a device can also be used for an
On-Path attack. The advantage in this case is that traffic can be captured before it gets
encrypted using TLS or any other mechanism. Therefore, having up to date antivirus/
antimalware software is critical.

Insider Threats

Insiders have always been a threat to organizations, and they always will be. They are the
most common threats and the most dangerous threats organizations face, but many people
forget because they have a tendency to think and believe that anyone who works for a

company would be "good" and not do anything "bad." However, threats are not about being "good" or "bad." An **insider threat** is a threat that originates from a trusted person within an organization.

It is obvious that an employee who downloads confidential corporate data to a USB flash drive and sells it to the highest bidder is jeopardizing confidentiality. It is obvious that an employee who manipulates data after hours for their advantage is jeopardizing integrity. It is also obvious that an employee who walks into the server room and unplugs everything is jeopardizing availability.

What is not obvious to many people is that a user downloading confidential corporate data to a USB flash drive so they can work on it at home is an insider threat as this action could jeopardize confidentiality. A user accidentally typing in $10000 instead of $100.00 is an insider threat as it could jeopardize integrity. A user clicking or typing the wrong command is an insider threat as this action could jeopardize availability. These are all insider threats, but they are not based on someone being "bad" or malicious; these actions are accidental or based on negligence.

Ex-employees or soon-to-be-ex-employees are also considered insider threats because they have existing knowledge of company systems, resources, and tools, and they had access or potentially still have access (I hope not!) to those systems.

The following are some examples of insider threats—some malicious and some that are just accidents or results of negligence:

- A disgruntled employee who is being terminated decides to exfiltrate data and post it on the Internet.

- An employee who is facing personal financial hardships decides to exfiltrate trade secrets and sell them to make some money on the side.

- An employee uses company systems to mine bitcoin or store illegal files, pictures, and videos.

- An employee falls for a phishing attack that leads to a massive ransomware attack.

- A remote worker falls for a vishing scam that costs the company thousands of dollars in gift cards.

- An ex-employee who still has access to a financial system skims money from the company and deletes financial records.

- A current employee makes a typing mistake that costs the company a lot of money.

- An employee who suspects they are about to be laid off installs a logic bomb on various data servers. The bomb is designed to delete all the records in the database one week after the employee is dismissed.

- A kind, friendly, trusted employee who has accepted a new job exfiltrates data and takes it with them to the new job and shares that information in order to gain a competitive edge.

- A remote worker has their house broken into, and company resources are stolen.

- An employee takes work home with them on a USB flash drive and misplaces it.

- An employee takes home papers containing confidential information and throws them in the trash when done reading them instead of shredding them.

- An employee accidentally sends an email with confidential information in it to the wrong person.

- An employee gives the wrong access permissions to a user for a file/folder/system/ network.

- An employee uses a personal email account for work-related activities.

- An employee uses a work-related account or system for personal activities.

- An employee uses their own phone, which is not up to date with the latest patches and fixes and does not have antivirus or antimalware software installed, on the corporate network.

As you can see from this short list, insider threats come in all shapes and sizes. As a security professional, one of the biggest challenges you will face is to reduce the likelihood of insider threats by creating various policies, procedures, and controls. Another challenge you will face is backlash/concern about those policies, procedures, and controls. So, being able to explain in a clear, nontechnical way why your policies, procedures, and controls are needed is critical.

As I sit here writing this, there are mass layoffs happening in the IT space with many of the largest IT companies that you interact with daily. Many news articles have been written about how poorly the layoffs have been handled. For example, employees have not been given advanced notice, they have been locked out of their accounts and unable to retrieve personal information they had on corporate systems, and they have been notified that they were laid off using a personal account like a personal email account or a message in a noncorporate chat tool. Now, leaving aside human emotion and considering the list of insider threats earlier, I want you to consider why these companies did things the way they did: It was all for the sake of security.

Imagine that you are a security professional for an organization, and your company is laying off 12,000 people at the same time. How would you recommend that the company handle the layoffs so that confidentiality, integrity, and availability are not jeopardized? Remember that out of these 12,000 people, all it takes is 1 disgruntled employee to cause a disaster. As a result, everyone has to be treated the same, and unfortunately, that is based on the assumption that they could all do something dangerous.

As another real-world example, Jack Teixeira, a 21-year-old airman first class of the Massachusetts Air National Guard's Intelligence Wing, leaked classified military documents related to Russia, Ukraine, North Korea, China, Iran, and the United Arab Emirates on a Discord server. So, insiders are your biggest threat, no matter what industry you are in.

Social Engineering Tactics

Key Topic

When cybersecurity incidents are analyzed, it is typically discovered that they began with **social engineering** attacks of some type that enable a cybercriminal to complete the first phase of a multi-phase attack. If you can eliminate social engineering attacks, you can typically prevent many other attacks from even happening. Take, for example, a ransomware attack. The end goal is to encrypt data and demand a ransom for the decryption key. How does the cybercriminal get access to the data? It could be through malware installed on the victim's machine or even by obtaining the victim's credentials and logging into the machine remotely. But how does the malware get installed, or how does the attacker get the credentials? Usually, the answer is a successful phishing attack, which is just one example of a social engineering attack.

As a cybersecurity professional, you need to be aware of various social engineering attacks. Social engineering attacks are accomplished through human interaction, taking advantage of people's tendency to be kind, helpful, curious, and then tricking them. Let's explore different types of social engineering attacks now.

Phishing

Phishing is an email-based social engineering attack. Its goal is to get the victim to click on a malicious attachment or a malicious link in an email. A malicious attachment may be any flavor of malware that will help the attacker continue their attack. Clicking a malicious link could take the user to a malicious site that has malware that can be downloaded and installed to the victim's system. Phishing emails and sites are typically creatively designed to look like emails and sites that users typically receive and visit; they make the victim feel like it's safe to enter their credentials. For example, a user might receive an email that looks like it came from their bank that asks them to reset their password. The user clicks a link that takes them to the malicious website where they proceed to enter their bank credentials; the attacker captures the credentials and forwards the user to the real site where they would have to log in again, potentially none the wiser.

Spear Phishing

Spear phishing is similar to phishing, but this type of attack is more focused. Whereas a phishing attack isn't focused on what it catches, a spear phishing attack targets only specific users. A spear phishing attacker is likely to craft their email more carefully, based on reconnaissance about their targets. By making their email more specific, the attacker is more apt to succeed.

Whaling

A **whaling** attack is also email based, and it's even more focused than a spear phishing attack, going after a "big fish," such as the CEO, CFO, CTO, CISO, or someone else who is high up in an organization.

Vishing

Vishing is a type of social engineering attack that relies on phone conversations. The attacker calls the potential victim and tries to persuade them to reveal information that would be beneficial to the attacker. It could be personal information, such as financial information or credential information, or it could be company-related information. You probably experience this type of attack all the time. My wife notified me that she received a phone call on her cell phone from "our bank," stating that there was a $1400 foreign transaction that had just occurred on our account, and we needed to divulge personal information for them to make it go away. She hung up, suspecting that it was a vishing attack because a bank official would not ask someone to "divulge personal information to make it go away." She went to our personal computer, logged into her account, and saw that there was no $1400 foreign transaction. I am so proud of her.

Smishing

Smishing is a type of social engineering attack that uses SMS messages to target a victim. The SMS message could contain malware that the victim downloads, but more often it is a malicious link that redirects the user to a malicious website that is designed to capture any credentials or information that the user types in.

Piggybacking/Tailgating

Piggybacking and **tailgating** are social engineering attacks that involve an unauthorized person—the attacker—gaining access to an authorized area by using an authorized person(s)—the victim(s). For example, an attacker who wants to get into a building that they are not authorized for might wait outside a service door, wearing a fake service uniform and holding a ladder, fumbling to get a fake access card to unlock the door. Then along comes a kind authorized employee, who badges into the authorized area with their own card and allows the unauthorized user in. This is known as piggybacking. As another example, an authorized user might enter a secured data center, and before the door closes, an attacker might slip in. This is known as tailgating. With piggybacking, the victim is aware that they are letting someone in, and with tailgating, the victim doesn't know someone slipped in.

Malvertising

Malvertising is a type of social engineering attack that takes advantage of people's curiosity or need to get a great deal. With advertisements splashed over every website today encouraging people to click on them to read a funny story, see a celebrity in a compromised act, or get a hard-to-find sought-after product for a fraction of the cost, it only makes sense that cybercriminals would take advantage of advertisements. Malvertising involves mimicking real ads or creating false ones so that when a user clicks, they download malware or are redirected to another site with malware or that has the ability to log what the user does.

As you can see, in all the different types of social engineering attacks, attackers are relying on and taking advantage of human fear, greed, curiosity, helpfulness, and urgency.

Physical Attacks

Physical attacks are attacks against physical security. Here are a few examples of physical attacks:

- **Piggybacking/tailgating:** As mentioned earlier, piggybacking and tailgating are social engineering attacks that involve an unauthorized person—the attacker—gaining access to an authorized area by using an authorized person(s)—the victim(s). For example, an attacker who wants to get into a building that they are not authorized for might wait outside a service door, wearing a fake service uniform and holding a ladder, fumbling to get a fake access card to unlock the door. Then along comes a kind authorized employee, who badges into the authorized area with their own card and allows the unauthorized user in. This is known as piggybacking. As another example, an authorized user might enter a secured data center, and before the door closes, an attacker might slip in. This is known as tailgating. With piggybacking, the victim is aware that they are letting someone in, and with tailgating, the victim doesn't know someone slipped in.

- **Dumpster diving:** This type of physical attack involves looking through the garbage of a victim to find information that could help with an additional attack. The attacker could be collecting garbage from small garbage cans, shredders, to even giant dumpsters outdoors (gross).

- **Cloning badges:** Electronic badges are pretty much the de facto standard for gaining authorized access to buildings and rooms in organizations today. If an attacker can get their hands on a valid electronic badge, with the right tools, they can clone the badge and make a copy for themself so they can gain access to areas that they are not authorized to access.

- **Jumping fences:** Not all fences offer the same level of protection. The wrong fence implementation could leave an organization vulnerable to fence jumping. Think about it. Could you climb over a 4-foot-tall chain-link fence? I am pretty sure you could. What about an 8-foot-tall chain-link fence? Now, it might be a little harder but not impossible. What about a 12-foot-tall chain-link fence? You might think twice about this, but if there is an enticing goal on the other side, you might still try. However, what about a 12-foot-tall fence where the top 2 feet angle outward at 45 degrees and are wrapped in barbed wire? Now we are getting very secure. The more difficult it is to scale your fence, the less likely you are to be subject to a fence jumping attack.

- **Lock picking/bumping/lock breaking:** An attacker might pick locks, bump lock pins, or break traditional locks to gain access to a locked area or item.

- **Vehicle ramming:** An attacker might ram a vehicle into a building to gain entry. It's not very stealthy, but it can be an effective physical attack.

- **Cable cutting:** An attacker might physically cut Internet cables or electrical cables to cause an outage and affect availability.

- **Theft:** An attacker might steal an asset from an organization, such as something from the corporate office or something from a remote employee's home.

- **Fire damage/water damage:** A building catching on fire or having its pipes burst and causing a flood are considered physical attacks. Regardless of whether they happen accidentally or on purpose, these are physical threats to an organization.

Advanced Persistent Threats (APTs)

Key Topic

Based on the name, you can tell that an **advanced persistent threat (APT)** is a threat. What kind of threat is it? Any kind of threat. So, what is so special about an APT? It is persistent, which means the threat will remain inside your organization, undetected, for a prolonged period of time, so that it could potentially result in severe damage to your organization. In addition, an APT uses advanced/sophisticated tactics and techniques, and it can be difficult to get all of an APT even if you detect it and attempt to clean it up. APTs typically leave remnants in various locations in your systems, including tiny backdoors and logic bombs that the attackers can take advantage of later. So, APTs are really bad for an organization, and the thought of them might keep you awake at night.

Because of the level of effort required to launch and maintain them, APTs are typically targeted at systems maintained by nations and large corporations. The primary long-term goal is typically to slowly steal a massive amount of data without being noticed. However, when the attackers are done, they typically cause damage or even execute a ransomware attack to try and cash in. Some well-known APTs include Titan Rain, Ghostnet, Stuxnet, and DarkSide24.

So, should security folks of small and medium organizations ignore APTs? Absolutely not. Small and medium businesses are often stepping-stones into larger organizations or nations. A small or medium organization may be part of the supply chain of the attacker's ultimate target. Therefore, small and medium businesses do have to be very concerned about APTs.

An APT typically occurs in stages, such as infiltration, escalation, and lateral movement. For example, an APT might start with some type of phishing attack that results in the attacker gaining undetected initial access to some system or systems. Then the attacker needs to dig in deeper by either elevating privileges or moving laterally through the organization, again remaining undetected. Once they find the true targets they are after (the systems with the data they want), they establish a long-term presence where they can look, learn, and remain for as long as they need to. As a cybersecurity professional, you have many opportunities to stop APTs in their tracks. Using a defense-in-depth strategy, you can prevent phishing attacks by implementing education, antivirus or antimalware software, and next-generation firewalls. In the event that the phishing attack is successful, you can use network and host IPSs as well as DLP to uncover abnormal behavior and stop the APT. With the right security strategy in place, you can significantly reduce the chances of being the victim of an APT.

Summary

It is imperative that from this day forward you constantly stay up to speed on the latest threats, attacks, and vulnerabilities that you will face. Common threats, attacks, and vulnerabilities include the following:

- **Malware** is any type of malicious software.

  - A **virus** inserts its code (payload) into a system's programs and files to cause harm.

  - A **worm** is standalone, self-replicating malware that doesn't inject its code into other programs or files like a virus and that does not require human interaction to spread or cause harm.

  - A **Trojan horse** is typically a program or file disguised as a legitimate program or file.

  - A **backdoor** is malicious software that allows an attacker to remotely access and control the system it has been installed on.

  - A **logic bomb** is malware with a timing component or associated conditions that cause it to go off.

  - **Downloaders** are designed to download other malicious software.

  - A **spammer** is designed to send unsolicited messages to as many people as it can, using tools like email, instant messaging, and newsgroups.

  - A **key logger** is designed to capture the user's keystrokes.

- **A rootkit** is designed to provide an attacker with administrative-level access to a system.

- **Ransomware** is malicious software that is designed to hold systems and data for ransom.

- **Internet of Things (IoT)** is the fancy name that has been given to Internet-enabled devices. IoT devices may have default accounts with passwords that are weak, guessable, posted to the Internet, or hardcoded in them. They may not get updates. They may have poorly developed applications or web interfaces that are used to manage, monitor, and maintain them. The backend systems that support the IoT devices may not be secure.

- A **denial of service (DoS)** is an attack against availability. The goal of this type of attack is to make a service unavailable.

- An **on-path attack** (formerly known as a man-in-the-middle attack) occurs when an attacker intercepts communication by placing themself between two communicating devices and eavesdropping on the conversation.

- **Insiders** are the most common and most dangerous threats organizations face. An insider threat is any threat that originates from someone trusted within the organization.

- **Social engineering** attacks are accomplished through human interaction, taking advantage of people's tendency to be kind and helpful and tricking them. These are some particular types of social engineering attacks:

  - **Phishing** is a type of social engineering attack that is email based. Its goal is to get the victim to click on a malicious attachment or a malicious link in an email.

  - **Spear phishing** is similar to phishing, but this attack is more focused on a specific target or targets.

  - **Whaling** is even more focused than spear phishing, going after a "big fish" such as a CEO, CFO, CTO, or CISO.

  - **Vishing** is a type of social engineering attack that relies on voice phone conversations.

  - **Smishing** is a type of social engineering attack that uses SMS messages to target victims.

  - **Piggybacking** and **tailgating** are social engineering attacks that involve an unauthorized person—the attacker—gaining access to an authorized area by using an authorized person(s)—the victim(s).

  - **Malvertising** takes advantage of people's curiosity or need to get a great deal.

- **Physical attacks** are attacks against physical security.

  - **Piggybacking** and **tailgating** are social engineering attacks that involve an unauthorized person—the attacker—gaining access to an authorized area by using an authorized person(s)—the victim(s).

  - **Dumpster diving** involves looking through the garbage of a victim to find information that could help with an additional attack.

- **Cloning badges** involves making copies of badges so an attacker can gain access to areas they are not authorized to access.

- **Jumping fences** involves climbing over a fence to gain access to an unauthorized area.

- **Lock picking/bumping/lock breaking** involves breaking traditional locks to gain access to a locked area or item.

- **Vehicle ramming** involves ramming a vehicle into a building to gain entry.

- **Cable cutting** involves physically cutting Internet or electrical cables.

- **Theft** is the act of stealing an asset from an organization.

- An **advanced persistent threat (APT)** is an undetected threat that is persistent within an organization.

Exam Preparation Tasks

As mentioned in the Introduction, you can customize your strategy for exam preparation. Suggested tasks include the exercises here, Chapter 16, "Final Preparation," and the exam simulation questions on the companion website.

Review All Key Topics

Review the most important topics in this chapter, noted with the Key Topics icon in the outer margin of the page. Table 2-2 lists these key topics and the page number on which each is found.

Table 2-2   Key Topics for Chapter 2

Key Topic Element	Description	Page Number
Section	Malware Variants	16
Paragraph	IoT devices	19
List	Denial of service attacks	19
Paragraph	Bots, botnets, as well as command and control servers	20
Section	On-Path Attacks	21
Section	Insider Threats	23
Section	Social Engineering Tactics	25
List	Physical attacks	27
Section	Advanced Persistent Threats (APTs)	28

Define Key Terms

Define the following key terms from this chapter and check your answers in the glossary:

malware, virus, worm, Trojan horse, remote access Trojan (RAT), backdoor, logic bomb, downloader, spammer, key logger, rootkit, ransomware, Internet of Things (IoT), denial of service (DoS), distributed denial of service (DDoS), botnet, bot, command and control server, C2 server, CnC server, C&C server, on-path attack, insider, insider threat, social engineering, phishing, spear phishing, whaling, vishing, smishing, piggybacking, tailgating, malvertising, Dumpster diving, cloning badges, jumping fences, lock picking, lock breaking, vehicle ramming, cable cutting, theft, fire damage, water damage, advanced persistent threat (APT)

Complete Tables and Lists from Memory

There are no memory tables for this chapter.

Review Questions

1. Which of the following BEST describes a backdoor?

   a. Malicious software that is designed to execute on its own at a specific time and date

   b. Malicious software that is standalone and self-replicating, does not need its code to be injected into other programs or files, and does not need human interaction to spread

   c. Malicious software disguised as a legitimate program or file that executes when the user attempts to access the software

   d. Malicious software that is designed to allow an attacker to remotely access and control the system it has been installed on

2. Which of the following are examples of IoT vulnerabilities? (Choose two.)

   a. Weak default account passwords

   b. Lack of updates

   c. Easily purchased from various stores

   d. Reliance on the cloud

3. Which of these are examples of DoS attacks? (Choose all that apply.)

   a. Malware is installed on a system and shuts down the system.

   b. A server is flooded with useless traffic that overwhelms the server's resources and crashes it.

   c. A user trips on a power cable and cuts power to various systems.

   d. A user exfiltrates data from a database.

4. Which of the following are examples of on-path attacks? (Choose two.)

   a. Trojan horse

   b. DHCP spoofing

   c. Logic bomb

   d. ARP cache poisoning

5. Which of the following are examples of insider threats? (Choose all that apply.)

   a. An employee falls for a simple phishing attack, which leads to a massive ransomware attack.

   b. A current employee accidentally types $10000 into the system instead of $100.00.

   c. A disgruntled employee who is being terminated exfiltrates data and posts it on the Internet.

   d. A cybercrime organization brute-forces a password for a system they have remote access to.

6. What is a phishing attack?

   a. An email-based social engineering attack that targets as many people as possible

   b. An email-based social engineering attack that targets a very specific group of people

   c. An email-based social engineering attack that targets the CEO or CFO of an organization

   d. An email-based social engineering attack that targets as many systems as possible

7. Which of the following are examples of physical attacks? (Choose two.)

   a. Cloning badges

   b. Whaling

   c. Cable cutting

   d. Logic bomb

8. What is the BEST way to defend against an APT?

   a. With a defense-in-depth strategy

   b. With education and training

   c. With a DLP solution

   d. With antimalware software

CHAPTER 3

Access Management

This chapter covers the following topics:

- **Introduction to AAA:** This section introduces you to the importance of AAA.

- **Authentication:** This section focuses on the various factors of authentication, the need for MFA, as well as passwords and password policies.

- **Authorization:** This section explores the need for authorization.

- **Accounting:** This section explores the need for accounting.

- **RADIUS:** This section examines the need for RADIUS and provides some sample use cases.

To provide confidentiality, integrity, and availability, you must be able to granularly control access to all resources and ensure that the access controls are upheld at all times. If the access controls ever break down, legitimate or non-legitimate users, applications, or services will have access to resources they should not have access to.

To provide an access management solution that maintains the appropriate levels of confidentiality, integrity, and availability, you must consider the AAA framework, which outlines the best practices you need to consider when it comes to authentication, authorization, and accounting.

This chapter introduces the AAA framework. It first focuses on authentication, MFA, and password policies. It then moves on to covering authorization, followed by accounting. It wraps up by examining a AAA service known as RADIUS.

This chapter covers information related to the following Cisco Certified Support Technician (CCST) Cybersecurity exam objective:

1.3. Explain access management principles.

"Do I Know This Already?" Quiz

The "Do I Know This Already?" quiz allows you to assess whether you should read this entire chapter thoroughly or jump to the "Exam Preparation Tasks" section. If you are in doubt about your answers to these questions or your own assessment of your knowledge of the topics, read the entire chapter. Table 3-1 lists the major headings in this chapter and their corresponding "Do I Know This Already?" quiz questions. You can find the answers in Appendix A, "Answers to the 'Do I Know This Already?' Quizzes and Review Questions."

Table 3-1 "Do I Know This Already?" Section-to-Question Mapping

Foundation Topics Section	Questions
Introduction to AAA	1
Authentication	2
Authorization	3
Accounting	4
RADIUS	5

CAUTION The goal of self-assessment is to gauge your mastery of the topics in this chapter. If you do not know the answer to a question or are only partially sure of the answer, you should mark that question incorrect for purposes of self-assessment. Giving yourself credit for an answer you correctly guess skews your self-assessment results and might provide you with a false sense of security.

1. Which of the following correctly defines AAA?
   a. A client/server protocol used for authentication, authorization, and accounting
   b. The process of verifying that someone or something is in fact truly who they say they are
   c. A framework that helps build the controls needed to access computing resources, enforce policies, and audit usage
   d. A type of MFA that encourages three factors

2. Which of the following correctly defines authentication?
   a. The process of adopting the least-privilege principle, the need-to-know principle, and the implicit-deny principle
   b. The process of granting privileges and controlling what a user is able to do
   c. The process of monitoring, recording, and auditing everything in an organization
   d. The process of verifying that someone or something is in fact truly who they say they are

3. Which of the following correctly defines authorization?
   a. The process of monitoring, recording, and auditing everything in an organization
   b. The process of granting privileges and controlling what a user is able to do
   c. The process of verifying that someone or something is in fact truly who they say they are
   d. The process of collecting, consolidating, and correlating log files

4. Which of the following correctly defines accounting?
   a. The process of using biometrics to allow access to a system
   b. The process of verifying that someone or something is in fact truly who they say they are

    c. The process of granting privileges and controlling what a user is able to do

    d. The process of monitoring, recording, and auditing everything in an organization

5. What is RADIUS?

    a. A client/server protocol used for accounting only

    b. A client/server protocol used for authentication only

    c. A client/server protocol used for authentication and authorization only

    d. A client/server protocol used for authentication, authorization, and accounting

Foundation Topics

Introduction to AAA

AAA, which is pronounced "triple A" and stands for *authentication, authorization, and accounting*, is a framework. A framework is a real or conceptual structure intended to serve as a support or guide for the building of something that expands the structure into something useful. The AAA framework is a guide that helps you build the controls needed to access computing resources, enforce policies, and audit usage. AAA plays a very important role in security.

Authentication is about verifying the identity of those who access your systems and data. Therefore, without authentication, you can't control access to your data, and so you can't protect confidentiality, integrity, and availability (CIA). Authorization is about controlling what can be done to your systems and data. Therefore, without authorization, you can't control what can be done with your data, and so you can't protect CIA. Accounting is about recording everything that is happening to your systems and data. Therefore, without accounting, you can't keep track of the who, what, where, when, why, and how of your data, and so you can't protect CIA.

As you can see, without AAA, it is impossible to meet the CIA needs of your organization.

Authentication

Authentication is about proving the identity of someone or something, or verifying that someone or something is in fact truly who they say they are. Why do I say "someone or something"? Well, *someone* refers to a person, and *something* refers to anything else that needs to be authenticated. Keep in mind that systems, devices, tools, applications, and so on need to be authenticated. If you are only focused on people, you are leaving your organization vulnerable to attack.

There are a multitude of factors that people, systems, devices, applications, and tools can use to authenticate. Table 3-2 explores these factors and provides examples.

Table 3-2 Authentication Factors

Factor	Description	Examples
Something you know	This is authentication based on knowledge.	A username, a password, a personal identification number (PIN) you have memorized, a passphrase you have memorized, CAPTCHA test, personal verification questions

Factor	Description	Examples
Something you have	This is authentication based on possession.	A security token that can provide you with a random PIN
		A random PIN, passphrase, or notification from your smartphone that you can accept or reject
		A swipe card, tap card, or passkey
Something you are	This is authentication based on unique aspects of yourself and relies on biometrics.	Your fingerprint, your facial geometry, your retina, your palm print
Somewhere you are	This is authentication based on location.	You are allowed or denied based on your connection to the corporate Wi-Fi versus coffee shop Wi-Fi versus airport Wi-Fi versus home Wi-Fi.
		You are allowed or denied based on your connection in the United States versus Canada versus any other country.
Something you do	This is authentication based on habits and characteristics.	The way you walk, the way you write, the way you talk, the path you take to work, the places you eat lunch, the sports you play and when
Time	This is authentication based on the time of day and/or day of the week.	You are allowed on the Internet between 9 a.m. and 5 p.m. and are not allowed on the Internet between 5 p.m. and 9 a.m.
		You are allowed to connect to the VPN Monday through Friday, 7 a.m. to 9 p.m. local time

Multifactor Authentication (MFA)

Using a single factor of authentication is no longer advisable. For example, relying on a username and password (a single factor: something you know) will not protect you as it once did. Cybercriminals have developed very creative ways to figure out your username and password (such as via a convincing phishing email), and once they know them, they will be able to access anything you can access with them. The same thing is true with PINs or passphrases that you have created and memorized. Once a cybercriminal has that information, they will have access to systems and data you don't want them to have access to.

One of the best ways to protect yourself today is with **multifactor authentication (MFA)**. MFA involves using two or more of the factors mentioned previously, in combination, to successfully authenticate (for example, combining something you know with something you have or combining something you have with something you are or combining something you have with somewhere you are). As of this writing, MFA is becoming closer to being the norm for every application and service that exists.

Now please note that MFA does not protect you from becoming the victim of a phishing attack that is designed to steal your credentials—or any other type of attack for that matter. It does, however, help prevent the cybercriminal from gaining access to your systems and data based only on the credentials they stole in the phishing attack. How so? Well, even though they may have stolen your username and password, they do not have the second factor that is needed to successfully authenticate to the systems and access the data. For example, let's say your first factor is a username and password. Regardless of how strong the password is, it could be stolen/captured during a phishing attack or a data breach targeting your authentication database. If you have a second factor that is required, like a one-time PIN generated by an application installed on your cell phone that is valid for only 30 seconds, the cybercriminal will not be able to access your systems and data because they do not have your cell phone and can't get the one-time PIN—and they also can't guess it or brute force it because it changes every 30 seconds.

Table 3-3 provides examples of MFA.

Key Topic

Table 3-3   Examples of MFA

Factor 1	Factor 2	Description
Your bank card	A memorized PIN	Your bank card is one factor (something you have), and the PIN is the other factor (something you know).
A swipe card	A retinal scan	The swipe card is one factor (something you have), and the retinal scan is the other factor (something you are).
A username and a password	A notification sent to your phone that asks you to click yes or no	The username/password is one factor (something you know), and your phone with the notification is the other factor (something you have).
A fingerprint scan	A PIN	The fingerprint scan is one factor (something you are), and the PIN is the other factor (something you know).
A username and a password	Your location	Your username/password is one factor (something you know), and your location is the other factor (somewhere you are).

Please be aware that true multifactor authentication requires two or more different factors, as shown in Table 3-3. So, having a username/password and a memorized PIN is not MFA as they are both something you know—and so count as only one factor. A retinal scan and a fingerprint scan are not MFA as they are also the same factor (something you are). Having your phone that generates a PIN that you enter and then an app on your phone that gives you a one-time password is not MFA as these are, again, the same factor (something you have). These are all examples of **two-step authentication** because two steps are needed for authentication, but only a single factor is being used. What I want you to realize from this is that if you implement MFA poorly, you might not be as protected as you think you are, and you would do better with other combinations. For example, what would you consider to be stronger?

Option 1.   A username/password and a six-digit one-time PIN generated at the time it is needed

Or

Option 2.   A USB authentication key that needs to be entered into the system and then a notification displayed on your phone that needs to be accepted or rejected

So, option 1 is an example of MFA as there are two different factors in use, and option 2 is an example of two-step authentication because the same factor is used twice. In this case, it is clear that it would be much harder for the cybercriminal to access your system with two-step authentication (the USB key and your phone) as they would need physical access to both those devices and the system they are accessing. Although option 1 is a great option and highly recommended, you can see that strength comes from the combinations and not necessarily from just different factors being used. So, for the CCST Cybersecurity exam, be clear about the difference between MFA and two-step authentication in case you have to pick them out of a lineup.

Key
Topic

Passwords and Password Policies

The most common way to authenticate today is with a username and password. Regardless of whether they are used as the only factor or as part of MFA or as part of two-step authentication, usernames and passwords are not going away anytime soon. Therefore, it is important to ensure that passwords meet certain requirements so that they are less apt to be easily guessed or determined using brute-force techniques and then reused by cybercriminals. In addition, they should be stored securely (hashed) in a database so that if the database is compromised, the likelihood of a cybercriminal being able to use any of the passwords in the database is significantly reduced.

So, what should a password be? It should be:

- Something that is not guessable

- Something that can't be brute forced

- Something that the user can remember without having to write it down

- Something that can be used for a long period of time

We used to encourage complexity by forcing users to include lowercase letters, uppercase letters, a digit, and special characters, but users would do the minimum to meet the requirements instead of creating complex passwords. For example, the password "password" would simply become "Password1!" which is not complex at all. We wanted them to use something like "Yt56R34w" but got "Password1!" instead. So, complexity requirements really haven't worked out as they were intended to and still result in passwords being guessable, brute forced, and written down.

Now we encourage length. The longer a password is, the harder it is to guess, and the harder it is to brute force. Users can now use passphrases or sentences for their passwords, which they can remember with ease without writing them down. For example, the password "We_Love_Oranges_And_Orange_Marmalade" is not easy to guess, it is impossible to brute force, and the user will not have to write it down. In addition, it will not have to be changed for a long time.

So, what would be a good password policy today? A good password policy would

- Encourage length (12 characters minimum with no maximum).

- Encourage the use of passphrases or sentences (something easy to remember but really long).

- Force the use of an uppercase letter, a special character, and a number and allow the rest to be all lowercase.

- Increase the number of days between password changes to a year or more.

Now a user can create a password such as "B3ing_A_CCST_Cybersecurity_Is_Awesome!" which would meet all the requirements of the password policy and more while being impossible to guess or brute forced, and the user will not have to write it down. If they don't want to use the special character _, then it would still be acceptable to use "B3ingACCSTCybersecurityIsAwesome!". You could even omit the special character ! or the number, and this would still be a very safe password.

In addition, because of the length requirement, a user could use their password for a longer period of time. Instead of forcing users to change their passwords every 30 to 90 days, you could let them change it every year or even every few years. According to the website How Secure Is My Password, at https://www.security.org/how-secure-is-my-password/, it would take a computer about 1 hundred tredecillion years to crack (brute force) the password "B3ingACCSTCybersecurityIsAwesome!". So using this password for a few years without changing it should be fine.

When it comes to storing passwords in a database, it is imperative that you use hashing and salting. Hashing is done so that the password is stored as a hash instead of plaintext. This way, if the database is ever exfiltrated, the cybercriminal will get all the hashes but will have a very difficult time converting the hashes back into the plaintext passwords. (We cover hashing in Chapter 4, "Cryptography.") Salting is a way to ensure uniqueness when storing a password as a hash and reduce the chances of a rainbow table being successful. Without salting, if two people have exactly the same plaintext password, the hash that is stored in the database will be exactly the same. However, if a salt is added (for example, four or more extra random characters) during the hashing process, then those two plaintext passwords would produce two different hashes that would be stored in the database. These extra random characters make it impossible for a cybercriminal to obtain the passwords by using a rainbow table.

Don't forget that a lengthy password does not eliminate the need for MFA. If by chance a cybercriminal tricks you into giving them your password via a phishing attack, MFA will save you, and then once you discover that you have given up your password, you can change the password and sleep better knowing that the cybercriminal did not get into your account.

Authorization

Authorization is the process of granting and controlling what an authenticated user is able to do. It is focused on permissions. When it comes to permissions, you should adopt three principles:

- The **least-privilege principle**, which is about giving users only the minimum permissions they need to accomplish their objectives

- The **need-to-know principle**, which is about only giving users access to what they absolutely need to do their jobs and perform their roles

- The **implicit-deny principle**, which means everyone is prevented from doing everything unless they are explicitly allowed

If you are careless with authorization, your users could do something they should not (by accident or on purpose), resulting in risks associated with CIA. A cybercriminal could gain control of an account with more privileges than they should have and move vertically (within a system) or laterally (between systems) and exfiltrate data, which would compromise CIA. Therefore, it is imperative that you control exactly what each user can access by establishing policies and rules and adopting the least-privilege principle (only giving users minimum permissions they need to do their job), the need-to-know principle (only giving users access to what they need to know to do their job), and the implicit-deny principle (denying by default unless explicitly allowed).

Accounting

Accounting is about keeping track of who, what, where, when, why, and how. It is the process of monitoring, recording, and auditing everything in your organization. By keeping track of who accessed what data, where and when they accessed it, why they accessed it, and how they accessed it, you will be more aware and in tune with what is happening (good or bad) in and around your organization. For a security professional, this is one of the most important A's of AAA, yet many fail to implement an appropriate level of accounting, or if they do, they are overwhelmed by it and fail to continually follow up on what needs to be done with the collected information. Accounting generates a lot of logs, and the logs will be your window into the happenings within and around your network and resources. So, having a **security information and event management (SIEM)** solution as well as a **security orchestration, automation, and response (SOAR)** tool will definitely help you stay in the loop and focused on continually monitoring and protecting your network. A SIEM solution helps you collect logs, consolidate logs, correlate logs, and get notified about abnormalities/threats in logs that are in breach of established policies. A SOAR tool helps you automate responses and reduce the amount of human intervention when an abnormality/threat has been detected.

For example, say that your SIEM solution collects logs, consolidates logs, correlates logs, and notifies you, but you have to manually react and respond. So from the moment of notification to the successful completion of the response, there may be a significant amount of time lost. With the help of a SOAR tool, you might have scripts or the help of artificial intelligence (AI) and machine learning (ML) to immediately respond to the notifications and threats without human intervention.

RADIUS

Remote Authentication Dial-In User Service (RADIUS) is a client/server protocol originally designed to give remote users the ability to access services via dial-up connections. (If you don't know what dial-up is, it is because you are too young. Back in my early days, we did not have always-on broadband or fiber connections to the Internet; we had to use our telephone landlines to dial in to the Internet.) RADIUS was a service used for remote authentication with dial-up network access. Because of its flexibility, over time RADIUS has evolved and been adopted and adapted for other scenarios as well. Today it is a protocol we use with AAA for authentication, authorization, and accounting purposes.

The best way to learn about RADIUS is through an example of its use. Refer to Figure 3-1 as we go through the following example.

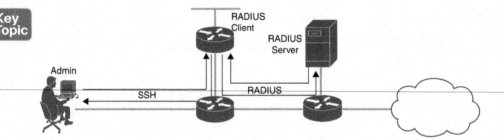

Figure 3-1   *Admin Using SSH to Manage a Router and Router Authenticating the Admin Using RADIUS*

On the right side of this figure is a RADIUS server. It is a server that contains a database of usernames and passwords, and it can communicate using the RADIUS protocol. You can implement RADIUS servers with several different options; in this example, we use Cisco Identity Services Engine (ISE). This is the server part of the client/server protocol.

In the middle of the figure is a router. This router is configured to communicate with the RADIUS server using the RADIUS protocol any time authentication needs to be performed. This is the client part of the client/server protocol.

Now focus on the left side of the figure, where you see the administrator of the router. The admin opens the SSH client and makes a connection to the router using SSH (port 22) for management purposes. They then need to provide their username and password to authenticate. When the router receives the username and password, it contacts the RADIUS server by using the RADIUS protocol so that the RADIUS server can determine if the admin is authenticated or not, based on the credentials provided. If the admin provided a username and password listed in the database, the RADIUS server tells the router to grant the admin access. If they did not provide a username and password listed in the database, the RADIUS server tells the router to deny the admin access.

With RADIUS, authentication and authorization happen at the same time. So, when the admin is being authenticated by the RADIUS server, the server can also be configured to tell the client (the router in Figure 3-1) what the user (the admin in Figure 3-1) is allowed and not allowed to do, based on a database of permissions that has been defined on the RADIUS server. For example, in Figure 3-1, once the user authenticates, they may only be authorized to configure, verify, and troubleshoot routing protocols on the router. Or maybe they are authorized to only perform verification tasks and no configuration tasks.

As mentioned earlier, because of its flexibility, RADIUS can be used in many different scenarios. For example, Figure 3-2 shows a wireless user, a wireless access point, and the RADIUS server.

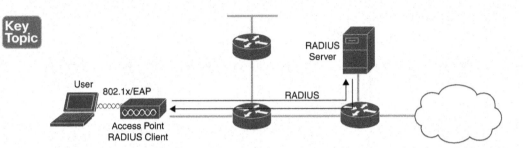

Figure 3-2 *Wireless User Authenticating to the Wireless Network Using 802.1x, EAP, and RADIUS*

For this scenario, the wireless user needs access to the network. When connecting, they provide their username and password to the wireless AP, using 802.1x and Extensible Authentication Protocol (EAP) messages. The wireless AP (RADIUS client) then sends those credentials to the RADIUS server, using the RADIUS protocol. The RADIUS server compares the username and password to those listed in the database. If the username and password are correct, the RADIUS server notifies the wireless AP that the user is authenticated and authorized, and the wireless AP can provide the user access to the network. If the username and password are not correct, the RADIUS server notifies the wireless AP that the user is not authenticated or authorized, and the wireless AP can prevent the user from accessing the network.

In addition to configuring authentication and authorization, you can also configure accounting with RADIUS. This gives you a centralized way of keeping track of who has been authenticated and who has not, when they were authenticated, and when they were not authenticated. This is important from a security standpoint as it gives you the ability to keep track of all successful and unsuccessful authentication and authorization sessions.

RADIUS uses UDP as its transport protocol. Traditionally, UDP port 1645 was used for authentication and authorization, and UDP port 1646 was used for accounting. However, today we typically see UDP port 1812 for authentication and authorization and UDP port 1813 for accounting. Why is this important? Many Cisco devices default to using 1645 and 1646 as the port numbers, but the RADIUS servers default to using 1812 and 1813 as the port numbers. So, when setting up RADIUS on many Cisco devices, you have to change the port numbers on those devices to 1812 and 1813.

If you are interested in reading more about RADIUS, you can check out RFC 2865, which covers authentication and authorization for RADIUS, and RFC 2866, which covers accounting for RADIUS.

Summary

To provide an access management solution that maintains the levels of confidentiality, integrity, and availability you need, consider the AAA framework, which includes authentication, authorization, and accounting:

- **Authentication** is about proving the identity of someone or something.
  - **Something you know** is authentication based on knowledge.
  - **Something you have** is authentication based on possession.
  - **Something you are** is authentication based on unique aspects of yourself and relies on biometrics.
  - **Somewhere you are** is authentication based on location.
  - **Something you do** is authentication based on habits and characteristics.
  - **Time** is authentication based on the time of day and/or day of the week.
  - **MFA** is about using two or more factors for authentication.

- **Authorization** is the process of granting and controlling what an authenticated user is able to do.
  - The **least-privilege principle** says to give users the minimum permissions they need to accomplish their objectives.
  - The **need-to-know principle** says to give users access only to what they absolutely need to do their jobs and perform their roles.
  - The **implicit-deny principle** says to ensure that everyone is prevented from doing everything unless explicitly allowed.

- **Accounting** is about keeping track of who, what, where, when, why, and how. It is the process of monitoring, recording, and auditing everything in an organization.
  - A **SIEM** solution helps you collect logs, consolidate logs, correlate logs, and get notified about abnormalities/threats in logs that are in breach of established policies.
  - A **SOAR** tool helps you automate responses and reduce the amount of human intervention required when an abnormality/threat has been detected.

- **Remote Authentication Dial-In User Service (RADIUS)** is a client/server protocol used with authentication, authorization, and accounting.

Exam Preparation Tasks

As mentioned in the Introduction, you can customize your strategy for exam preparation. Suggested tasks include the exercises here, Chapter 16, "Final Preparation," and the exam simulation questions on the companion website.

Review All Key Topics

Review the most important topics in this chapter, noted with the Key Topics icon in the outer margin of the page. Table 3-4 lists these key topics and the page number on which each is found.

Key Topic

Table 3-4   Key Topics for Chapter 3

Key Topic Element	Description	Page Number
Paragraph	The AAA framework	36
Paragraph	Authentication	36
Table 3-2	Authentication Factors	36
Paragraph	MFA	37
Table 3-3	Examples of MFA	38
Section	Passwords and password policies	39
Section	Authorization	41
Section	Accounting	41
Paragraph	RADIUS	42
Figure 3-1	Admin Using SSH to Manage a Router and Router Authenticating the Admin Using RADIUS	42
Figure 3-2	Wireless User Authenticating to the Wireless Network Using 802.1x, EAP, and RADIUS	43

Define Key Terms

Define the following key terms from this chapter and check your answers in the glossary:

AAA; authentication; something you know; something you have; something you are; somewhere you are; something you do; multifactor authentication (MFA); two-step authentication; authorization; least-privilege principle; need-to-know principle; implicit-deny principle; accounting; security information and event management (SIEM); security orchestration, automation, and response (SOAR); Remote Access Dial-In User Service (RADIUS)

Complete Tables and Lists from Memory

Print a copy of Appendix B, "Memory Tables," found on the companion website, or at least the section for this chapter, and complete the tables and lists from memory. Appendix C, "Memory Tables Answer Key," includes completed tables and lists you can use to check your work.

Review Questions

1. What does AAA stand for?

   a. Authentication, accessibility, and availability

   b. Availability, authentication, and authorization

   c. Authentication, authorization, and accounting

   d. Authentication, availability, and accounting

2. Which of the following are examples of MFA? (Choose two.)

   a. A USB authentication key that needs to be connected to the USB port on the system and a notification displayed on your phone that needs to be accepted or rejected

   b. A bank card and a memorized PIN

   c. A fingerprint scan followed by a facial scan

   d. A username/password and a four-digit PIN that you have memorized

   e. A username/password and a notification sent to your phone that requires you to click yes or no

3. Which of the following are authorization principles? (Choose three.)

   a. Enable MFA

   b. Least privilege

   c. Need to know

   d. Implicit deny

   e. Record all activity

4. Which of the following is a system that can help you collect logs, consolidate logs, correlate logs, and get notified about abnormalities and threats in logs that are in breach of established policies.

   a. SIEM

   b. SOAR

   c. RADIUS

   d. MFA

5. What port numbers are typically used with RADIUS?

   a. 20 and 21

   b. 22 and 23

   c. 1812 and 1813

   d. 3388 and 3389

CHAPTER 4

Cryptography

This chapter covers the following topics:

- **Cryptography Overview:** This section introduces you to encryption and decryption concepts as well as states of data.

- **Symmetric Cryptography:** This section explores symmetric cryptography.

- **Asymmetric Cryptography:** This section explores asymmetric cryptography.

- **Using Symmetric and Asymmetric Cryptography:** This section discusses when to use symmetric cryptography and when to use asymmetric cryptography.

- **Types of Ciphers:** This section provides descriptions and examples of various symmetric and asymmetric ciphers.

- **Certificates and PKI:** This section explores the need for certificates and PKI for cryptography.

- **Hashing:** This section covers hashing and provides examples of when to use hashing.

- **Cryptography in the Real World:** This section explores how to use cryptography for secure web browsing, VPNs, and remote management.

- **Cisco Next-Generation Cryptography:** This section introduces Cisco next-generation cryptography.

As a security professional, you must be an expert at cryptographic concepts. Cryptography ensures confidentiality and integrity. In modern networks, cryptography is mandatory; there is no excuse for not using it.

This chapter begins by introducing cryptography and then jumps right in to exploring symmetric and asymmetric cryptography. Next, it discusses when to use symmetric cryptography and when to use asymmetric cryptography. Since there are many different types of symmetric and asymmetric ciphers, this chapter introduces some of the most common ones in use today. To conclude the symmetric and asymmetric discussion, this chapter describes the need for certificates and PKI. It also covers hashing and provides a few examples of when hashing is beneficial and the various hashing algorithms that exist. Finally, this chapter provides some real-world cryptographic examples and wraps up with coverage of Cisco next-generation cryptography.

This chapter covers information related to the following Cisco Certified Support Technician (CCST) Cybersecurity exam objective:

1.4. Explain encryption methods and applications.

"Do I Know This Already?" Quiz

The "Do I Know This Already?" quiz allows you to assess whether you should read this entire chapter thoroughly or jump to the "Exam Preparation Tasks" section. If you are in doubt about your answers to these questions or your own assessment of your knowledge of the topics, read the entire chapter. Table 4-1 lists the major headings in this chapter and their corresponding "Do I Know This Already?" quiz questions. You can find the answers in Appendix A, "Answers to the 'Do I Know This Already?' Quizzes and Review Questions."

Table 4-1 "Do I Know This Already?" Section-to-Question Mapping

Foundation Topics Section	Questions
Cryptography Overview	1
Symmetric Cryptography	2
Asymmetric Cryptography	3
Using Symmetric and Asymmetric Cryptography	4
Types of Ciphers	5
Certificates and PKI	6
Hashing	7
Cryptography in the Real World	8
Cisco Next-Generation Cryptography	9

CAUTION The goal of self-assessment is to gauge your mastery of the topics in this chapter. If you do not know the answer to a question or are only partially sure of the answer, you should mark that question incorrect for purposes of self-assessment. Giving yourself credit for an answer you correctly guess skews your self-assessment results and might provide you with a false sense of security.

1. Which of the following statements are true? (Choose two.)

   a. Decryption is the act of taking a plaintext message and turning it into ciphertext so it is unreadable.

   b. Encryption is the act of taking unreadable ciphertext and turning it back into its original plaintext message.

   c. Encryption is the act of taking a plaintext message and turning it into ciphertext so it is unreadable.

   d. Decryption is the act of taking unreadable ciphertext and turning it back into its original plaintext message.

2. Which of the following describes symmetric cryptography?

   a. It requires the use of a single key for both encryption and decryption.

   b. It requires the use of different keys for encryption and for decryption.

   c. It takes variable-length information and turns it into a fixed-length output.

   d. It is used to securely generate and exchange cryptographic keys.

3. Which of the following is true about asymmetric cryptography?

   a. It uses shared secret keys.

   b. It uses a private key pair.

   c. It uses a public key pair.

   d. It uses a public/private key pair.

4. Which are examples of using symmetric cryptography? (Choose two.)

   a. You need to encrypt data at rest on a server.

   b. You need to generate and exchange cryptographic keys.

   c. You need to encrypt data that is being transferred over a VPN.

   d. You need to prove that the data exchanged is from an authentic source.

5. Which of the following are symmetric ciphers? (Choose two.)

   a. DH

   b. AES

   c. RSA

   d. DSA

   e. 3DES

6. What is the purpose of a digital certificate?

   a. To prove the identity and ownership of a public key

   b. To prove the identity and ownership of a private key

   c. To generate and store public keys

   d. To share private keys

7. Which of the following are reasons you would use hashing algorithms? (Choose all that apply.)

   a. You need to store passwords in a database.

   b. You need to verify that data has not changed during transmission.

   c. You need to verify that data has not changed while at rest.

   d. You need to provide confidentiality for data at rest and in transit.

8. Why is cryptography used with remote management? (Choose two.)

   a. To conceal management traffic as it moves from a management PC and the device being managed.

   b. To verify that management traffic has not been altered while in transit from a management PC and the device being managed.

   c. To increase the transfer speed between the management PC and the device being managed.

   d. To improve the availability and reliability of the connection between the management PC and the device being managed.

9. What is the purpose of Cisco next-generation cryptography?

   a. It is a new all-in-one Cisco next-generation firewall.

   b. It is a set of Cisco-proprietary cryptographic features and services supported only on Cisco devices.

   c. It is a NIST best practice that has become a standard for implementing cryptographic algorithms.

   d. It is meant to ensure that there is a widely accepted and consistent set of cryptographic algorithms that provide strong security and good performance for everyone.

Foundation Topics

Cryptography Overview

The National Institute of Standards and Technology (NIST) defines cryptography as follows:

> **Cryptography** uses mathematical techniques to transform data and prevent it from being read or tampered with by unauthorized parties. That enables exchanging secure messages even in the presence of adversaries. (https://www.nist.gov/cryptography)

For example, cryptography makes it possible to take a plaintext message, turn it into ciphertext by encrypting it, transfer the ciphertext over an untrusted or trusted network, and then decrypt it on the other side back into the plaintext message—all while maintaining the confidentiality of the plaintext message.

Another example of cryptography is to encrypt data that is stored in a database so if it is ever accessed or exfiltrated by a cybercriminal, it will be unreadable and unusable by them. This is a way of maintaining the confidentiality of the data.

Encryption and Decryption

Using encryption enables us to enforce confidentiality. **Encryption** is the act of taking a plaintext message and turning it into ciphertext so it is unreadable. **Decryption** is the act of taking unreadable ciphertext and turning it back into its original plaintext message.

To encrypt and decrypt data, we need unique information that is used for encryption and decryption and a set of rules that are followed to perform encryption and decryption. The unique information is called a *key*. The set of rules is called an *algorithm*.

Let's say Alice has the following message she wants to send to Bob secretly:

Hi Bob,

How was your weekend?

Alice

Alice has decided to encrypt this message with the unique key 73ethqbk837468 and the AES algorithm. The resulting ciphertext is as follows:

4eywtHGjiwj

Syi872jakdakdjasdnwnq3ie3ui3hadano13q238923

sfhsfhfsdbwe

> **NOTE** This is not the exact result of using that key and algorithm. It is just a representation of what would occur for your learning.

Now Alice sends the encrypted message to Bob over the network. If anyone captures it by using an on-path attack, they can't make sense of it because they don't know the key that was used. Once Bob gets the message, Bob will need to decrypt the ciphertext using the same key Alice used to encrypt it (73ethqbk837468) and the same algorithm (AES). The result would be the same plaintext message Alice encrypted:

Hi Bob,

How was your weekend?

Alice

States of Data

Today, cryptography is more important than it has ever been for data in transit, data at rest, and data in use.

Data in transit refers to data that is being transmitted over a wired or wireless network, regardless of whether that network is a private trusted network or a public untrusted network. Data that is in plaintext while in transit will easily be read by a cybercriminal if they are able to capture it (for example, by using an on-path attack). However, if the data is encrypted while in transit, then if and when the cybercriminal captures it, it will be ciphertext, and the only way they will be able to read it is if they have the key to decrypt it back to plaintext, which they should not have. In addition, we should be adding a hash to all data in transit. With a hash, we can verify the integrity (accuracy) of the data that has been transmitted to ensure that it has not been modified during transit. (You'll learn more about hashing later in this chapter.)

Data at rest refers to data that is being stored (using any type of storage, such as a local hard drive, a flash drive, a NAS, a SAN, or multitude of cloud-based options). Data that is stored in plaintext will easily be read by those who access it, whether they are authorized to have it or not. Consider a data breach. If a cybercriminal accesses your system and exfiltrates your plaintext data, they can easily read it. But if they access your system and exfiltrate your encrypted data, they will not be able to read it unless they also have the decryption key, which they should not have. In addition, we should be adding a hash to all our data at rest. With a hash, we can verify the integrity (accuracy) of the data at rest because we can determine whether the data has been modified by accident or on purpose. (You'll learn more about hashing later in this chapter.)

Data in use refers to data that is being processed by the CPU or stored in RAM. Most systems only have the ability to process data that is in plaintext. They are not able to process data that is encrypted. So, most systems have to take the encrypted data in RAM and decrypt it before they can process it, and then they need to re-encrypt it after processing. While the data is being processed, it is vulnerable because it is in plaintext. However, there are systems out there that can process data without having to decrypt it. So this is something that you may have to consider, depending on the sensitivity of the system and data in question.

Symmetric Cryptography

Symmetric cryptography requires the use of a single key for both encryption and decryption.

For example, let's pretend that Alice wants to send a message to Bob secretly. Using symmetric cryptography, Alice encrypts the plaintext message with a key, creating ciphertext (an encrypted message). Then Alice sends the ciphertext to Bob any way she wants. Upon receiving the ciphertext, Bob must decrypt it by using the same key Alice used to encrypt the message. Once Bob decrypts the ciphertext, the plaintext message will be revealed. So, for this to work, Alice and Bob both need a copy of the same key. How do Alice and Bob share the key with each other? Well, that is a story you will have to wait for (see the section "Using Symmetric and Asymmetric Cryptography," later in this chapter).

Asymmetric Cryptography

Asymmetric cryptography requires the use of two different keys, but these keys are related to each other. We call these keys a public key and a private key, and together they are a **public/private key pair**.

The private key is the key that you need to protect with your life. It needs to be kept safe and secure and used only by the person, application, or service that it was created for. You do not share your private key with anyone.

However, the public key is for anyone to use. You can share your public key with anyone or anything, and that is perfectly fine, because that is what it is intended for.

Now, with all this in mind, it is really important to understand the following about these keys:

- If you encrypt with a public key, only the private key can decrypt it.

- If you encrypt with a private key, only the public key can decrypt it.

Let's look at both of these in more detail, with examples, to see how to get both confidentiality and authentication with asymmetric cryptography. We will begin with confidentiality.

Confidentiality with Asymmetric Cryptography

Say that Alice wants to send a private message to Bob using asymmetric cryptography. Bob has a public/private key pair. Recall that if you encrypt with a public key, only the private key can decrypt it. So, if Bob sends his public key to Alice, Alice can use Bob's public key to encrypt the message and then send the encrypted message to Bob. Since Bob is the only one who has the corresponding private key, Bob will be the only one able to decrypt it. If anyone else gets a copy of the encrypted message, they will not be able to decrypt it, even if they have Bob's public key (as Alice does). Why? Recall that *if you encrypt with a public key, only the private key can decrypt it*. So, no one but Bob can decrypt, and therefore Alice has successfully sent Bob a secret message that only Bob can read. That is why we get confidentiality in this scenario.

Just to be clear, recall that Alice used Bob's public key, not her own public key. She used Bob's public key to encrypt, and Bob used his private key to decrypt. With that in mind, if Bob wanted to send Alice an encrypted confidential message, he would use Alice's public key to encrypt (not his own), and Alice would use her private key to decrypt. So, for bidirectional encryption to occur with confidentiality, Alice would have her own public/private key pair, and Bob would have his own public/private key pair. Alice would share her public key with Bob, and Bob would share his public key with Alice. How do they share their public

4

keys with each other? In this case, they can do so any way they want. I am serious. Why? Because the public key is meant to be public and shared with anyone or anything you want so that they can use it to encrypt traffic that they need to send to you with privacy/confidentiality. So that means you can send it via email, chat, GitHub, post it in an AWS public S3 bucket, even put it on your home page for anyone to download. As I said, it does not matter who sees it because when it is used, the only person who can decrypt anything encrypted with your public key is the person with your private key, and that should only be you.

Authentication with Asymmetric Cryptography

Now let's look at what the result is if you encrypt with the private key and decrypt with the public key—the opposite of the last discussion. The short answer is authentication.

Recall earlier that we stated that if you encrypt with a private key, only the public key can decrypt it. This is important because it allows you to use this process for authentication—not for confidentiality, as in the previous example. So how do you get authentication with this? Well, consider that Alice would have her own public/private key pair, and Bob would have his own public/private key pair. Alice would share her public key with Bob, and Bob would share his public key with Alice. Again, it does not matter how the public keys are shared, as long as the private key is safe and secure. So, in this scenario, Alice wants to send a message to Bob, and she wants to make sure that Bob can confirm (authenticate) that the message actually came from Alice. For this to happen, Alice will encrypt the message with her private key (yes, her private key) and send the encrypted message to Bob. By now, you must remember what I've said a few times:

If you encrypt with a private key, only the public key can decrypt it.

This is important because Bob will use Alice's public key to decrypt the message, and since the public key is the only key that can decrypt anything encrypted with the private key, this will prove to Bob that Alice sent the message because Alice's public key is able to decrypt it. So this is how we get authentication.

Now you might be thinking, "But wait, what if someone else intercepts the message and has Alice's public key (because anyone can get a copy of it, since it is "public")? Won't they be able to decrypt the message?" Absolutely. That is why this process is for authentication not confidentiality.

Combining Confidentiality and Authentication with Asymmetric Cryptography

So could you combine these two scenarios of confidentiality and authentication? Oh, yeah! Are you ready? Here it is.

Alice has a public/private key pair, and Bob has a public/private key pair. Alice shares her public key with Bob, and Bob shares his public key with Alice. Alice wants to send an encrypted and authenticated message to Bob. So, Alice encrypts the plaintext message with Bob's public key for privacy, creating the encrypted ciphertext, and then Alice encrypts the encrypted ciphertext with her private key for authentication. She now sends the message to Bob. Bob decrypts the message with Alice's public key, first proving that the message came from Alice. Now Bob is left with the ciphertext and decrypts it with his private key, revealing the plaintext message.

In the previous example, could Alice have encrypted with her private key first and then Bob's public key second? Sure, that would have worked as well. So, as you can see from these last two scenarios, knowing what was done first and second would be important for the person/device decrypting on the other end so they know the order in which to use the keys.

 ## Using Symmetric and Asymmetric Cryptography

Symmetric ciphers are very fast compared to asymmetric ciphers because asymmetric ciphers are very resource intensive. So, when encrypting large amounts of data, it makes sense to use symmetric ciphers (for example, when encrypting data at rest in a database or when encrypting data in transit over a VPN). Now, don't get me wrong. You could technically use asymmetric ciphers for the same thing, but it would be so resource intensive that many systems would not be able to handle the processing involved with encrypting or decrypting large amounts of data with asymmetric ciphers.

So, when would it make sense to use asymmetric ciphers? When the amount of data is very minimal, such as when trying to share/exchange a symmetric key.

Let's go back to Alice and Bob and the symmetric example from earlier. Recall that Alice and Bob both need an exact copy of the symmetric key. I told you I'd let you know how Alice and Bob share the key with each other. It's now time.

For Alice and Bob to have the same symmetric key, one of them has to generate it and share it with the other. It does not matter who generates it, as long as they both have a copy of it. So, let's say Alice generates the symmetric key. How can Alice send it to Bob? She could email it, SMS it, chat it over Teams, place it in a shared folder that Bob can download it from, call Bob and dictate it over the phone, put it in an envelope and mail it to Bob using the postal service, or write it on a sticky note and give it to Bob. All of these would work, but they are not secure or convenient. We do not want anyone other than those who need to encrypt or decrypt using this key to have a copy of it. If anyone else gets a copy of it, confidentiality will be compromised as that individual would be able to decrypt and read the data that was encrypted with it. So, secure exchange of the symmetric key is our number-one priority, and none of the methods just listed will work. So do not use them to exchange symmetric keys.

So, what will work? Our asymmetric ciphers for secure key exchange. In this scenario, Alice has her asymmetric public/private key pair, and Bob has his asymmetric public/private key pair. Alice also has a symmetric key that she needs to securely send to Bob. So, Alice gets Bob's asymmetric public key and uses it to encrypt the symmetric key. She then sends the encrypted symmetric key to Bob, and he decrypts it with his asymmetric private key. The result is that Bob now has a copy of the symmetric key that was sent to him in a safe and secure way that upholds confidentiality. Now Alice can take any data she needs to send to Bob and encrypt it with the symmetric key and then send the encrypted data to Bob. Bob can then decrypt it with the symmetric key he got from Alice. Bob can also encrypt messages with the symmetric key and send them to Alice, and Alice can decrypt them with the symmetric key.

Notice that the asymmetric public/private keys are only used to share/exchange the symmetric key. Once the symmetric key is exchanged, Alice and Bob can encrypt and decrypt massive amounts of data back and forth with each other using just the symmetric key.

NOTE   Without a doubt, this is a lot of information. If you are overwhelmed, I get it. I felt the same at one point in my career. I encourage you to reread this information on symmetric and asymmetric ciphers so that you have a better understanding of them moving forward. If you feel comfortable enough, move on. But if you start to struggle with the topics being covered at any point, coming back to review this information may be the best thing for you to do.

Types of Ciphers

In this section, we will briefly explore the different types of symmetric and asymmetric ciphers and identify which of them are commonly used today. Keep in mind that in the real world, symmetric ciphers are typically used to encrypt large amounts of data and the asymmetric ciphers are used for key exchange, to encrypt small amounts of data, or to authenticate the sender of exchanged information.

Symmetric Ciphers

Table 4-2 defines a few of the prominent symmetric algorithms.

Key Topic

Table 4-2   Symmetric Algorithms

Symmetric Algorithm	Description
DES	**Data Encryption Standard (DES)** is a symmetric key encryption algorithm that was developed by IBM in the 1970s. It is a block cipher that encrypts data in blocks of 64 bits.
3DES	**Triple Data Encryption Standard (3DES)** is an extension of DES that uses three keys instead of one to encrypt data. It is more secure than DES but slower.
AES	**Advanced Encryption Standard (AES)** is a symmetric block cipher that encrypts data in blocks of 128, 192, or 256 bits. Today we typically use 256. It is faster and more secure than DES and 3DES. It was established by NIST in 2001 and is the most widely used encryption standard for protecting sensitive data from unauthorized access. You use AES every day when encrypting data over the Internet and VPNs.
IDEA	IDEA was designed as a replacement for DES, but AES is more secure, and IDEA is not highly utilized today.
RC2, RC4, RC5, RC6	RC2, RC4, RC5, and RC6 were designed by Ron Rivest, but AES has proven to be more secure, and the RC options listed here are not highly utilized today.

As you can see from the information provided in Table 4-2, AES is the most commonly used symmetric algorithm today. It is used to protect Internet communications using HTTPs, private communications with IPsec VPNs, and management connections with SSH.

> **NOTE**   For more information on cryptographic algorithms, see the Cisco Next Generation Cryptography website, at https://sec.cloudapps.cisco.com/security/center/resources/next_generation_cryptography#2. This site provides a table that lists asymmetric algorithms and describes the intended operation, status, and any alternative recommendations for each.

Types of Asymmetric Algorithms

Table 4-3 describes a few of the prominent asymmetric algorithms.

Key Topic

Table 4-3   Asymmetric Algorithms

Asymmetric Algorithm	Description
Rivest, Shamir, and Adleman (RSA)	The primary use of this asymmetric algorithm today is for authentication. The key length may be from 512 to 4096, and a minimum size for good security is at least 1024, but 2048 is now being recommended because when it comes to security, bigger is better. RSA was named after the three people who created the algorithm: Rivest, Shamir, and Adleman.
Digital Signature Algorithm (DSA)	The primary use of this asymmetric algorithm today is to generate digital signatures, authenticate the sender of a digital message, and prevent message tampering. It was proposed by NIST and developed by the U.S. National Security Agency (NSA). As with RSA, key lengths of 2048 or greater are recommended.
Diffie-Hellman (DH)	DH is referred to as a key exchange protocol. It allows two devices to negotiate and establish shared secret keying material (symmetric keys) over an untrusted network. This is very interesting because although the algorithm itself is asymmetric, the keys generated by the exchange are symmetric keys that can then be used with symmetric algorithms such as 3DES and AES. It is used with TLS for HTTPs connections, IPsec for VPN connections, and SSH for management connections.
Elliptic-curve cryptography (ECC)	Elliptic-curve cryptography is public-key cryptography based on the algebraic structure of elliptic curves over finite fields. It is used to create faster, smaller, and more efficient cryptographic keys. It is an alternative to the RSA cryptographic algorithm. ECC is most often used for digital signatures in cryptocurrencies, such as bitcoin and Ethereum, as well as for one-way encryption of emails, data, and software. ECC allows smaller keys compared to non-elliptic-curve cryptography to provide equivalent security. It is therefore great for mobile products that do not have the processing capabilities needed for RSA computations. As a result, there are elliptic-curve versions of DH (ECDH) and DSA (ECDSA).

All the asymmetric algorithms listed in Table 4-3 are in common use today.

NOTE   For more information on cryptographic algorithms, see the Cisco Next Generation Cryptography website, at https://sec.cloudapps.cisco.com/security/center/resources/next_generation_cryptography#2. This site provides a table that lists asymmetric algorithms and describes the intended operation, status, and any alternative recommendations for each.

Certificates and PKI

Recall that with asymmetric cryptography, you need to share your public key. Alice has a public/private key pair, and Bob has a public/private key pair, and they share their public keys with each other, as discussed earlier in this chapter. But there is an issue with this in the real world.

How does Alice know 100% without any doubt that the public key she received is Bob's, and how does Bob know 100% without a doubt that the public key he received is Alice's?

In a small office between peers, they could simply share the public key with each other via email or a Microsoft Teams chat, and they would know 100% (give or take 1% or 2%) that the public key belongs to the other.

However, think bigger for a moment. How big? Internet BIG. Consider Alice and Bob again, but now say that they don't know each other but need to perform a secure private transaction with each other over the Internet. When Alice gets Bob's public key, how does she know 100% without a doubt that it belongs to Bob and not some cybercriminal who has hijacked the conversation? When Bob gets Alice's public key, how does he know 100% without a doubt that it belongs to Alice and not some cybercriminal who has hijacked the conversation? The last thing Alice or Bob wants to do is use the wrong public key. If they use the public key of the cybercriminal who hijacked the session, then the cybercriminal will be able to decrypt the transaction.

This is where public key infrastructure (PKI) and certificates come into play.

- **Public key infrastructure (PKI)** is a set of identities, roles, policies, and actions for the creation, use, management, distribution, and revocation of digital certificates.

- A **digital certificate** (also known as a public key certificate) is used to cryptographically link ownership of a public key with the entity that owns it.

So, the whole point behind PKI and digital certificates is to 100% without a doubt provide the proof that the public key you are about to use belongs to the entity that you are about to perform a secure conversation/transaction with.

This is not a new concept. We have been using this concept in other aspects of our lives for ages. For example, your driver's license for this discussion is going to be your "digital certificate." Let's say you are going for a night on the town with your close friends. You arrive at a club, and the bouncer wants you to prove your identity and your age. So, you pull out your driver's license and give it to him. He uses the driver's license to verify that it is really you, based on your picture, and to ensure that you are of legal age to enter the establishment. Now why in the world would the bouncer accept this as your proof? How can the bouncer be confident 100% without a doubt that the information is accurate and that you are, in fact, who you say you are? It is because they trust the issuer of the driver's license. Recall that when you got your driver's license, you had to visit the Department of Motor Vehicles (DMV) and go through a rigorous process to prove your identity and age with them. Once everything was approved, they issued you a driver's license, which is a signed trusted government document. The bouncer at the door has been informed that they can use the driver's license (a signed trusted government document) to verify 100% without a doubt the identity and age of anyone that wants to enter the club. So, to recap, you have a driver's license that is signed by the government, and the bouncer trusts the government, so the bouncer can use your driver's license to prove that you are who you say you are, and you are the right age.

Now let's get back to Alice and Bob. With PKI, Alice can have her public key signed by a trusted entity called a **certificate authority (CA)**, and Bob can have his public key signed by the same CA or a different one. In addition, Alice and Bob must both trust the CAs that the other has used for this to work. Now when Alice sends Bob her public key, Bob can contact the trusted CA and determine if it truly belongs to Alice and if it is still valid and not revoked. When Bob sends Alice his public key, Alice can contact the trusted CA and determine if it truly belongs to Bob and if it is still valid and not revoked. If the public keys truly belong to the correct entity, then they will be used. But if they don't or if they have been revoked, they can be ignored, and the communication/transaction can be stopped before it goes any further.

For this to work, we need trusted CAs. A CA is an entity that creates and issues digital certificates. You can build your own CAs for issuing and verifying certificates in your own organizations, and you can use trusted third-party CAs to issue and verify certificates of others (such as on the Internet). Here is a sampling of some of the trusted third-party CAs as of writing this book:

- GoDaddy
- AWS
- Thawte
- DigiCert
- Global Sign
- Symantec
- Verisign
- Entrust

If you are wondering how you trust a CA, Figure 4-1 shows an example of preloaded trusted root CAs in a Windows 10 PC. This list allows the PC (and you as well) to trust a CA so that when the CA signs someone else's public key, it is possible to confirm 100% without a doubt using that trusted CA certificate that the public key really is from that person.

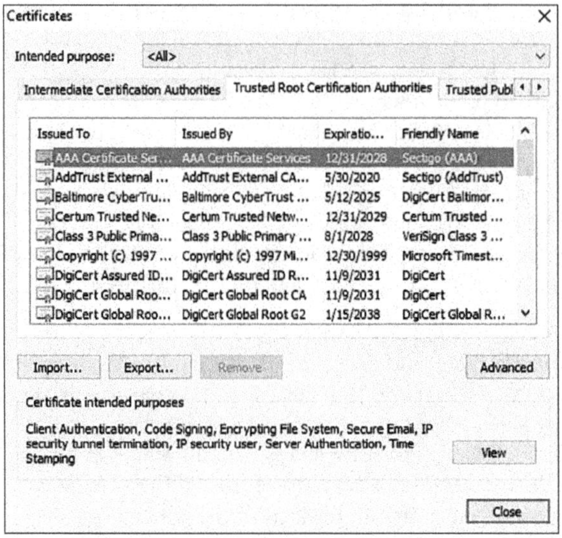

Figure 4-1   *Example of Preloaded Trusted Root CAs in a Windows 10 PC*

So how would this work for Alice and Bob? Alice has a public/private key pair. Alice takes her public key, contacts any of the CAs she chooses to pay for this service (such as GoDaddy, AWS, Thawte, DigiCert, Global Sign, Symantec, Verisign, or Entrust), and requests an identity digital certificate for that public key. The digital certificate includes information about the identity of the entity, such as its IP address, and fully qualified domain name (FQDN), as well as the public key that Alice submitted. The digital certificate is also assigned a serial number by the CA. Finally, the CA signs the digital certificate with its own digital signature, using its private key, and since Alice has the public key of the CA in her trusted root CA list (like the one in Figure 4-1), Alice can verify that the certificate is from that CA by decrypting the signature with the public key.

NOTE   In the following examples, we use www.cisco.com, but if it makes it easier for you to follow along, you can replace *www.cisco.com* with *Alice*.

Figure 4-2 shows the public key in the www.cisco.com digital certificate signed by IdenTrust Commercial Root CA 1, and Figure 4-3 shows the serial number in the www.cisco.com digital certificate signed by IdenTrust Commercial Root CA 1. Figure 4-4 shows the signature in the www.cisco.com digital certificate signed by IdenTrust Commercial Root CA 1. Note that IdenTrust Commercial Root CA 1 would be listed as a trusted root certification authority in Figure 4-1.

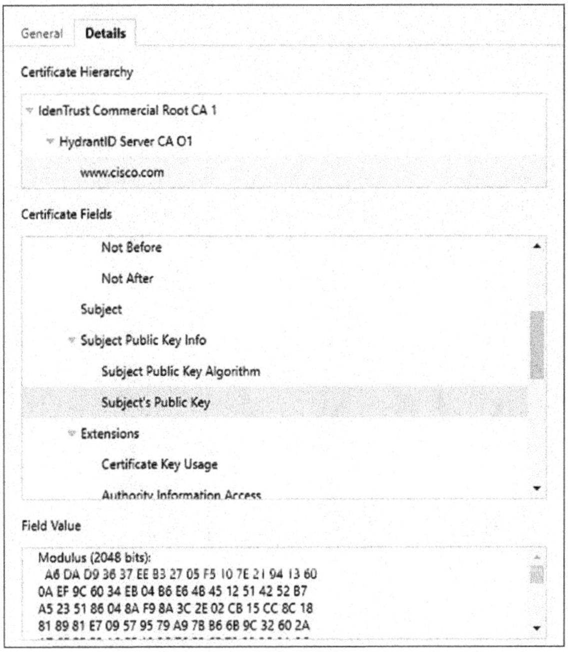

Figure 4-2 *Example of a Public Key Listed in a Digital Certificate*

Figure 4-3 *Example of a Serial Number Listed in a Digital Certificate*

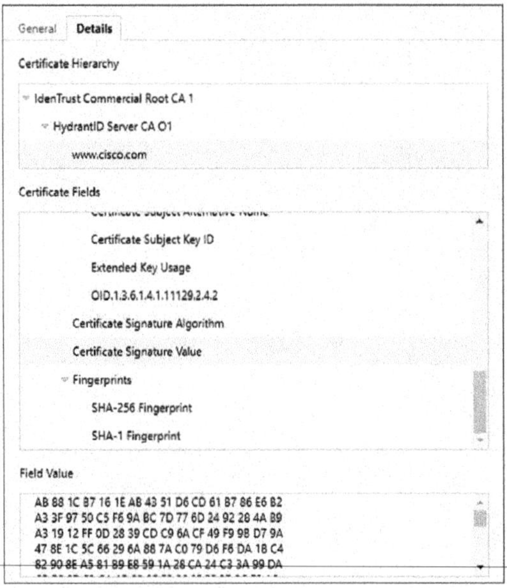

General   **Details**

Certificate Hierarchy

▽ IdenTrust Commercial Root CA 1

   ▽ HydrantID Server CA O1

      www.cisco.com

Certificate Fields

      Certificate Subject Alternative Name
      Certificate Subject Key ID
      Extended Key Usage
      OID.1.3.6.1.4.1.11129.2.4.2
      Certificate Signature Algorithm
      Certificate Signature Value
   ▽ Fingerprints
      SHA-256 Fingerprint
      SHA-1 Fingerprint

Field Value

AB 88 1C 87 16 1E AB 43 51 D6 CD 61 87 86 E6 82
A3 3F 97 50 C5 F6 9A 8C 7D 77 6D 24 92 28 4A 89
A3 19 12 FF 0D 28 39 CD C9 6A CF 49 F9 98 D7 9A
47 8E 1C 5C 66 29 6A 88 7A C0 79 D6 F6 DA 18 C4
82 90 8E A5 81 89 88 59 1A 28 CA 24 C3 3A 99 DA

Figure 4-4   *Example of the CA's Signature in a Digital Certificate*

After the CA has generated and signed the digital certificate for www.cisco.com, the CA sends it to Cisco so it can be used. Now let's say you need to do a secure transaction with www.cisco.com. You open your browser and type in www.cisco.com to contact Cisco, and Cisco sends you their digital certificate, which includes the public key, as you saw in Figure 4-2. Now you can 100% trust that the public key belongs to Cisco, and you (via your computer) can verify this by using the CA's public key to verify that they were the ones who signed the certificate, as in Figure 4-4.

SCEP

The process of authenticating a CA server, generating a public/private key pair, requesting an identity certificate, and then verifying and implementing the identity certificate can take several steps. Cisco, in association with a few other vendors, developed the Simple Certificate Enrollment Protocol (SCEP), which can automate most of the process for requesting and installing an identity certificate. Although it is not an open standard, it is supported by most Cisco devices and makes getting and installing both root and identity certificates convenient.

Digital Certificates

There are many different types of digital certificates that can be used for different purposes. Table 4-4 lists a few of the different types of digital certificates and what you would use them for; keep in mind that this is not an exhaustive list.

Table 4-4   Digital Certificate Types

Digital Certificate	Use Case
root (CA certificate)	Used to identify CAs
ssl/tls (third-party)	Used to validate website domains and secure data in transit over the Internet

Digital Certificate	Use Case
code signing	Used to ensure the authenticity of code developed for a software application
user/client	Used to authenticate people or devices that request access to sensitive corporate data or services instead of using usernames and passwords
object-signing	Used to digitally sign any digital item, providing a means to validate the item's integrity and ownership

Certificates are based on the X.509 public key certificates standard. This standard defines the structure and format of digital certificates. A digital certificate contains the information listed in Table 4-5 (refer to Figures 4-2, 4-3, and 4-4).

Table 4-5   Digital Certificate Information

Certificate Information	Description
Subject	The person or entity that is being identified
Signature algorithm	The specific algorithm used for signing the digital certificate
Signature	The digital signature from the certificate authority, which is used by devices that want to verify the authenticity of the certificate issued by that CA
Issuer	The entity or CA that created and issued the digital certificate
Valid from	The date the certificate became valid
Valid to	The expiration date of the certificate
Key usage	The functions for which the public key in the certificate may be used
Public key	The public portion of the public and private key pair generated by the host whose certificate is being looked at
Thumbprint algorithm	The hash algorithm used for data integrity
Thumbprint	The actual hash
Certificate revocation list location	The URL that can be checked to see whether the serial number of any certificates issued by the CA have been revoked

Lifetime of a Digital Certificate

A digital certificate has a lifetime. This lifetime is critical because of what we use digital certificates for. Recall that we use them to verify that the public key we are about to use is in fact the public key of the entity that we want to use it with for a safe and secure exchange of data. Therefore, it is imperative that we only use a certificate if it is valid. Therefore, we only use a digital certificate if the current time is within the validity period, which can be found in the certificate as the Valid From information and the Valid To information, as described earlier, in Table 4-5. Outside that window, you do not use it.

Consider a scenario: What happens if the certificate is compromised by a cybercriminal? How might that happen? Well, let's go back to Alice and Bob. Remember that Alice has a public/private key pair, and she has a digital certificate for the public key signed by a CA that she gives to Bob. Let's say the cybercriminal has been able to compromise Alice and get their hands on her private key. Now the cybercriminal has the ability to decrypt anything that is encrypted with Alice's public key/digital certificate. Therefore, the digital certificate is now said to be compromised. So how would Bob know this and ensure that he does not use Alice's current digital certificate?

Well, first, Alice has to report this to the CA so the CA can revoke the certificate and make it invalid. But how does Bob check to see if a digital certificate he is about to use has been revoked? He can check a certificate revocation list (CRL) or an Online Certificate Status Protocol (OCSP) database. A **certificate revocation list (CRL)** is a list of all the digital certificates that have been revoked by the certificate authority (CA) that issued them so that the validity and trustworthiness of the certificates can be verified. **Online Certificate Status Protocol (OCSP)** is an Internet protocol defined in RFC 6960 that can be used to get the current revocation status of a single X.509 certificate.

NOTE   OCSP is considered faster and more efficient than CRLs because it only returns the real-time current status of a single certificate instead of a static listing of all revoked certificates, as a CRL does.

Any revoked certificates will be listed based on their serial number so that any certificate that is about to be used by anyone (like Bob) can be checked against the list. If the serial number of the certificate that is about to be used is on it, it is not used, and communication stops. Bob then has to get a new updated valid noncompromised digital certificate from Alice. Figure 4-5 shows how the certificate contains a CRL Distribution Points field that contains the URL for a CRL that can be used to verify whether the certificate has been revoked. Notice that the certificate is maintained by the CA (IdenTrust) in this case.

Certificate Hierarchy

▽ IdenTrust Commercial Root CA 1

   ▽ HydrantID Server CA O1

      www.cisco.com

Certificate Fields

   ▽ Extensions

      Certificate Key Usage

      Authority Information Access

      Certification Authority Key ID

      Certificate Policies

      CRL Distribution Points

      Certificate Subject Alternative Name

      Certificate Subject Key ID

      Extended Key Usage

Field Value

Not critical
URI: http://validation.identrust.com/crl/hydrantidcao1.crl

Figure 4-5   *Example of the CRL URL of a Digital Certificate*

PKI Infrastructure

Public key infrastructure (PKI) is based on a hierarchy of servers. At the top, there is a root CA. This is the case regardless of whether the PKI is a private solution you set up in your organization or a public setup on the Internet maintained by a well-known trusted CA. Under that root CA are subordinate and intermediate levels of CAs. Figure 4-6 shows an example of this hierarchy. In addition, if you go back to Figure 4-5, you can see at the top the certificate hierarchy in the actual certificate. In that case, for www.cisco.com, the root CA is IdenTrust Commercial Root CA 1, and the intermediate CA is HydrantID Server CA 01. Figure 4-7 shows another example of a certificate for www.microsoft.com. Notice that the root CA is DigiCert Global Root G2, and the intermediate CA is Microsoft Azure TLS Issuing CA 06.

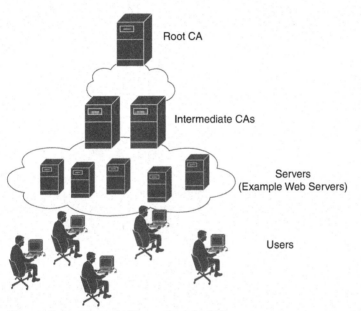

Figure 4-6 *Example Hierarchy of a PKI*

Why is this important? Because for all of this to work successfully, the client must be able to verify the "chain" of trust/authority, and the only way to do this is for the client to have access to all the certificates that are part of the chain. So, the client needs both the intermediate CA's certificate and the root certificate. For example, the root certificate (along with its public key) is required to verify the digital signature of the intermediate CA, and the intermediate CA's certificate (along with its public key) is required to verify the digital certificate. If there are multiple levels of intermediate CAs, a client needs the certificates of all the devices in the chain, from the root all the way to the intermediate CA that issued the client's certificate.

Figure 4-7   *Example of the Certificate Hierarchy at the Top of a Digital Certificate*

Hashing

Hashing can be used for different purposes. For example, you can use it to verify the integrity of data, as shown in Figure 4-8, you can use it for authentication purposes (signing), as shown in Figure 4-9, and you can even use it to conceal data as it is stored, as shown in Figure 4-10 for Raymond's and Shane's passwords.

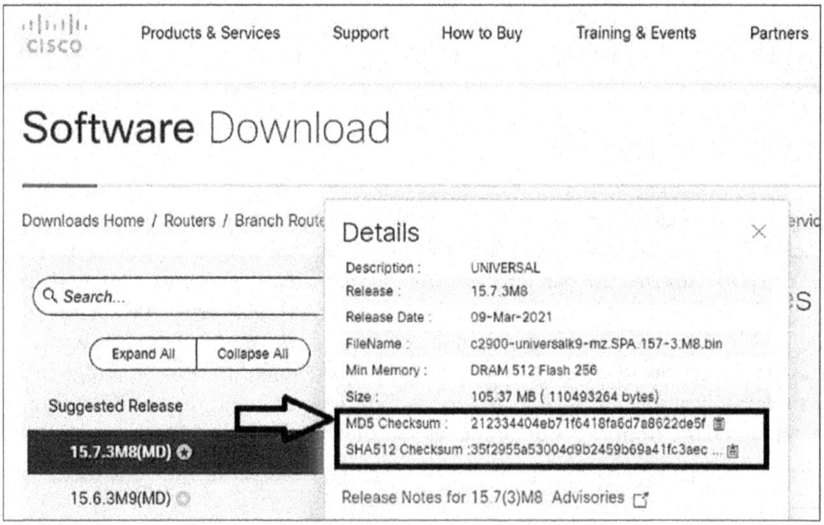

Figure 4-8   *Examples of a Message Digest 5 (MD5) and Secure Hash Algorithm (SHA) Hash to Verify the Integrity of Data*

Figure 4-9   *Examples of a Hash That Is Used for Authentication Purposes (Signing)*

```
R2#show run | section username
username raymond secret 5 $1$namr$F5XIICckSsEGDyY0QBATh/
username shane secret 8 $8$fZMRdR4G3y5SDU$viYycxvE43DLi4HgHX3zghO0mInqPKWP7HN6QMJSePM
```

Figure 4-10   *Examples of Hashing Used to Conceal Stored Data*

Key Topic

Hashing and encryption are similar in the sense that they both involve taking some amount of data and transforming it so that it is no longer plaintext. However, hashing is a one-way process, whereas encryption is a two-way process. For example, with encryption, you encrypt the data, and then you can decrypt the data to read it again. But with hashing, once you hash the data, you can't return it back to its plaintext. This is why none of the examples in the previous figures show hashing and then unhashing. They are all about hashing something to conceal it and use it for verification and integrity purposes. You still need encryption to protect the data in transit if you want privacy.

With hashing, you use hashing algorithms, which are different from encryption algorithms. Table 4-6 provides a list of hashing algorithms.

Key Topic

Table 4-6   Hashing Algorithms

Hashing Algorithm	Description
MD5	Takes any amount of data as input and creates a 128-bit hash value that can be used as a checksum to verify the integrity of data. Due to vulnerabilities, it is recommended that you use it only for noncryptographic purposes.

Hashing Algorithm	Description
SHA-1	Takes any amount of data as input and creates a 160-bit hash value that can be used as a checksum to verify the integrity of data. It was designed by the NSA and is a U.S. Federal Information Processing Standard. Due to vulnerabilities, it is recommended that you use it only for noncryptographic purposes.
SHA-256	Part of the SHA-2 family designed by the NSA. Takes any amount of data as input and creates a 256-bit hash value that can be used as a cryptographic function to conceal data or for verifying the integrity of data. It is the minimum recommended hash function today.
SHA-384	Part of the SHA-2 family designed by the NSA. Takes any amount of data as input and creates a 384-bit hash value that can be used as a cryptographic function to conceal data or for verifying the integrity of data.
SHA-512	Part of the SHA-2 family designed by the NSA. Takes any amount of data as input and creates a 512-bit hash value that can be used as a cryptographic function to conceal data or for verifying the integrity of data.

You can run plaintext data through any of these hashing algorithms and produce a hash of that data. Pay close attention to the fact that I said "produce a hash of that data," which means that, in this case, the original data is still in plaintext, but now you also have a hash that was produced based on the exact state of that data at that specific moment in time.

Look again at Figure 4-8. The MD5 hash and SHA hash were both produced by using the Cisco IOS software and running it through each hashing algorithm listed in the figure. The software was unmodified in this case. All Cisco did was produce an MD5 and SHA hash of that software and put the hash on the website for all to see. When someone downloads the Cisco IOS software, they can run the software through the same hashes on their local machine, using any application that can create hashes. If the hashes produced on the local machine are the same as the ones listed on the Cisco website, they know the Cisco IOS software has not been maliciously or accidentally modified since Cisco uploaded it to the site. This gives you a way to verify the integrity of the data.

Now go back to Figure 4-10, which shows the hashed passwords. In this case, the hash has actually modified the plaintext. Instead of being stored in plaintext, the password is being stored as a hash. So, if someone ever exfiltrates the password database, all they have is the hashes, and remember that the hashes are one-way hashes, and it would be very difficult for a cybercriminal to figure out the plaintext password from the hashes. So, now when a user logs in and provides their plaintext password, the system hashes the password provided, and if the result of the hash is exactly the same as what is stored in the database, then the user is authenticated. But if the result is different, the user is denied.

Shared Secret Keys and Salting with Hashing

Hashing by just using a hashing algorithm can be made even more secure by adding a shared secret key or a salt to the hashing process. A **shared secret key** is a password, passphrase, or random characters that all parties know. When hashing, you take the shared secret key, along with the actual data and the hashing algorithm, and produce the hash. Therefore, only those who know the shared secret key are able to produce and verify the hash. So, it is much harder for a cybercriminal to break or reverse the hash or modify any packets because they do not know the shared secret to calculate a proper hash. This is referred to as a hashed message authentication code (HMAC).

Salting means adding random characters on the fly as part of the hashing process. It is typically used when storing passwords in a database to ensure that every hash is unique. This is important because when you hash exactly the same data with the same hashing algorithm, the resulting hash is exactly the same. For example, if Alice uses the password "cisco," and Bob uses the password "cisco," and they are both using MD5, the passwords will have exactly the same hash created. To better understand this, let's pretend that the result of hashing is "q^%tyrfg5543j". However, if a salt is added to each password during the hashing process, then the results would be different. For example, Alice might get a random salt of "yt6r," and Bob might get a random salt of "0u4f." Once hashing occurs, in the database, Alice's password will be hashed as "6req6yhgft67," and Bob's will be hashed as "thyw653yh891." So, the same plaintext password now appears completely different in the database. In Figure 4-10, you can see the salt used for Raymond's password, "namr," and you can see the salt used for Shane's password, "fZMRdR4G3y5SDU." The difference in the length of the salts is due to the fact that Raymond's password is hashed with MD5, and Shane's is hashed with SHA-256.

Cryptography in the Real World

This section briefly explores three examples of how symmetric cryptography, asymmetric cryptography, and hashing play out in the real world with web browsing, VPNs, and remote management. Note that these are not all-inclusive examples that explore the intricate details. They are very high-level overviews to help bring together everything we have discussed so far.

Web Browsing

The most common reason to use SSL/TLS is to secure communications between a client and a server. For example, when you visit https://www.cisco.com, SSL/TLS is used to secure the traffic that is going back and forth between your PC and the Cisco server hosting https://www.cisco.com.

At a very high level, how would this work? When you type in www.cisco.com, your browser (PC) reaches out to the server hosting www.cisco.com, introduces itself, and indicates what it supports when it comes to cryptography, such as the various cipher suites and the maximum SSL version, so the server is aware of what it can use. The server responds with similar information, so the client knows what the server supports. Once they know each other and what they support, it is time for the server to provide the PC with its digital certificate, which contains its public key. Now the PC can verify if the server is truly the server it wants to make a secure connection with, as discussed earlier in this chapter. Now comes Diffie-Hellman (DH), an asymmetric algorithm that is used to dynamically generate and exchange a symmetric key that will be used to encrypt any data exchanged between the server and the client. Once the DH process is complete, the client and the server will have the same dynamically generated symmetric key, which can be used with AES to encrypt and decrypt data that is exchanged between them.

VPNs

The most common reason to use IPsec VPNs is to secure the connections between a remote user's PC and a corporate network over the Internet or to secure the communication between branch offices and the corporate network over the Internet.

At a very high level, how would this work? An asymmetric algorithm such as DH is used to securely create and exchange a symmetric key between a device at the HQ site and a device at the branch site. Once the exchange is complete, the devices each have a dynamically generated key that is needed for AES to successfully encrypt and decrypt the data that will be exchanged between the two devices over the untrusted network (the Internet). In addition, using SHA, hashing can be done so each device has the opportunity to verify the integrity of the data that has been exchanged.

Remote Management

The most common reason to use SSH is to secure communication between a device you need to manage, such as a Linux server or a Cisco router or switch, and a management station, such as your PC.

At a very high level, how would this work? When you open your SSH client and attempt to make an SSH connection to a device (an SSH server in this case), a communication channel is opened, and the server sends the client a list of supported cryptographic algorithms and its public key/digital certificate. The client can use this information to verify the identity of the server. Next, the asymmetric algorithm DH is used to securely create and exchange a symmetric key between the client and the server. Once the exchange is complete, the devices each have a dynamically generated key that is needed for AES to successfully encrypt and decrypt the data that will be exchanged between the two devices. In addition, using SHA, hashing can be done so each device has the opportunity to verify the integrity of the data that has been exchanged.

Cisco Next-Generation Cryptography

Key Topic

I need to make sure that before you read this section, you are clear on what next-generation cryptography is. It is purely a marketing name by Cisco and not some up-and-coming out-of-this-world starship that will boldly go where no one has gone before in relation to cryptography. However, although the name may be marketing based, the purpose behind the name is what makes Next-Generation Cryptography very important for each and every one of us.

Cisco next-generation cryptography is about keeping up with the ever-changing security landscape and ensuring that there is a widely accepted and consistent set of cryptographic algorithms that provide strong security and good performance for everyone. It is about defining best standards and setting an industry trend that everyone can implement today to meet their security and scalability requirements for years to come and ensure that the best technologies exist for future-proof cryptography.

At some point, the widely accepted algorithms will become obsolete due to vulnerabilities, and a new set will be needed to replace them. Everyone needs to be aware of and have the option to use the latest, greatest, and safest cryptographic algorithms that provide strong security and good performance.

For example, today, should you use DES or not? According to the "Recommendations for Cryptographic Algorithms" table at https://sec.cloudapps.cisco.com/security/center/

resources/next_generation_cryptography#2, you should avoid it. But what about something like AES that comes in a few different flavors, like AES-CBC mode and AES-GCM mode? According to the same site, AES-CBC mode is acceptable, but for next-generation cryptography, AES-GCM mode is the way to go.

So based on the site just mentioned, these are the current next-generation encryption (NGE) recommendations about the algorithms that are expected to meet the security and scalability requirements of the next two decades:

- AES-GCM-256 for authenticated encryption

- SHA-256, SHA-384, or SHA-512 for integrity (with SHA-384 or SHA-512 preferred over SHA-256)

- HMAC-SHA-256 for integrity

- ECDH-384 for key exchange

- ECDSA-384 for authentication

Obviously, this list will change in years to come, and with changes to the NGE recommendations, devices will be designed to support the changes as well as give you access to the latest, greatest, and safest cryptographic algorithms that provide strong security and good performance.

Summary

Cryptography ensures that confidentiality and integrity are established and maintained. It uses mathematical techniques to transform data and prevent it from being read or tampered with by unauthorized parties. In this chapter, you've learned about the following cryptography-related concepts:

- **Encryption** is the act of taking a plaintext message and turning it into ciphertext so it is unreadable.

- **Decryption** is the act of taking unreadable ciphertext and turning it back into its original plaintext message.

- **Data in transit** refers to data that is being transmitted over a wired or wireless network.

- **Data at rest** refers to data that is being stored.

- **Data in use** refers to data that is being processed by a CPU or sitting in RAM.

- **Symmetric cryptography** requires the use of a single key for both encryption and decryption.

  - **DES, 3DES,** and **AES** are examples of symmetric algorithms.

- **Asymmetric cryptography** requires the use of two different keys, but these keys are related to each other. We call these keys a public key and a private key, and together they are a public/private key pair.

  - If you encrypt with a public key, only the private key can decrypt it.

■ If you encrypt with a private key, only the public key can decrypt it.

■ **RSA, DSA,** and **DH** are examples of asymmetric algorithms.

■ **Public key infrastructure (PKI)** is a set of identities, roles, policies, and actions for the creation, use, management, distribution, and revocation of digital certificates. It is based on a hierarchy of servers.

■ A **digital certificate** (also known as a public key certificate) is used to cryptographically link ownership of a public key with the entity that owns it.

■ A **certificate revocation list (CRL)** is a list of all the digital certificates that have been revoked by the certificate authority (CA) that issued them so that the validity and trustworthiness of the certificates can be verified.

■ **Online Certificate Status Protocol (OCSP)** is an Internet protocol defined in RFC 6960 that can be used to get the current revocation status of a single X.509 certificate.

■ **Hashing** can be used for different purposes. You can use it to verify the integrity of data, and you can use it for authentication purposes (signing).

■ **MD5** and **SHA** are examples of hashing algorithms

■ **Salting** involves adding random characters on the fly as part of the hashing process.

■ **Cisco next-generation cryptography** is about keeping up with the ever-changing security landscape and ensuring that there is a widely accepted and consistent set of cryptographic algorithms that provide strong security and good performance for everyone.

Exam Preparation Tasks

As mentioned in the Introduction, you can customize your strategy for exam preparation. Suggested tasks include the exercises here, Chapter 16, "Final Preparation," and the exam simulation questions on the companion website.

Review All Key Topics

Review the most important topics in this chapter, noted with the Key Topics icon in the outer margin of the page. Table 4-7 lists these key topics and the page number on which each is found.

Table 4-7   Key Topics for Chapter 4

Key Topic Element	Description	Page Number
Terms	Encryption	51
Section	States of Data	52
Section	Symmetric Cryptography	52
Section	Asymmetric Cryptography	53
List	Asymmetric keys	53

Key Topic Element	Description	Page Number
Section	Confidentiality with Asymmetric Cryptography	53
Section	Authentication with Asymmetric Cryptography	54
Section	Using Symmetric and Asymmetric Cryptography	55
Table 4-2	Symmetric Algorithms	56
Table 4-3	Asymmetric Algorithms	57
Paragraph	The primary purpose of the PKI and digital certificates	58
Paragraph	CAs	59
Section	Digital Certificates	62
Paragraph	Hashing	67
Table 4-6	Hashing Algorithms	67
Paragraph	Salting	69
Section	Cryptography in the Real World	69
Section	Cisco Next-Generation Cryptography	70

Complete Tables and Lists from Memory

Print a copy of Appendix B, "Memory Tables," found on the companion website, or at least the section for this chapter, and complete the tables and lists from memory. Appendix C, "Memory Tables Answer Key," includes completed tables and lists you can use to check your work.

Define Key Terms

Define the following key terms from this chapter and check your answers in the glossary:

cryptography; encryption; decryption; data in transit; data at rest; data in use; symmetric cryptography; asymmetric cryptography; public/private key pair; Data Encryption Standard (DES); Triple Data Encryption Standard (3DES); Advanced Encryption Standard (AES); Rivest, Shamir, and Adleman (RSA); Digital Signature Algorithm (DSA); Diffie-Hellman (DH); elliptic-curve cryptography (ECC); public key infrastructure (PKI); digital certificate, certificate authority (CA); certificate revocation list (CRL); Online Certificate Status Protocol (OSCP); hashing, Message Digest 5 (MD5); Secure Hash Algorithm (SHA); shared secret key, salting, Cisco next-generation cryptography

Review Questions

1. Which of the following correctly defines data at rest?
    a. Data that is being exfiltrated
    b. Data that is being processed by a CPU
    c. Data that is being stored in any type of storage
    d. Data that is being transmitted over a wired or wireless network

2. Which of the following is an example of symmetric cryptography?

   a. Alice sends Bob a message that has been encrypted using a private key that has been shared with Bob so they can both encrypt and decrypt information they have exchanged with each other.

   b. Alice sends Bob a message that has been encrypted with Bob's public key, and Bob decrypts the message with his private key.

   c. Alice sends Bob a message that has been encrypted with her private key, and Bob uses Alice's public key to decrypt it.

   d. Alice sends Bob a message that has been encrypted with her public key, and Bob uses Alice's public key to decrypt it.

3. Which of the following are true about asymmetric cryptography? (Choose two.)

   a. If you encrypt with a public key, only the corresponding private key can decrypt it.

   b. If you encrypt with a public key, only the corresponding public key can decrypt it

   c. If you encrypt with a private key, only the corresponding private key can decrypt it.

   d. If you encrypt with a private key, only the corresponding public key can decrypt it.

4. Which of the following are examples of using asymmetric cryptography? (Choose two.)

   a. You need to encrypt data at rest on a server.

   b. You need to generate and exchange symmetric cryptographic keys.

   c. You need to encrypt data that is being transferred over a VPN.

   d. You need to prove that the data exchanged is from an authentic source.

5. Which of the following are asymmetric ciphers? (Choose three.)

   a. DH

   b. AES

   c. RSA

   d. DSA

   e. 3DES

6. Which of the following is a list of all the digital certificates that have been revoked by the certificate authority (CA) that issued them?

   a. SCEP

   b. OSCP

   c. CRL

   d. PKI

7. Which of the following are examples of hashing algorithms? (Choose two.)

   a. MD5

   b. SHA

   c. AES

   d. RSA

   e. DH

8. Why is cryptography used with web browsing? (Choose two.)

   a. To conceal the data traffic as it moves from an end user's device to a web server

   b. To verify that the web server an end user device is connecting to is in fact the correct device

   c. To increase the transfer speed between an end user's device and a web server

   d. To improve the availability and reliability of the connection between an end user's device and a web server

9. Which of the following are Cisco next-generation cryptography recommendations? (Choose two.)

   a. ECDH-384 for key exchange

   b. SHA1 for integrity

   c. AES-GCM 256 for encryption

   d. RSA for authentication

4

CHAPTER 5

Introduction to Networking, Addressing, and TCP/IP Protocols

This chapter covers the following topics:

- **The TCP/IP Stack:** This section discusses the TCP/IP stack and the OSI reference model.

- **Common TCP/IP Protocols and Their Vulnerabilities:** This section discusses vulnerabilities and vulnerability mitigation techniques for various TCP/IP protocols and services.

- **Network Addressing and Its Impact on Security:** This section examines various addressing and addressing services and how they impact security.

To provide secure network communications, you must be familiar with the fundamentals of network communications. In addition, you have to be familiar with the different types of protocols and services that are required for network communication so that you can uncover any and all vulnerabilities associated with them and mitigate those vulnerabilities.

This chapter begins by introducing the TCP/IP stack and the OSI reference model. You will learn what each layer provides for network communication. This chapter also explores vulnerabilities and vulnerability mitigation techniques for various TCP/IP protocols and services, such as TCP, UDP, HTTP, ARP, ICMP, DHCP, and DNS. In addition, this chapter explores how network addressing impacts network security. It covers IPv4 and IPv6 addresses, MAC addresses, network segmentation, CIDR notation, NAT, and public versus private networks.

This chapter covers information related to the following Cisco Certified Support Technician (CCST) Cybersecurity exam objectives:

2.1. Describe TCP/IP protocol vulnerabilities (TCP, UDP, HTTP, ARP, ICMP, DHCP, DNS).

2.2. Explain how network addresses impact network security (IPv4 and IPv6 addresses, MAC addresses, network segmentation, CIDR notation, NAT, public vs. private networks).

"Do I Know This Already?" Quiz

The "Do I Know This Already?" quiz allows you to assess whether you should read this entire chapter thoroughly or jump to the "Exam Preparation Tasks" section. If you are in doubt about your answers to these questions or your own assessment of your knowledge of the topics, read the entire chapter. Table 5-1 lists the major headings in this chapter and their corresponding "Do I Know This Already?" quiz questions. You can find the answers in Appendix A, "Answers to the 'Do I Know This Already?' Quizzes and Review Questions."

Table 5-1 "Do I Know This Already?" Section-to-Question Mapping

Foundation Topics Section	Questions
The TCP/IP Stack	1
Common TCP/IP Protocols and Their Vulnerabilities	2
Network Addressing and Its Impact on Security	3

CAUTION The goal of self-assessment is to gauge your mastery of the topics in this chapter. If you do not know the answer to a question or are only partially sure of the answer, you should mark that question incorrect for purposes of self-assessment. Giving yourself credit for an answer you correctly guess skews your self-assessment results and might provide you with a false sense of security.

1. Which layer of the TCP/IP stack is responsible for IPv4 and IPv6 addressing and the routing of data packets across interconnected networks?
   a. Application
   b. Transport
   c. Internet
   d. Link

2. Which of the following protocols are vulnerable to eavesdropping? (Choose three.)
   a. HTTP
   b. FTP
   c. Telnet
   d. SSH
   e. TCP

3. Which of the following are characteristics of private addressing? (Choose three.)
   a. Accessible to the general public or a large user base
   b. Restricted to specific users or organizations
   c. Owned and operated by third-party entities
   d. Owned and controlled by the organization or entity using them
   e. Susceptible to eavesdropping, data interception, and unauthorized access by malicious actors
   f. Allows organizations to enforce strict access controls, limiting connectivity to authorized devices and users

Foundation Topics

The TCP/IP Stack

The TCP/IP stack, also known as the Internet Protocol suite, is a set of communication protocols that form the foundation of the Internet and many other computer networks. Think of it as a blueprint, but one that outlines a standardized way for devices to communicate and exchange data over networks, ensuring reliable and efficient transmission of information. The purpose of the **TCP/IP stack** is to facilitate reliable, scalable, and interoperable communication between devices on a network. It enables the Internet and other networks to function by providing a standardized set of protocols that define how data is transmitted, routed, and received.

The TCP/IP stack is named for its two primary protocols: Transmission Control Protocol (TCP) and Internet Protocol (IP). These protocols work together and operate at specific layers of the protocol stack to handle various aspects of network communication.

Development of the TCP/IP stack was a collaborative effort involving numerous researchers and engineers, primarily associated with the U.S. Department of Defense (DoD) and its Advanced Research Projects Agency (ARPA) in the 1970s—and we still use it to this day. Figure 5-1 provides a visual representation of the TCP/IP stack. Notice that it consists of four distinct named layers; each of them is responsible for specific communication tasks.

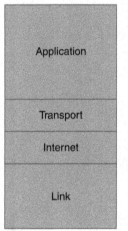

Figure 5-1   *The TCP/IP Stack*

There is another communications model that is commonly used: the OSI reference model. The **OSI (Open Systems Interconnection) reference model** is a conceptual framework that standardizes and describes the functions and interactions of a communication system. It was developed by the International Organization for Standardization (ISO) around the same time the TCP/IP stack was developed. However, every time you are working with a networking device, you are dealing with TCP and IP, so really you are using TCP/IP in the real world, and the OSI reference model is really more theoretical. Figure 5-2 provides a visual example of the OSI reference model. Notice how it is made of seven distinct layers that are numbered and named; each of them is responsible for specific communication tasks.

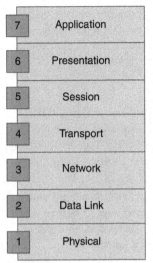

Figure 5-2 *The OSI Reference Model*

These two different communication models are closely related, as you can see in Figure 5-3. Notice how the application layer of the TCP/IP stack is an amalgamation of the application, presentation, and session layers of the OSI reference model. The transport layer is still just the transport layer. The network layer of the OSI reference model is called the Internet layer in the TCP/IP stack. The data link and physical layers of the OSI reference model are amalgamated as the link layer in the TCP/IP stack.

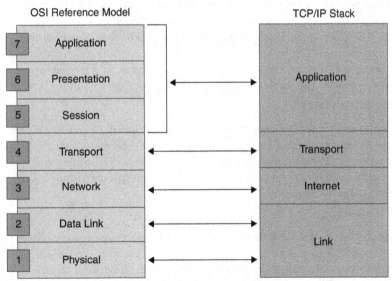

Figure 5-3 *Comparing the TCP/IP Stack and the OSI Reference Model*

It is important to note that although we use the TCP/IP stack in the real world on all our networking devices, when we discuss network communications, we typically speak of the layers of the OSI reference model because they are broken out in a more granular way, which simplifies our understanding and learning and aids in more detailed troubleshooting. As a result, this chapter provides information about the seven layers of the OSI reference model for learning purposes instead of just describing the four layers of the TCP/IP stack. However, at any time, you can take a peek at Figure 5-3 to visually see how the layers relate:

- TCP/IP stack application layer

  7. **Application layer:** The **application layer** is the topmost layer of the TCP/IP stack and of the OSI model. It provides a means for applications to communicate with each other over the network. Protocols such as Hypertext Transfer Protocol (HTTP), File Transfer Protocol (FTP), Simple Mail Transfer Protocol (SMTP), and Domain Name System (DNS) operate at this layer.

  6. **Presentation layer:** The **presentation layer** is responsible for data representation, encryption, and compression. It ensures that data exchanged between applications is in a format that both can understand. It also handles data encryption and decryption, as well as data compression and decompression.

  5. **Session layer:** The **session layer** establishes, manages, and terminates communication sessions between applications. It enables processes running on different devices to establish a dialogue and coordinate their communication. This layer provides mechanisms for session establishment, maintenance, and synchronization.

- TCP/IP stack transport layer

  4. **Transport layer:** The **transport layer** ensures reliable or unreliable and efficient end-to-end data delivery between applications running on different devices. The most widely used transport protocol in the TCP/IP stack is Transmission Control Protocol (TCP), which provides features such as error correction, flow control, and congestion control. Another transport protocol is User Datagram Protocol (UDP), which is a connectionless and lightweight alternative. TCP is reliable, and UDP is best-effort or unreliable.

- TCP/IP stack Internet layer

  3. **Network layer:** The **network layer** is where Internet Protocol (IP) operates. This layer also handles the routing and forwarding of data packets across interconnected networks. IP assigns unique addresses (IPv4 and/or IPv6 addresses) to devices and is used by routers to determine the best path for data to travel from the source to the destination.

- TCP/IP stack link layer

  2. **Data link layer:** The **data link layer** is responsible for the transmission of data frames between adjacent network nodes over a physical medium and the addressing of those frames. It provides mechanisms for error detection, flow control, and data framing. Ethernet is a commonly used protocol in this layer, and MAC addressing is used to address the sources and destinations of the frames. This is the layer where switches forward frames within a subnet/VLAN/broadcast domain.

1. **Physical layer:** The **physical layer** deals with the physical transmission of data through network cables, wireless signals, or other media. It defines the electrical, mechanical, and functional specifications for transmitting raw bits across the network.

Common TCP/IP Protocols and Their Vulnerabilities

As an up-and-coming security professional, it is important that you start to build your understanding of the purpose behind an assortment of common TCP/IP protocols and services. However, it is even more important that you take the time to understand various vulnerabilities associated with them and how to mitigate those vulnerabilities. This section introduces some of the most common TCP/IP protocols and services, the vulnerabilities associated with them, and how you can mitigate those vulnerabilities.

Transmission Control Protocol (TCP)

Transmission Control Protocol (TCP) is a reliable and connection-oriented transport protocol that you find at the transport layer of the TCP/IP stack. It ensures that data sent over the network reaches the intended destination accurately and in the correct order. TCP provides features like error correction, flow control, and congestion control. TCP enables robust and dependable communication between applications across networks, such as the Internet.

A number of vulnerabilities are associated with TCP, including the following:

- **TCP SYN flood attacks:** Attackers flood a target server with TCP SYN packets, exhausting server resources and preventing legitimate connections.

  - **Mitigation:** Implementing firewall rules and rate limiting to detect and mitigate TCP SYN flood attacks

- **TCP sequence number prediction:** Attackers can predict TCP sequence numbers, which enables them to hijack TCP connections or inject malicious data.

  - **Mitigation:** Enforcing strict randomization of TCP sequence numbers to prevent prediction attacks

- **TCP session hijacking:** Attackers intercept and manipulate TCP sessions to gain unauthorized access or modify data.

  - **Mitigation:** Employing encryption and strong authentication mechanisms to protect against TCP session hijacking

User Datagram Protocol (UDP)

User Datagram Protocol (UDP) is a connectionless and lightweight transport protocol that operates at the transport layer of the TCP/IP stack. It provides for faster transmission of data between communicating devices compared to TCP but does not offer the reliability and error-correction mechanisms of TCP. Therefore, UDP is commonly used for real-time streaming, VoIP, and DNS.

Since UDP lacks built-in reliability mechanisms, the vulnerabilities associated with UDP include the following:

- **UDP flood attacks:** Attackers flood a target server with a large volume of UDP packets, causing network congestion and denial of service.

  - **Mitigation:** Implementing rate-limiting and traffic-filtering mechanisms to detect and block UDP flood attacks

- **UDP amplification attacks:** Attackers exploit vulnerable UDP services to generate a large response to a small request, resulting in network congestion and amplification of the attack traffic.

  - **Mitigation:** Configuring network devices to disable or restrict vulnerable UDP services to mitigate UDP amplification attacks

- **Lack of reliability:** UDP does not provide built-in mechanisms for detecting errors, retransmitting lost packets, or ensuring the ordered delivery of packets. This can lead to data loss or inconsistent data transmission.

  - **Mitigation:** Implementing error-detection and error-handling mechanisms at the application layer, such as checksums or acknowledgment protocols

Key Topic

Internet Protocol Version 4 (IPv4)

Internet Protocol version 4 (IPv4) is the fourth version of the Internet Protocol and is responsible for addressing and routing packets with routers across networks. It uses 32-bit addresses, allowing for approximately 4.3 billion unique addresses for devices around the world. You will find IPv4 at the Internet layer of the TCP/IP stack. It is the foundation of Internet communication.

Vulnerabilities associated with IPv4 include the following:

- **IP spoofing:** IPv4 allows the source IP address in a packet to be easily spoofed, which can lead to impersonation, unauthorized access, or distributed denial of service (DDoS) attacks.

  - **Mitigation:** Implementing packet filtering or ingress filtering such as IP Source Guard at network boundaries to verify the authenticity of IP packets and discard spoofed packets

- **IP fragmentation attacks:** Attackers exploit IP fragmentation mechanisms to evade detection or cause resource exhaustion on target systems.

  - **Mitigation:** Enforcing fragmentation controls and monitoring for abnormal or malicious IP fragmentation patterns

- **Limited address space:** IPv4 has a limited address space, with a maximum of approximately 4.3 billion unique IP addresses. This scarcity can lead to challenges in providing unique IP addresses for all devices in a network.

  - **Mitigation:** Adopting IPv6 (Internet Protocol version 6), which offers a significantly larger address space, allowing for the allocation of unique addresses to a larger number of devices

Internet Protocol Version 6 (IPv6)

Internet Protocol version 6 (IPv6), which is the successor to IPv4, is designed to overcome the limitations of address exhaustion in IPv4. It uses 128-bit addresses, allowing for a significantly larger number of unique addresses. It is responsible for addressing and routing packets across networks, and you will find IPv6 at the Internet layer of the TCP/IP stack.

While IPv6 was designed with security improvements, it does have some vulnerabilities, including the following:

- **Increased attack surface:** IPv6 introduces a larger address space and additional features, which can increase the attack surface for potential vulnerabilities. Attackers may exploit new or less-familiar protocols and features in IPv6, including extension headers, autoconfiguration mechanisms, or multicast communication.

    - **Mitigation:** Implementing network segmentation, firewall policies, and intrusion detection systems (IDSs) and staying updated with IPv6 security best practices and recommendations

- **Address scanning:** Attackers scan IPv6 address ranges to identify vulnerable systems or discover network topologies.

    - **Mitigation:** Implementing network access controls and monitoring mechanisms to prevent unauthorized scanning and reconnaissance activities

- **Neighbor Discovery Protocol (NDP) security:** NDP is the IPv6 equivalent of ARP (Address Resolution Protocol) in IPv4, and it can be vulnerable to various attacks, such as neighbor solicitation/advertisement spoofing and router advertisement spoofing.

    - **Mitigation:** Implementing techniques such as secure neighbor discovery mechanisms, NDP snooping, and ingress filtering to validate and secure neighbor relationships

- **Transition mechanisms:** The coexistence of IPv4 and IPv6 introduces complexities and potential vulnerabilities during the transition period.

    - **Mitigation:** Ensuring that secure transition mechanisms are implemented during the coexistence of IPv4 and IPv6

Media Access Control (MAC)

Media Access Control (MAC) addresses are unique identifiers assigned to network interface cards (NICs) at the data link layer. They facilitate the identification of devices within a local network, and switches use the destination MAC address listed in a frame to make forwarding decisions.

MAC addresses are not typically exposed outside the local network, so vulnerabilities associated with them are limited to local network attacks, including the following:

- **MAC address spoofing:** Attackers can spoof or change their MAC addresses to impersonate legitimate devices on a network. This can lead to unauthorized access, network disruption, or unauthorized monitoring.

5

- **Mitigation:** Implementing MAC address filtering, port security, or network access control mechanisms to validate and restrict MAC address assignments

- **MAC flooding:** An attacker floods a switch with a large number of forged MAC addresses, causing the switch to enter a fail-open mode, where it starts forwarding packets to all ports. This is known as a CAM table overflow, and it can lead to a denial of service (DoS) situation or enable unauthorized monitoring of network traffic.

  - **Mitigation:** Implementing features such as MAC address limiting, dynamic MAC address aging, or switch port security measures such as port security

- **ARP (Address Resolution Protocol) spoofing:** Also known as ARP poisoning or ARP cache poisoning, ARP spoofing is a type of network attack in which an attacker manipulates the ARP tables (mappings of IP addresses to MAC addresses) on a local area network (LAN).

  - **Mitigation:** Implementing port security mechanisms, such as MAC address filtering and Dynamic ARP Inspection, to prevent unauthorized access and ARP spoofing

Key Topic | Address Resolution Protocol (ARP)

Address Resolution Protocol (ARP) is used to map IP addresses to MAC addresses in a local network. It enables devices to determine the MAC address associated with an IP address for direct communication in a subnet/VLAN/broadcast domain. ARP is a data link layer protocol.

Vulnerabilities associated with ARP include the following:

- **ARP spoofing:** Attackers forge or manipulate ARP messages, associating their MAC address with a legitimate IP address in order to intercept or modify network traffic.

  - **Mitigation:** Implementing mechanisms like ARP inspection and Dynamic ARP Inspection

- **ARP cache poisoning:** Attackers send false ARP messages to update the ARP caches on network devices, redirecting traffic to their own malicious systems.

  - **Mitigation:** Configuring static ARP entries or using techniques like ARP cache timeout to reduce the impact of ARP cache poisoning attacks

Key Topic | Hypertext Transfer Protocol (HTTP)

Hypertext Transfer Protocol (HTTP) is an application-layer protocol used for transmitting and receiving web-based content. It enables communication between web clients (such as web browsers) and web servers. HTTP operates at the application layer of the TCP/IP stack.

Vulnerabilities associated with HTTP include the following:

- **On-path attacks:** Attackers intercept HTTP traffic to eavesdrop on or modify data exchanged between the client and the server.

  - **Mitigation:** Implementing secure HTTP (HTTPS) with Transport Layer Security (TLS) to encrypt and authenticate communication between clients and servers

- **Cross-site scripting (XSS):** Attackers inject malicious scripts into web pages, and those scripts are then executed by unsuspecting users' browsers, enabling various attacks.

  - **Mitigation:** Employing input validation and output encoding techniques to prevent XSS attacks

- **SQL injection:** SQL injection vulnerabilities occur when an attacker can manipulate or inject malicious SQL queries into an HTTP(s) application's database. This can lead to unauthorized access, data leakage, or manipulation of the database.

  - **Mitigation:** Using prepared statements or parameterized queries, input validation, and proper input sanitization to prevent SQL injection attacks for HTTP(s) applications and regularly performing security testing and vulnerability scanning to identify and fix potential SQL injection vulnerabilities

- **Cross-site request forgery (CSRF):** Attackers trick users into performing unintended actions on web applications by exploiting the trust relationship between the user's browser and the target website.

  - **Mitigation:** Implementing anti-CSRF tokens and enforcing strict policies to mitigate CSRF attacks

Internet Control Message Protocol (ICMP)

Internet Control Message Protocol (ICMP) is primarily used for diagnostics and error reporting in IP networks. It allows network devices to send control messages, such as echo requests (pings) and error notifications, and even trace the path through a network (traceroute). ICMP is an Internet layer protocol.

ICMP vulnerabilities include the following:

- **ICMP flood attacks:** Attackers flood a target system with ICMP echo requests, consuming network resources and causing denial of service.

  - **Mitigation:** Applying rate limiting or filtering mechanisms to prevent ICMP flood attacks

- **ICMP redirect attacks:** Attackers send false ICMP redirect messages to modify the routing table of a victim system, redirecting its traffic to a malicious gateway.

  - **Mitigation:** Configuring devices to ignore ICMP redirect messages to mitigate ICMP redirect attacks

Dynamic Host Configuration Protocol (DHCP)

Dynamic Host Configuration Protocol (DHCP) is used for dynamically assigning IP addresses and network configuration parameters to devices on a network. It simplifies network management and reduces manual configuration. DHCP is an application layer protocol.

Vulnerabilities associated with DHCP include the following:

- **DHCP spoofing:** Attackers impersonate legitimate DHCP servers, providing incorrect IP addresses or malicious configuration information to devices.

- **Mitigation:** Implementing DHCP snooping or DHCP server authentication to detect and prevent DHCP spoofing attacks

- **DHCP starvation attacks:** Attackers exhaust the available pool of IP addresses in a DHCP server by requesting a large number of IP addresses, preventing legitimate devices from obtaining addresses.

  - **Mitigation:** Enforcing rate limiting and lease duration controls to mitigate DHCP starvation attacks

Domain Name System (DNS)

Domain Name System (DNS) translates domain names (such as www.example.com) into IP addresses (such as 203.0.113.10), facilitating the use of easy-to-remember names when referring to resources. It is an application layer protocol.

Vulnerabilities associated with DNS include the following:

- **DNS spoofing:** Attackers manipulate DNS responses to redirect users to malicious websites or intercept and modify DNS queries.

  - **Mitigation:** Implementing DNSSEC (DNS Security Extensions) to provide data integrity and authentication of DNS responses and using DNS filtering and monitoring solutions to detect and block DNS spoofing attempts

- **DNS amplification attacks:** Attackers exploit misconfigured DNS servers to amplify their attack traffic, causing network congestion and denial of service.

  - **Mitigation:** Configuring network devices to prevent open DNS resolvers and ensure proper DNS server configuration to mitigate DNS amplification attacks

File Transfer Protocol (FTP)

File Transfer Protocol (FTP) is used to facilitate the transfer of files between computers on a network. It provides a standard set of commands and protocols for uploading, downloading, and managing files on remote servers. FTP allows users to efficiently exchange files over networks, making it useful for tasks like file sharing, website publishing, and remote file management. FTP is an application layer protocol.

Vulnerabilities associated with FTP include the following:

- **Lack of encryption:** FTP transmits data in plaintext, which makes it susceptible to eavesdropping and unauthorized access.

  - **Mitigation:** Implementing FTP over SSL/TLS (FTPS) or using the more secure SSH File Transfer Protocol (SFTP), to provide encryption for data transmission

- **Weak authentication:** FTP relies on basic username and password authentication, which can be vulnerable to brute-force attacks and password interception.

  - **Mitigation:** Enforcing strong passwords, implementing two-factor authentication (2FA), and using more secure authentication methods, such as public key authentication for SFTP

- **Data tampering:** Since FTP does not provide built-in integrity checks, data transferred via FTP can be tampered with during transmission.

    - **Mitigation:** Using file integrity verification techniques such as checksums or digital signatures to ensure that the files have not been modified or tampered with

Telnet

Key Topic

Telnet establishes a remote terminal connection between a client and a server over a network. It allows users to log into a remote host and access its command-line interface. Telnet facilitates remote management, troubleshooting, and text-based communication with network devices or systems.

Vulnerabilities associated with Telnet include the following:

- **Lack of encryption:** Telnet sends data, including login credentials, in plaintext, which can be intercepted (eavesdropping) and exposed.

    - **Mitigation:** Replacing Telnet with an encrypted alternative like Secure Shell (SSH), which provides secure encrypted communication between client and server

- **Weak authentication:** Telnet typically relies on basic username and password authentication, which can be vulnerable to brute-force attacks or password interception.

    - **Mitigation:** Enforcing strong passwords, implementing two-factor authentication (2FA), and using more secure authentication mechanisms available with SSH

- **On-path attacks:** Telnet connections are susceptible to interception and tampering by attackers positioned on the network path.

    - **Mitigation:** Implementing SSH or using virtual private networks (VPNs) to mitigate the risk of on-path attacks by providing encrypted communication channels between clients and servers

Secure Shell (SSH)

Key Topic

Secure Shell (SSH) provides secure encrypted communication and secure remote administration of network devices and systems. It allows users to establish secure command-line, file transfer (SFTP), and tunneling sessions over an unsecured network. SSH ensures confidentiality, integrity, and authentication of data transmitted between a client and a server, offering a secure alternative to protocols like Telnet and FTP.

Vulnerabilities associated with SSH include the following:

- **Weak authentication:** SSH is vulnerable to weak authentication practices such as using weak passwords or relying solely on username and password authentication.

    - **Mitigation:** Enforcing strong password policies, using public key authentication, and implementing multifactor authentication (MFA) for SSH connections

- **Vulnerabilities in SSH implementations:** Like any other software, SSH implementations may have vulnerabilities that can be exploited by attackers.

5

- **Mitigation:** Keeping SSH software and systems up to date with the latest security patches to mitigate known vulnerabilities and regularly monitoring and applying security updates to protect against potential exploits

- **Misconfigured access controls:** Improperly configured access controls can lead to unauthorized access or privilege escalation.

  - **Mitigation:** Implementing proper access controls and restricting SSH access to only authorized users and systems and using firewall rules or network segmentation to limit SSH access to trusted networks or specific IP addresses

Network Addressing and Its Impact on Security

For devices to communicate over any network, they need various addresses. Specifically, when using devices on Ethernet networks, IPv4 or IPv6 public and private addressing is needed, and so is MAC addressing. This section explores the impact IPv4, IPv6, and MAC addressing have on security. It also examines NAT for IPv4 and its relationship with security.

IPv4 and IPv6

Network addressing, both IPv4 and IPv6, plays a crucial role in network security and has a significant impact on various aspects of network security, including network visibility, access control, vulnerability management, and the network attack surface. As a future security professional, it is important for you to grasp how network addresses impact these various aspects of network security.

For starters, a network address provides a unique identifier for a device connected to a network. This visibility allows network administrators to monitor and track network traffic, identify authorized and unauthorized devices, and detect potential security threats. It also enables organizations to implement network monitoring tools, intrusion detection systems (IDSs), and intrusion prevention systems (IPSs) to identify malicious activities and unauthorized access attempts.

Network addresses are also used in access control mechanisms to determine which devices or users are granted access to network resources. By leveraging IP-based access control lists (ACLs) or firewall rules, organizations can enforce security policies, restrict access to sensitive resources, and prevent unauthorized access. Properly configured access control based on network addresses can help mitigate the risks of unauthorized access, data breaches, and insider threats.

Network addresses are also essential for vulnerability management processes. Security teams can perform network scans, vulnerability assessments, and penetration testing to identify security weaknesses and vulnerabilities within the network infrastructure. By correlating identified vulnerabilities with network addresses, organizations can prioritize remediation efforts, apply necessary patches or security updates, and implement mitigations to protect vulnerable systems from exploitation.

Finally, network addresses contribute to the network attack surface—that is, the potential points of entry for attackers. Each IP address represents a potential target that can be probed, scanned, or attacked. With the increasing prevalence of connected devices and the growth of the Internet of Things (IoT), more devices are being assigned unique IP addresses, and the attack surface is expanding. It is crucial for organizations to implement proper security controls, such as network segmentation, intrusion detection systems, and network access controls, to reduce the attack surface and protect against external threats.

CIDR Notation

CIDR (classless interdomain routing) notation is a method used to represent IP addresses and their associated network prefixes (for example, 192.168.0.0/24). In this example, 192.168.0.0 represents the network address, and /24 indicates the subnet mask or the number of significant network bits in the network prefix. The /24 notation indicates that the first 24 bits of the IP address are the network address, and the remaining 8 bits (32 bits total in IPv4 – 24 network bits = 8) are available for host addresses within that network.

CIDR notation impacts network security in several ways. For starters, it allows for efficient allocation and utilization of IP addresses. With CIDR, networks can be divided into smaller subnets by varying the prefix length, allowing organizations to allocate IP addresses based on their specific needs. This flexibility helps optimize IP address allocation and reduces waste, ensuring that IP addresses are used effectively. Therefore, CIDR notation enables network administrators to define and enforce network segmentation and to create distinct segments with different security requirements. This segmentation enhances network security by isolating sensitive systems or departments, controlling access between segments, and limiting the potential impact of security breaches.

CIDR notation is often used in access control lists (ACLs) to specify the range of IP addresses allowed or denied access to specific resources. By defining CIDR ranges in ACLs, network administrators can enforce granular control over network traffic, allowing or restricting access based on the source IP addresses. This helps prevent unauthorized access attempts and provides an additional layer of security. In addition, CIDR notation is commonly used in firewall configurations to define IP address ranges for filtering incoming and outgoing traffic. Firewalls can be configured to allow or block traffic from specific network ranges using CIDR notation, helping to protect against malicious activities such as denial of service (DoS) attacks, intrusion attempts, and unauthorized access from specific IP address ranges.

Finally, CIDR notation plays a vital role in routing protocols such as Border Gateway Protocol (BGP) and OSPF. It allows networks to advertise and exchange routing information more efficiently, resulting in optimized routing decisions. Properly configuring network ranges using CIDR notation in routing tables and implementing appropriate routing security measures helps prevent route hijacking, IP prefix spoofing, and other routing-based security vulnerabilities.

Network Segmentation

As stated earlier, you can use network addressing to segment a network by dividing it into smaller, isolated subnetworks/subnets or segments. This segmentation helps improve network performance, enhance security, and simplify network management because in the end, you can ensure that what happens in a subnet stays in a subnet or what happens in a subnet does not affect another subnet.

Subnetting involves dividing a large network into smaller, more manageable subnets. For example, you might subnet the 10.0.0.0/8 network into 65,536 smaller, more manageable /24 networks. By doing so, you create 65,536 distinct subnetworks within the larger network, each with its own range of IP addresses. Why would you care to do this? Because subnetting allows for better allocation of IP addresses, reduces broadcast traffic, and provides logical separation between different departments, locations, or security zones so you can implement tighter security controls between the devices in the different subnets.

Each subnet created through subnetting is assigned a specific range of IP addresses. This range defines the valid IP addresses that can be assigned to devices within the subnet. By allocating different IP address ranges to different subnets, network administrators can easily identify devices belonging to specific segments and enforce security policies accordingly. For example, an administrator could implement an ACL to control which traffic is allowed to enter or leave the subnet, based on source and destination IP addressing.

VLANs are a form of network segmentation that operates at the data link layer (Layer 2) of the OSI model. VLANs allow logical grouping of devices across different physical LAN segments, regardless of their physical location. VLANs are created by configuring network switches to assign specific ports to a particular VLAN. Devices within the same VLAN can communicate with each other as if they were connected to the same physical LAN, and devices in different VLANs are isolated from each other and can only communicate with each other if the traffic is routed using a router. VLANs provide enhanced security by segregating sensitive systems and restricting network access between VLANs.

As mentioned in an earlier example, an administrator could implement an ACL to control which traffic is allowed to enter or leave a subnet based on source and destination IP addressing. Using ACLs allows administrators to define and enforce access policies based on IP addresses or address ranges. ACLs can be applied to routers, firewalls, or other network devices to control traffic flow between different segments. By specifying which IP addresses or address ranges are allowed or denied access to specific segments, ACLs help ensure that only authorized traffic is allowed to pass through, enhancing network security.

You can think of network segmentation based on network addressing as a way to define security zones within a network. Each security zone consists of a separate network segment with its own IP address range. By assigning devices to specific security zones based on their IP addresses, network administrators can implement different security measures and access controls based on the zone. For example, a screened subnet or demilitarized zone (DMZ) is a security zone that separates publicly accessible servers from internal networks to protect critical internal resources.

Keep in mind that segmenting a network using network addressing enables organizations to isolate different departments, control access between segments, reduce the impact of security incidents, and improve overall network performance. It provides a structured and organized approach to network design and management, allowing for better resource allocation, scalability, and security management.

Public Versus Private Networks

When it comes to securing your networks, keeping your data and communications private is critical. Therefore, it is imperative that you have the ability to clearly demarcate where a private network begins and ends and where public networks begin and end.

Public and private networks are distinct in terms of their accessibility, ownership, and security implications. Understanding the differences between public and private networks is crucial for maintaining robust security measures. Table 5-2 provides a comparison of public and private networks.

Key Topic

Table 5-2   Characteristics of Public and Private Networks

Characteristic	Public Networks	Private Networks
Addressing	Public IPv4 addresses from the Class A, B, or C ranges Global IPv6 unicast addresses	Private RFC 1918 addresses from the Class A, B, or C ranges Unique local IPv6 unicast addresses and link-local IPv6 unicast addresses
Accessibility	Public networks are accessible to the general public or a large user base. They are typically provided by Internet service providers (ISPs) or managed by organizations for public access.	Private networks are restricted to specific users or organizations. They are typically used within corporate environments, educational institutions, or government entities.
Ownership and control	Public networks are owned and operated by third-party entities, such as ISPs, that maintain and manage the network infrastructure.	A private network is owned and controlled by the organization or entity using it. This ownership and control give administrators of private networks more authority over the implementation of security measures and policies tailored to their specific needs.
Security	Public networks, such as the Internet and public Wi-Fi hotspots, present increased security risks due to their open nature. These are some of the key security implications: **Increased exposure:** Public networks are susceptible to eavesdropping, data interception, and unauthorized access by malicious actors. The lack of control over the network infrastructure and the multitude of connected devices make public networks prime targets for attacks. **On-path attacks:** Public networks provide an opportunity for attackers to intercept and manipulate network traffic, potentially compromising sensitive information transmitted between devices.	Private networks offer several security advantages over public networks, including the following: **Controlled access:** Private networks allow organizations to enforce strict access controls, limiting connectivity to authorized devices and users. This reduces the exposure to potential threats and unauthorized access attempts. **Network segmentation:** Private networks enable segmentation into separate subnets or VLANs, allowing for isolation of sensitive systems, departments, or security zones. This segregation limits the impact of security incidents and contains potential breaches within specific network segments.

5

Characteristic	Public Networks	Private Networks
	Lack of trust: Public networks are inherently untrusted environments, as they are shared among numerous users. Trusting the security and integrity of public networks can be challenging. **Vulnerability to attacks:** Public networks may be especially susceptible to various attacks, including phishing, malware distribution, and network-based attacks, due to the potential presence of compromised devices or malicious actors.	**Enhanced monitoring and management:** Private networks provide greater visibility into and control over network traffic, facilitating effective monitoring, logging, and incident response. Network administrators can implement security measures such as intrusion detection systems (IDSs) and firewalls to protect the network and quickly identify and respond to security events. **Compliance and regulatory requirements:** Private networks allow organizations to meet specific compliance requirements, such as data privacy regulations, by implementing appropriate security controls and safeguarding sensitive information.

In summary, public and private networks differ in terms of accessibility, ownership, and security implications. Public networks, while providing widespread connectivity, present higher security risks due to their open nature. Private networks offer greater control, segmentation, and the ability to implement tailored security measures, reducing the exposure to potential threats and unauthorized access attempts. Organizations should carefully consider the security implications and implement appropriate security measures for both public and private networks to protect their sensitive data and resources.

NAT

By default, users within organizations cannot access the Internet due to the fact that private networks use RFC 1918 addresses. In order to provide connectivity from private networks to public networks, you need a service called **Network Address Translation (NAT)**. NAT has the ability to take a private RFC 1918 address that is routable only on a private network and convert it into a public IP address that is routable on the Internet.

For example, let's say you are on your work PC in a private subnet, and it has the RFC 1918 address 10.0.10.37. Every time your PC sends a packet, the source of that packet will be your private IP address 10.0.10.37. However, this is not an address that is allowed on the Internet. The addresses allowed on the Internet are public IP addresses. Therefore, at the edge of your network, you need to set up a device (such as a router) that is capable of performing NAT. When your packet arrives at the edge device and needs to go to a server on the Internet, the NAT device converts your IP address 10.0.10.37 that is in the packet into a public IP address, such as 203.0.113.91, and then forwards the packet onto the Internet. Your PC has no idea that this is happening. When the return packet from the server is coming back to your PC, the NAT device converts that public IP address (203.0.113.91) back to your private address (10.0.10.37) in the packet and then forwards the packet to you. Again, your PC has no idea that this is happening. So, NAT is a service that is completely transparent to users.

In addition, modern networks have a massive imbalance when it comes to private versus public addressing. For example, you might have 5700 devices that need private IP addresses and access to the Internet but only 7 public IP addresses. This means all 5700 devices need to share the 7 public IP addresses. Great news: NAT can perform this sharing for you.

NAT can translate multiple private IP addresses to a single public IP address by using a feature called Port Address Translation (PAT). This simplifies network configuration and reduces the need for obtaining multiple public IP addresses from Internet service providers. NAT acts as an intermediary between the private network and the Internet, facilitating communication while maintaining the privacy of internal IP addresses.

NAT provides a level of security by hiding the private IP addresses of devices within the network. When communicating with external networks, the source IP address is translated to the public IP address assigned by the NAT device. Therefore, only the public IP address is known by outsiders. This obfuscation of internal IP addresses makes it difficult for attackers to directly target specific devices within the network. However, NAT is not really a real-world security solution as sophisticated attackers will still be able to get the information they need with the correct tools; NAT is just replacing the private IP address with a public IP address. So don't get overly confident about the security provided by just NAT as this would be considered a weak security solution. However, for the sake of the CCST Cybersecurity exam, if you are asked if NAT provides security, the best answer is yes because it does provide a very low level of security.

NAT devices often function as firewalls as well, providing a form of network protection. They filter incoming and outgoing traffic based on the stateful inspection of network connections. NAT devices maintain a state table that tracks active connections, allowing only established or related incoming traffic to pass through. This filtering capability helps protect against unauthorized incoming connections and can prevent certain types of network-based attacks.

PAT, a variant of NAT, allows multiple devices within a private network to share a single public IP address by using different port numbers. This process introduces an additional layer of security as it makes it more challenging for attackers to target specific devices within the network.

By default, NAT devices do not allow inbound connections unless they are explicitly configured. This provides a level of protection against unsolicited incoming traffic, such as port scanning or direct attacks targeting internal devices. NAT devices act as a barrier, preventing external entities from initiating connections to devices within the private network unless specific port forwarding or NAT traversal rules are configured.

As stated before, while NAT provides certain security benefits, it is not a comprehensive security solution on its own. Organizations should still implement additional security measures, such as firewalls, IDSs, and network monitoring, to enhance network security.

For the CCST Cybersecurity exam, remember that NAT conserves public IP addresses, enables Internet access for devices within a private network, and has implications for network security. It hides internal IP addresses, acts as a firewall, facilitates network segmentation, introduces port-based differentiation, and limits inbound connections. These aspects of NAT contribute to the overall security posture of a network, but organizations should adopt a layered approach to security to ensure comprehensive protection.

5

MAC Addressing

MAC (Media Access Control) addresses operate at the data link layer of the OSI model and are primarily used for communication between devices in the same subnet/VLAN/broadcast domain. When it comes to security, you need to consider the following:

Key Topic

- A MAC address serves as a unique identifier for a network interface card (NIC) at the data link layer. This identification allows network administrators to track and identify individual devices within a local network. By associating MAC addresses with specific devices, organizations can enforce MAC-based access control and MAC address filtering, ensuring that only authorized devices are allowed to connect to the network. This helps prevent unauthorized access and reduces the risk of potential security breaches.

- MAC addresses play a crucial role in ARP, a protocol used to resolve IP addresses to MAC addresses within a local network. ARP spoofing attacks involve manipulating the mapping between IP addresses and MAC addresses, leading to potential security vulnerabilities. To mitigate ARP spoofing, network security measures like ARP inspection, Dynamic ARP Inspection, and ARP cache validation can be implemented. These measures validate the consistency between IP and MAC address mappings, ensuring the integrity of network communications and preventing unauthorized ARP manipulations.

- In wireless networks, MAC addresses are used as a security measure to allow or deny access to Wi-Fi networks based on the MAC addresses of wireless devices. MAC address filtering in wireless access points allows network administrators to specify which devices are permitted to connect to the network. This control helps prevent unauthorized devices from connecting to the wireless network and strengthens the overall security posture.

Overall, MAC addresses impact network security by facilitating device identification, network access control, network segmentation, ARP security, and wireless network security within a local network. Organizations should leverage MAC addresses as part of their security strategies, along with other network security measures, to enhance the overall security posture of their networks.

Summary

To provide secure network communications, you must be familiar with the fundamentals of network communications. In addition, you have to be familiar with the different types of protocols and services that are required for network communication so that you can uncover any and all vulnerabilities associated with them and mitigate those vulnerabilities. This chapter discusses the following concepts related to networking, addressing, and TCP/IP protocols:

- The **TCP/IP stack** is a set of communication protocols that form the foundation of the Internet and many other computer networks. The **OSI (Open Systems Interconnection) reference model** is a conceptual framework that standardizes and describes the functions and interactions of a communication system. These models have a number of layers:

- The **application layer** is the topmost layer of the TCP/IP stack and the OSI model. It provides a means for applications to communicate with each other over the network.

- The **presentation layer** of the OSI model is responsible for data representation, encryption, and compression.

- The **session layer** of the OSI model establishes, manages, and terminates communication sessions between applications.

- The **transport layer** of the OSI model and the TCP/IP stack ensures reliable or unreliable and efficient end-to-end data delivery between applications running on different devices.

- The **network layer** of the OSI model is where Internet Protocol (IP) operates. It also handles the routing and forwarding of data packets across interconnected networks.

- The **data link layer** of the OSI model is responsible for the transmission of data frames between adjacent network nodes over a physical medium and the addressing of those frames.

- The **physical layer** of the OSI model deals with the physical transmission of data through network cables, wireless signals, or other media.

- Being aware of **common TCP/IP protocols** that exist in modern networks and the **vulnerabilities** associated with them will help you protect your network from threats associated with them:

  - **TCP (Transmission Control Protocol)** is a reliable and connection-oriented transport protocol that operates at the transport layer of the TCP/IP stack. Vulnerabilities include TCP SYN flood attacks, TCP sequence number prediction, and TCP session hijacking.

  - **UDP (User Datagram Protocol)** is a connectionless and lightweight transport protocol that operates at the transport layer of the TCP/IP stack. Vulnerabilities include UDP flood attacks, UDP amplification attacks, and lack of reliability.

  - **IPv4 (Internet Protocol version 4)** is the fourth version of the Internet Protocol and is responsible for addressing and routing packets with routers across networks. Vulnerabilities include IP spoofing, IP fragmentation attacks, and limited address space.

  - **IPv6 (Internet Protocol version 6)** is the successor to IPv4, designed to overcome the limitations of address exhaustion in IPv4. Vulnerabilities include increased attack surface, address scanning, Neighbor Discovery Protocol (NDP) security, and transition mechanisms.

5

- **MAC (Media Access Control) addresses** are unique identifiers assigned to network interface cards (NICs) at the data link layer. Vulnerabilities include MAC address spoofing, MAC flooding, and ARP (Address Resolution Protocol) spoofing.

- **ARP (Address Resolution Protocol)** is used to map IP addresses to MAC addresses in a local network. Vulnerabilities include ARP spoofing and ARP cache poisoning.

- **HTTP (Hypertext Transfer Protocol)** is an application-layer protocol used for transmitting and receiving web-based content. Vulnerabilities include on-path attacks, cross-site scripting (XSS), SQL injection, and cross-site request forgery (CSRF).

- **ICMP (Internet Control Message Protocol)** is primarily used for diagnostics and error reporting in IP networks. Vulnerabilities include ICMP flood attacks and ICMP redirect attacks.

- **DHCP (Dynamic Host Configuration Protocol)** is used for dynamically assigning IP addresses and network configuration parameters to devices on a network. Vulnerabilities include DHCP spoofing and DHCP starvation attacks.

- **DNS (Domain Name System)** translates domain names (such as www.example.com) into IP addresses (such as 203.0.113.10), facilitating the use of easy-to-remember names when referring to resources. It is an application layer protocol. Vulnerabilities include DNS spoofing and DNS amplification attacks.

- **FTP (File Transfer Protocol)** is used to facilitate the transfer of files between computers on a network. Vulnerabilities include lack of encryption, weak authentication, and data tampering.

- **Telnet** establishes a remote terminal connection between a client and a server over a network. Vulnerabilities include lack of encryption, weak authentication, and on-path attacks.

- **SSH (Secure Shell)** is used to provide secure encrypted communication and secure remote administration of network devices and systems. Vulnerabilities include weak authentication, vulnerabilities in SSH implementations, and misconfigured access controls.

- **CIDR** notation allows for efficient allocation and utilization of IP addresses. CIDR notation enables network administrators to define and enforce network segmentation.

- **Network segmentation** helps improve network performance, enhance security, and simplify network management because it makes it possible to ensure that what happens in a subnet stays in a subnet or what happens in a subnet does not affect another subnet.

- **Public IP addresses** are used on the Internet.

- **Private IP addresses** are used everywhere else.

- **NAT** takes a private RFC 1918 address that is only routable on a private network and converts it into a public IP address that is routable on the Internet.

■ **MAC (Media Access Control) addresses** operate at the data link layer of the OSI model and are primarily used for communication between devices in the same subnet/VLAN/broadcast domain.

Exam Preparation Tasks

As mentioned in the Introduction, you can customize your strategy for exam preparation. Suggested tasks include the exercises here, Chapter 16, "Final Preparation," and the exam simulation questions on the companion website.

Review All Key Topics

Review the most important topics in this chapter, noted with the Key Topics icon in the outer margin of the page. Table 5-3 lists these key topics and the page number on which each is found.

Table 5-3   Key Topics for Chapter 5

Key Topic Element	Description	Page Number
List	TCP/IP stack application layer	80
List	TCP/IP stack transport layer	80
List	TCP/IP stack Internet layer	80
List	TCP/IP stack link layer	80
Section	Transmission Control Protocol (TCP)	81
Section	User Datagram Protocol (UDP)	81
Section	Internet Protocol version 4 (IPv4)	82
Section	Internet Protocol version 6 (IPv6)	83
Section	Media Access Control (MAC)	83
Section	Address Resolution Protocol (ARP)	84
Section	Hypertext Transfer Protocol (HTTP)	84
Section	Internet Control Message Protocol (ICMP)	85
Section	Dynamic Host Configuration Protocol (DHCP)	85
Section	Domain Name System (DNS)	86
Section	File Transfer Protocol (FTP)	86
Section	Telnet	87
Section	Secure Shell (SSH)	87
Paragraph	How CIDR notation impacts security	89
Paragraph	How network segmentation impacts security	90
Table 5-2	Characteristics of Public and Private Networks	91
Paragraph	The impact of NAT on security	93
List	Security considerations of MAC addressing	94

5

Complete Tables and Lists from Memory

There are no memory tables for this chapter.

Define Key Terms

Define the following key terms from this chapter and check your answers in the glossary:

TCP/IP stack, OSI (Open Systems Interconnection) reference model, application layer, presentation layer, session layer, transport layer, network layer, data link layer, physical layer, Transmission Control Protocol (TCP), User Datagram Protocol (UDP), Internet Protocol version 4 (IPv4), Internet Protocol version 6 (IPv6), Media Access Control (MAC) address, Address Resolution Protocol (ARP), Hypertext Transfer Protocol (HTTP), Internet Control Message Protocol (ICMP), Dynamic Host Configuration Protocol (DHCP), Domain Name System (DNS), File Transfer Protocol (FTP), Telnet, Secure Shell (SSH), CIDR (classless interdomain routing), Network Address Translation (NAT)

Review Questions

1. Which of the following TCP/IP stack layers is responsible for the addressing of frames?
    a. Application
    b. Transport
    c. Internet
    d. Link

2. How would you mitigate an HTTP on-path attack?
    a. By employing input validation and output encoding techniques
    b. By applying rate limiting or filtering mechanisms
    c. By enforcing strong passwords and implementing two-factor authentication (2FA)
    d. By implementing secure HTTP (HTTPS) with Transport Layer Security (TLS)
    e. By ensuring that software and systems are up to date with the latest security patches

3. Which of the following is a form of network segmentation that allows you to divide up a physical local area network into multiple virtual local area networks?
    a. IPv4 and IPv6
    b. CIDR
    c. DHCP
    d. NAT
    e. VLAN
    f. ACL
    g. Screened subnet

CHAPTER 6

Network Infrastructure

This chapter covers the following topics:

- **The Network Security Architecture:** This section introduces the Cisco SAFE Security Reference Architecture.

- **Screened Subnets, Virtualization, and the Cloud:** This section describes the benefits of using a screened subnet, explains the benefits of virtualization, and introduces various security considerations for the cloud.

- **Proxy servers:** This section discusses forward and reverse proxy servers as well as the Cisco WSA.

- **Honeypots:** This section discusses how honeypots can be used to attract and deceive attackers.

- **Intrusion Detection/Prevention Systems:** This section discusses host- and network-based intrusion detection systems and intrusion prevention systems.

Networks are designed to move data from one location to another. Networks can be wired as well as wireless, and it is imperative that a network be designed with a security-first mindset. When security is an afterthought, the likelihood of a security breach is significant. However, when security is first and foremost, it significantly reduces the risk a of security breach that jeopardizes confidentiality, integrity, and availability of your data.

This chapter introduces the Cisco SAFE (Security Access for Everyone) Security Reference Architecture, which can guide you as you create layered defenses and enforce security policies to safeguard your network infrastructure and data from potential risks. SAFE focuses on security domains and places in your network (PINs). In addition, this chapter discusses the benefits of using a screened subnet, the several security benefits that virtualization offers, and various security considerations for the cloud.

This chapter also focuses on proxy servers. It describes the differences between a forward proxy and a reverse proxy. It also talks about Cisco's very own proxy server, Cisco WSA (Web Security Appliance). This chapter covers honeypots, which you can use to attract and deceive attackers in order to gain better insights into their tactics and techniques. This chapter wraps up by exploring host-based and network-based intrusion detection and prevention systems.

This chapter covers information related to the following Cisco Certified Support Technician (CCST) Cybersecurity exam objective:

2.3. Describe network infrastructure and technologies (network security architecture, DMZ, virtualization, cloud, honeypot, proxy server, IDS, IPS).

"Do I Know This Already?" Quiz

The "Do I Know This Already?" quiz allows you to assess whether you should read this entire chapter thoroughly or jump to the "Exam Preparation Tasks" section. If you are in doubt about your answers to these questions or your own assessment of your knowledge of the topics, read the entire chapter. Table 6-1 lists the major headings in this chapter and their corresponding "Do I Know This Already?" quiz questions. You can find the answers in Appendix A, "Answers to the 'Do I Know This Already?' Quizzes and Review Questions."

Table 6-1 "Do I Know This Already?" Section-to-Question Mapping

Foundation Topics Section	Questions
The Network Security Architecture	1
Screened Subnets, Virtualization, and the Cloud	2
Proxy Servers	3
Honeypots	4
Intrusion Detection/Prevention Systems	5

CAUTION   The goal of self-assessment is to gauge your mastery of the topics in this chapter. If you do not know the answer to a question or are only partially sure of the answer, you should mark that question incorrect for purposes of self-assessment. Giving yourself credit for an answer you correctly guess skews your self-assessment results and might provide you with a false sense of security.

1. Which of the following are PINs in relation to the Cisco SAFE Security Reference Architecture? (Choose four.)

    a. Secure services

    b. Internet edge

    c. Security intelligence

    d. WAN

    e. Campus

    f. Segmentation

    g. Data center

2. Which of the following correctly describes a screened subnet?

    a. A hardware or virtual appliance offered by Cisco Systems that provides web security and content filtering capabilities.

    b. A security mechanism used to detect, deflect, or study unauthorized access attempts or malicious activity within a network or system.

    c. A separate network segment that acts as a buffer zone between an internal trusted network and an external untrusted network, such as the Internet.

    d. A security technology designed to monitor network traffic, detect malicious activities or potential security breaches, and take appropriate actions to protect the network.

3. What is the purpose of a forward proxy server?

    a. It is a server that is used to detect, deflect, or study unauthorized access attempts or malicious activity within a network or system.

    b. It is a server in a network that is used to create a separate network segment that acts as a buffer zone between an internal trusted network and an external untrusted network, such as the Internet.

    c. A server that acts as an intermediary between client devices and the Internet, evaluating communications to ensure that they are valid and forwarding client requests to the Internet on behalf of the client and returning the response back to the client.

    d. A server that acts as an intermediary between devices on the Internet and servers in a server farm, forwarding requests to the servers on behalf of the devices on the Internet and returning the response back to the devices on the Internet.

4. Which of the following is used to detect, deflect, or study unauthorized access attempts or malicious activity within a network or system?

    a. WSA

    ~~**b.** IDS/IPS~~

    c. Honeypot

    d. Screened subnet

5. Which of the following is a security technology that is designed to monitor network traffic, detect malicious activities or potential security breaches, and take appropriate actions to protect the network?

    a. WSA

    b. Screened subnet

    c. IPS

    d. Honeypot

Foundation Topics

The Network Security Architecture

A network security architecture refers to the design and implementation of a comprehensive framework that provides security measures and controls to protect a network's infrastructure and assets from unauthorized access, threats, and attacks. It involves the integration of various security components, technologies, policies, and procedures to ensure the confidentiality, integrity, and availability of network resources. A network security architecture typically includes components such as firewalls, intrusion detection and prevention systems, virtual private networks (VPNs), access controls, encryption, network segmentation, and monitoring mechanisms, among others.

The goal with a network security architecture is to create layered defenses and enforce security policies to safeguard the network infrastructure and data from potential risks.

The **Cisco SAFE Security Reference Architecture** is a security reference architecture developed by Cisco to help you design a secure infrastructure for your entire network. The framework encompasses operational domains such as management, security intelligence, compliance, segmentation, threat defense, and secure services. Figure 6-1 provides a visual representation of SAFE as a key. The SAFE key organizes security by using two core concepts: places in the network (PINs) and secure domains.

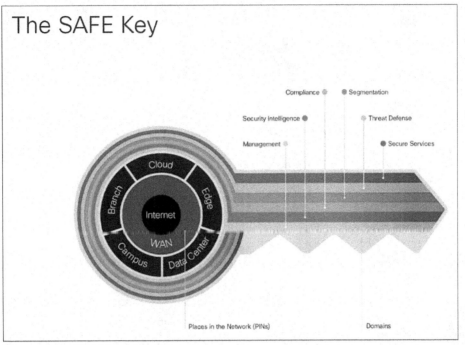

Figure 6-1 *The Cisco Safe Key*

PINs are on the left side of the key. These are places in the network that you need to secure, such as a data center, a branch office or small office/home office (SOHO), the campus, the WAN, the cloud, and the Internet edge.

Secure domains speak to the security concepts that you need to consider in order to protect the PINs, including management, security intelligence, compliance, segmentation, threat defense, and secure services.

For more detailed coverage of SAFE, check out Cisco's website, at https://www.cisco.com/c/en/us/solutions/enterprise/design-zone-security/landing_safe.html#~overview.

Screened Subnets, Virtualization, and the Cloud

This section discusses the benefits of using a screened subnet, the security benefits of virtualization, and various security considerations for the cloud.

Screened Subnet (DMZ)

A **DMZ (demilitarized zone)**, or **screened subnet**, is a separate network segment that acts as a buffer zone between an internal trusted network and an external untrusted network, such as the Internet. The purpose of a DMZ is to provide an additional layer of security by isolating publicly accessible services and systems from the internal network. Figures 6-2 and 6-3 provide examples of how you could deploy a screened subnet. In Figure 6-2, notice how the screened subnet is inline with the traffic flow, and in Figure 6-3, notice how the screened subnet is not inline with the traffic flow.

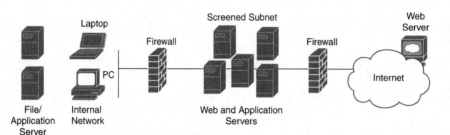

Figure 6-2 *An Inline Screened Subnet (DMZ)*

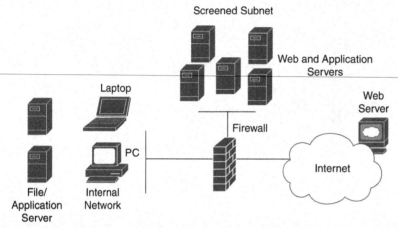

Figure 6-3 *A Three-Armed Firewall Screened Subnet*

In a typical network architecture, the internal network contains sensitive resources, such as databases, application servers, and other critical systems. The DMZ sits between the internal network and the external network, as shown in Figure 6-2, or it can be off to the side, as shown in Figure 6-3. A screened subnet hosts services that need to be accessed from the outside, such as web servers, email servers, and public-facing applications. Therefore, anything that needs to be accessed by both the Internet and the internal users can be in a screened subnet, and anything that only needs to be accessed by internal users can be kept in the internal network.

The main idea behind a DMZ is to create a controlled environment that limits direct access to the internal network. By placing publicly accessible servers in the DMZ, an organization can enforce stricter security policies and reduce the risk of unauthorized access to sensitive data or systems. It acts as a "screen" between the external and internal networks, providing an additional layer of protection against potential threats.

Typically, firewalls and other security devices are deployed to enforce access control and filtering rules between the different network segments. The firewall rules are configured to allow specific traffic to pass from the Internet to the DMZ, while restricting direct access to the internal network. This way, even if a server in the DMZ is compromised, the attacker's access is limited to the DMZ and does not extend to the internal network.

Virtualization

Virtualization is a technology that plays a significant role in modern network infrastructure and has implications for network security. It involves creating virtual instances or virtual machines (VMs) that run on a single physical server, allowing multiple operating systems and applications to run independently on the same hardware.

From a network security perspective, virtualization offers several benefits:

Key Topic

- **Segmentation and isolation:** Virtualization allows for the creation of isolated virtual networks within a single physical network infrastructure. This segmentation enhances security by separating different types of traffic and isolating potential vulnerabilities or breaches within specific virtual environments.

- **Network virtualization:** Network virtualization abstracts the underlying physical network infrastructure, enabling the creation of virtual networks (overlay networks) on top of it. This approach provides flexibility, scalability, and the ability to define network policies and security controls specific to each virtual network.

- **Virtual firewalls and security appliances:** Virtualization allows the deployment of virtual instances of firewalls, intrusion detection systems (IDSs), and other security appliances. These virtual security devices can be centrally managed, easily scaled, and dynamically provisioned to protect virtualized workloads.

- **Sandboxing and testing:** Virtualization enables the creation of virtual sandboxes for testing and analyzing potentially malicious software or suspicious network traffic. By running these elements in isolated virtual environments, the risk of compromising the underlying network infrastructure is minimized.

- **Disaster recovery and high availability:** Virtualization facilitates disaster recovery and high-availability solutions. Virtual machines can be easily migrated or replicated across physical servers, often with zero downtime, ensuring continuity of operations in the event of hardware failure or other disruptions. This helps maintain network security by minimizing downtime and allowing for rapid recovery.

- **Network function virtualization (NFV):** NFV leverages virtualization to replace dedicated network appliances with software-based virtual network functions (VNFs) running on standard servers. This approach offers agility, scalability, and cost savings, while allowing for centralized management and easier implementation of security policies.

It's important to note that while virtualization brings numerous benefits, it also introduces new security considerations. Organizations need to ensure proper configuration, access controls, and monitoring of virtualized environments to mitigate risks associated with shared resources, virtual machine escape, and vulnerabilities within hypervisors or virtualization management systems.

Cloud

Cloud computing has transformed the landscape of network infrastructure and introduced new security considerations for organizations. Here's a look at how cloud computing relates to basic network security concepts:

- **Shared responsibility model:** In a cloud environment, such as infrastructure as a service (IaaS), platform as a service (PaaS), or software as a service (SaaS), the responsibility for security is shared between the cloud service provider (CSP) and the customer. The cloud environment that has been chosen and the service within that cloud model will ultimately determine your level of security responsibility and the cloud provider's level of security responsibility. However, in almost all scenarios, the CSP is responsible for securing the underlying infrastructure, while the customer is responsible for securing access to their applications and data. Understanding and defining these shared responsibilities is crucial for ensuring comprehensive security.

- **Data protection:** Cloud services involve storing and processing data on remote servers owned and managed by the CSP. This necessitates robust data protection mechanisms, including encryption, access controls, and data backup and recovery processes. Customers must understand the data protection measures implemented by their CSP and ensure that they align with their security requirements.

- **Network isolation and segmentation:** Cloud service providers use network isolation techniques to separate the infrastructure and data of different customers. Virtual private clouds (VPCs) and virtual networks (VNs) can be created to isolate and segment network traffic between different tenants. Properly configured network isolation helps mitigate risks associated with unauthorized access and data breaches.

- **Identity and access management (IAM):** IAM is crucial in cloud environments to ensure secure access to resources and data. Implementing strong authentication mechanisms, multifactor authentication (MFA), and access control policies helps prevent unauthorized access. In addition, implementing the least-privilege principle ensures that users only have access to the resources they need.

- **Security monitoring and logging:** Effective security in the cloud depends on comprehensive monitoring and logging. CSPs typically offer logging services, allowing customers to monitor activities and detect potential security incidents. Customers should leverage these capabilities to proactively identify and respond to security events.

- **Compliance and auditing:** Compliance requirements vary across industries and geographic regions. Organizations must ensure that their chosen cloud service provider meets the necessary compliance standards and regulations. In addition, cloud environments offer auditing capabilities that allow customers to track and review system changes, access logs, and security events.

- **Incident response and business continuity:** Cloud environments should have incident response plans and business continuity measures in place. This includes processes for detecting, responding to, and recovering from security incidents. Regular testing of incident response plans and backups is essential to ensure readiness and minimize potential downtime.

- **Cloud security best practices:** Organizations should follow cloud security best practices, which include keeping systems and software up to date, regularly patching vulnerabilities, performing security assessments, and implementing secure coding practices for applications deployed in the cloud.

It's important to note that cloud security is a shared responsibility. While cloud service providers offer robust security measures, customers also have a responsibility to implement security controls specific to their applications, data, and user access.

Proxy Servers

Proxy servers play a vital role in network security by acting as intermediaries between client devices and the resources they are trying to access. They enhance security and provide additional functionalities that help protect the network infrastructure. Here's an overview of proxy servers in relation to basic network security concepts:

- **Anonymity and privacy:** Proxy servers can be configured to provide anonymity and privacy by masking the client's IP address. When clients connect to the Internet through a proxy server, their requests are forwarded by the proxy, and the target server sees the proxy's IP address instead of the client's. This can help protect the privacy of users and prevent direct exposure of their IP addresses.

- **Content filtering and access control:** Proxy servers can be used to enforce content filtering policies and restrict access to specific websites or types of content. By intercepting and inspecting web requests, proxy servers can block or allow access based on predefined rules. This capability helps organizations enforce acceptable use policies, protect against malicious or inappropriate content, and prevent unauthorized access to certain resources.

- **Caching:** Proxy servers can cache frequently accessed web content, such as images, files, or web pages. By storing this content locally, subsequent requests for the same content can be served directly from the proxy's cache, reducing bandwidth usage and improving performance. Caching also provides a layer of protection against distributed denial of service (DDoS) attacks by absorbing traffic before it reaches the origin server.

- **Load balancing:** Proxy servers can act as load balancers by distributing incoming network traffic across multiple servers. This helps optimize resource utilization, prevent overloading of individual servers, and improve overall performance and availability. Load-balancing proxies enhance network security by ensuring high availability and mitigating the impact of DDoS attacks by distributing the traffic across multiple servers.

- **Application layer security:** Proxy servers can provide application layer security services, such as protocol filtering, intrusion detection and prevention, and data loss prevention. By analyzing the content of network traffic, proxies can detect and block malicious activities, including malware downloads, SQL injection attempts, and cross-site scripting (XSS) attacks. Proxies also enable the implementation of SSL/TLS encryption and decryption, enhancing the security of data transmitted over the network.

■ **Logging and auditing:** Proxy servers can log and audit network traffic passing through them, providing valuable insights into user activity, attempted connections, and potential security incidents. These logs can be used for troubleshooting, incident response, and compliance purposes.

It's worth noting that while proxy servers offer security benefits, they should be properly configured, regularly updated, and monitored to ensure their effectiveness. In addition, organizations must consider the performance impact of proxy servers and ensure that they are appropriately sized and optimized for the network's needs.

Key Topic

Forward Proxy

A **forward proxy server**, also known as an outbound proxy server, is a server that acts as an intermediary between client devices and the Internet. When a client device, such as a computer or mobile device, requests access to a resource on the Internet, it sends the request to the forward proxy instead of directly connecting to the target server. The forward proxy then forwards the request to the target server on behalf of the client and returns the response back to the client, as shown in Figure 6-4.

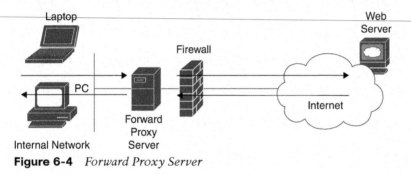

Figure 6-4 *Forward Proxy Server*

Here are the key aspects of a forward proxy:

■ **Client communication:** Forward proxies are configured in client devices or network gateways to redirect outbound Internet traffic through the proxy server. The client device is typically unaware that it is communicating with the proxy server since the proxy transparently handles the communication.

■ **Anonymity and privacy:** One of the primary functions of a forward proxy is to provide anonymity and privacy. By forwarding client requests, the proxy server masks the client's IP address and other identifying information from the target server. This helps protect the client's privacy and can be useful for bypassing network restrictions or accessing content anonymously.

■ **Caching:** Forward proxies can cache frequently accessed web content. When a client requests a resource that is already cached on the proxy server, the proxy can serve the content directly from its cache instead of fetching it from the Internet. Caching improves performance by reducing bandwidth usage and decreasing the response time for subsequent requests.

■ **Content filtering and access control:** Forward proxies can implement content filtering and access control policies. They can inspect and analyze client requests, block or allow access based on predefined rules, and filter out malicious or inappropriate content. Organizations often use forward proxies to enforce acceptable use policies, block access to specific websites or categories of content, and prevent unauthorized access to certain resources.

- **Network optimization:** Forward proxies can optimize network traffic by compressing data, reducing the size of transferred files, or stripping unnecessary elements from web pages. These optimization techniques help improve network performance, especially in bandwidth-constrained environments.

- **Security:** Forward proxies can enhance security by acting as a barrier between client devices and the Internet. They can filter out malicious content, scan for viruses or malware, and enforce security policies. Proxies can also provide an additional layer of protection by performing SSL/TLS encryption and decryption, allowing for secure communication between clients and target servers.

- **Logging and auditing:** Forward proxies often maintain logs of client requests and server responses passing through them. These logs can be used for auditing, troubleshooting network issues, and analyzing user activity. They provide valuable insights into the traffic patterns, potential security incidents, and usage statistics.

It's important to note that while forward proxies offer advantages, they can also introduce latency and impact network performance. Proper configuration, sizing, and monitoring are essential to ensure a proxy server's effectiveness and to address any performance issues.

Reverse Proxy

A **reverse proxy server** is a server that sits between client devices on the Internet and web servers in your data center, acting as an intermediary for inbound Internet traffic. Unlike a forward proxy that handles outbound traffic, a reverse proxy manages incoming requests from Internet clients and forwards them to the appropriate backend servers. The reverse proxy receives the requests on behalf of the servers and sends back the responses to the clients, as shown in Figure 6-5.

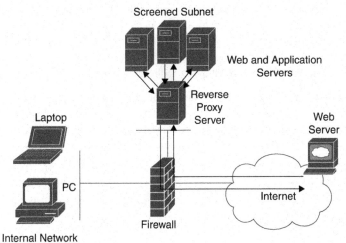

Figure 6-5 *Reverse Proxy Server*

Here are the key aspects of a reverse proxy:

- **Client communication:** Reverse proxies are configured to accept incoming client requests on a specific port or URL. When a client device sends a request to access a resource, such as a website or an application, it connects to the reverse proxy server, unaware of the backend servers handling the request. The reverse proxy transparently handles the communication and forwards the request to the appropriate server.

- **Load balancing:** One of the primary functions of a reverse proxy is load balancing. When multiple backend servers are available to handle incoming requests, the reverse proxy distributes the traffic among them based on predefined algorithms, such as round-robin or least connections. Load balancing helps distribute the workload evenly, optimize resource utilization, and ensure high availability and scalability of the web application.

- **SSL/TLS termination:** Reverse proxies can handle SSL/TLS encryption and decryption. When clients make secure requests, the reverse proxy decrypts the SSL/TLS traffic, forwards the unencrypted request to the backend server, and re-encrypts the response before sending it back to the client. This offloading of SSL/TLS processing from the backend servers reduces their computational load and improves performance.

- **Caching:** Reverse proxies can cache content from the backend servers. When clients request a resource that is already stored in the proxy's cache, the reverse proxy serves the content directly from the cache, eliminating the need to fetch it from the backend servers. Caching improves response time, reduces bandwidth usage, and helps handle traffic spikes more efficiently.

- **Security:** Reverse proxies enhance security by acting as a protective layer between clients and backend servers. They can filter and inspect incoming requests, apply security policies, and block malicious traffic. Reverse proxies can mitigate DDoS attacks by absorbing and distributing the traffic across multiple backend servers.

- **Application layer security:** Reverse proxies can provide additional application layer security. They can analyze and filter requests for malicious content, perform deep packet inspection, and apply rules to prevent common attacks such as XSS, SQL injection, or request forgery. Reverse proxies also enable the implementation of security controls and access restrictions specific to the web application.

- **Logging and auditing:** Reverse proxies often maintain logs of incoming requests, backend server responses, and client interactions. These logs are valuable for troubleshooting, monitoring traffic patterns, identifying potential security incidents, and analyzing user behavior. They aid in auditing, compliance, and forensic investigations.

- **Web server shielding:** By acting as a frontend server, a reverse proxy shields the backend servers from direct exposure to the Internet. The reverse proxy's IP address is visible to clients, providing an additional layer of protection for the backend servers, which remain hidden and isolated from direct public access.

Key
Topic

Cisco WSA

The **Cisco Web Security Appliance (WSA)** is a hardware or virtual appliance offered by Cisco Systems that provides web security and content filtering capabilities. It is designed to protect organizations from web-based threats, enforce acceptable use policies, and ensure secure and compliant web browsing for users within the network. It is Cisco's version of a proxy server.

Key features and functionalities of the Cisco Web Security Appliance include

- **Web filtering:** The WSA enables organizations to control and filter web content accessed by users. It uses various techniques, such as URL filtering, category-based filtering, and reputation analysis, to block or allow access to specific websites or categories of content. This helps enforce acceptable use policies, prevent access to malicious or inappropriate content, and protect against web-based threats.

- **Malware protection:** The WSA includes robust malware protection capabilities to safeguard the network from web-based threats, including viruses, ransomware, and other forms of malware. It uses real-time threat intelligence, advanced malware detection techniques, and integration with security services to identify and block malicious web content.

- **Data loss prevention (DLP):** The WSA can be configured to enforce data loss prevention policies. It scans web content and prevents the transmission of sensitive or confidential data, such as credit card numbers or personally identifiable information (PII), through web forms, file uploads, or other web-based channels. DLP policies help organizations protect sensitive data from accidental or intentional leaks.

- **Secure web gateway:** The WSA acts as a secure web gateway, providing a secure and encrypted connection between users and web resources. It supports SSL/TLS inspection, which allows the appliance to decrypt and inspect encrypted web traffic for potential threats or policy violations. SSL/TLS inspection helps organizations detect and mitigate threats hidden within encrypted communication.

- **Reporting and analytics:** The WSA offers comprehensive reporting and analytics capabilities, providing insights into web usage patterns, threat activity, and policy violations. It generates detailed logs and reports, allowing administrators to monitor user activity, investigate security incidents, and analyze web traffic trends. These insights help organizations make informed decisions, assess risks, and enforce security policies effectively.

- **Integration with Cisco security solutions:** The WSA integrates with other Cisco security solutions, such as Cisco Advanced Malware Protection (AMP), Cisco Identity Services Engine (ISE), and Cisco Security Intelligence Operations (SIO). This integration enhances the overall security posture, allows for centralized management and policy enforcement, and enables coordinated threat response across the Cisco security ecosystem.

- **Scalability and performance:** The Cisco WSA is designed to handle high volumes of web traffic and support large user populations. It offers scalability options, such as clustering and load balancing, to ensure performance and availability in enterprise environments. Organizations can deploy multiple appliances to distribute the load and provide redundancy for uninterrupted web security services.

■ **Centralized management:** Cisco provides a centralized management interface, known as Cisco Security Management Appliance (SMA), to manage and configure multiple Cisco security appliances, including the WSA. The SMA simplifies administration, policy management, and reporting across distributed deployments.

The Cisco Web Security Appliance is a comprehensive web security solution that combines web filtering, malware protection, data loss prevention, and secure web gateway capabilities. It helps organizations protect their network, users, and data from web-based threats, enforce security policies, and ensure a secure and productive web browsing experience.

Honeypots

A **honeypot** is a security mechanism used to detect, deflect, or study unauthorized access attempts or malicious activity within a network or system. It is essentially a decoy or trap designed to attract and deceive attackers, providing valuable insights into their methods, motives, and techniques.

A honeypot is intentionally designed to appear as a vulnerable or valuable target within a network. It may simulate a server, application, or network device that would be of interest to attackers. By mimicking a real system or service, the honeypot lures attackers to interact with it, diverting their attention from actual production systems and away from critical systems and resources. By presenting an attractive target that appears vulnerable, the honeypot encourages attackers to focus their efforts on it instead of on your actual production systems. This diversionary tactic buys time for security teams to detect and respond to attacks, mitigating potential damage.

When attackers engage with the honeypot, their activities are closely monitored and logged. This includes capturing network traffic, analyzing command inputs, and observing their behavior. By observing and analyzing these activities, security professionals can gain insights into attack techniques, identify new threats, and understand the tools and methodologies used by attackers. As a result, honeypots can serve as an early warning system, alerting security teams to potential threats or ongoing attacks. Any interaction with the honeypot triggers an alert, allowing security personnel to respond quickly and proactively. This early warning can help prevent further compromise of the network and reduce the impact of attacks as well as improve defensive measures, develop countermeasures, and enhance incident response capabilities.

Honeypots also provide valuable evidence for legal or law enforcement purposes. The captured data and logs from the honeypot can be used to identify attackers, gather intelligence, and support investigations. The information gathered can aid in prosecuting attackers and building stronger cases against them.

It's important to note that deploying and maintaining a honeypot requires careful planning and consideration. It should be done in a controlled and isolated environment separate from production systems to prevent unintended consequences. A honeypot should be regularly monitored, updated with the latest vulnerabilities, and configured with proper security measures to prevent the honeypot itself from being compromised.

Intrusion Detection/Prevention Systems

Intrusion detection systems (IDSs) and intrusion prevention systems (IPSs) are security tech-nologies designed to monitor network traffic, detect malicious activities or potential secu-rity breaches, and, in the case of an IPS, take appropriate actions to protect the network. An IDS/IPS can be a physical device or a virtual device (software running on a server, such as a VM). In addition, an IDS/IPS can be deployed as a network-based device or as a host-based device. In most instances today, an IDS/IPS is a single device or software application, and it is how you license and configure the device or software application that makes it an IDS or IPS. This section discusses IDSs and IPSs from both host and network standpoints. In addi-tion, it introduces detection methods offered by both IDSs and IPSs.

Intrusion Detection Systems (IDSs)

An **intrusion detection system (IDS)** passively monitors network traffic, looking for suspicious patterns or indicators of malicious activity. It analyzes network packets, system logs, and other data sources to identify potential security incidents. When an IDS detects an anomaly or a known attack signature, it generates an alert to notify administrators or secu-rity personnel. An IDS does not actively block or prevent attacks because it is not placed inline with the flow of traffic. Therefore, it receives a copy of all traffic to analyze and focuses on detection and raising alarms instead of prevention. It is possible for the malicious traffic to reach the destination as the IDS does not stop it.

Intrusion Prevention Systems (IPSs)

An **intrusion prevention system (IPS)** goes beyond the capabilities of an IDS, actively preventing and blocking malicious activities by taking automated actions to stop attacks in real time. This can involve blocking network traffic, dropping malicious packets, or reconfig-uring network devices to protect against the identified threats. This is possible because IPSs can operate in inline mode, where they actively intercept and analyze network traffic and prevent any malicious traffic from continuing to the destination device.

Network-Based and Host-Based IDSs/IPSs

Both IDSs and IPSs can be implemented as network-based or host-based systems:

- **Network-based IDSs/IPSs:** These systems are deployed at key points in the network infrastructure, such as at network gateways or within network segments, to monitor and protect network traffic flowing through those points. They analyze network pack-ets and can detect attacks targeting multiple systems or network-wide vulnerabilities.

- **Host-based IDSs/IPSs:** These systems are installed on individual hosts or servers to monitor and protect the specific systems they are installed on. They focus on the activities and vulnerabilities specific to a host, such as detecting unauthorized access attempts, monitoring file integrity, and monitoring abnormal system behavior.

Signature-Based and Behavioral-Based Detection

IDSs/IPSs can use signature-based or behavioral-based detection methods:

- **Signature-based detection:** This method involves using a database of known attack signatures or patterns to identify malicious activity. The IDS/IPS compares incoming network traffic or system behavior against the signature database to detect matches and raise alerts. Signature-based detection is effective against known attacks but may struggle to detect new or evolving threats.

■ **Behavioral-based detection:** This method involves analyzing normal patterns of network traffic or system behavior and detects deviations from those patterns. It first establishes a baseline of normal activity and then is able to alert you and block traffic when anomalies or suspicious behavior are detected. Behavioral-based detection is useful for identifying unknown or zero-day attacks but may have a higher rate of false positives.

Summary

It is imperative that a network be designed with a security-first mindset. When security is an afterthought, the likelihood of a security breach is significant. However, when security is first and foremost, you significantly reduce the risk a of security breach that jeopardizes confidentiality, integrity, and availability of your data. This chapter discusses the following topics related to network infrastructure:

■ The **Cisco SAFE** is a security reference architecture developed by Cisco to help you design a secure infrastructure for an entire network.

   ■ **PINs** are places in a network that you need to secure, such as a data center, a branch office or small office/home office (SOHO), the campus, the WAN, the cloud, and the Internet edge.

   ■ **Secure domains** are the security concepts that you need to consider in order to protect the PINs. Management, security intelligence, compliance, segmentation, threat defense, and secure services are all critical domains that need to be explored.

■ A **DMZ (demilitarized zone)**, or screened subnet, is a separate network segment that acts as a buffer zone between an internal trusted network and an external untrusted network, such as the Internet. The purpose of a DMZ is to provide an additional layer of security by isolating publicly accessible services and systems from the internal network.

■ **Virtualization** brings numerous benefits, but it also introduces new security considerations. Organizations need to ensure proper configuration, access controls, and monitoring of virtualized environments to mitigate risks associated with shared resources, virtual machine escape, and vulnerabilities in hypervisors or virtualization management systems.

■ **Cloud security** is a shared responsibility. While cloud service providers offer robust security measures, customers also have a responsibility to implement security controls specific to their applications, data, and user access.

■ **Proxy servers** act as intermediaries between client devices and the resources they are trying to access. They enhance security and provide additional functionalities that help protect the network infrastructure.

   ■ A **forward proxy server**, also known as an outbound proxy, is a server that acts as an intermediary between client devices and the Internet.

- A **reverse proxy server** is a server that sits between client devices on the Internet and web servers in a data center, acting as an intermediary for inbound Internet traffic.

- **Cisco Web Security Appliance (WSA)** is a hardware or virtual appliance offered by Cisco Systems that is designed to protect organizations from web-based threats, enforce acceptable use policies, and ensure secure and compliant web browsing for users within the network. It is Cisco's version of a proxy server.

- A **honeypot** is a security mechanism used to detect, deflect, or study unauthorized access attempts or malicious activity within a network or system. It is essentially a decoy or trap designed to attract and deceive attackers, providing valuable insights into their methods, motives, and techniques.

- **Intrusion detection systems (IDSs)** and **intrusion prevention systems (IPSs)** are security technologies designed to monitor network traffic, detect malicious activities or potential security breaches, and take appropriate actions to protect the network.

  - An **IDS** passively monitors network traffic, looking for suspicious patterns or indicators of malicious activity and generating alerts to notify administrators or security personnel.

  - An **IPS** actively monitors network traffic, looking for suspicious patterns or indicators of malicious activity and taking automated actions to stop attacks by blocking network traffic, dropping malicious packets, or reconfiguring network devices to protect against the identified threats.

- **Signature-based detection** involves using a database of known attack signatures or patterns to identify malicious activity.

- **Behavioral-based detection** involves analyzing normal patterns of network traffic or system behavior and detecting deviations from those patterns.

Exam Preparation Tasks

As mentioned in the Introduction, you can customize your strategy for exam preparation. Suggested tasks include the exercises here, Chapter 16, "Final Preparation," and the exam simulation questions on the companion website.

Review All Key Topics

Review the most important topics in this chapter, noted with the Key Topics icon in the outer margin of the page. Table 6-2 lists these key topics and the page number on which each is found.

Table 6-2 Key Topics for Chapter 6

Key Topic Element	Description	Page Number
Paragraph	Cisco SAFE Security Reference Architecture	102
Paragraph	Screened subnet (DMZ)	103

Key Topic Element	Description	Page Number
List	Benefits of virtualization	105
Section	Forward Proxy	108
Section	Reverse Proxy	109
Section	Cisco WSA	111
Paragraph	Honeypots	112
Section	Intrusion Detection Systems (IDSs)	113
Section	Intrusion Prevention Systems (IPSs)	113
List	Signature-based detection and behavioral-based detection	113

Complete Tables and Lists from Memory

There are no memory tables for this chapter.

Define Key Terms

Define the following key terms from this chapter and check your answers in the glossary:

Cisco SAFE Security Reference Architecture, screened subnet, DMZ, demilitarized zone, forward proxy server, reverse proxy server, Cisco Web Security Appliance (WSA), honeypot, intrusion detection system (IDS), intrusion prevention system (IPS)

Review Questions

1. Which of the following are secure domains in relation to the Cisco SAFE Security Reference Architecture? (Choose three.)

   a. Data center

   b. Management

   c. Cloud

   d. Compliance

   e. Campus

   f. Threat defense

2. Which of the following are benefits of virtualization? (Choose two.)

   a. It enables you to provide relaxed security measures so you do not have to worry about the underlying hardware.

   b. It enables you to create isolated virtual networks within a single physical network infrastructure.

   c. It enables you to eliminate all physical equipment from your environment, reducing your overall attack surface.

   d. It enables you to create virtual sandboxes for testing and analyzing potentially malicious software or suspicious network traffic.

3. Which of the following is designed to protect organizations from web-based threats, enforce acceptable use policies, and ensure secure and compliant web browsing for users within the network?

    a. IPS/IDS

    b. Cloud

    c. Honeypot

    d. WSA

    e. Screened subnet

4. You need to gain insight into attack techniques, identify new threats, and understand the tools and methodologies used by attackers as they attempt to attack your network. What would be the BEST solution?

    a. Implement a WSA and enable content filtering.

    b. Implement an IPS to monitor network traffic.

    c. Implement a honeypot to attract and deceive attackers.

    d. Implement a screened subnet to segment and isolate resources.

5. You need a solution that will establish a baseline of normal activity and that can then alert you and block traffic when anomalies or suspicious behavior are detected. What would be the BEST solution?

    a. Implement a WSA.

    b. Implement an IPS.

    c. Implement a honeypot.

    d. Implement a screened subnet.

6

CHAPTER 7

Controlling Network Access

This chapter covers the following topics:

■ **Virtual Private Networks:** This section explores site-to-site and remote-access VPNS as well as introduces you to Cisco AnyConnect and IPsec.

■ **Firewalls:** This section introduces firewalls and then focuses on the power of next-generation firewalls, including Cisco Firepower Next-Generation Firewall.

■ **Access Control Lists:** This section explores how to read and understand standard and extended IPv4 ACLs.

■ **Network Access Control:** This section introduces network access control (NAC) concepts and how Cisco Identity Services Engine (ISE) is a great option for all your NAC needs.

Controlling network access is a critical part of maintaining the confidentiality, integrity, and availability of your data. If users gain access to a network or portions of a network that they should not have access to, then they could read information they should not be able to read, change information they should not be able to change, and even delete or remove information that should not be deleted or removed.

This chapter discusses how VPNs, both site-to-site and remote-access VPNs, can be used to provide secure network access. You will discover how firewalls can be used to control access and, more importantly, how modern next-generation firewalls can do even more. You will also dig into how to read and understand standard and extended IPv4 ACLs. At the end of the chapter, you will have an opportunity to learn about the importance of NAC and specifically how ISE can help with that.

This chapter covers information related to the following Cisco Certified Support Technician (CCST) Cybersecurity exam objective:

2.5. Implement secure access technologies (ACL, firewall, VPN, NAC).

"Do I Know This Already?" Quiz

The "Do I Know This Already?" quiz allows you to assess whether you should read this entire chapter thoroughly or jump to the "Exam Preparation Tasks" section. If you are in doubt about your answers to these questions or your own assessment of your knowledge of the topics, read the entire chapter. Table 7-1 lists the major headings in this chapter and their corresponding "Do I Know This Already?" quiz questions. You can find the answers in Appendix A, "Answers to the 'Do I Know This Already?' Quizzes and Review Questions."

Table 7-1 "Do I Know This Already?" Section-to-Question Mapping

Foundation Topics Section	Questions
Virtual Private Networks	1
Firewalls	2
Access Control Lists	3
Network Access Control	4

CAUTION The goal of self-assessment is to gauge your mastery of the topics in this chapter. If you do not know the answer to a question or are only partially sure of the answer, you should mark that question incorrect for purposes of self-assessment. Giving yourself credit for an answer you correctly guess skews your self-assessment results and might provide you with a false sense of security.

1. You are creating a site-to-site IPsec VPN tunnel over the Internet from HQ to Branch. Which of the following should you use? (Choose two.)
   a. Transport mode
   b. Tunnel mode
   c. Authentication Header
   d. Encapsulating Security Payload

2. Which of the following BEST describes the purpose of a firewall?
   a. It plays a vital role in securing networks and ensuring that only trusted and compliant devices connect and interact with critical resources.
   b. It is used to permit or deny traffic that is flowing through the network, based on source and destination IP addresses and port numbers.
   c. It controls incoming and outgoing network traffic based on predefined security rules and policies.
   d. It is used to provide centralized policy management, authentication, and access control for network devices.

3. Which of the following BEST describes the evaluation logic for an ACL?
   a. Top-down processing, immediate execution upon a match, implicit deny all
   b. Immediate execution upon a match, top-down processing, implicit deny all
   c. Implicit deny all, top-down processing, immediate execution upon a match
   d. Top-down processing, implicit deny all, immediate execution upon a match

4. Which of the following BEST describes network access control? (Choose two.)
   a. It controls incoming and outgoing network traffic based on predefined security rules and policies.
   b. It is used to permit or deny traffic that is flowing through the network, based on source and destination IP addresses and port numbers.
   c. It is used to provide centralized policy management, authentication, and access control for network devices.
   d. It plays a vital role in securing networks and ensuring that only trusted and compliant devices connect and interact with critical resources.

Foundation Topics

Virtual Private Networks

A **virtual private network (VPN)** is a technology that allows you to create a secure and encrypted connection over a less secure network, such as the Internet. It essentially extends a private network across a public network, enabling users to send and receive data as if their devices were directly connected to the private network.

When you create a VPN, two devices—typically in different geographic locations—establish a secure tunnel over an untrusted network. All the traffic between the two devices is routed through this VPN on top of the untrusted network. The VPN encrypts the data, verifies the integrity of the data, and hides the original IP addressing information in the process. This encryption and rerouting of data provide several benefits:

- **Confidentiality:** A VPN encrypts data before the data is sent on the VPN tunnel and decrypts it once it is received at the other end of the tunnel. You can protect your privacy by using modern encryption algorithms such as AES-256 to encrypt your data. By doing so, you ensure that the data will be unreadable if it is captured.

- **Integrity:** A VPN uses hashing algorithms such as SHA-256 or SHA-512 to verify the integrity of the data. Using these algorithms means that a hash can be generated before the data is sent across the VPN. When the data is sent, the hash is sent with the data. When the other end of the VPN receives the data, it computes a hash of the data. If the hash computed by the receiving device matches the hash that was included with the message, you know that the data has not been modified in transit, and therefore, the integrity of the data is confirmed.

- **Authentication:** A VPN uses authentication to ensure that the start and the end of the VPN tunnel are authentic and that someone has not maliciously created a separate fake malicious VPN tunnel with one of the VPN tunnel endpoints. This ensures that your data is flowing over a 100% legitimate VPN tunnel.

- **Anti-replay protection:** A replay attack is a form of network attack in which a valid data transmission is maliciously or fraudulently recorded and later repeated. A VPN tunnel provides **anti-replay protection** by sequencing the packets that flow over the tunnel. This ensures that if someone or something hijacks the VPN tunnel and tries to use existing packets to take over one of your sessions, they won't succeed, because the hijacker's attempt will mess up all the sequencing and the tunnel will not be happy about it, so it will terminate the session or simply drop the packets that are out of sequence.

It's worth noting that while VPNs provide enhanced security and privacy, they are not foolproof. It is up to you to build them using the strongest protocols and algorithms to ensure that they are as safe and secure as they can possibly be. In addition, you need to continuously monitor them for abnormal activity so that you can prevent any security breaches from occurring.

Site-to-Site

A **site-to-site VPN**, also known as a network-to-network VPN or branch-to-branch VPN, is a type of VPN connection that allows two or more separate networks in different physical locations to securely communicate with each other over the Internet.

In a site-to-site VPN setup, each network has its own local network infrastructure, including routers, switches, and other networking devices. The VPN connection establishes a secure tunnel between these networks, as shown in Figure 7-1, enabling data to be transmitted securely between them as if they were directly connected through a private network.

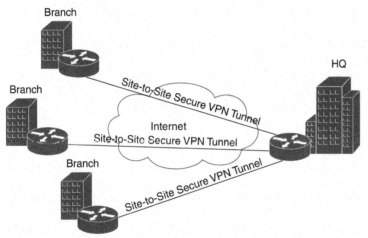

Figure 7-1   *Site-to-Site Secure VPN Tunnel*

Here's how a site-to-site VPN typically works: Each network involved in the VPN connection has a VPN gateway or router that is responsible for handling the encryption and decryption of data and managing the secure connection. These gateways establish a VPN tunnel between them. The VPN gateways authenticate each other to ensure the security of the connection. They exchange encryption keys and establish a secure tunnel using protocols such as IPsec (Internet Protocol Security) or SSL/TLS (Secure Sockets Layer/Transport Layer Security). Once the VPN tunnel is established, data can be transmitted between the networks in an encrypted form. The VPN gateways encrypt the data at the sending end and decrypt it at the receiving end, ensuring confidentiality and integrity. With the site-to-site VPN in place, the connected networks can communicate with each other as if they were part of the same local network. Devices in one network can access resources in the other network securely and vice versa.

Site-to-site VPNs are commonly used by businesses and organizations with multiple branches or remote offices. They provide a secure and cost-effective way to connect geographically dispersed networks, allowing for seamless data sharing, access to shared resources, and centralized management of network services. Therefore, it's important to configure the VPN gateways properly and implement strong security measures to ensure the privacy and integrity of the transmitted data. The choice of VPN protocols, encryption algorithms, and authentication methods should be carefully considered to meet the specific security requirements of the network.

Remote-Access

A **remote-access VPN**, also known as a client-to-site VPN or a remote VPN, is a type of VPN connection that enables individual users or devices to securely access a private network from a remote location over the Internet. It allows remote users to establish a secure connection to a corporate network or any private network as if they were directly connected to it, as shown in Figure 7-2.

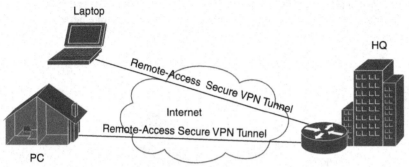

Figure 7-2   *Remote-Access Secure VPN Tunnel*

Here's how a remote-access VPN typically works: The remote user's device, such as a laptop, smartphone, or tablet, requires VPN client software. This software creates a secure connection to the VPN server or gateway. The VPN server or gateway is the endpoint in the private network that handles the remote connections. It authenticates the remote user's credentials and establishes a secure tunnel for data transmission. The remote user provides their credentials, such as a username and password or digital certificate, to authenticate themselves to the VPN server. Once authenticated, the VPN server encrypts the data transmitted between the remote device and the private network to ensure its confidentiality. After the secure tunnel is established, all data transmitted between the remote user's device and the private network is encrypted. This protects the data from unauthorized access or interception while it traverses the Internet. Once connected to the remote-access VPN, a user can access resources within the private network, such as files, applications, printers, or internal websites, as if they were physically present on the network.

Organizations commonly use remote-access VPNs to provide secure remote access to their employees or authorized users. A remote-access VPN allows employees to work remotely while maintaining secure access to internal resources and systems. It offers benefits such as enhanced security, data privacy, and flexibility for remote workers. Therefore, it's important for organizations to implement appropriate security measures, such as strong authentication methods and encryption protocols, to protect a remote-access VPN and the private network from unauthorized access or attacks.

Cisco AnyConnect is a secure remote-access software application developed by Cisco Systems. Organizations commonly use it to provide secure and encrypted remote access to their networks for employees or authorized users.

AnyConnect allows users to establish a secure connection to a corporate network or VPN gateway, enabling them to access network resources, files, applications, and internal systems as if they were physically present on the network. It supports various operating systems, including Windows, macOS, Linux, iOS, and Android, making it versatile for a wide range of devices.

AnyConnect is now part of Cisco Secure Client, as shown in Figure 7-3.

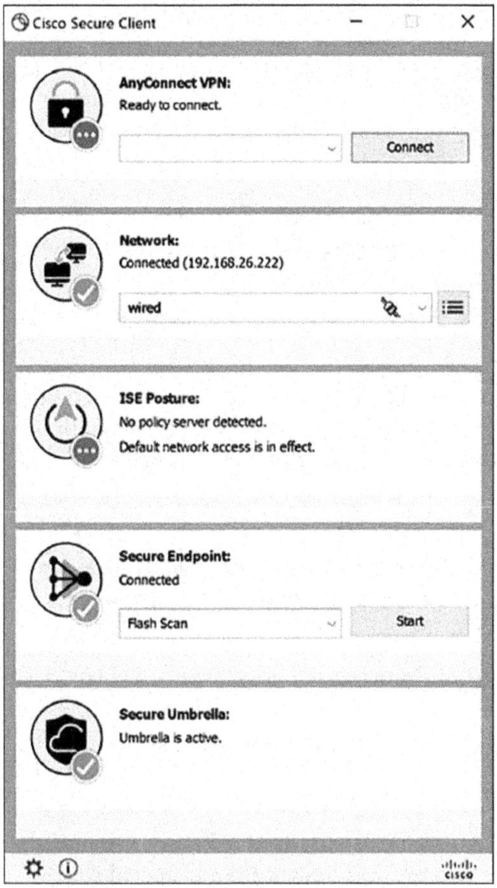

Figure 7-3   *Cisco Secure Client*

Here are some key features and functionalities of Cisco AnyConnect:

- **Secure VPN connectivity:** AnyConnect uses strong encryption protocols such as IPsec and SSL/TLS to establish secure connections between remote devices and the VPN gateway. This ensures the confidentiality and integrity of data transmitted over the VPN.

- **Multifactor authentication (MFA):** AnyConnect supports multiple authentication methods, including username and password, digital certificates, and integration with third-party authentication systems. This helps enhance the security of remote access by requiring additional factors for user authentication.

- **Endpoint security posture assessment:** AnyConnect can perform endpoint security assessments to ensure that remote devices meet certain security requirements before allowing access to the network. It can check for the presence of antivirus software, firewall settings, and other security configurations.

- **Web security and malware protection:** AnyConnect can provide web security features, including web filtering and blocking of malicious websites, to protect users from web-based threats. It can also scan downloaded files for malware.

- **Network visibility and monitoring:** AnyConnect provides administrators with visibility into the connected devices, their activities, and network traffic. This helps in monitoring and troubleshooting network connections and ensuring compliance with security policies.

Cisco AnyConnect is a widely adopted remote-access solution due to its robust security features, cross-platform compatibility, and management capabilities. It offers a comprehensive set of tools to establish secure remote connections while maintaining the integrity and confidentiality of data transmitted over the network.

IPsec

IPsec (Internet Protocol Security) is a framework that helps provide secure communication over IP networks. It is widely used for establishing virtual private networks (VPNs)—both site-to-site and remote-access VPNs—to ensure confidentiality, integrity, and authentication of all network traffic.

IPsec operates at the network layer (Layer 3) of the OSI model and consists of a set of protocols and cryptographic algorithms that can be used to protect data transmitted over the Internet or other IP-based networks, such as local-area networks (LANs) or wide-area networks (WANs).

The main components of IPsec are protocols, confidentiality, integrity, modes, and key management:

- **Protocols:** Two protocols exist for IPsec. Each protocol is designed to serve a specific purpose. So choosing the correct one based on the scenario is important.

  - **Authentication Header (AH):** AH provides integrity, authentication, and protection against replay attacks. It ensures that the data has not been tampered with during transmission and verifies the identity of the sender. It is a perfect option for when you are not worried about privacy. For example, you might use AH in scenarios where you are creating a VPN over a trusted network, and you want to use VPN technology for integrity checking, authentication, and anti-replay protection.

  - **Encapsulating Security Payload (ESP):** ESP provides confidentiality, integrity, authentication, and anti-replay protection for data. It encrypts the payload of IP packets, protecting the data from eavesdropping or unauthorized access. It is perfect for when you are worried about privacy, such as when creating a VPN over the Internet.

NOTE Because ESP provides encryption and AH does not, ESP is used for all VPN tunnels over unsecured networks, especially the Internet.

Key Topic

- **Confidentiality:** As mentioned earlier, VPNs provide confidentiality by using encryption algorithms. When setting up a VPN tunnel, you specify the encryption algorithm and key you want to use to scramble the data being sent over the tunnel into ciphertext, making it unintelligible to anyone who intercepts it. When the encrypted packets reach the receiving IPsec peer, they are decrypted using the appropriate decryption algorithm and the corresponding decryption key. For modern VPN deployments, AES-256 is recommended.

- **Integrity:** As mentioned earlier, VPNs provide integrity checks using hashing algorithms. When setting up a VPN tunnel, you specify the hashing algorithm and key you want to use to create a hash. Before the data is sent over the VPN, a hash is created and sent with the data. When the hashed packets reach the receiving IPsec peer, the receiving IPsec peer generates a hash, and if it matches the one sent with the data, the integrity of the data is verified. If it does not match, the integrity of the data is compromised, and the packet will be ignored. For modern VPN deployments, SHA-256 or SHA-512 is recommended.

Key Topic

- **Modes:** IPsec can be implemented in two modes:

  - **Transport mode:** In transport mode, only the payload of the IP packet is encrypted and authenticated, and the IP header remains intact. This mode is typically used for host-to-host communication within a network.

  - **Tunnel mode:** In tunnel mode, the entire IP packet, including the original IP header, is encapsulated within a new IP packet with a new IP header. This mode is commonly used for site-to-site and remote-access VPNs, where the entire packet is protected and encrypted.

- **Key management:** IPsec requires a mechanism for securely exchanging and managing encryption keys between the communicating parties. This can be done using manual keying (pre-shared keys) or automated key exchange protocols such as Internet Key Exchange (IKE) or IKEv2.

Firewalls

Key Topic

A **firewall** is a network security device that acts as a barrier between an internal network and external networks, such as the Internet. It monitors and controls incoming and outgoing network traffic based on predefined security rules and policies. Firewalls play a critical role in network security by protecting the network from unauthorized access, malicious activities, and potential threats.

You would want to use one or more firewalls in your network for a number of reasons, including the following:

- **Network security:** Firewalls provide a strong line of defense against unauthorized access and external threats. They examine network traffic and enforce security policies to block malicious packets or connections. By filtering and inspecting traffic, firewalls prevent unauthorized users, hackers, or malicious software from gaining access to your network and compromising your systems or data.

7

■ **Access control:** Firewalls enable you to define and control which network traffic is allowed or denied based on specific criteria, such as source/destination IP addresses, ports, protocols, and application types. This allows you to restrict access to certain resources, services, or applications within your network, enhancing security and enforcing network segmentation.

■ **Threat prevention:** Firewalls can detect and prevent various types of threats, such as viruses, worms, malware, and intrusion attempts. They use techniques like stateful packet inspection, application-level gateways, and intrusion detection/prevention systems (IDSs/IPSs) to analyze traffic patterns, identify suspicious activity, and block or alert on potential threats in real time.

■ **Network monitoring:** Firewalls provide valuable insights into network traffic by generating logs and reports. These logs capture information about incoming and outgoing connections, blocked traffic, and security events. By monitoring firewall logs, administrators can identify patterns, analyze network activity, and investigate security incidents or anomalies.

■ **Content filtering:** Firewalls can enforce content filtering policies to control the types of content that can be accessed from or delivered to your network. This includes blocking access to specific websites, filtering web content based on categories (for example, adult content, social media, gambling), and preventing the transfer of sensitive data through specific protocols. Content filtering helps enforce acceptable use policies, improve productivity, and mitigate risks associated with inappropriate or malicious content.

■ **Virtual private network (VPN) support:** Many firewalls include VPN capabilities, allowing secure remote access to a network. VPN tunnels create encrypted connections over public networks, enabling remote users or branch offices to access internal resources securely. Firewalls with built-in VPN support ensure that remote access is secure, authenticated, and protected from unauthorized access.

■ **Compliance and regulatory requirements:** Firewalls play a crucial role in meeting compliance standards and regulatory requirements. Many industries have specific security regulations that mandate the use of firewalls to protect sensitive data and ensure privacy. Implementing firewalls helps demonstrate adherence to these requirements and mitigates the risk of noncompliance penalties.

■ **Scalability and network segmentation:** As a network grows, firewalls can be deployed to create network segments or zones and enforcing security policies between different segments. This segmentation helps contain the impact of a security breach, restrict lateral movement of threats, and reduce the attack surface. Firewalls also support the scalability of a network by providing a flexible and manageable security framework as the network expands.

In summary, firewalls are essential network security devices that protect a network from unauthorized access, threats, and malicious activities. By using firewalls, you can establish access control, prevent threats, monitor network traffic, enforce content filtering, support secure remote access, meet compliance requirements, and enhance the overall security and resilience of the network infrastructure.

NGFW

A **next-generation firewall (NGFW)** builds on the capabilities of a traditional firewall by incorporating additional features and technologies to provide enhanced security and advanced threat protection. While both traditional firewalls and NGFWs share the objective of protecting networks, NGFWs offer several key advancements:

Key Topic

- **Deep packet inspection:** NGFWs perform deep packet inspection (DPI) that goes beyond traditional packet filtering to analyze the contents of network packets. NGFWs inspect not only the header information but also the payload of each packet. DPI enables NGFWs to identify specific applications and protocols and even detect and block threats that may be hidden within legitimate traffic.

- **Application awareness and control:** NGFWs have advanced application-aware capabilities. They can identify specific applications or application categories within network traffic, even if the traffic is encrypted. NGFWs can then enforce granular policies based on application usage, such as allowing or blocking specific applications or controlling bandwidth allocation for different applications.

- **Intrusion prevention system (IPS) integration:** NGFWs often include integrated IPS functionality. This means that in addition to using traditional firewall rules, NGFWs can actively inspect traffic for known attack signatures, detect and block malicious activities, and provide intrusion prevention capabilities. By combining firewall and IPS functionalities, NGFWs offer enhanced protection against a wide range of network-based threats.

- **Advanced threat detection and prevention:** NGFWs leverage advanced threat detection and prevention mechanisms, such as antivirus, antimalware, and sandboxing. These technologies allow NGFWs to detect and block sophisticated threats, including zero-day attacks and advanced malware, by analyzing traffic patterns, file content, and behaviors. NGFWs may also integrate threat intelligence feeds to stay updated with the latest known threats.

- **Identity and user-based policies:** NGFWs can integrate with identity management systems, such as Active Directory, to enforce policies based on user identities. This allows for more granular control and the ability to apply different security policies to different user groups or individuals. User-based policies can be enforced regardless of the user's location or device, improving security in dynamic and distributed environments.

- **Centralized management and reporting:** NGFWs often come with centralized management consoles that provide a unified view of security policies, events, and reporting across multiple firewall instances. This simplifies administration, allows for policy consistency, and provides comprehensive visibility into network security status. Centralized management also facilitates efficient incident response and auditing.

- **Integration with the security ecosystem:** NGFWs can integrate with other security technologies and platforms, such as security information and event management (SIEM) systems, endpoint protection solutions, or threat intelligence feeds. This integration allows for a coordinated and cohesive security ecosystem, enabling more effective threat detection, incident response, and overall security posture.

7

In summary, NGFWs offer advanced features beyond traditional firewalls. They provide deep packet inspection, application awareness, intrusion prevention, advanced threat detection and prevention capabilities, identity-based policies, centralized management, and integration with other security technologies. NGFWs are designed to address the evolving threat landscape and provide enhanced security and visibility for modern network environments.

Cisco Firepower Next-Generation Firewall (NGFW)

Cisco Firepower Next-Generation Firewall (NGFW) is a comprehensive network security solution that combines the functionality of a traditional firewall with advanced threat detection and prevention capabilities. It provides organizations with enhanced visibility, control, and protection against modern threats. Here are the key features and components of the Cisco Firepower NGFW:

Key Topic

- **Firewall functionality:** Cisco Firepower NGFW acts as a traditional firewall, securing network traffic by inspecting and filtering it based on predefined security policies. It allows administrators to define rules to permit or deny traffic based on various criteria such as source/destination IP addresses, ports, protocols, and applications.

- **Intrusion prevention system (IPS):** Cisco Firepower NGFW incorporates a powerful IPS that monitors network traffic in real time, detecting and blocking known and unknown threats. It uses signature-based detection, anomaly detection, and behavioral analysis techniques to identify and prevent network-based attacks, including malware, exploits, and vulnerabilities.

- **Advanced Malware Protection (AMP):** Cisco Firepower NGFW integrates with Cisco AMP, a cloud-based threat intelligence platform. This integration enables the detection and blocking of advanced malware, zero-day threats, and fileless attacks. The NGFW can leverage file reputation analysis, sandboxing, and retrospective security analysis to identify and mitigate threats.

- **Application visibility and control:** Cisco Firepower NGFW provides deep visibility into network traffic and application usage. It can identify and categorize thousands of applications, allowing administrators to define granular policies based on application characteristics. This level of control helps organizations enforce security policies, optimize network performance, and prioritize critical applications.

- **URL filtering:** Cisco Firepower NGFW includes URL filtering capabilities that enable administrators to control web access and block or allow specific websites or website categories based on predefined policies. This feature helps prevent users from accessing malicious or inappropriate content defined by an organization's security policy, improving security and productivity.

- **Network-based malware detection:** Cisco Firepower NGFW can detect malware communications within a network. It monitors network traffic patterns, command-and-control (C2) communications, and other indicators of compromise to identify and block malware that may be present within the network, even if it bypasses other security layers.

- **Threat intelligence and security analytics:** Cisco Firepower NGFW benefits from Cisco Talos, one of the largest threat intelligence research organizations. Talos provides up-to-date threat intelligence and security analytics, enabling Cisco Firepower NGFW to stay ahead of emerging threats and provide proactive protection against known and unknown attacks.

- **Network segmentation and virtualization:** Cisco Firepower NGFW supports network segmentation and virtualization, allowing organizations to create multiple logical firewalls within a single physical device. This capability enables network isolation and helps enforce security policies based on different user groups, departments, or applications.

- **Centralized management:** Cisco Firepower NGFW is managed through Cisco Firepower Management Center (FMC), a centralized management platform. FMC provides a unified interface for configuration, policy management, monitoring, and reporting across multiple Firepower NGFW devices. It streamlines security operations and provides comprehensive visibility into network security posture.

Cisco Firepower NGFW combines advanced security features with robust network performance, scalability, and ease of management. It helps organizations protect their networks from a wide range of threats, enhance visibility and control, and simplify security management across their infrastructure.

Access Control Lists

An **access control list (ACL)** is a set of rules or filters that define the permissions and restrictions applied to network traffic. It acts as a security mechanism, allowing or denying access to network resources based on specific criteria, such as source/destination IP addresses, port numbers, protocols, and other factors.

ACLs are commonly used in routers, firewalls, and other network devices to control the flow of traffic and enforce security policies. They are typically configured on network interfaces or applied to specific network objects, such as IP addresses or subnets.

Key Aspects and Uses of Access Control Lists

As a security professional, you will be dealing with ACLs daily. Therefore, it is important that you familiarize yourself with them now and become comfortable with them. The more comfortable you are with them early in your career, the easier other topics and concepts that rely on them will become for you.

ACLs can filter network packets based on various criteria, such as source and destination IP addresses, transport layer protocols (TCP/UDP), port numbers, or other header fields. By examining these parameters, ACLs can permit or deny traffic flow based on predetermined rules. As a security-conscious network administrator, you will be able to manage network traffic by controlling its movement using rules that prioritize certain types of traffic. You will be able to protect network resources by limiting access to certain services, ports, or protocols and restricting access to specific resources, and you will even be able to throttle bandwidth for particular applications or IP addresses.

ACLs allow for the segregation of network traffic by enabling you to create different rules for different network segments or user groups. This helps improve network performance, isolate sensitive data, or systems, and enhance overall network security.

7

It's important to carefully plan and configure ACLs to ensure that they align with the organization's security requirements and network architecture. Regular auditing and updates of ACLs are necessary to maintain an effective security posture.

 ## ACL Entries

ACLs are often implemented using a rule-based structure. Each rule (**access control entry [ACE]**) consists of a condition or match criteria, such as source/destination IP addresses or port numbers, and an action to be taken, such as permit or deny. ACEs are evaluated in sequence, and the first matching rule is applied to the traffic.

Each ACE within an ACL contains the following information:

- **Subject:** The subject of an ACE identifies the entity to which the permission or restriction applies. It can be a user, a group of users, a network device, or any other entity defined in the access control policy. In typical networking cases, the subject is a source IP addressing range, such as a subnet, a VLAN, or a group of subnets or VLANs.

- **Permissions:** ACEs specify the permissions granted or denied to the subject. These permissions can include read, write, execute, delete, or other actions, depending on the context and the resource being protected. Permissions determine what actions the subject is allowed to perform or prohibited from performing. In typical network scenarios, the permissions are usually either permit or deny.

- **Object:** The object of an ACE represents the resource or target to which the access control applies. It can be a file, a directory, a network share, a printer, or any other network resource. The object is usually identified by its unique identifier, such as an IP address, a filename, or a uniform resource identifier (URI). In typical networking cases, the subject is a destination IP address or range of IP addresses, such as the IP address of a server, or the subnet or VLAN the server is in, or a group of subnets or VLANs.

- **Conditions:** ACEs may include additional conditions or qualifiers that further define when the permissions or restrictions are applicable. These conditions can be based on factors such as time of day, IP addresses, protocols, or other relevant parameters. For example, you may specify that TCP port 22 or TCP port 443 is permitted and TCP port 23 and TCP port 80 are denied. Or you may even have entries that include QoS markings so that you only match traffic based on those specific QoS values.

Let's look at an example of an ACL with six entries that you might find in a network.

Entry 1:

```
Subject: Source IP: 192.168.0.10

Permissions: Allow

Object: Destination IP: 10.0.0.0/24

Conditions: Protocol: TCP, Destination Port: 80

Description: This entry allows the source IP address 192.168.0.10
to access the destination network 10.0.0.0/24 specifically on TCP
port 80, which is commonly used for HTTP traffic.
```

Here is an example of how entry 1 would be entered in the CLI of a Cisco IOS XE router:

```
access-list 100 permit tcp host 192.168.0.10 10.0.0.0 0.0.0.255 eq 80
```

Entry 2:

Subject: Source IP: 192.168.0.0/16

Permissions: Allow

Object: Destination IP: Any

Conditions: Protocol: Any

Description: This entry allows any source IP address within the 192.168.0.0/16 subnet to access any destination IP address on any protocol. It provides general access to the network for all devices within the specified subnet.

Here is an example of how entry 2 would be entered in the CLI of a Cisco IOS XE router:

```
access-list 100 permit ip 192.168.0.0 0.0.255.255 any
```

Entry 3:

Subject: Source IP: Any

Permissions: Deny

Object: Destination IP: 172.16.0.0/12

Conditions: Protocol: Any

Description: This entry denies any source IP address from accessing the destination network 172.16.0.0/12 on any protocol. It blocks all traffic to this network, which is typically used for private IP addresses.

Here is an example of how entry 3 would be entered in the CLI of a Cisco IOS XE router:

```
access-list 100 deny ip any 172.16.0.0 0.15.255.255
```

Entry 4:

Subject: Source IP: 10.1.1.5

Permissions: Allow

Object: Destination IP: Any

Conditions: Protocol: UDP, Destination Port: 53

Description: This entry allows the source IP address 10.1.1.5 to access any destination IP address specifically on UDP port 53, which is commonly used for DNS (Domain Name System) traffic.

Here is an example of how entry 4 would be entered in the CLI of a Cisco IOS XE router:

```
access-list 100 permit udp host 10.1.1.5 any eq 53
```

Entry 5:

Subject: Source IP: Any

Permissions: Deny

Object: Destination IP: 192.168.10.50

Conditions: Protocol: ICMP

Description: This entry denies any source IP address from accessing the specific destination IP address 192.168.10.50 on ICMP (Internet Control Message Protocol). It blocks ICMP traffic to this specific IP address.

Here is an example of how entry 5 would be entered in the CLI of a Cisco IOS XE router:

```
access-list 100 deny icmp any host 192.168.10.50
```

Entry 6:

Subject: Source IP: Any

Permissions: Allow

Object: Destination IP: Any

Conditions: Protocol: Any

Description: This entry allows any source IP address to access any destination IP address on any protocol. It provides a fallback rule that allows general access to the network when no other specific entries match.

Here is an example of how entry 6 would be entered in the CLI of a Cisco IOS XE router:

```
access-list 100 permit ip any any
```

> **NOTE** Keep in mind that these are examples, and the actual ACL entries you need will depend on the network's specific requirements, the security policies in place, and the types of traffic that need to be controlled or restricted. For example, let's say you needed to make sure that users on networks could not spoof the IP addresses used by other networks. Then you would have to create an ACL that permits only legitimate IP addresses for the network and denies all other addresses that are not part of that network.

Standard and Extended ACLs

Standard IPv4 ACLs and extended ACLs are two types of ACLs used in network devices, such as routers or firewalls, to control network traffic. They differ in terms of the criteria they use for filtering and the range of functions they offer.

Standard ACL

A **standard ACL** filters network traffic based on the source IP address only. It doesn't consider other factors, such as destination IP address, protocols, or port numbers. Standard

ACLs are identified by numbers ranging from 1 to 99 or 1300 to 1999 on Cisco IOS XE devices.

Here is an example of a standard ACL entry:

```
access-list 10 permit 192.168.0.0 0.0.255.255
```

This ACL entry permits traffic that is sourced from the IP address range 192.168.0.0 through 192.168.255.255

Standard ACLs are generally used in situations where you need to apply a simple, broad filtering rule, based on the source IP address. For example, you might use a standard ACL to block or permit traffic from specific subnets or hosts. However, since standard ACLs don't consider other factors, they should be applied with caution to avoid unintended consequences and should be placed as close to the destination as possible.

Extended ACL

An **extended ACL** is an access control list that provides more granular control over network traffic filtering. It can filter based on source and destination IP addresses, protocols (TCP, UDP, ICMP), port numbers, and other factors. Extended ACLs are identified by numbers ranging from 100 to 199 or 2000 to 2699 on Cisco IOS XE devices.

Here is an example of an extended ACL entry:

```
access-list 100 permit tcp any host 192.168.0.10 eq 80
```

This ACL entry permits TCP traffic from any source device going to a specific device at IP address 192.168.0.10 as long as the destination port is 80. Therefore, this entry permits WWW or HTTP traffic from anyone to a specific web server.

Compared to standard ACLs, extended ACLs offer more flexibility and control. Extended ACLs allow you to define specific filtering rules based on various criteria, such as allowing or denying traffic to specific ports or protocols. They are commonly used to enforce security policies, control access to specific services or applications, or filter traffic based on specific requirements.

When deciding between a standard ACL and an extended ACL, consider the level of granularity and specificity required for your filtering rules. If you only need to filter traffic based on source IP addresses, a standard ACL may be sufficient. However, if you require more complex filtering based on multiple criteria, such as source/destination IP addresses, port numbers, or protocols, an extended ACL is more appropriate. In addition, keep in mind that extended ACLs should be placed as close to the source of traffic as possible.

ACL Evaluation

When an access request is made, an ACL that contains multiple ACEs is evaluated in the order in which it has been configured. For example, let's say you have the following ACL, which has six entries:

```
access-list 100 permit tcp host 192.168.0.10 10.0.0.0 0.0.0.255 eq 80

access-list 100 permit ip 192.168.0.0 0.0.255.255 any

access-list 100 deny ip any 172.16.0.0 0.15.255.255

access-list 100 permit udp host 10.1.1.5 any eq 53
```

```
access-list 100 deny icmp any host 192.168.10.50

access-list 100 permit ip any any
```

The order of processing will be from the top down in this case. We refer to this as "top-down processing." Consider traffic that needs to be evaluated against this list. The traffic will be compared with the first entry, and then the second one, and then the third one, and so on.

However, it is important to note that once it is determined that the traffic matches an entry, the processing stops, and that entry applies. We refer to this as "immediate execution upon a match." So, let's say the traffic matches the third entry. What would be the result? Since it is a deny entry, the traffic would be denied/dropped. This is important to grasp because even if a future entry matches, it does not matter because processing occurs from the top down and immediately executes upon a match.

Finally, what happens if the traffic does not match any of the entries in the ACL? It is automatically denied/dropped. The reason for this is the "implicit deny all" entry at the end of every single ACL. You can't see it because it is not listed in the ACL, but it is there (implicit), and you must always remember that it exists. Therefore, if the traffic does not match any entry, it is automatically denied/dropped.

So, to summarize, when evaluating an ACL to see how network traffic will be treated or affected by the ACL, the following order is followed:

1. Top-down processing
2. Immediate execution upon a match
3. Implicit deny all

Network Access Control

Key Topic

From a network security standpoint, NAC stands for **network access control**. NAC is a security framework that ensures only authorized and compliant devices gain access to a network infrastructure. It helps organizations enforce security policies, mitigate risks, and protect against unauthorized access and threats.

NAC typically involves a combination of hardware and software components that work together to establish and enforce access control policies. These are the key aspects and benefits of network access control:

■ **Endpoint authentication:** NAC verifies the identity and security posture of devices attempting to connect to the network. It ensures that only authorized devices, such as laptops, desktops, smartphones, or IoT devices with valid credentials, digital certificates, or other authentication mechanisms are granted access.

■ **Access control policies:** NAC allows administrators to define granular access control policies based on various criteria, including user roles, device types, operating systems, patch levels, antivirus status, and more. These policies determine what level of access each device or user is granted and what resources they can access once connected to the network.

■ **Health assessment:** NAC solutions often include health assessment or posture assessment capabilities. This involves checking the security posture of devices, such as the presence of up-to-date antivirus software, the installation of security patches, and compliance with organizational security policies. Devices that fail a health assessment can be placed in a restricted network segment or denied access until they meet the security requirements.

■ **Network segmentation:** NAC enables network segmentation, dividing the network into different segments or VLANs based on security policies. This segmentation helps contain threats and limits the lateral movement of attackers in the network. NAC can dynamically assign devices to appropriate network segments based on their authentication and health status.

■ **Threat mitigation:** NAC solutions can integrate with other security tools, such as firewalls, IPSs, and SIEM systems. This integration allows for real-time threat detection and response, including blocking or isolation of devices that exhibit suspicious behavior or pose security risks.

■ **Guest access management:** NAC solutions often provide capabilities for managing guest access to the network. Organizations can set up self-registration portals or temporary guest accounts with limited access rights. NAC can enforce policies to ensure that guest devices are segregated from the internal network and provide time-limited access for visitors.

■ **Centralized management:** NAC solutions typically offer centralized management consoles or platforms that allow administrators to configure policies, monitor network activity, and generate reports. This centralized approach simplifies policy enforcement, provides visibility into network access activities, and helps with compliance requirements.

NAC allows organizations to enhance their network security by enforcing access control, validating device health, and reducing the risk of unauthorized access, data breaches, and malware propagation. NAC plays a vital role in securing networks and ensuring that only trusted and compliant devices connect and interact with resources needed to complete required tasks.

One example of NAC using Cisco devices is Cisco **Identity Services Engine (ISE)**. Cisco ISE is a comprehensive NAC solution that provides centralized policy management, authentication, and access control for network devices.

Here's an overview of how Cisco ISE can be used as a NAC solution:

■ **Authentication and authorization:** Cisco ISE acts as a central authentication and authorization server for network devices. It supports various authentication methods, such as 802.1X, MAC Authentication Bypass, and Web Authentication. When a device attempts to connect to the network, Cisco ISE verifies its credentials and authorizes access based on defined policies.

■ **Endpoint profiling:** Cisco ISE can perform endpoint profiling, which involves gathering information about the connected devices, such as the operating system, installed applications, and security posture. This information helps determine the appropriate access control policies for each device.

- **Policy enforcement:** Based on the authentication and profiling results, Cisco ISE enforces access control policies. These policies can be highly granular, considering factors such as user roles, device types, time of day, and location. Access can be granted, restricted, or redirected to a guest network based on the defined policies.

- **Guest access:** Cisco ISE provides guest access management capabilities. It allows organizations to create self-service guest portals where visitors can request network access. Guest users are assigned limited access rights and can be provided with time-limited accounts. Cisco ISE ensures that guest access is segregated from the main network and complies with security policies. In addition, it allows the organization to get agreement that the guest will adhere to network policies when using the network.

- **Posture assessment:** Cisco ISE can perform health or posture assessments on devices connecting to the network. It checks for compliance with security policies, such as the presence of up-to-date antivirus software, security patches, or specific configurations. Noncompliant devices can be placed in a quarantine network, prompted to remediate the issues, or denied access until they meet the security requirements.

- **Centralized management and reporting:** Cisco ISE provides a centralized management console for configuring and managing NAC policies. It offers real-time monitoring of network access activities, generating detailed reports on user authentication, device compliance, and security incidents. This centralized approach simplifies policy administration, improves visibility, and aids compliance efforts.

- **Integration with network devices:** Cisco ISE integrates with network infrastructure devices, such as switches and wireless controllers, through protocols like RADIUS (Remote Authentication Dial-In User Service) and IEEE 802.1X. This integration enables dynamic enforcement of access control policies at the network edge.

- **Threat-centric NAC:** Cisco ISE integrates with Cisco's threat intelligence solutions, such as Cisco Threat Grid and Cisco Umbrella, to provide threat-centric NAC. This integration allows ISE to make access control decisions based on real-time threat intelligence, protecting the network from compromised or malicious devices.

- **Integration with security ecosystem:** Cisco ISE can integrate with other security solutions and third-party platforms, such as SIEM systems, threat intelligence platforms, and mobile device management (MDM) solutions. This integration enables organizations to leverage existing security investments and enhance their overall security posture.

- **Context-based access control:** Cisco ISE supports context-based access control, where access decisions are made based on contextual information such as user identity, device type, location, time of day, and behavior. This fine-grained control enables organizations to enforce policies specific to different user groups or network segments.

- **TrustSec integration:** Cisco ISE integrates with Cisco TrustSec, a security framework that enables secure group-based access control and segmentation. TrustSec allows organizations to define security groups based on business requirements, simplifying policy management and improving network segmentation.

- **BYOD enablement:** Cisco ISE supports bring-your-own-device (BYOD) initiatives by providing secure onboarding and policy enforcement for employee-owned devices. It offers self-registration portals, certificate provisioning, and device compliance checks to ensure that user devices adhere to security policies before they are able to gain network access.

Cisco ISE offers a comprehensive and scalable NAC solution with a wide range of features and integrations. By leveraging Cisco ISE as a NAC solution, you can achieve centralized control over network access, enforce security policies, and gain visibility into network activities. It will enhance your network security by ensuring that only authorized and compliant devices connect to the network, mitigating risks associated with unauthorized access and compromised endpoints.

Summary

Controlling network access is a critical part of maintaining the confidentiality, integrity, and availability of your data. This chapter discusses the following concepts related to controlling network access:

- A **virtual private network (VPN)** is a technology that allows you to create a secure and encrypted connection over a less secure network, such as the Internet, providing confidentiality, integrity, and availability for data.

  - A **site-to-site VPN**, also known as a network-to-network VPN or branch-to-branch VPN, is a type of VPN connection that allows two or more separate networks in different physical locations to securely communicate with each other over the Internet.

  - A **remote-access VPN**, also known as a client-to-site VPN or a remote VPN, is a type of VPN connection that enables individual users or devices to securely access a private network from a remote location over the Internet. It allows remote users to establish a secure connection to a corporate network or any private network as if they were directly connected to it.

  - **Cisco AnyConnect** is a secure remote-access software application developed by Cisco Systems that organizations commonly use to provide secure and encrypted remote access to their networks for employees or authorized users.

- **IPsec (Internet Protocol Security)** is a framework that helps provide secure communication over IP networks. It is widely used for establishing VPNs to ensure confidentiality, integrity, and authentication of all network traffic.

- A **firewall** is a network security device that acts as a barrier between an internal network and external networks, such as the Internet. It monitors and controls incoming and outgoing network traffic based on predefined security rules and policies.

  - A **next-generation firewall (NGFW)** builds on the capabilities of a traditional firewall by incorporating additional features and technologies to provide enhanced security and advanced threat protection.

7

- **Cisco Firepower Next-Generation Firewall (NGFW)** is a comprehensive network security solution that combines the functionality of a traditional firewall with advanced threat detection and prevention capabilities. It provides organizations with enhanced visibility, control, and protection against today's threats.

- An **access control list (ACL)**, commonly used in routers, firewalls, and other network devices, is a set of rules or filters that define the permissions and restrictions applied to network traffic.

  - A **standard ACL** filters network traffic based on the source IP address only. It doesn't consider other factors, such as destination IP address, protocols, or port numbers. Standard ACLs are identified by numbers ranging from 1 to 99 or 1300 to 1999 on Cisco IOS XE devices.

  - An **extended ACL** is an access control list that provides more granular control over network traffic filtering. It can filter based on source and destination IP addresses, protocols (TCP, UDP, ICMP), port numbers, and other factors. Extended ACLs are identified by numbers ranging from 100 to 199 or 2000 to 2699 on Cisco IOS XE devices.

  - When evaluating an ACL to see how network traffic will be treated or affected by the ACL, the following order is followed:

    1. Top-down processing

    2. Immediate execution upon a match

    3. Implicit deny all

- **Network access control (NAC)** is a security framework that ensures only authorized and compliant devices gain access to a network infrastructure. It helps organizations enforce security policies, mitigate risks, and protect against unauthorized access and threats.

  - One example of NAC using Cisco devices is **Cisco Identity Services Engine (ISE)**. Cisco ISE is a comprehensive NAC solution that provides centralized policy management, authentication, and access control for network devices.

Exam Preparation Tasks

As mentioned in the Introduction, you can customize your strategy for exam preparation. Suggested tasks include the exercises here, Chapter 16, "Final Preparation," and the exam simulation questions on the companion website.

Review All Key Topics

Review the most important topics in this chapter, noted with the Key Topics icon in the outer margin of the page. Table 7-2 lists these key topics and the page number on which each is found.

Table 7-2   Key Topics for Chapter 7

Key Topic Element	Description	Page Number
List	VPN confidentiality, integrity, authentication, and anti-replay	120
Paragraph	Site-to-site VPNs	121
Paragraph	Remote-access VPNs	122
Paragraphs	Cisco AnyConnect VPN	122
List	IPsec AH and ESP protocols	124
List	IPsec confidentiality and integrity	125
List	IPsec modes transport and tunnel	125
Paragraph	Definition of a firewall	125
List	General features and advancements of NGFWs	127
List	Cisco Firepower NGFW	128
Paragraph	Definition of access control list	129
Section	ACL Entries	130
Section	Standard ACL	132
Section	Extended ACL	133
Section	ACL Evaluation	133
Section	Network Access Control	134

Complete Tables and Lists from Memory

There are no memory tables for this chapter.

Define Key Terms

Define the following key terms from this chapter and check your answers in the glossary:

virtual private network (VPN), anti-replay protection, site-to-site VPN, remote-access VPN, Cisco AnyConnect, IPsec (Internet Protocol Security), Authentication Header (AH), Encapsulating Security Payload (ESP), transport mode, tunnel mode, firewall, next-generation firewall (NGFW), Cisco Firepower Next-Generation Firewall (NGFW), access control list (ACL), access control entry (ACE), standard ACL, extended ACL, network access control (NAC), Identity Services Engine (ISE)

Review Questions

1. Which of the following statements about VPNs are true? (Choose three.)

   a. A site-to-site VPN allows two or more separate networks in different physical locations to securely communicate with each other over the Internet.

   b. A remote-access VPN allows remote users to establish a secure connection to a corporate network or any private network as if they were directly connected to it.

   c. Cisco AnyConnect is an automation feature that allows for the dynamic creation and termination of site-to-site VPN connections.

    d. The IPsec AH protocol is best suited for remote-access and site-to-site VPN connections.

    e. IPsec tunnel mode encapsulates an entire IP packet, including the original IP header.

2. Which of the following features of Cisco Firepower NGFW enables the detection and blocking of advanced malware, zero-day threats, and fileless attacks?

    a. Firewall

    b. URL filtering

    c. IPS

    d. AMP

3. Which of the following can an extended ACL use to filter traffic on a network? (Choose four.)

    a. Ingress interface of the packet

    b. QoS markings

    c. Application port number

    d. IPv4 address

    e. Layer 4 protocol

    f. Application layer header information

4. Which of the following are reasons for implementing a NAC solution? (Choose two.)

    a. To gain access to a SIEM and SOAR system

    b. To provide an intrusion prevention system and AMP solution

    c. To provide simplified and centralized endpoint authentication

    d. To enforce a corporate wide end user device posture assessment solution

CHAPTER 8

Wireless SOHO Security

This chapter covers the following topics:

- **Hardening Wireless Routers and Access Points:** This section explores the need to protect the administrative interface on wireless routers and access points as well as the need to keep wireless routers and access points up to date.

- **Wireless Encryption Standards:** This section covers WEP, WPA, WPA2, and WPA3.

- **Wireless Authentication:** This section addresses Personal mode and Enterprise mode.

- **Wi-Fi Protected Setup, SSIDs, and MAC Address Filtering:** This section explores WPS, SSID, and MAC address filtering.

- **Common Wireless Network Threats and Attacks:** This section dives into a few different wireless network threats and attacks and wraps up with a discussion of best practices you should consider to protect yourself.

In today's interconnected world, **small office/home office (SOHO)** environments heavily rely on wireless networks for their day-to-day operations. SOHO refers to a type of work setup where individuals or businesses operate from their residences or small office spaces. It allows professionals to work remotely and independently, often utilizing technology and digital tools to facilitate their work. SOHO setups are popular among freelancers, entrepreneurs, and individuals seeking flexibility in their work arrangements. Wireless networks provide flexibility, convenience, and increased productivity. However, they also introduce unique security challenges that need to be addressed to protect sensitive information and maintain the integrity of the network.

This chapter begins by exploring the need to harden your wireless routers and access points. Specifically, it focuses on hardening your administrative interface and keeping your wireless routers and APs up to date. It then discusses wireless encryption standards and wireless authentication, covering the differences between WEP, WPA, WPA2, and WPA3, as well as Personal mode versus Enterprise mode. Near the end of the chapter, you will learn about Wi-Fi Protected Setup, service set identifiers, and MAC address filtering. The chapter wraps up by discussing common wireless network threats and attacks as well as a multitude of best practices to protect yourself from these attacks.

This chapter covers information related to the following Cisco Certified Support Technician (CCST) Cybersecurity exam objective:

2.4. Set up a secure wireless SOHO network (MAC address filtering, encryption standards and protocols, SSID).

"Do I Know This Already?" Quiz

The "Do I Know This Already?" quiz allows you to assess whether you should read this entire chapter thoroughly or jump to the "Exam Preparation Tasks" section. If you are in doubt about your answers to these questions or your own assessment of your knowledge of the topics, read the entire chapter. Table 8-1 lists the major headings in this chapter and their corresponding "Do I Know This Already?" quiz questions. You can find the answers in Appendix A, "Answers to the 'Do I Know This Already?' Quizzes and Review Questions."

Table 8-1 "Do I Know This Already?" Section-to-Question Mapping

Foundation Topics Section	Questions
Hardening Wireless Routers and Access Points	1
Wireless Encryption Standards	2
Wireless Authentication	3
Wi-Fi Protected Setup, SSIDs, and MAC Address Filtering	4
Common Wireless Network Threats and Attacks	5

CAUTION The goal of self-assessment is to gauge your mastery of the topics in this chapter. If you do not know the answer to a question or are only partially sure of the answer, you should mark that question incorrect for purposes of self-assessment. Giving yourself credit for an answer you correctly guess skews your self-assessment results and might provide you with a false sense of security.

1. Which of the following should you consider when hardening the administrative interface of a wireless router or access point? (Choose two.)

    a. Use Enterprise mode for authentication.

    b. Use the WPA3 wireless encryption standard.

    c. Only allow encrypted communication using protocols such as HTTPs or SSH.

    d. Avoid using the default password and set a strong, unique custom password.

2. Which of the following wireless encryption standards use AES? (Choose two.)

    a. WEP

    b. WPA

    c. WPA2

    d. WPA3

3. Which of the following are characteristics of Personal mode? (Choose two.)

    a. Uses a pre-shared key

    b. Uses 802.1x and RADIUS

    c. Suitable for enterprise deployments

    d. Suitable for small office/home office deployments

4. What is an SSID?

    a. A type of wireless network attack in which an attacker creates a fake wireless access point

    b. A security feature used on wireless networks to control access

    c. A unique name assigned to a wireless network to identify it

    d. A network security standard designed to simplify the process of connecting devices to a Wi-Fi network

5. Which of the following should you consider when connecting to a public Wi-Fi network at a coffee shop?

    a. Use a VPN.

    b. Disable WPS.

    c. Disable SSID broadcasting.

    d. Use strong passwords.

Foundation Topics

Hardening Wireless Routers and Access Points

By default, wireless SOHO routers and access points are not as safe and secure as they need to be. In addition, they have flaws that emerge as time passes that, if left unchanged, could easily jeopardize confidentiality, integrity, and availability. This section explores how you can protect the administrative interface and why you should keep your SoHo routers and access points up to date.

Administrative Interface

The administrative interface, also known as the admin interface, the management interface, or the configuration interface, is a web-based portal or CLI provided by a wireless router or access point. Administrators use this interface to configure and manage various settings of wireless routers and access points, such as wireless network parameters, security settings, and overall device functionality settings.

From a security standpoint, the admin interface is a critical component to consider as it grants access to the device's configurations and settings. Therefore, it is imperative that you take the time and energy needed to secure the admin interface. If not, you will be vulnerable to an assortment of attacks.

One of the first essential steps is to set a strong, unique password for accessing the admin interface. Using weak or default passwords makes it easier for unauthorized individuals to gain access to the device and make malicious changes. The password should be complex, consisting of a combination of uppercase and lowercase letters, numbers, and special characters and should never be shared with anyone who does not need it.

Next, you should consider using multifactor authentication (MFA), if supported, as it adds an extra layer of security to the admin interface. MFA requires users to provide additional verification, such as a one-time password or biometric authentication, in addition to the password. This helps prevent unauthorized access even if the password is compromised.

When communicating from your admin PC to the SOHO router or access point for administrative purposes, you need to ensure that the admin interface is accessible only through secure communication channels. For example, you should use Hypertext Transfer Protocol Secure (HTTPs) instead of HTTP so that all transmitted data is encrypted between the device and the administrator's browser. This prevents eavesdropping and protects against on-path attacks. If you are using a command-line interface (CLI), you should use Secure Shell (SSH) instead of Telnet.

When it comes to access control and user roles, the admin interface should offer granular access control, allowing administrators to assign different roles and permissions to different users. Limiting access to only necessary functionalities based on user roles reduces the risk of unauthorized changes and potential security breaches. In addition, you should consider enabling intrusion detection and prevention mechanisms within the admin interface. These features can monitor and detect suspicious activity, such as repeated failed login attempts or unusual configuration changes and take appropriate actions to mitigate potential security threats.

Finally, you need to enable logging and auditing capabilities within the admin interface to track and monitor administrative activities. This helps in identifying any unauthorized changes or suspicious behavior and aids in investigating security incidents, if necessary.

Updates

Firmware is software code embedded in electronic devices that provides instructions for their operation. It is a combination of hardware-specific software and low-level software that acts as the device's operating system. Firmware controls the device's functionality, behavior, and interactions with other hardware components. It is stored in nonvolatile memory and remains persistent even after power loss. Firmware can be found in various devices, including routers, smartphones, cameras, and IoT devices. Since firmware serves as a crucial component in the overall functionality and reliability of electronic devices, it is important to update firmware to uphold security, fix bugs, improve performance, introduce new features, and maintain compatibility with evolving technologies.

Firmware updates include security patches that address vulnerabilities or exploits discovered in the device's software. Updating firmware helps protect against potential security breaches or unauthorized access. In addition, firmware updates can fix bugs or software glitches that may affect the device's performance, stability, or compatibility with other devices. The updates may also introduce performance improvements or new features, and as technology evolves, the updates will ensure that wireless devices remain compatible with new standards, protocols, or encryption methods.

If you don't keep your firmware up to date, it is possible that your SOHO routers or access points may no longer be eligible for manufacturer support. In the event of technical issues or troubleshooting needs, having outdated firmware increases the likelihood of not receiving assistance from the manufacturer. Therefore, it is imperative that you keep the firmware up to date. Also note that in certain industries or environments, compliance regulations, IT insurance policies, and third-party vendor contracts may mandate regular firmware updates as part of security best practices. Adhering to these requirements helps maintain compliance and demonstrate a commitment to security.

Since cybersecurity threats and attack techniques are constantly evolving, keeping firmware up to date is essential for maintaining the security, performance, and compatibility of wireless devices. Therefore, you need to regularly check for firmware updates from the manufacturer and promptly apply them to protect yourself from vulnerabilities and exploits. Doing so will also reduce your risk of being targeted by attackers.

Wireless Encryption Standards

Encryption on a wireless network is essential for protecting sensitive data, ensuring confidentiality, and maintaining privacy. It prevents unauthorized access and interception of data transmitted over the network, safeguarding against eavesdropping and data theft. Encryption also helps maintain the integrity of data by detecting any tampering or modifications during transmission. It plays a critical role in authentication, ensuring that only authorized devices can connect to the network. Compliance with legal and industry regulations often requires encryption to protect sensitive information. This section explores WEP, WPA, WPA2, and WPA3.

Key Topic

WEP

Wired Equivalent Privacy (WEP) is an encryption protocol used to secure wireless networks. It was introduced as the first standard encryption method for Wi-Fi networks. WEP operates by encrypting data transmitted between wireless devices using a shared key. However, WEP has significant security flaws and vulnerabilities. It uses a relatively short encryption key (40 or 104 bits) that can be easily cracked using various techniques. WEP's encryption algorithm suffers from weaknesses that allow attackers to recover the key and gain unauthorized access to the network. Due to these vulnerabilities, WEP is no longer considered secure, and its use in wireless networks is strongly discouraged. It has been largely replaced by more robust encryption standards, such as WPA, WPA2, and WPA3. Never use it, and if you have devices that support it, maybe it is time to consider upgrading the devices. Later in this section, Table 8-2 compares key features of WEP and other wireless encryption standards to help you prepare for the CCST Cybersecurity exam.

Key Topic

WPA

Wi-Fi Protected Access (WPA) is a security protocol designed to improve the security of wireless networks. It is the successor to the vulnerable WEP encryption standard. WPA introduced stronger encryption and security mechanisms, such as Temporal Key Integrity Protocol (TKIP), which dynamically generates and encrypts individual data packets. WPA also implements message integrity checks to prevent tampering with data. It supports both personal (pre-shared key) and enterprise (RADIUS server-based) authentication methods. WPA improves the overall security of wireless networks by addressing the weaknesses of WEP and providing stronger encryption and authentication. However, WPA is still susceptible to certain attacks, and it has largely been superseded by the more secure WPA2 and WPA3 protocols. So, as with WEP, you are encouraged to avoid WPA and never use it. Later in this section, Table 8-2 compares key features of WPA and other wireless encryption standards to help you prepare for the CCST Cybersecurity exam.

Key Topic

WPA2

Wi-Fi Protected Access 2 (WPA2) is a current standard for wireless network security. It is an improvement over WPA and offers stronger encryption and authentication methods. WPA2 uses the Advanced Encryption Standard (AES) algorithm for secure data transmission, replacing the vulnerable TKIP used in WPA. It supports both personal (pre-shared key) and enterprise (RADIUS server-based) authentication modes. WPA2 also introduces the four-way handshake process, which ensures secure key exchange between wireless devices and access points. Despite being widely adopted, WPA2 is still susceptible to certain vulnerabilities, such as KRACK attacks. However, it remains a recommended and widely implemented security protocol for protecting wireless networks. WPA2 has replaced the older and less secure WEP and WPA standards. Therefore, it would be the minimal starting point for security when implementing a modern wireless network. Later in this section, Table 8-2 compares key features of WPA2 and other wireless encryption standards to help you prepare for the CCST Cybersecurity exam.

Key Topic

WPA3

Wi-Fi Protected Access 3 (WPA3) is the latest-generation wireless security protocol. It uses AES and provides enhanced security features compared to its predecessors, WPA and WPA2. WPA3 introduces individualized data encryption, ensuring that even if one device's encryption is compromised, the security of other devices remains intact. It strengthens the process of initial key exchange, making it more resistant to offline dictionary and brute-force attacks. WPA3 also offers a simplified mode for easier device setup, reducing the risk of misconfiguration. It includes protections against potential threats like brute-force password cracking attempts and phishing attacks. WPA3 is designed to provide stronger security measures for open, personal, and enterprise wireless networks, addressing the vulnerabilities of previous standards. While WPA3 adoption is gradually increasing, hardware upgrades may be required to fully support its features.

Table 8-2 compares and contrasts the key features of WEP, WPA, WPA2, and WPA3. Keep in mind that this table provides a simplified overview and does not include all the technical details and nuances of each security protocol.

Key Topic

Table 8-2   Comparing WEP, WPA, WPA2, and WPA3

Security Protocol	Encryption Algorithm	Key Length	Authentication Method(s)	Notes
WEP	RC4	40/104 bits	Pre-shared key	Weak encryption, vulnerable to key cracking, easily susceptible to attacks
WPA	TKIP	128 bits	Personal mode (pre-shared key) Enterprise mode (802.1x with EAP and RADIUS)	Improved encryption compared to WEP but still susceptible to some attacks
WPA2	AES-CCMP	128 bits	Personal mode (pre-shared key) Enterprise mode (802.1x with EAP and RADIUS)	Strong encryption, supports enterprise (RADIUS) authentication, susceptible to KRACK attacks

8

Security Protocol	Encryption Algorithm	Key Length	Authentication Method(s)	Notes
WPA3	AES-CCMP SAE	192/256 bits	Enhanced Open Personal mode (Simultaneous Authentication of Equals [SAE]) Enterprise mode (802.1x with EAP and RADIUS)	Enhanced security, individualized data encryption, strengthened key exchange, and protection against certain attacks and vulnerabilities

Wireless Authentication

This section begins by exploring why authentication is critical for wireless networks and then dives into an examination of Personal mode and Enterprise mode authentication, which are introduced in the previous section.

Authentication is critical for wireless SOHO security. Authentication ensures that only authorized users or devices can connect to the wireless network, protecting against unauthorized access and minimizing the risk of insider threats by ensuring that only authorized employees or individuals with legitimate credentials can access the network and resources on it. This ensures that sensitive data transmitted over the network is only accessible to authorized individuals, safeguarding against data theft or interception. Authentication also helps with performance, preventing unauthorized users from consuming bandwidth that they should not be able to consume.

In addition, authenticating every user makes accountability possible, ensuring that each user accessing the network can be uniquely identified and traced, and they cannot deny having done something. This aids in any security analysis or investigations that may be needed in the event of security incidents or policy violations.

Always remember that authentication serves as a fundamental building block for overall network security. It forms the basis for implementing additional security measures and controls to protect wireless SOHO networks against various threats and attacks. Since many industry regulations and data protection standards mandate the use of strong authentication methods to ensure compliance and to protect sensitive information, authentication can't be an afterthought or something that is ignored. It needs to be considered first and implemented with the highest levels of security so that CIA can be maintained in the organization.

Personal Mode

Personal authentication, in relation to wireless networks, refers to the method of authenticating individual users or devices accessing the network. It is commonly used in SOHO environments to secure personal Wi-Fi networks using WPA, WPA2, or WPA3.

With **Personal mode**, a shared key or passphrase, known as the **pre-shared key (PSK)**, is used to authenticate users. Each user or device connecting to the wireless network must provide the correct PSK to gain access. This PSK, commonly known as the "Wi-Fi password," is manually configured on the wireless router or access point. When a user attempts to connect to the network, they are prompted to enter the Wi-Fi password. If the entered password matches the preconfigured PSK, the authentication is successful, and the user is granted access to the network. If the entered password doesn't match, the user is denied access.

While personal authentication is simple to set up and suitable for SOHO environments, it may have limitations in larger organizations or situations where more granular control over user access is required. A big issue with Personal mode in enterprise networks is accountability. Since everyone is using the same PSK, it is difficult to know who is who on the wireless network. In addition, the security of personal authentication depends on the strength of the PSK in addition to making sure that people don't share it with others who don't need it. So, using a strong, complex, and unique password is crucial to prevent unauthorized access and protect the wireless network, but that is only true if people don't share it with the wrong people.

Enterprise Mode

Key Topic

Enterprise mode, in the context of wireless networks, is a method of authentication that is typically used in larger organizations, businesses, or institutions. It offers benefits such as centralized user management, strong security through various authentication methods, user accountability through logging and auditing, and the ability to integrate with existing authentication infrastructure, such as Active Directory. It is commonly employed in larger-scale deployments where network security and access control are critical considerations.

Enterprise authentication involves the use of a centralized authentication server, such as a RADIUS (Remote Authentication Dial-In User Service) server, EAP, and the 802.1X authentication standard:

- A **RADIUS server** acts as a central authority responsible for authenticating and authorizing users attempting to connect to the wireless network.

- **Extensible Authentication Protocol (EAP)** is an authentication framework that enables multiple authentication methods within the enterprise environment. It allows for the integration of various authentication protocols, including username/password, digital certificates, smart cards, and token-based authentication. EAP provides flexibility in choosing the most suitable authentication method based on the organization's requirements.

- The **802.1X** standard is a network access control framework that operates in conjunction with EAP. It defines the process for authenticating devices attempting to connect to a network and enforcing access policies. With 802.1X, each user or device must authenticate before being granted network access.

With Enterprise mode, when a user or device attempts to connect to the network, they first communicate with the wireless access point using 802.1X. The access point acts as a supplicant and requests authentication from the authentication server (the RADIUS server). The server, acting as an authenticator, verifies the user's credentials through EAP.

Enterprise authentication can also use various authentication methods, such as username/password, digital certificates, or other strong authentication mechanisms, like two-factor authentication (2FA) or MFA. These methods add an extra layer of security by requiring additional verification beyond just a password.

8

Table 8-3 provides a comparison of Personal mode and Enterprise mode features.

Table 8-3   Features of Personal Mode and Enterprise Mode

Feature	Personal Mode	Enterprise Mode
Authentication	PSK	802.1X with EAP and RADIUS
User management	Limited control and individual PSK usage	Centralized user management and authentication server
Security	Shared PSK, vulnerable to brute-force attacks	Robust security, supports various authentication methods
Granularity	Limited control over access policies	Fine-grained control over user access and policies
Scalability	Suitable for small-scale deployments	Suitable for large-scale organizations
Guest networks	Limited segregation options	Supports dedicated guest networks with separate access
User accountability	Difficult to trace specific user actions	Provides detailed logs and accountability for each user
Integration	No integration with external directories	Integration with existing authentication infrastructure
Complexity	Simple setup and configuration	More complex setup and configuration
Compliance	May not meet specific regulatory requirements	Supports compliance standards with stronger authentication options

WPA3 Enhanced Open

As you have already seen, WPA3, like WPA2, has various forms (Personal and Enterprise modes) to meet the usage and security needs of different organizations. In addition, WPA3 also has an Enhanced Open mode.

WPA3 Enhanced Open is for public networks and is based on Opportunistic Wireless Encryption (OWE). The purpose is to provide encryption and privacy on open, non-password-protected networks, such as those in cafes, hotels, restaurants, and libraries, to prevent passive eavesdropping. This mode uses 256-bit authenticated encryption, 384-bit key derivation and confirmation, and 256-bit management frame protection.

Keep in mind that WPA3 Enhanced Open doesn't provide authentication, but it does provide encryption.

Wi-Fi Protected Setup, SSIDs, and MAC Address Filtering

This section explores three wireless concepts that you need to be familiar with for the CCST Cybersecurity exam: Wi-Fi Protected Setup (WPS), service set identifiers (SSIDs), and MAC address filtering.

Wi-Fi Protected Setup

Wi-Fi Protected Setup (WPS) is a network security standard designed to simplify the process of connecting devices to a Wi-Fi network. It aims to make the setup process more user-friendly by allowing users to easily add devices to a network using a PIN, a push-button configuration, or near-field communication (NFC).

However, WPS has faced significant security concerns over the years. The PIN-based authentication method in particular has been found to be vulnerable to brute-force attacks, where an attacker can systematically guess the PIN to gain unauthorized access to the network. In addition, flaws in the implementation of WPS have allowed for the exploitation of security weaknesses, making it easier for attackers to bypass network security measures.

Due to these vulnerabilities, it is generally recommended to avoid using WPS, especially the PIN-based method. Disabling WPS on a wireless router is considered a best practice for enhancing network security. Most modern routers provide the option to disable WPS entirely or disable the PIN-based method specifically. By disabling WPS, you eliminate the potential security risks associated with its vulnerabilities.

SSID

A **service set identifier (SSID)** is a unique name assigned to a wireless network to identify it. It acts as the wireless network's name and distinguishes it from other nearby networks. Users can see the available SSIDs when scanning Wi-Fi networks on their devices. An SSID is used to differentiate one network from another and helps users connect to the intended network. It can be a string of alphanumeric characters or a customized name chosen by the network administrator. While an SSID does not directly provide security, hiding or not broadcasting the SSID can add a layer of obscurity to the network. However, this is not a foolproof security measure and should be used in conjunction with other security measures, such as encryption and authentication.

Using multiple SSIDs can enhance security in certain scenarios. Here are some ways in which multiple SSIDs can contribute to enhanced security:

- **Network segmentation:** By creating separate SSIDs for different groups or purposes, such as guest networks, IoT devices, or employee networks, you can isolate traffic and prevent unauthorized access between segments.

- **Access control:** Different SSIDs can be associated with different access control policies, allowing administrators to apply specific security measures, such as firewall rules or bandwidth limitations, to each SSID.

- **Resource allocation:** By assigning specific SSIDs to critical resources or sensitive data, you can prioritize bandwidth allocation or implement more stringent security measures for those networks.

- **Compliance requirements:** In regulated industries, separate SSIDs can help meet specific compliance requirements by segmenting and isolating data or systems according to compliance guidelines.

- **Client isolation:** Multiple SSIDs can enable client isolation, where devices connected to one SSID cannot directly communicate with devices on other SSIDs, adding an extra layer of security against unauthorized access or lateral movement.

8

■ **Guest networks:** Creating a dedicated guest network with its own SSID can keep guest traffic separate from internal resources, mitigating the risk of unauthorized access or potential attacks from guest devices.

■ **Ease of management:** Assigning different SSIDs can simplify network management by allowing administrators to apply specific configurations, monitor usage, or trouble-shoot network issues on a per-SSID basis.

As a final note, using multiple SSIDs should be accompanied by other security measures, such as strong encryption, robust authentication protocols, and regular security updates, to ensure the overall security of the wireless network.

MAC Address Filtering

MAC address filtering is a security feature used on wireless networks to control access based on the unique Media Access Control (MAC) addresses (hardware addresses) of devices. It involves creating a whitelist or blacklist of MAC addresses that are either allowed or denied access to the network. When MAC address filtering is enabled, only devices with MAC addresses listed in the whitelist are permitted to connect, while those in the blacklist are blocked. It adds an extra layer of access control by filtering devices at the hardware level. However, MAC addresses can be spoofed or easily changed, making MAC address filtering less effective as a standalone security measure. However, it is better to use it than not as part of an overall security implementation.

Common Wireless Network Threats and Attacks

Various security risks and malicious activities commonly target wireless networks and devices. These threats exploit vulnerabilities in wireless protocols, configurations, or user behavior to compromise network security.

This section explores a number of these common wireless threats and attacks, including rogue access points, evil twins, war driving, and password cracking, and discusses how you can mitigate them.

Rogue Access Points and Evil Twins

A **rogue access point** is an unauthorized wireless access point (AP) that has been deployed within a network without proper authorization or knowledge. It may act as a deceptive device, often impersonating a legitimate AP, to lure users into connecting to it. Or, it may have been added by someone to improve connectivity or test features without considering the security risks introduced by doing so. Whether such an AP is malicious or not, it is still considered a rogue AP.

Rogue access points pose a significant security risk as they can facilitate various malicious activities, such as eavesdropping, data interception, and unauthorized access to sensitive information—even if that isn't their intended purpose. Detecting and removing rogue access points is crucial to maintaining a secure and reliable network environment, typically requiring network administrators to employ specialized tools and monitoring systems. Implementing strong security measures, such as strong encryption, network segmentation, and regular security audits, can help mitigate the risks associated with rogue access points.

Rogue APs are particularly concerning in public spaces, such as airports, cafes, or hotels, where users often connect to open or unsecured Wi-Fi networks without verifying their authenticity. However, rogue access points can also be deployed within corporate environments, where attackers exploit security vulnerabilities or lack of proper network monitoring.

An **evil twin attack** is a type of wireless network attack in which an attacker creates a fake wireless AP that appears identical to a legitimate one. This is 100% malicious. The attacker typically uses specialized software to clone the network name (SSID) and encryption settings of the legitimate AP, tricking users into connecting to the malicious AP unknowingly by ensuring that it has the best connection and signal strength. Once a user is connected, the attacker can intercept and manipulate the user's network traffic, potentially gaining unauthorized access to sensitive information such as login credentials or financial data.

Evil twin attacks often exploit the trust users place in familiar network names, making it challenging for them to distinguish between legitimate and malicious APs. Evil twin attacks are often carried out in public places with free Wi-Fi access, such as cafes, airports, or hotels, where users are more likely to connect to open networks without verifying their authenticity. However, they can happen in Enterprise networks as well.

To protect against evil twin attacks, users should exercise caution when connecting to wireless networks and verify the authenticity of the AP by comparing the network details with trusted sources. In addition, using strong encryption protocols, regularly updating wireless device firmware, and employing virtual private networks (VPNs) can help mitigate the risk of falling victim to an evil twin attack.

While rogue access points and evil twin attacks are related, there are some distinct differences between them (see Table 8-4).

Table 8-4   Comparing Rogue APs and Evil Twins

Characteristic	Rogue Access Point	Evil Twin
Scope	Any unauthorized wireless access point within a network, whether maliciously created or mistakenly deployed.	A fake access point set up to deceive users.
Intent	May or may not be created with malicious intent. It can be a result of misconfiguration or an unintentional deployment.	Always implemented with malicious intent. The attacker aims to deceive and exploit unsuspecting users.
Deception	Employs various techniques, such as using different SSIDs or broadcasting signals on unauthorized channels.	Specifically involves cloning a legitimate network's SSID and encryption settings to make the fake access point appear identical to the real one.
User interaction	May be discovered by users if they notice unfamiliar network names or experience connectivity issues.	Designed to deceive users, making it difficult for them to distinguish between legitimate and fake access points.

Characteristic	Rogue Access Point	Evil Twin
Security risk	Depends on whether the AP was deployed with malicious or non-malicious intent. Either way, it can have a negative effect on CIA.	Specifically focused on exploiting users who connect to the fake access point. Attackers can intercept and manipulate their network traffic, potentially compromising sensitive information and jeopardizing CIA.

War Driving

War driving is a technique used to discover and map wireless networks by driving around in a vehicle equipped with a Wi-Fi-enabled device, such as a laptop or smartphone. The purpose of war driving is to identify vulnerable or unsecured wireless networks for potential exploitation or unauthorized access.

During war driving, the Wi-Fi-enabled device scans for available wireless networks, logging information such as SSIDs, signal strength, and encryption settings. This information helps the attacker identify networks with weak security configurations, default or easily guessable passwords, or outdated encryption protocols.

War driving poses a significant threat as it allows attackers to gather information about wireless networks without physically accessing them. Armed with this knowledge, attackers can target specific networks for further attacks, such as cracking passwords or launching more sophisticated exploits.

Wireless Password Cracking

Wireless password cracking refers to the process of attempting to discover or guess the password used to secure a wireless network. Attackers use various techniques to crack passwords, with the intention of gaining unauthorized access to the network and potentially compromising the connected devices or stealing sensitive information.

The following is a list of different methods employed for wireless password cracking:

- **Brute-force attack:** An attacker systematically tries every possible combination of characters until they find the correct password. Brute-force attacks can be time-consuming but are effective against weak or short passwords.

- **Dictionary attack:** An attacker uses pre-generated lists of common passwords or words from dictionaries and systematically tries each one against the target network. This method is faster than a brute-force attack and relies on users' tendencies to choose easily guessable passwords.

- **Rainbow table attack:** A rainbow table is a precomputed set of hash values for different possible passwords. Attackers compare captured password hashes with entries in the rainbow table to quickly determine the password corresponding to a specific hash.

- **WPS PIN attack:** If a Wi-Fi network uses Wi-Fi Protected Setup (WPS), attackers can exploit vulnerabilities in the WPS PIN authentication process to gain access to the network. This involves trying different PIN combinations until the correct one is discovered.

Key Topic

Protecting Yourself from Wireless Attacks

It is imperative that you protect yourself from the multitude of wireless attacks that exist. Consider these best practices for protecting yourself from wireless attacks:

- **Use strong encryption protocols:** Implement robust encryption standards, such as WPA2 or WPA3, with strong and unique passwords.

- **Use strong passwords:** Avoid common words and easily guessable information.

- **Enable network lockout policies:** Implement mechanisms that lock out users after a certain number of failed login attempts to deter brute-force attacks.

- **Disable SSID broadcasting:** Hide the network's SSID to make it less visible to casual war drivers. Although this alone is not a foolproof security measure, it may help.

- **Disable WPS:** If it is not necessary, disable WPS on the wireless router, as it is often a target for password cracking attacks.

- **Encrypt guest network traffic:** All wireless traffic needs to be encrypted—even guest network traffic. It is imperative that this not be overlooked.

- **Regularly update firmware and security patches:** Keeping wireless devices and routers up to date with the latest firmware and security patches helps protect against known vulnerabilities.

- **Implement intrusion detection systems:** Using wireless intrusion detection systems (WIDSs) can help identify unauthorized access points or suspicious activity on the network.

- **Perform regular security audits:** Conducting periodic assessments of wireless network security, including vulnerability scanning and penetration testing, helps identify and address potential weaknesses.

- **Monitor network activity:** Regularly monitoring network traffic and logs can help detect and respond to any unauthorized access or suspicious behavior.

- **Educate users:** Users should be educated about the risks of connecting to unsecured networks and the importance of verifying the legitimacy and security of Wi-Fi networks before connecting to them.

- **Use VPNs:** When connecting to public Wi-Fi networks, consider using a VPN so you can encrypt all your traffic inside the VPN as it is transmitted over the wireless network.

By considering these best practices, you can strengthen your wireless network and protect it from the multitude of wireless attacks that exist.

Summary

Wireless networks provide flexibility, convenience, and increased productivity. However, they also introduce unique security challenges that need to be addressed to protect sensitive information and maintain the integrity of the network. This chapter discussed the following concepts related to wireless SOHO security:

8

- **Hardening wireless routers and access points** is a critical part of security. Failing to do so jeopardizes confidentiality, integrity, and availability. Consider these tips:

  - Set a strong, unique password for accessing the admin interface.

  - Consider using multifactor authentication (MFA).

  - Use secure protocols like HTTPs.

  - Use granular access controls.

  - Keep the firmware up to date.

  - Keep the software up to date.

- **Encryption** on a wireless network is essential for protecting sensitive data, ensuring confidentiality, and maintaining privacy. It prevents unauthorized access and interception of data transmitted over the network, safeguarding against eavesdropping and data theft.

  - **Wired Equivalent Privacy (WEP)** and **Wi-Fi Protected Access (WPA)** are older encryption protocols used to secure wireless networks. Due to their weaknesses, they should not be used anymore.

  - **Wi-Fi Protected Access 2 (WPA2)** is a current standard for wireless network security that uses AES and provides Personal and Enterprise modes.

  - **Wi-Fi Protected Access 3 (WPA3)** is the most recent standard for wireless network security. It uses AES and provides Enhanced Open, Personal, and Enterprise modes.

  - With **Personal mode**, a shared key or passphrase, known as a pre-shared key (PSK), is used to authenticate users.

  - **Enterprise** authentication involves the use of a centralized authentication server, such as a RADIUS (Remote Authentication Dial-In User Service) server, EAP (Extensible Authentication Protocol), and the 802.1X authentication standard.

  - **WPA3 Enhanced Open** is for public networks and is based on Opportunistic Wireless Encryption (OWE). The purpose is to provide encryption and privacy on open, non-password-protected networks, such as those in cafes, hotels, restaurants, and libraries, to prevent passive eavesdropping.

- **Wi-Fi Protected Setup (WPS)** is a network security standard designed to simplify the process of connecting devices to a Wi-Fi network. It aims to make the setup process more user-friendly by allowing users to easily add devices to a network using a PIN, a push-button configuration, or near-field communication (NFC).

- A **service-set identifier (SSID)** is a unique name assigned to a wireless network to identify it among other nearby networks. It acts as the wireless network's name. Users can see the available SSIDs when scanning Wi-Fi networks on their devices.

- **MAC address filtering** is a security feature used on wireless networks to control access based on the unique Media Access Control (MAC) addresses (hardware addresses) of devices.

- A **rogue access point** is an unauthorized wireless AP that has been deployed within a network without proper authorization or knowledge. It could be deployed accidentally or on purpose.

- An **evil twin attack** is a type of wireless network attack in which an attacker creates a fake wireless AP that appears identical to a legitimate one to lure people to connect so that traffic can be captured. This is 100% malicious.

- **War driving** is a technique used to discover and map wireless networks by driving around in a vehicle equipped with a Wi-Fi-enabled device, such as a laptop or smartphone. The purpose of war driving is to identify vulnerable or unsecured wireless networks for potential exploitation or unauthorized access.

- **Wireless password cracking** refers to the process of attempting to discover or guess the password used to secure a wireless network.

Exam Preparation Tasks

As mentioned in the Introduction, you can customize your strategy for exam preparation. Suggested tasks include the exercises here, Chapter 16, "Final Preparation," and the exam simulation questions on the companion website.

Review All Key Topics

Review the most important topics in this chapter, noted with the Key Topics icon in the outer margin of the page. Table 8-5 lists these key topics and the page number on which each is found.

Table 8-5   Key Topics for Chapter 8

Key Topic Element	Description	Page Number
Paragraph	The importance of protecting the administrative interface	144
Paragraph	The importance of updating wireless routers and access points	145
Section	WEP	146
Section	WAP	146
Section	WAP2	146
Section	WAP3	147
Table 8-2	Comparing WEP, WPA, WPA2, and WPA3	147
Section	Personal Mode	148
Section	Enterprise Mode	149
Table 8-3	Features of Personal Mode and Enterprise Mode	150
Paragraph	WPA3 Enhanced Open	150
Section	Wi-Fi Protected Setup, SSIDs, and MAC Address Filtering	150
Table 8-4	Comparing Rogue APs and Evil Twins	153
Section	War Driving	154
Section	Wireless Password Cracking	154
Section	Protecting Yourself from Wireless Attacks	155

Complete Tables and Lists from Memory

Print a copy of Appendix B, "Memory Tables," found on the companion website, or at least the section for this chapter, and complete the tables and lists from memory. Appendix C, "Memory Tables Answer Key," includes completed tables and lists you can use to check your work.

Define Key Terms

Define the following key terms from this chapter and check your answers in the glossary:

small office home office (SOHO), firmware, Wired Equivalent Privacy (WEP), Wi-Fi Protected Access (WPA), Wi-Fi Protected Access 2 (WPA2), Wi-Fi Protected Access 3 (WPA3), Personal mode, pre-shared key (PSK), Enterprise mode, RADIUS server, Extensible Authentication Protocol (EAP), 802.1X, WPA3 Enhanced Open, Wi-Fi Protected Setup (WPS), service set identifier (SSID), MAC address filtering, rogue access point, evil twin attack, war driving, brute-force attack, dictionary attack, rainbow table attack, WPS PIN attack

Review Questions

1. Why is it necessary to keep your SOHO routers and APs up to date? (Choose two.)
   a. So they don't get physically stolen from your SOHO network.
   b. So the administrative interface password can't be brute-forced or easily guessed.
   c. To ensure that your organization is in compliance with various security best practices.
   d. To enforce secure communication between your management station and the wireless router or AP.
   e. To ensure that flaws that emerge as time passes are not easily exploited by an attacker.

2. Which of the following are characteristics of WPA3? (Choose three.)
   a. It uses the RC4 encryption algorithm.
   b. It uses the TKIP encryption algorithm.
   c. It uses the AES encryption algorithm.
   d. It has a key length of 104 bits.
   e. It has a key length of 128 bits.
   f. It has a key length of 256 bits.
   g. It supports only Personal mode.
   h. It supports only Enterprise mode.
   i. It supports both Personal and Enterprise mode.

3. Which of the following are characteristics of Enterprise mode authentication? (Choose three.)
   a. Uses 802.1x with EAP and RADIUS
   b. Uses pre-shared keys
   c. Provides fine-grained control over user access and policies
   d. Makes it difficult to trace specific user actions
   e. Uses a centralized user management and authentication server

4. Which of the following is a method that can be used to control access to a Wi-Fi network using hardware addresses?

   a. 802.1x with EAP and RADIUS

   b. Pre-shared keys

   c. MAC address filtering

   d. SSIDs

   e. WPS

5. Which of the following correctly defines war driving?

   a. A network security standard designed to simplify the process of connecting devices to a Wi-Fi network

   b. A type of wireless network attack in which an attacker creates a fake wireless access point (AP) that appears identical to a legitimate one

   c. The process of attempting to discover or guess the password used to secure a wireless network

   d. A technique used to discover and map wireless networks by driving around in a vehicle equipped with a Wi-Fi-enabled device, such as a laptop or smartphone

8

CHAPTER 9

Operating Systems and Tools

This chapter covers the following topics:

- **Host Security Features:** This section discusses common host security concepts and terminology.

- **Windows:** This section discusses security controls specific to Microsoft Windows, including Defender, NTFS permissions, and BitLocker.

- **Linux:** This section discusses security controls available in Linux, such as firewalls, file system permissions, and disk encryption.

- **macOS:** This section discusses security controls integrated into macOS, including its firewall, file system permissions, and FileVault.

- **Tools:** This section discusses fundamental software and technologies for cybersecurity professionals.

So far in this book, we've focused heavily on network protocols and security. However, these are only one part of the cybersecurity equation. No ACL, network security appliance, or encrypted protocol can protect our computers if the computers themselves are compromised! With that in mind, this chapter introduces common endpoint operating systems and their security features. We begin our tour with Windows, a heavy hitter in the business realm. Then we discuss Linux, an open-source operating system frequently used for server applications. The final operating system we cover is macOS, a UNIX-based operating system maintained by Apple. The chapter concludes with some information about **netstat**, **nslookup**, **tcpdump**, and other tools that are available in some form on any OS. They may not be the most glamorous security tools, but you'll use them often.

This chapter covers information related to the following Cisco Certified Support Technician (CCST) Cybersecurity exam objective:

3.1. Describe operating system security concepts.

3.2. Demonstrate familiarity with appropriate endpoint tools that gather security assessment information.

3.4. Implement software and hardware updates.

3.5. Interpret system logs.

"Do I Know This Already?" Quiz

The "Do I Know This Already?" quiz allows you to assess whether you should read this entire chapter thoroughly or jump to the "Exam Preparation Tasks" section. If you are in doubt about your answers to these questions or your own assessment of your knowledge of the topics, read the entire chapter. Table 9-1 lists the major headings in this chapter and their corresponding "Do I Know This Already?" quiz questions. You can find the answers in Appendix A, "Answers to the 'Do I Know This Already?' Quizzes and Review Questions."

Table 9-1 "Do I Know This Already?" Section-to-Question Mapping

Foundation Topics Section	Questions
Host Security Features	1
Windows	2–3
Linux	4–6
macOS	7
Tools	8–10

CAUTION The goal of self-assessment is to gauge your mastery of the topics in this chapter. If you do not know the answer to a question or are only partially sure of the answer, you should mark that question incorrect for purposes of self-assessment. Giving yourself credit for an answer you correctly guess skews your self-assessment results and might provide you with a false sense of security.

1. What technology do operating systems use to control access to data stored on hard drives or SSDs?
   a. RADIUS
   b. Malware scanning
   c. Syslog
   d. File system permissions

2. An attacker exploits a vulnerability in the Apache web server and gains limited access to the system as the www-data user. What would their next step be to obtain unfettered control?
   a. Pivoting
   b. Port scanning
   c. Privilege escalation
   d. On-path attack

3. You are configuring a Windows 10 Professional laptop for a new user and want to ensure that its data is secure if the device is lost or stolen. What is the best option for securing its data?
   a. FileVault
   b. NTFS Permissions
   c. Windows Defender
   d. BitLocker

4. Which command displays file system permissions in Linux?

    a. ls

    b. show-perm

    c. ls -l

    d. get-acl

5. What directory does Linux use by default to store log files?

    a. /log

    b. /tmp/log

    c. /audit

    d. /var/log

6. What Linux feature uses a system of labeling and policies to restrict how users, services, sockets, and files can interact?

    a. SELinux

    b. firewalld

    c. FileVault

    d. LUKS

7. What graphical tool, analogous to Event Viewer, allows you to review logs in macOS?

    a. LogViewer

    b. Console

    c. Zsh

    d. Auditor

8. What command lists the sockets a Linux system is waiting for connections on?

    a. ls

    b. ls -l

    c. netstat -o

    d. netstat- l

9. Which tool is best suited to capturing traffic while connected to a server with no GUI?

    a. Snort

    b. Wireshark

    c. tcpdump

    d. nc

10. Which of the following commands queries for cisco.com from a specific DNS server at 208.67.222.222?

    a. nslookup 208.67.222.222 cisco.com

    b. nslookup cisco.com 208.67.222.222

    c. nslookup 208.67.222.222@cisco.com

    d. nslookup cisco.com@208.67.222.222

Foundation Topics

Host Security Features

We achieve defense-in-depth by applying multiple, complementary security controls. At the broadest levels, we implement network-wide technical controls and business-wide security policies. Zooming in, we also secure individual systems with any tools we have at our disposal. Layering security controls ensures that we aren't reliant on any one thing. In this chapter, we'll look at the tools and security features available to Windows, Linux, and macOS endpoints. With a few exceptions, they fall into the following six categories:

- **Host-based firewall:** In contrast to network-based firewalls, **host-based firewalls** filter traffic at each endpoint. Host- and network-based firewalls protect against different threats and complement each other. Network firewalls restrict traffic at network boundaries, but they can't filter traffic between hosts within a subnet, nor can they protect devices that roam between networks. In contrast, host-based firewalls protect devices regardless of their location.

- **Command-line interface:** A command-line interface (CLI) is a text-based shell that provides an administrator with numerous tools that are unavailable in graphical interfaces. This chapter explains the essential characteristics of CLI, such as their prompts and privilege elevation.

- **File system permissions: File system permissions** dictate which actions are allowed on directories and files and are defined on a user-by-user or group-by-group basis. According to the principle of least privilege, users should have the bare minimum access to do their jobs and no more. Lenient permissions put data at risk, but draconian permissions can undermine productivity. Threading that needle requires a solid understanding of how file system permissions work.

- **Full-disk encryption: Full-disk encryption (FDE)** is a potent confidentiality control that wraps stored data in strong encryption. FDE protects against attackers with physical access to a device because plaintext data is inaccessible without a decryption key. Unless attackers can guess the key—which is virtually impossible—the stored data is indistinguishable from random noise.

- **Update mechanisms:** Update mechanisms help fix bugs in operating system components, applications, and drivers. Software updates remove vulnerabilities and bugs as they're discovered. They're not a panacea, but they might make attackers' jobs more difficult. Promptly and regularly applying updates is an important facet of endpoint security.

- **Log data:** Log data, which provides a record of events on a system, provides a clear picture of what happened (and what's happening). Finding and parsing log information is a fundamental skill in IT and cybersecurity. It helps you detect issues, anomalies, or attacks and determine root causes.

9

Windows

Windows is a closed-source operating system maintained and sold by Microsoft. There are client versions of Windows, such as Windows 10 and 11, and server versions, such as Windows Server 2016 and 2019. Client versions come in different *editions*, including Home, Pro, Education, and Enterprise. Many Windows security and management features are only available on non-Home editions. For example, the ability to centrally manage Windows devices using Active Directory (one reason for Microsoft's dominance in the business realm) is not available for Windows Home editions. Similarly, Microsoft restricts BitLocker drive encryption to Pro, Education, and Enterprise editions. We don't muddy the waters in this chapter by dwelling on Windows licensing, but it is important to pay attention to the different capabilities of Windows editions. A highly abridged summary of Windows 10 and 11 editions, accurate as of 2023, is provided in Table 9-2.

Table 9-2   Windows 10 and 11 Editions

Feature	Home Edition	Pro Edition	Enterprise Edition
Active Directory	—	✓	✓
Workgroups	✓	✓	✓
BitLocker	—	✓	✓

Before diving into Windows security features and tools, it is worth discussing two mechanisms Windows can use to share data and services over networks: workgroups and domains.

A workgroup provides a simple mechanism for sharing resources like files and printers between endpoints. By default, new Windows installations are members of a workgroup imaginatively called WORKGROUP. Workgroups are simple and available in all Windows editions, but they have significant drawbacks. They use a peer-to-peer model and therefore lack centralized management. If Alice might log in to any of five computers, you need to create her account on each system individually. Likewise, file or printer shares must be configured and managed locally on each system. Workgroups suit small offices, but administrative complexity grows geometrically with new users and endpoints.

Active Directory domains use a centralized client/server architecture. At their core are on-premises or cloud-based domain controllers. These servers centrally manage authentication, authorization, and machine and user configurations (via Group Policy). By default, domain controllers also handle time synchronization and DNS. Windows clients join domains to utilize these services. Additional Windows servers (not acting as domain controllers) may also become domain members to provide additional services like file shares, printers, update management, and RADIUS. Two strengths of Active Directory are its manageability and scalability. Active Directory improves manageability by defining users and configurations in a single place: the domain controller. Unlike with a workgroup, our user Alice can immediately use her Active Directory account to log in to domain-joined workstations. Active Directory is also more scalable: As domains grow, deploying additional controllers is a breeze. Active Directory also supports multiple sites and the creation of trust relationships between multiple domains. In all but the smallest environments, Active Directory is preferable to workgroups. Table 9-3 compares workgroups and domains.

Table 9-3 Windows Workgroups and Domains

Factor	Workgroups	Active Directory Domains
Architecture	Peer-to-peer	Client/server
Authentication	System-local accounts	Domain-wide accounts
Configuration and management	Systems configured and managed individually	Central configuration and management via Group Policy
Suitability	Small, simple environments	Scalable to gigantic environments

Now that we've covered some basic Windows terminology and concepts, let's delve into some of its tools and features. We will begin with Microsoft Defender.

Microsoft Defender

Defender is a constellation of security features that can be difficult to summarize cleanly due to constant changes to branding and user interface. Most Defender components are managed in the Settings app by browsing to Update & Security > Windows Security (see Figure 9-1). The following sections examine some of the key sections in Windows Security.

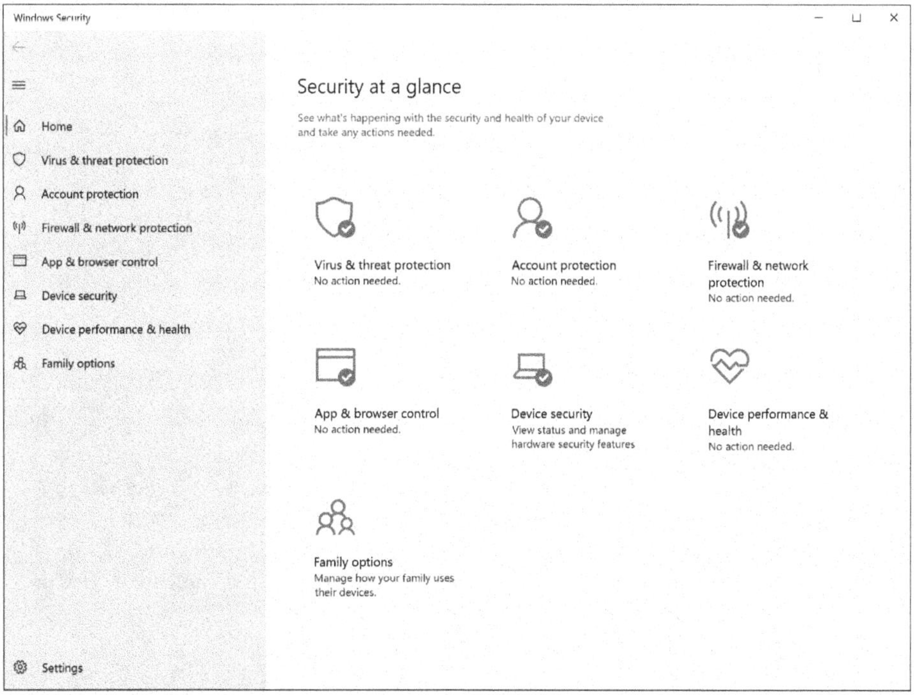

Figure 9-1 *Windows Security Settings*

Virus & Threat Protection

In the Virus & Threat Protection section of Windows Security, you can review previous scans and their results, perform new scans, and manage settings for Microsoft Defender Antivirus. It includes the following important tools (see Figure 9-2):

- The Scan Options link beneath the Quick Scan button allows you to trigger more intensive full or offline scans.

- The Manage Settings link beneath Virus & Threat Protection Settings allows you to toggle features like real-time protection and automatic sample submission.

- The Check for Updates link beneath Virus & Threat Protection Updates allows you to manually update malware signatures (although this typically occurs automatically).

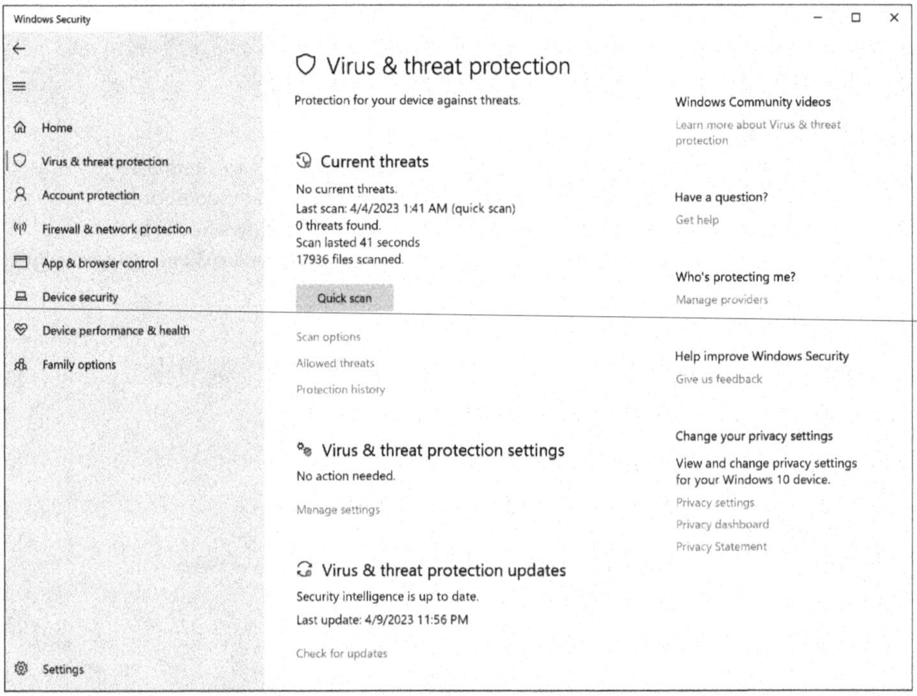

Figure 9-2 *Virus & Threat Protection*

Firewall & Network Protection

In the Firewall & Network Protection section of Windows Security, you can review and manage Windows Defender Firewall. It displays whether you're on a public, private, or domain network and whether the firewall is enabled for each profile (see Figure 9-3). You can toggle the firewall for any profile, but disabling the firewall is never recommended. This section includes the following useful links:

- Allow an App Through Firewall allows you to specify whether specific apps should be allowed to communicate on public, private, or domain networks.

- Advanced Settings allows you to define very specific firewall rules based on direction (inbound or outbound), source and destination IP addresses and ports, program paths, and more.

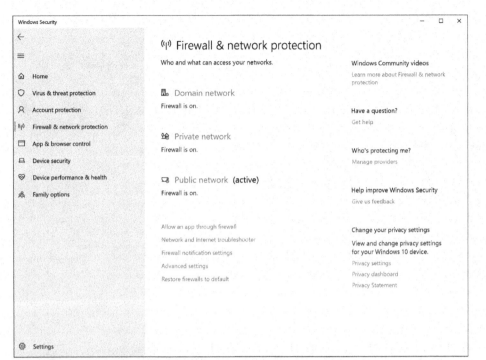

Figure 9-3   *Firewall & Network Protection*

You might have wondered why Windows asks for the network type whenever it connects to a new LAN. It requests this information because different firewall rules are applied based on a network's trustworthiness. The Public profile has more restrictive rules than Domain or Private profiles; after all, who else might be connected? You can customize any of these profiles to meet your security needs in different network contexts.

App & Browser Control

The App & Browser Control section of Windows Security contains security options for SmartScreen, Edge sandboxing, and several enhanced exploit mitigations (see Figure 9-4). As a group, these settings constrain what applications can do, limiting the impact if applications are compromised. In the App & Browser Control section, Reputation-Based Protection Settings allows you to manage settings for Microsoft Defender SmartScreen. SmartScreen uses reputational data about URLs, certificates, and file hashes to evaluate the trustworthiness of websites and downloaded applications. It warns the user if it can't verify a resource's trustworthiness. SmartScreen can block low-reputation files and applications, URLs (if using Edge), and nuisance software like potentially unwanted programs (PUPs). Figure 9-5 shows its settings.

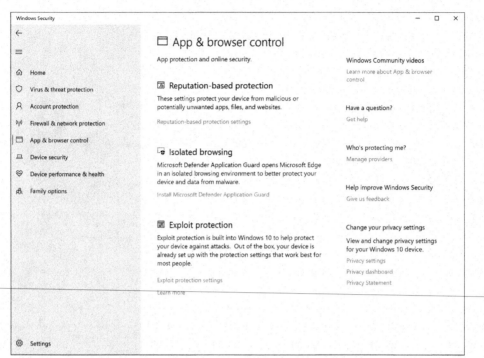

Figure 9-4 *App & Browser Control*

Figure 9-5 *Reputation-Based Protection*

CMD and PowerShell

Windows ships with two command-line interface (CLI) environments: the older CMD and the newer PowerShell. **CMD** is a dated but dependable relic of the MS-DOS days. It has less functionality, less intuitive syntax, and reduced scripting functionality compared to Power-Shell. **PowerShell** has more bells and whistles. It is largely backward compatible, inheriting most CMD commands, but it adds an entire command set of its own. PowerShell commands (called *cmdlets*) follow a standard verb-object naming convention, dramatically improving readability. PowerShell also sports friendlier syntax, robust scripting constructs, and a helpful Integrated Scripting Environment (ISE). Table 9-4 compares analogous commands between CMD and PowerShell. Particularly for scripting and automation, PowerShell is the obvious choice.

Table 9-4   Comparing Simple Tasks in CMD and PowerShell

Task	CMD	PowerShell
List all services	sc queryex type=service state=all	Get-Service
Show current location	cd	Get-Location
Change locations	cd *location*	Set-Location *location*
Create new file	type NUL > *filename*	New-Item *filename*
Delete a file	del *filename*	Remove-Item *filename*

Both CMD and PowerShell can be launched with standard or elevated privileges. If you ever receive an "Access is denied" message when running a command, you need to elevate your privileges. There are two ways to invoke elevated shells:

- Via the Windows GUI, locate the CMD or PowerShell program, right-click it, and select Run as Administrator. Privileges are elevated for all commands run within this shell.

- In an existing unprivileged CMD or PowerShell session, the command **runas /user:***user* { *command* } launches a command with the privileges of the specified user. The **runas** command is handy for one-off administrative commands.

The CMD and PowerShell prompts (the text to the left of where you type commands) are simple. They display where you are in the file system. Unlike in macOS and Linux, the prompts don't indicate which device you're on, your username, or whether you're operating with elevated privileges. All you see is your current location. To glean additional information, you can use the **hostname** command to view the system's name or **whoami** to view your username. As for whether you're using standard or elevated privileges, there are a few indicators to look for.

If the windows' title bars state simply Command Prompt or Windows PowerShell, you're running as a standard user; if they are prepended with Administrator:, you're running with administrative privileges. Standard and administrative shells also start in different file system locations. If you open a shell as a regular user, you'll begin in that user's home profile (for example, C:\Users\student). As an administrator, you'll find yourself starting in C:\Windows\system32.

9

Obtaining administrative privileges is naturally something that authorized IT and cyberse-curity personnel should understand. If we were confined to standard user accounts, our jobs would be a morass of "Access is denied" messages and frustration! Attackers feel the same way. They'll often gain access to systems by compromising unprivileged accounts that con-strain their nefarious activities. To sidestep those limitations, attackers use exploit techniques to achieve **privilege escalation** and gain greater (or total) control of a host. Privilege eleva-tion and privilege escalation are nearly synonymous, but the latter term has more malicious connotations.

NTFS Permissions

Most Windows systems use Microsoft's New Technology File System (NTFS). NTFS incor-porates numerous improvements over prior FAT file systems, including

- Support for larger files and partitions

- A higher upper limit on file count

- Improved reliability

- Encryption or compression of individual files and folders

- Granular permissions

The last item, NTFS permissions, is particularly important. File system permissions are applied to directories and files and dictate what principals (users or groups of users) can do. Essentially, they are lists of who can (or can't) do what. Table 9-5 presents a summary of NTFS permissions. Note that some permissions have different effects on folders than on files.

Table 9-5 NTFS Permissions

Permission Name	Description
Full Control	User or group has total control over a folder or file
Modify	User or group can modify folder contents or individual files (but cannot change their permissions or take ownership)
Read and Execute	**Folder:** User or group can read or execute files within a directory **File:** User or group can read or execute a file
List Folder Contents	User or group can view the contents of a folder
Read	**Folder:** User or group can read (but not execute) files in a directory **File:** User or group can read (but not execute) a file
Write	**Folder:** User or group can create files and folders in a directory **File:** User or group can modify the contents of a file

Figure 9-6 shows an example of folder permissions. The Accounting group can read and execute (as well as list folder contents). Lily has the same permissions with added write permissions. Hulk and Student (the folder's owner) have full control.

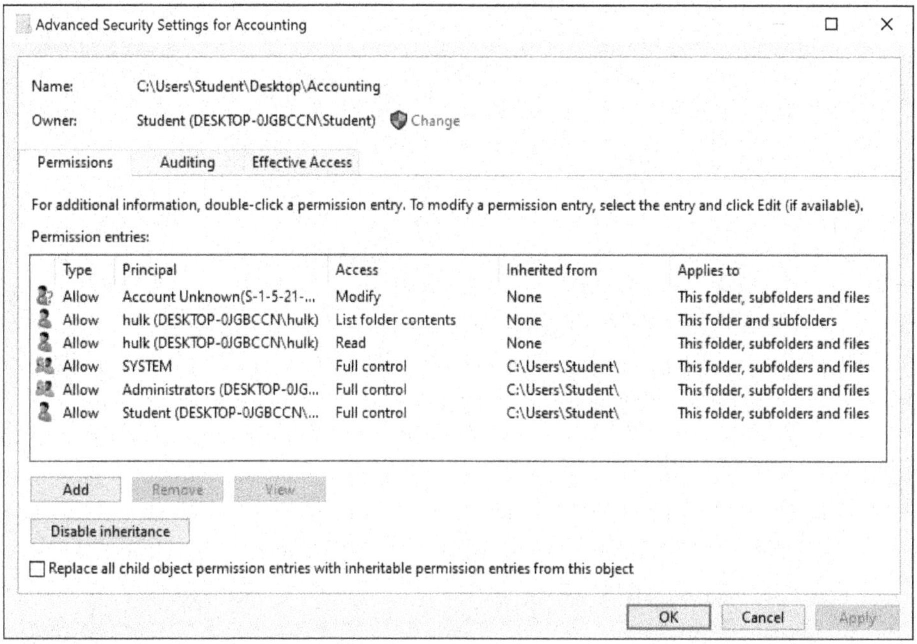

Figure 9-6   *NTFS Permissions*

Windows permissions grow in complexity when directories are shared over a network. In network shares, two distinct sets of rules apply: NTFS permissions and Share permissions. The most restrictive of the two wins, and it can be challenging to understand how they interact. The Effective Access tab (see Figure 9-7) is a lifesaver for troubleshooting. For any user or group, it lists the effective permissions (after NTFS and Share permissions are applied) and informs you which of the two is limiting access.

One weakness of file system permissions is that they require something to enforce them. Generally, operating systems evaluate permissions for each access attempt and then allow or deny them accordingly. If the operating system ignores permissions, they're as useless as laws without a justice system. For example, mounting an NTFS-formatted volume in Linux yields unfettered access to the file system. Linux doesn't recognize the jurisdiction of Windows permissions. Furthermore, simply copying a file within Windows or between systems can affect the original permissions. By default, copied files inherit permissions from the directories they're copied to, which can result in unintentional exposure of data. These caveats lead us to another, far stronger data protection technology: BitLocker.

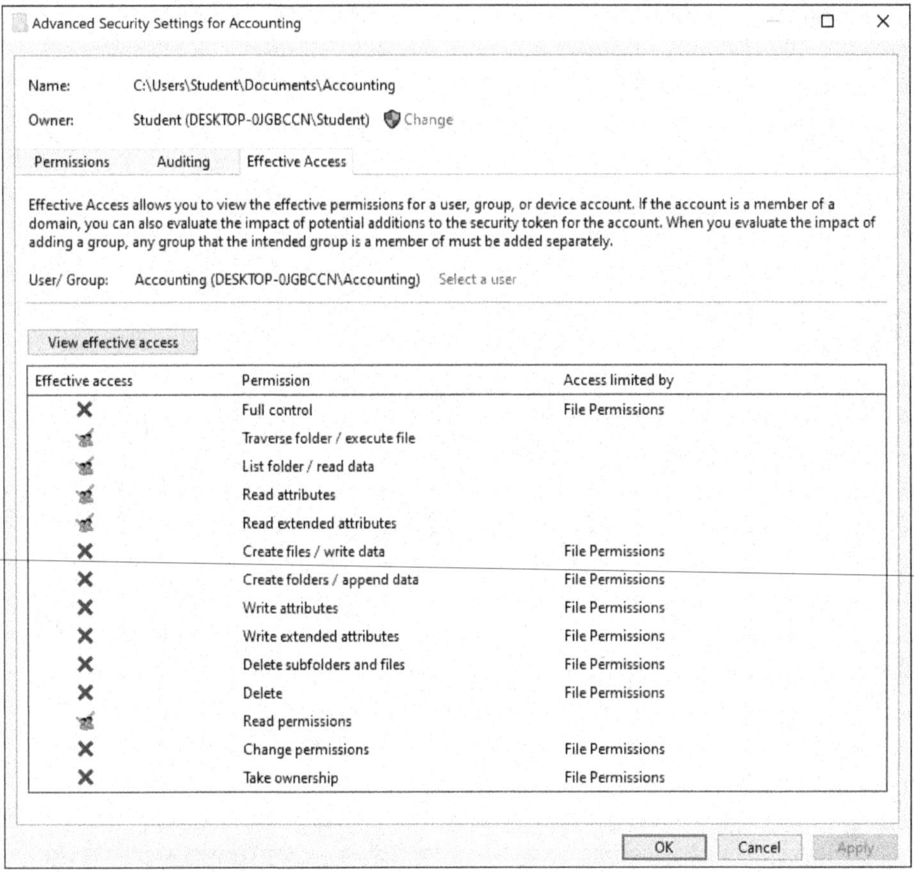

Figure 9-7   *Effective Access*

BitLocker

Key Topic

BitLocker is Microsoft's full-disk encryption (FDE) technology that (as it says on the tin) encrypts all data written to a hard drive or solid-state drive. Using FDE technologies like BitLocker is inherently more secure than encrypting individual files. Piecemeal data encryption risks accidental exposure. Plaintext data may leak into unencrypted temporary files or caches. BitLocker and other FDE technologies prevent data leakage by encrypting everything.

BitLocker is available on Pro and higher editions of Windows. It supports several deployment models, depending on the computer's capabilities and security requirements. You can secure BitLocker devices with a Trusted Platform Module (TPM) chip, PIN, USB key, or combinations of these methods. Using the TPM in conjunction with a PIN or USB key is common. In these configurations, the encryption keys are stored securely on the motherboard's TPM chip. To release the keys to decrypt a volume, you must prove your identity with something you know (a PIN) or something you have (a USB key).

When enabling BitLocker, recording and securely storing the recovery key is critical. On non-domain systems, you may need to physically print the key and store it safely. It can also be stored online if you're using a Microsoft account. On domain-joined systems, administrators can back up BitLocker recovery keys and keep them in Active Directory. Whichever method you select, don't neglect this step! BitLocker uses strong encryption, and getting locked out of your drive functionally destroys any data stored locally.

Windows Updates

Windows Update is a built-in utility for Windows operating systems that keeps their components current. It provides new features, bug fixes, and security patches. Windows vulnerabilities are constantly being discovered and disseminated, and it's important to correct vulnerable software before attackers exploit it. Many attacks succeed long after patches are available—because they were simply overlooked! Regular updates protect systems from privilege escalation exploits, malware, and other attacks.

Windows Update can download and install updates automatically, or you can manually check for updates and install them yourself. Automatic updates help reduce the chances of applying security patches too late (or not at all). However, in production environments, blindly updating software can be dangerous. Windows updates occasionally break software and have even destroyed user data. For example, a Windows update that inadvertently broke remote-access VPNs was released during the Covid-19 pandemic. Most of the country was working remotely, and there was pandemonium and scramble to roll the update back! Therefore, it's wise to strike a balance between testing updates and ensuring that they're promptly applied. In Active Directory environments, features like Windows Server Update Services (WSUS) help to centrally manage the approval and deployment of Windows updates.

Alas, Windows Update does not handle updates to third-party applications. Some programs, such as Chrome and Firefox, can automatically update themselves. Others may require you to manually trigger updates through their interface. Many do not have built-in update mechanisms: You must download and run installers for newer versions. These differences make it important to maintain an accurate inventory of installed programs and their respective update mechanisms.

Event Viewer and Audit Logs

Windows **Event Viewer** is a graphical utility for monitoring, filtering, and organizing log entries from many sources on Windows systems. Logs are arranged into a hierarchical tree, and the most-used section is Windows Logs, which has Application, Security, Setup, System, and Forwarded Events subsections. Figure 9-8 shows the Event Viewer interface, and Table 9-6 describes the purpose of each category in Event Viewer.

9

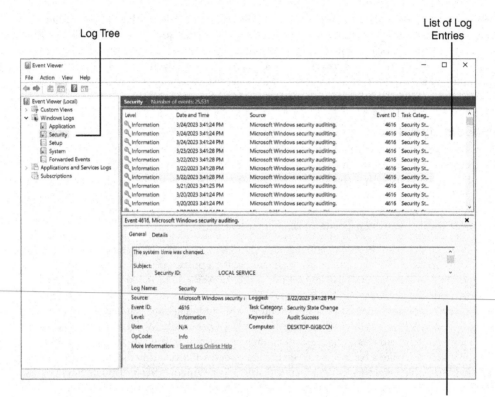

Figure 9-8 *Windows Event Viewer*

Table 9-6 Windows Event Viewer Log Categories

Log Category	Description and Example
Application	Application events ■ Background service events (Licensing, Defender) ■ Application events (automatic browser updates)
Security	All security-relevant events ■ Successful logons ■ Unsuccessful logons ■ Other events based on audit policy
Setup	Windows installation and update events ■ Windows update(s) installed ■ Windows update(s) removed
System	System and component events ■ System shut down or powered on ■ New services created ■ Time synchronization events ■ Driver events
Forwarded Events	Events generated on other systems and transmitted here

It's no surprise that our primary focus is on the Security log. By default, the Security log is filled mainly with successful and unsuccessful authentication attempts, but Windows supports monitoring of many other security events. Using either Group Policy (in domains) or Local Security Policy (on non-domain computers), you can choose to audit many security-relevant events including the following:

- Successful or failed account management attempts

- Successful or failed policy changes

- Successful or failed process events

- Successful or failed file system events

- Successful or failed kernel events

It might be tempting to audit everything, but it is important to consider the signal-to-noise ratio. Which log data will be most helpful? If you monitor all possible events, you can expect hundreds of log entries per second. Such a volume of log events makes it more challenging to investigate issues, causes your logs to balloon in size, and may even degrade system performance. As ever, it is important to balance the quantity and quality of information

Linux

Linux is an open-source operating system, which means its code is freely available to anyone. It began as Linus Torvalds' hobby in 1991. At the time, Unix operating systems were closed-source and inaccessible to most people. Torvalds began Linux to create a free, open-source, and Unix-compliant operating system. Since then, Linux's worldwide footprint has grown dramatically, particularly in the server space.

Because Linux has a permissive open-source license, anyone can download, modify, and redistribute its code. Consequently, there is no one "true" Linux. It has many branching variants, called *distributions*. Some are short-lived, and some have been popular for decades. Think of Linux as an expansive family tree of related distributions with a handful of "granddaddy" distributions that have spawned entire families. We focus here on two such families: Debian distributions and Red Hat distributions. One of their primary differences is which package manager they use. Package managers are tools that install, remove, and update operating system components and applications. In many cases, the package manager is either **apt**, **yum**, or **dnf**:

- Debian distributions, including Ubuntu, use **apt** (Advanced Package Tool).

- Red Hat distributions like RHEL, Fedora, and CentOS use **yum** (Yellowdog Updater, Modified) or **dnf** (Dandified YUM). The tool used largely depends on the age of the Linux installation, and **dnf** is gradually supplanting **yum**. The syntax with these two tools is essentially identical.

firewalld and UFW

Modern Linux distributions use a component called nftables to inspect and filter network traffic. While nftables is very powerful, it isn't particularly user-friendly. Various front ends exist to simplify the configuration and management of the nftables subsystem. UFW and firewalld are the most common. While not a hard-and-fast rule, Red Hat distributions tend to use firewalld, and Ubuntu systems often use UFW. The full syntaxes used to manage firewalld and UFW are beyond the scope of the CCST Cybersecurity certification, but in case you are curious, Table 9-7 provides some comparative examples.

Table 9-7   Comparison of firewalld and UFW

Task	Firewalld Syntax	UFW Syntax
Allow TCP port 80	firewall-cmd --add-port=80/tcp	sudo ufw allow 80/tcp
Deny TCP port 23	firewall-cmd --remove-port=23/tcp	sudo ufw deny 23/tcp
Allow all from 10.0.0.0/8	firewall-cmd --add-source=10.0.0.0/8	sudo ufw allow from 10.0.0.0/8 to any
View current firewall rules	firewall-cmd --list-all	sudo ufw status

Bash

Linux has many graphical user interfaces (GUIs), generally called *desktop environments*. These include GNOME, KDE, Cinnamon, and MATE. Unlike with Windows and macOS, you can swap Linux desktop environments or even install more than one on the same system. However, like nuclear fusion, the "year of the Linux desktop" is perpetually just around the corner. Especially on servers, the CLI is king.

In addition to being rich in distributions and desktop environments, Linux has many shells, including the Bourne Shell (sh), Bourne Again Shell (Bash), C shell, KornShell, and Zsh. Thankfully, you don't have to learn all their intricacies unless you want to. Bash is almost universally the default shell in Linux. Like PowerShell, Bash is very robust. It supports command history, tab completion, scripting, and more. Unlike PowerShell, it wasn't designed for consistency from the ground up. The names and syntaxes of commands are more variable and reflect UNIX-like operating systems' long and storied history. In addition, unlike Windows, Linux is case-sensitive (so that, for example, cat.txt and Cat.txt are two separate files). Put simply: There is a learning curve to Bash and Linux. The learning curve is worth scaling, however. There may be graphical tools to administer different components of Linux systems, but in many cases, there aren't. As your fluency in Bash grows, you'll probably find working with the CLI more efficient than using the GUI. Given Linux's pervasiveness in the GUI-less realm of servers, getting comfortable with Bash is recommended.

The Bash prompt provides several important pieces of information. Its prompt is customizable and varies slightly across distributions, but the default components are predictable. They tell you which user you are, the host you're on, and your current directory. Finally, a single character is appended to the prompt to indicate whether you're running with standard or root (administrative) privileges. A dollar sign ($) is present in user sessions, and a pound sign (#) tells you that you're logged in as root. Figure 9-9 show a typical Bash prompt. The user in this example starts as a normal user ("student"), as indicated by a dollar sign appended to the prompt. After they switch to being the root user with **su**, the dollar sign changes to a pound sign. (You'll learn about elevating privileges by becoming the root user in a moment.)

```
● ● ●   ⌥⌘1              student@redhat1              ⌘1
[student@redhat1 Documents]$ whoami
student
[student@redhat1 Documents]$ su
Password:
[root@redhat1 Documents]# whoami
root
[root@redhat1 Documents]#
```

Figure 9-9 *The Bash Prompt*

Understanding whether you're running with elevated permissions is important. Next, we'll look at how you can become root to perform administrative tasks.

One of the most important parts of working with Bash (or any other shell) is elevating permissions. Normal users cannot, for instance, modify firewall rules, install applications, or modify certain configuration files. You can assume administrative (or root privileges) in three ways:

- **Log in as the root user:** If you log in as root, you don't have to worry about permissions because there are few limits on what the root user can do. However, this approach is strongly discouraged. Best practice dictates that you elevate your privileges as needed. Lingering as the root user can cause major damage if you make a minor typo or inadvertently run a malicious program.

- **Log in as a normal user and switch users to root:** If you know the root user's password, you can use the **su** command to switch to the root user and perform tasks with elevated privileges. The **su** ("switch user") command enables you to log in to other accounts, if they are specified and root if no other accounts are specified. Using **su** is subject to the same issues as simply logging in as root: You'll wield expansive privileges until you switch back to operating as a standard user.

- **Log in as a normal user and execute commands with the sudo command:** sudo is the preferred approach. Prepending commands with **sudo** enables you to run them with root privileges—but only for the duration of the command. Each time you need to elevate permissions, you must include **sudo**. One benefit of using **sudo** is that you do not linger as the root user. Another major advantage is that, unlike with the previous two methods, all **sudo** commands are logged. An audit trail records users' actions (see Figure 9-10). Not all users can invoke **sudo**. By default, you must be a member of the **sudo** group on Debian systems or the **wheel** group on Red Hat systems.

9

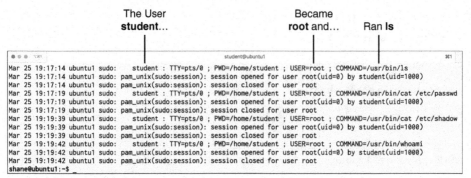

Figure 9-10   sudo *Usage Is Recorded and Allows You to Audit User Activities*

Linux Permissions

Linux's approach is clean and simple compared to NTFS's granular (but slightly complicated) permissions system. In Linux, there are three principals (users or groups of users), and each principal can have three permissions. The principals used in Linux are user, group, and others. Table 9-8 describes each of them.

Table 9-8   Principals Used by Linux File System Permissions

Ownership	Description
User (u)	User (owner) associated with a file
Group (g)	Group associated with a file
Others (o)	Everyone else on the system

Each principal (user, group, and others) has permissions dictating what it can (or can't) do. These are read, write, and execute. So, there are nine basic permissions in Linux: three per principal. Table 9-9 summarizes the available permissions. Note that they have different meanings when applied to files or directories.

Table 9-9   Permissions Used by Linux File System Permissions

Permission	Description
Read (r)	Read file contents.
	List the directory contents.
Write (w)	Edit a file.
	Create or delete files within a directory.
Execute (x)	Execute a file (for example, a script or binary).
	Enter a directory.

Putting all this together, let's dissect the output of **ls -l**. The **ls** command lists the contents of a directory; adding the **-l** flag adds print permissions and other pertinent information (see Figure 9-11).

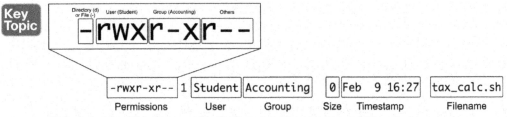

Figure 9-11 *The Output of* **ls -l**, *Showing Ownership and Permissions*

The user associated with tax_calc.sh is Student, and the group is Accounting. Anyone who is not Student or a member of the Accounting group belongs to "others." Now, let's walk through the permissions. The first character indicates whether the object is a file or a directory: Files have dashes, and directories have a d. The next three positions are user permissions, followed by three group permissions, and ending with three permissions for all other principals. Translated to plain English, the output in Figure 9-11 says

- Student can read, write to, and execute the script.

- Members of Accounting can read and execute the script but not modify it.

- Anyone else on the system can only read the script's contents.

SELinux and AppArmor

File system permissions are examples of discretionary access control (DAC). In DAC, the owner of a resource (such as a file or directory) may change its permissions at their discretion. In Figure 9-11, Student has total control over the permissions of tax_calc.sh. This gives the resource owner flexibility but can also be a security issue. Imagine if Student solves an "Access Denied" issue by allowing read, write, and execute across the board. It would be open season: Anyone could tamper with and execute the script.

DAC's weaknesses can be attenuated by employing a complementary system called mandatory access control (MAC). MAC allows administrators to define access policies that users cannot override. It can restrict which users or services can access specific directories, the TCP or UDP ports that services bind to, and how system components are allowed to interact. MAC and DAC policies are additive: Principals must be permitted by both to take certain actions. Thus, even with worryingly lax file system permissions, a restrictive MAC policy can protect tax_calc.sh.

There are two common MAC implementations for Linux: SELinux and AppArmor.

SELinux

SELinux is a security module that began as a U.S. National Security Agency (NSA) project. The NSA works with highly classified information and requires far more access control than DAC provides. It developed SELinux to meet its needs. SELinux assigns labels to many system objects (for example, users, network ports, directories, processes, and hardware). Actions are allowed or denied based on the SELinux policy. Here are a few examples of SELinux in action:

- The SSH daemon (sshd) can only bind to port 22 by default. To move SSH to port 2222, you must add it to the ssh_port_t type.

- The Apache webserver (httpd) can access files labeled as httpd_sys_content_t. However, it cannot access the /etc/passwd file, which contains user information, because /etc/passwd is labeled passwd_file_t.

- A user account labeled user_u cannot elevate permissions with **su** or **sudo**, but a user account labeled sysadm_u can.

This is only a very basic introduction to SELinux, which has capabilities far beyond what we have discussed here. Highly sensitive environments, for instance, can utilize SELinux's multilevel security functionality to restrict data flow between classification levels. For example, SELinux can block a user with Top Secret clearance from writing to an unclassified file in order to prevent accidental disclosure of sensitive information.

AppArmor

AppArmor is a MAC module that is currently maintained by Canonical, the publisher of Ubuntu. Compared to SELinux, which has a comprehensive and complex labeling and enforcement system, AppArmor is simpler and more intuitive. It applies profiles on a per-program basis. For instance, you can write (or generate) a profile to restrict an application's ability to access the network or to enter specific directories. Unlike SELinux, which blocks everything that's not explicitly allowed, AppArmor enforces profiles only when they're applied to specific programs. AppArmor is generally more straightforward and targeted than SELinux.

dm-crypt and LUKS

Linux systems support disk encryption using two complementary tools: dm-crypt and LUKS. The dm-crypt component is a Linux subsystem that provides encryption functionality for block storage devices. It is a low-level module—and not something you'd want to manage directly. Linux Unified Key Setup (LUKS) is a popular tool that utilizes and expands on dm-crypt. LUKS uses a special header that supports multiple decryption keys and simplifies key rotation.

There are approaches to applying LUKS to disks and partitions after the fact (that is, after operating system installation), but they can be tedious and involved. In most situations, encryption is configured during Linux installation. Most distributions' installers support this, although you must explicitly enable it during the disk partitioning phase.

Sometimes, you may not want to encrypt an entire operating system installation. For instance, you may encrypt and mount a separate partition to store sensitive documents. However, remember that, in any operating system, selective disk encryption can expose data. Consider Linux's swap partition, a portion of the disk set aside as an overflow area for RAM. If the system's memory is at capacity, Linux may write some of the less-accessed data in memory to the swap partition to free up capacity. Nothing prevents sensitive data from being shuffled from RAM to unencrypted swap space. For this reason, best practice is to encrypt everything.

Updates: yum, dnf, and apt

As previously stated, one of the major differences between different Linux distribution families is which package manager they use. Three common package managers are **yum** and **dnf** (for Red Hat distributions) and **apt** (for Debian and Ubuntu distributions). If you are new to Linux, this may seem complex, but it isn't. Package managers are one of the joys of using Linux. The command syntaxes are similar (or identical) between these tools, although they operate differently under the hood. You can also use package managers for nearly all updates: operating system, application, drivers, and so on. Unlike in Windows, where you update the OS in one place and update applications all over the place, Linux package managers provide a one-stop shop for maintaining a system.

Red Hat distributions such as RHEL, Rocky Linux, CentOS, and Fedora use **yum** and **dnf**. Their syntax is identical, although **dnf** has some performance and simplicity improvements. You will generally see **yum** on older versions of Red Hat distributions and **dnf** on more recent releases. In Debian and Ubuntu distributions, **apt** is the default package manager. Its syntax is similar but not identical to that of **yum** and **dnf**. Table 9-10 compares some equivalent commands. An important distinction between **yum**, **dnf**, and **apt** is shown in the "Update system" and "Install Apache" rows of this table. **yum** and **dnf** automatically check which packages are available from online repositories, so updates and installations are performed with a single command. **apt** requires an additional step. You must first run **apt update** to check what's new in available repositories. Then you can upgrade the system or install packages. Omitting **apt update** may result in out-of-date packages being installed.

Table 9-10   Comparing Package Managers

Task	yum/dnf Commands	apt Commands
Update system	yum update dnf upgrade	apt update apt upgrade
Install Apache	yum install httpd dnf install httpd	apt update apt install apache2
Remove Apache	yum remove httpd dnf remove httpd	apt remove apache2

Linux Logs

What log files are present in a Linux system depends on its distribution, installed packages, and how you configure logging. However, log files are generally stored in the same location (/var/log/) as simple text files. Finding, searching, and analyzing Linux log data is relatively easy using built-in commands. Table 9-11 provides an overview of important log files. Apache web server logs, shown in Figure 9-12, are a good example of how log files are arranged.

Table 9-11   Linux Log Files by Family

Purpose	Red Hat Files	Debian/Ubuntu Files
Authentication	/var/log/secure	/var/log/auth.log
General messages	/var/log/messages	/var/log/syslog
MAC (SELinux/AppArmor)	/var/log/audit/audit.log	/var/log/syslog
Apache web server logs	/var/log/httpd/	/var/log/apache2/

9

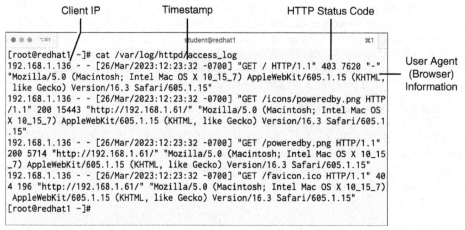

Figure 9-12   *Reading Apache Web Server Logs*

Their layouts may differ somewhat, but log files typically contain the following information:

- A timestamp

- The user or system that invoked a command or made a request

- The command or action taken

- The resource acted upon

- A description or additional information

When I introduced Linux logs, I described finding, searching, and analyzing data as "relatively easy." This is true for those familiar with Linux, but what if it's a brand-new world for you? Some fundamental tools for working with text files (including logs) in Linux are **cat**, **head**, **tail**, and **grep**:

- **cat** displays the contents of all files you specify. **cat file1** prints out the contents of file1. **cat file1 file2** prints out the contents of both file1 and file2. On its own, **cat** can produce far too much output. For instance, **cat /var/log/syslog** may spew out thousands of log entries simultaneously.

- **head**, by default, prints the first 10 lines of a file or the number of lines you specify with the **-n** flag. For example, **head audit.log** shows the first 10 lines of this file, and **head -n 25 audit.log** outputs the first 25 lines. This is handy in some scenarios, but because log files fill up chronologically, you'll use its sibling command, **tail**, more often.

- **tail**, the inverse of the **head** command, prints out the last 10 lines of a file unless otherwise specified. In log files, these would be the 10 most recent entries. It also supports the **-n** flag, so, for example, **tail -n 500 audit.log** will display the 500 most recent SELinux entries. You can also use **tail -f** to view new lines as they are appended to a file.

- **grep** enables you to search for specific text patterns in a file. Any line containing the text pattern is printed to the screen. This command can search for literal strings or use a matching language called regex (regular expressions). You will often use **grep** with one of the previously mentioned commands and the pipe operator (|) to redirect one command's output to the input of the next command. For instance, you might run **tail -n 2500 audit.log | grep "sudo"** to collect the last 2500 lines of the file and search for **sudo** in those lines. Depending on the size of your logs, you may need to get more specific than this.

macOS

Apple's macOS is a Unix operating system that has many similarities to Linux under the hood.

Firewall

Like Windows and Linux operating systems, macOS has a built-in host firewall. Under the hood, macOS uses pf (packet filter), a powerful firewall commonly used by other BSD distributions. The pf firewall is robust and configurable, but full coverage of it is beyond the scope of the CCST Cybersecurity certification. At a minimum, you'll want to ensure that the firewall is enabled on macOS. Depending on the version of macOS, this is accomplished in System Settings, under Network or Security & Privacy. You can also choose to enable additional security settings, such as the ones explained Table 9-12 and shown in Figure 9-13.

Table 9-12   Basic macOS pf Settings

Setting	Description
Block All Incoming Connections	Restricts incoming connections to those required for basic connectivity.
Enable Stealth Mode	Prevents the device from responding to ICMP echo requests.
Service List	Allows or blocks connections on a service-by-service basis.
Automatically Allow Built-in Software to Receive Incoming Connections	Enables programs and services packaged with the operating system to receive inbound traffic.
Automatically Allow Downloaded Signed Software to Receive Incoming Connections	Enables applications with trusted digital signatures to receive inbound connections.

9

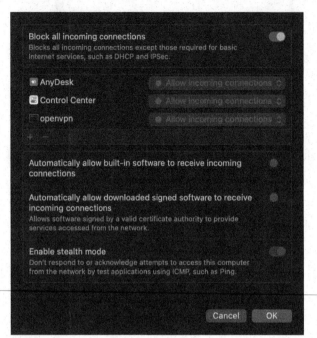

Figure 9-13 *Firewall Settings in macOS Ventura 13*

Zsh

The default shell on macOS was Bash for years, but Apple recently replaced it with Zsh (possibly for licensing reasons). If you are familiar with Bash, you'll feel comfortable with Zsh. They are mostly compatible, and commands work the same way. Most differences between them are in advanced features (such as scripting syntax), glob qualifiers to match files with specific characteristics, and wildcard patterns to match filenames. These are worth investigating if you frequently work with Zsh or macOS, but you won't see them on the CCST Cybersecurity exam. One of the most noticeable changes is in the final prompt character indicating whether you are a standard user or root. In Bash, standard users are tagged with a dollar sign; in Zsh, they have a percent sign (%). Both environments, however, display a pound sign if you are root.

APFS Permissions

macOS's Apple File System (APFS) is already familiar to you. That is because, like Linux's file systems, APFS uses standard Unix file system permissions. Each file or directory has an associated user and group, and read, write, or execute permissions are assigned to the user, group, and everyone else. You can use the **ls -l** command to view permissions, although you may notice a few differences in the output. Specifically, permissions may be marked with @ or + to indicate that more information is available:

- An @ appended to the permissions string indicates that extended attributes are applied to the object. These commonly contain type information for file system objects.

- A + appended to the permissions string indicates that a file system access control list (FACL) is applied to the object. FACLs can be applied to improve the granularity of permissions. For instance, some files in your home directory will have FACLs denying the group "everyone" the ability to delete objects.

FileVault

FileVault, which is technically FileVault 2, is Apple's built-in full-disk encryption technology. You enable FileVault in the System Settings app under Security & Privacy. When toggled on, it transparently encrypts your disk contents in the background, and you can continue to use your computer. It is important to note that, as with all other FDE technologies, you should store the provided recovery key in a secure location locally or in iCloud. If you lose both the login password and recovery key, your data is also lost.

Updates

In macOS, you manage updates in a few places. For applications you've installed via the App Store, you can browse to the App Store Updates tab to check whether any newer versions are available. Applications installed from other sources, such as those downloaded from vendors' websites, often have built-in update mechanisms. However, you may need to manually check for updates in some cases. Finally, operating system updates can be checked and installed via the System Settings application, under Software Update (see Figure 9-14). The Software Update utility applies global updates, including operating system patches, drivers, and firmware. You may also enable automatic updates to ensure that your system remains current with minimal interaction.

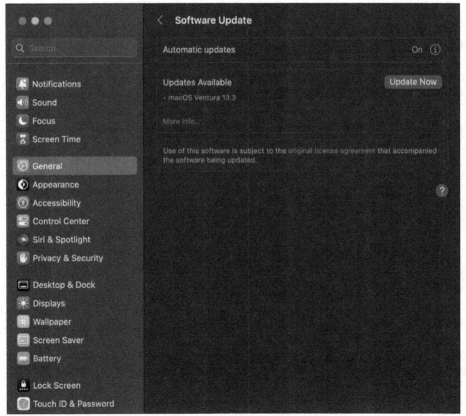

Figure 9-14 *Updating macOS*

macOS Logs: Console

You can access macOS logs directly by navigating to their file system location or by using the Console tool for convenience. The Console tool has two sections, which you can find along the left-hand panel of the window. The first section, Devices, allows you to monitor log entries for your computer or other connected devices. Select the computer name (such as Student's MacBook Pro) and then click Start to begin collecting log data. By default, all messages being generated are shown. To reduce the volume of output, you might apply filter conditions. For example, you may decide to display only errors and faults. The second section, Reports, gives you access to crash, diagnostic, analytic, and other information. It also enables you to view specific log files. The Log Reports option is a good place to explore. These are some of the most security-relevant log files:

- ppp.log, which includes VPN logs

- access.log, which records traffic, including HTTP requests

- appfirewall.log, which records firewall activity

Console provides a convenient interface for searching and organizing log data, but you can also open files directly. Most macOS log files are in /private/var/log.

Tools

A discussion of endpoint operating systems and security wouldn't be complete without an explanation of some useful network security utilities. Commands and their syntax may vary between operating systems, but these tools fall into distinct categories:

- **netstat** and **ss** help uncover connections, listeners, interface statistics, and other data.

- **nslookup** and **dig** are excellent tools for testing and analyzing DNS.

- **tcpdump** and Wireshark are used to capture and analyze network traffic.

- Syslog is a standard or a protocol that you can use to centrally aggregate log data from many hosts and network devices, enhancing visibility into a network.

netstat and ss

As you might have gleaned from its name, **netstat** is a tool for viewing network statistics. It enables you to view per-protocol statistics, enumerate active connections and listeners, and identify the executable or process identifier (PID) of an application that is using the network. netstat's syntax differs somewhat between Windows and "Unixy" operating systems, such as macOS and Linux. Table 9-13 compares how the same tasks can be accomplished in Windows and macOS.

Key Topic

Table 9-13 The **netstat** Command

Task	Windows Command	Linux Command
List all sockets.	netstat -a	netstat -a
List TCP sockets.	netstat -p tcp	netstat -t
List UDP sockets.	netstat -p udp	netstat -u
List sockets and the associated processes.	netstat -o	netstat -p

netstat's output is formatted as a set of columns, as shown in Figure 9-15. Some columns are self-explanatory. The Proto (protocol) column tells you which protocol is used (for example, TCP or UDP). The Local Address and Foreign Address columns list IP addresses and port numbers for each side of the connection. Finally, the State column tells the status of each connection. Connection states bear some additional explanation:

- **LISTENING:** The socket is waiting for a connection.

- **ESTABLISHED:** A connection has been established.

- **CLOSE_WAIT:** The connection is currently being torn down.

- **CLOSED:** The connection is closed.

```
student@ubuntu1:~$ netstat -l
Active Internet connections (only servers)
Proto Recv-Q Send-Q Local Address            Foreign Address         State
tcp        0      0 localhost:domain         0.0.0.0:*               LISTEN
tcp        0      0 0.0.0.0:ssh              0.0.0.0:*               LISTEN
tcp6       0      0 [::]:ssh                 [::]:*                  LISTEN
tcp6       0      0 [::]:http                [::]:*                  LISTEN
udp        0      0 localhost:domain         0.0.0.0:*
udp        0      0 rocky-server-2.s:bootpc  0.0.0.0:*
raw6       0      0 [::]:ipv6-icmp           [::]:*                  7
```

Figure 9-15 *The Output of* **netstat -l,** *Which Lists Listening Ports*

The CCST Cybersecurity objectives mention only **netstat**, but you'll also see the **ss** ("socket statistics") tool. **netstat** has been deprecated on most Linux systems in favor of **ss** because **ss** is faster and more detailed than **netstat**. The syntax of **ss** is similar to that of **netstat.** Table 9-14 provides some examples.

Table 9-14   The **ss** Command

Task	Command
List all sockets.	**ss -a**
List TCP sockets.	**ss -at**
List UDP sockets.	**ss -au**
List sockets and the associated processes.	**ss -p**

nslookup and dig

There is a grain of truth to the adage that "it's always DNS." DNS issues are a common source of degraded network connectivity, and attackers may abuse DNS to redirect traffic to malicious servers. Let's discuss two useful tools for analyzing DNS records: **nslookup** and **dig.**

nslookup

nslookup is available on Windows, macOS, and Linux (though, depending on the distribution, it may need installation). In its simplest form, **nslookup** queries a DNS server for the name you specify and then prints out the IP address(es). Conversely, you can provide an IP address to find a name. **nslookup** also enables you to specify the DNS server to query, which can be useful for examining DNS records on specific DNS servers. Table 9-15 provides some examples of **nslookup** commands.

Table 9-15   nslookup Commands

Command	Description
nslookup cisco.com	Query the default DNS server for cisco.com's IP addresses.
nslookup cisco.com 208.67.222.222	Query a specific DNS server (208.67.222.222) for cisco.com's IP addresses.
nslookup -type=a cisco.com	Query for cisco.com A records (IPv4 addresses).
nslookup -type=mx cisco.com 208.67.222.222	Query a specific DNS server (208.67.222.222) for cisco.com's MX records (mail servers).

dig

dig is like **nslookup** in functionality: It enables you to review DNS records. It is commonly used on Unix and Linux systems and provides more capabilities than nslookup. By default, its output is more verbose than **nslookup**'s, and it includes information about the DNS query, the corresponding answer, and various statistics. Table 9-16 shows the **dig** commands that correspond to the **nslookup** commands in Table 9-15.

Table 9-16   The dig Command

Command	Description
dig cisco.com	Query the default DNS server for cisco.com's IP addresses.
dig @208.67.222.222 cisco.com	Query a specific DNS server (208.67.222.222) for cisco.com's IP addresses.
dig cisco.com a	Query for cisco.com A records (IPv4 addresses).
dig @208.67.222.222 cisco.com mx	Query a specific DNS server (208.67.222.222) for cisco.com's MX records (mail servers).

tcpdump and Wireshark

Capturing, storing, and analyzing network traffic is incredibly useful for cybersecurity professionals. **tcpdump** is a command-line tool that allows you to record all traffic (or specific traffic you choose) traversing a NIC. Depending on your needs, you may print this information to the screen or store it in a **packet capture (PCAP)** file. Wireshark also allows you to sniff network traffic, but it provides a powerful GUI for filtering and dissecting the collected data. On CLI operating systems, such as many Linux servers, you might use **tcpdump** to capture traffic and then send the file to another system for analysis with Wireshark.

tcpdump

Like many other topics in CCST Cybersecurity, **tcpdump** could fill a book. Thankfully, a basic understanding of its usage will prepare you for the exam. First, and crucially, **tcpdump** requires unhindered access to the NICs it sniffs: You must run **tcpdump** with root privileges. Remember that the preferred way to elevate your privileges in Linux is with the **sudo** command. If you are using a **tcpdump** clone for Windows, ensure that it's launched from an administrative command prompt. You can begin capturing traffic from an interface by using the **-i** flag followed by the interface name. The default behavior of **tcpdump** is to output packets to the screen in real time. This can be useful, but you'll commonly want to save the information to a file. You can do so with the **-w** flag.

When capturing traffic, you might get overwhelmed by the volume of information that **tcp-dump** spews out. Most of the time, our systems are quite talkative! Consider using capture filters whenever possible to tell **tcpdump** "I want to capture only this specific traffic." In this way, you can reduce the size of the output (or file), which makes analysis easier later. Table 9-17 provides examples of **tcpdump** commands and what they accomplish. Note that **tcpdump** supports "and" and "or" conditions, as displayed in the last two rows.

Key Topic

Table 9-17   The **tcpdump** Command (Remember to Elevate Privileges)

Command	Description
tcpdump -i ens18	Capture traffic on the ens18 interface and print to the screen.
tcpdump -i ens18 -w traffic.pcap	Capture traffic on the ens18 interface and save it to traffic.pcap file.
tcpdump -i ens18 host 208.67.222.222	Capture traffic to or from 208.67.222.222 on ens18.
tcpdump -i ens18 tcp port 80	Capture TCP port 80 traffic on ens18.
tcpdump -i ens18 tcp dst port 80 and dst 10.0.0.5	Capture only TCP traffic to host 10.0.0.5 port 80 on ens18.
tcpdump -i ens18 tcp dst port 80 or tcp dst port 443	Capture HTTP or HTTPS traffic to web servers on ens18.

Wireshark

Wireshark provides traffic-capturing capabilities, complemented by a highly customizable GUI that you can tailor to suit your needs. When you open Wireshark, you see a list of interfaces you may capture from. After you initiate a packet capture, Wireshark displays a three-paned interface for analyzing the collected traffic (see Figure 9-16).

As with **tcpdump**, applying filters can make your life much easier. Unlike **tcpdump**, Wireshark has two kinds of filters with different syntaxes:

- **Capture filters:** These filters are applied before you begin a packet capture. They use the same syntax as the **tcpdump** filters covered earlier. Only traffic that matches the capture filter is stored in memory, and the rest is discarded. Capture filters reduce RAM consumption and PCAP size and limit your dataset to relevant traffic.

- **Display filters:** These filters don't affect which traffic is captured or stored. They simply dictate which traffic Wireshark shows. You can apply display filters during or after a capture and remove them at any time to show the entire contents. Display filters tease out and analyze specific threads within the larger dataset.

9

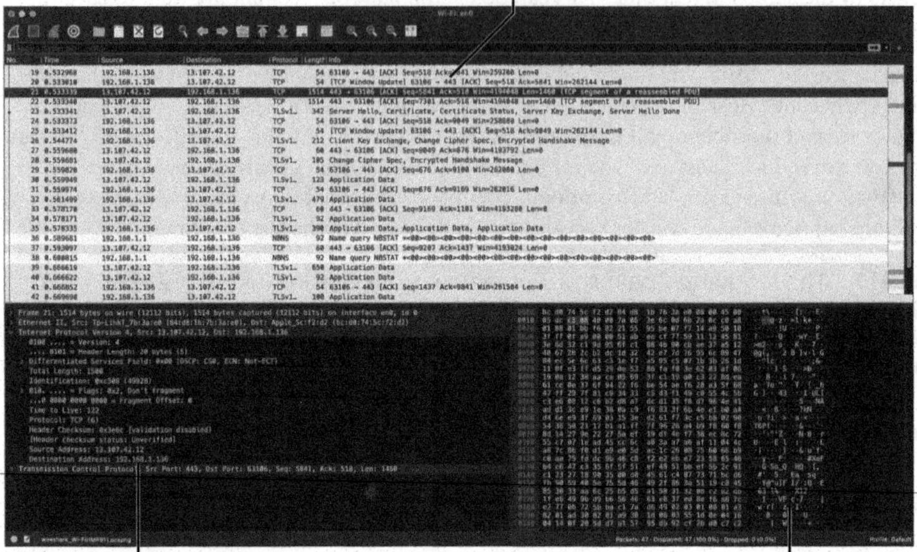

The **packet list** pane provides
a list of all captured packets.

The **packet details** pane displays
information about each network
layer of the selected packet.

The **packet bytes** pane displays
raw packet bytes as hexadecimal.

Figure 9-16 *Wireshark Panes*

syslog

Syslog is a common means of formatting and transmitting log messages. It may be used
locally, internal to a host, or sent to a collector on the network. Although syslog has been
around since the 1980s, it was only formally standardized in 2009. For this reason, you may
occasionally see slight variations in its formatting and implementation. Several core components of syslog messages are worth detailing:

- Timestamps indicate when systems generated each log entry. When aggregating logs
  from many systems, it is vital to ensure that their clocks are synchronized (for example, with NTP) to avoid time offsets when viewing logs.

- Device IDs, such as host names or IP addresses, identify which system generated the
  log entries.

- Facilities indicate which service or system component a message pertains to. The
  available facilities depend on the type of endpoint or appliance generating the log
  messages.

- Severity values range from 0 to 7. A value of 0 is an emergency, and 7 indicates verbose debugging entries. Table 9-18 explains the syslog levels.

- Messages describe the event that occurred.

Key Topic

Table 9-18 Syslog Levels

Level	Name	Description
0	Emergency	A system is not functioning or usable.
1	Alert	An event requires an immediate response.
2	Critical	An event needs a response.
3	Error	A system remains up, but something is degrading its functionality.
4	Warning	A more severe event may occur.
5	Notice	Regular but important events are occurring.
6	Informational	Routine events are occurring.
7	Debug	Verbose details about system operation are provided.

In addition to defining the formatting of log messages, syslog is a network protocol for transmitting them. It uses a client/server architecture, where the hosts generating logging information transmit that information to a syslog server, where the information is centrally stored. Using a syslog server can be very helpful to IT professionals because it provides a single repository of log data for many devices. It simplifies monitoring, searching, and analysis of events on a network. Syslog data is commonly transmitted unencrypted over UDP port 514. Being plaintext, this data may be a juicy source of information for eavesdroppers! It's worth considering implementing additional controls, such as transmitting syslog messages in a separate VLAN or wrapping the traffic in SSL/TLS encryption.

Summary

Endpoint operating systems have a constellation of administrative tools and security mechanisms. Some, like Windows Defender and SELinux, are unique to their operating systems. Most are variations on similar themes:

- **Host-based firewalls** restrict inbound or outbound traffic on individual systems.
    - **Windows** uses Windows Defender Firewall.
    - **Linux** uses firewalld or UFW as front ends to nftables.
    - **macOS** uses Firewall as a front end to pf.
- **Command-line interfaces (CLIs)** allow you to interact with systems textually.
    - **Windows** offers CMD and PowerShell.
    - **Linux** most often uses Bash.
    - **macOS** uses Zsh.
- **Full-disk encryption (FDE)** encrypts all data written to storage devices.
    - **Windows** uses BitLocker.
    - **Linux** provides dm-crypt/LUKS.
    - **macOS** integrates FileVault 2.

9

- **Updates** remediate bugs and vulnerabilities as they are discovered.

    - **Windows** has Windows Update (and per-application updates).

    - **Linux** uses package managers such as **dnf** or **yum**.

    - **macOS** provides the App Store and Software Update utility.

- **Logs** record events occurring on a host.

    - **Windows** provides Event Viewer.

    - **Linux** stores logs as text files in /var/log/.

    - **macOS** offers the Console utility.

Exam Preparation Tasks

As mentioned in the Introduction, you can customize your strategy for exam preparation. Suggested tasks include the exercises here, Chapter 16, "Final Preparation," and the exam simulation questions on the companion website.

Review All Key Topics

Review the most important topics in this chapter, noted with the Key Topics icon in the outer margin of the page. Table 9-19 lists these key topics and the page number on which each is found.

Key Topic

Table 9-19   Key Topics for Chapter 9

Key Topic Element	Description	Page Number
Paragraph	Privilege escalation	170
Paragraph	Full-disk encryption (FDE)	172
Table 9-6	Windows Event Viewer Log Categories	174
Figure 9-11	The Output of **ls -l**, Showing Ownership and Permissions	179
Table 9-13	The **netstat** Command	186
Table 9-15	**nslookup** Commands	188
Table 9-17	The **tcpdump** Command (Remember to Elevate Privileges)	189
Table 9-18	Syslog Levels	191

Complete Tables and Lists from Memory

Print a copy of Appendix B, "Memory Tables," found on the companion website, or at least the section for this chapter, and complete the tables and lists from memory. Appendix C, "Memory Tables Answer Key," includes completed tables and lists you can use to check your work.

Define Key Terms

Define the following key terms from this chapter and check your answers in the glossary:

host-based firewall, file system permissions, full disk encryption (FDE), Defender, CMD, PowerShell, privilege escalation, BitLocker, Event Viewer, FileVault, **netstat**, **nslookup**, packet capture (PCAP), **tcpdump**, syslog

Review Questions

1. Which command lists network connections, listening ports, and protocol statistics?
   a. nslookup
   b. netstat
   c. tcpdump
   d. Wireshark

2. BitLocker, FileVault 2, and LUKS are all examples of what security technology?
   a. Host-based firewall
   b. Protocol encryption
   c. FDE
   d. File system permissions

3. What is the difference between a syslog error and a syslog warning?
   a. A syslog error is a possible issue, and a syslog warning is an actual issue.
   b. A syslog error is an actual issue, and a syslog warning is a possible issue.
   c. A syslog error is a complete system outage, and a syslog warning is a partial outage.
   d. A syslog error is a partial system outage, and a syslog warning is a complete outage.

4. What command tests DNS requests and responses?
   a. tcpdump
   b. dnf
   c. name
   d. nslookup

5. What Linux tool enables you to execute single commands with elevated privileges?
   a. sudo
   b. su
   c. dnf
   d. root

6. Which of the following are major log categories in Event Viewer? (Choose three.)
   a. System
   b. Application
   c. Defender
   d. Security

9

7. After running **ls -l**, you see that a file has the permissions -rwxr-----. What permissions does the owner have in this case?

   a. r

   b. rw

   c. rwx

   d. No permissions

8. Which of the following utilities generate PCAP files? (Choose two.)

   a. ezcappr

   b. tcpdump

   c. deeptap

   d. Wireshark

9. Which of the following is the largest potential pitfall of automatic updates?

   a. The updates may be applied too slowly.

   b. The updates may be missed if the system isn't online during the update window.

   c. The updates may unintentionally break things.

   d. The updates may slow down systems while they're in use.

10. Which of the following operating systems offers a unified OS and application update utility?

   a. Windows

   b. Linux

   c. macOS

   d. None of these

CHAPTER 10

Endpoint Policies and Standards

This chapter covers the following topics:

- **Asset Management:** This section discusses the importance of tracking devices and maintaining inventories for cybersecurity professionals.

- **Program Deployment:** This section discusses manual and automated methods for deploying programs to endpoints.

- **Backups:** This section discusses classification of backups based on their locations and how they function.

- **Bring Your Own Device (BYOD):** This section discusses the benefits and drawbacks of BYOD, implementation considerations, and supporting management tools.

- **Regulatory Compliance:** This section discusses the relevance of PCI-DSS, HIPAA, and GDPR to endpoint security

Networks make little sense without the endpoints that communicate across them, and without endpoint security, network security is just a nice thought. Numerous tools and techniques help us keep endpoints secure. Inventories and asset management improve visibility into our environments. Mobile device management (MDM) and other tools help us enforce security policies on disparate devices (which we may not even own). The topics in this chapter center around how we can keep endpoints aligned with internal policies and compliant with certain standards and regulations.

This chapter covers information related to the following Cisco Certified Support Technician (CCST) Cybersecurity exam objective:

3.3. Verify that endpoint systems meet security policies and standards.

"Do I Know This Already?" Quiz

The "Do I Know This Already?" quiz allows you to assess whether you should read this entire chapter thoroughly or jump to the "Exam Preparation Tasks" section. If you are in doubt about your answers to these questions or your own assessment of your knowledge of the topics, read the entire chapter. Table 10-1 lists the major headings in this chapter and their corresponding "Do I Know This Already?" quiz questions. You can find the answers in Appendix A, "Answers to the 'Do I Know This Already?' Quizzes and Review Questions."

Table 10-1 "Do I Know This Already?" Section-to-Question Mapping

Foundation Topics Section	Questions
Asset Management	1
Program Deployment	2
Backups	3

Foundation Topics Section	Questions
Bring Your Own Device (BYOD)	4
Regulatory Compliance	5

CAUTION The goal of self-assessment is to gauge your mastery of the topics in this chapter. If you do not know the answer to a question or are only partially sure of the answer, you should mark that question incorrect for purposes of self-assessment. Giving yourself credit for an answer you correctly guess skews your self-assessment results and might provide you with a false sense of security.

1. Which of the following are endpoints? (Choose two.)
   a. Server
   b. Switch
   c. Firewall
   d. Workstation

2. Which of the following is a Windows-specific tool that can be used for program deployment?
   a. Intune
   b. GPO
   c. ManageEngine
   d. MaaS360

3. Which backup strategy is appropriate if you're concerned about natural disasters?
   a. Full
   b. Remote
   c. Local
   d. Differential

4. Which of the following operating systems support full disk encryption? (Choose three.)
   a. Android
   b. macOS
   c. iOS
   d. Windows 10 Home

5. Which standard or regulation specifically requires "data protection by design and by default"?
   a. PCI-DSS
   b. HIPAA
   c. GDPR
   d. FISMA

Foundation Topics

Asset Management

In recent years, networks have supported increasingly motley crews of endpoint systems. **Endpoints** are devices that connect to a network. They can include workstations, laptops, mobile devices, and servers. They use different processor architectures and operating systems and provide varied management features. To add to the confusion, many environments have a mishmash of corporate and personal devices that come and go with employees. In all the hustle and bustle of modern networks, asset management has become an essential process for cybersecurity.

Asset management is the process of deploying, maintaining, and decommissioning IT resources and tracking assets throughout their lifecycle. An asset is anything of value to an organization, although this chapter is focused on hardware and software. It may initially seem to be a bland managerial concern, but asset management imparts several security benefits, including the following:

- **Improved visibility:** Visibility enables you to know what is and isn't on a network.

- **System maintenance:** It is important to ensure that all assets are updated with the latest security patches.

- **Asset prioritization:** A complete picture of assets is the first step in evaluating system priorities and choosing security controls.

- **Better auditing and detection:** A centralized asset database provides an accurate corporate network baseline. It simplifies the process of finding unapproved devices or distinguishing between personal and company devices.

- **Legal exposure:** Asset inventories help you keep up with licensing and avoid fines or lawsuits.

Theoretically, you could track assets in a notebook or spreadsheet, but better options are available. Asset management software enables you to keep track of assets throughout their lifecycle. With this software, related assets, such as a workstation and its software, can be linked. Assets can be labeled with bar or QR codes and tracked, and costs can be accurately evaluated.

Regardless of the approach, maintaining hardware and software inventories simplifies life for cybersecurity professionals. Consider performing the following security activities with and without an accurate inventory of hardware and software:

- **Vulnerability management:** Vulnerability scanners can't see all software on the network, and they are not perfectly reliable at determining software versions. An updated list of software and versions can be quickly consulted to find vulnerabilities in your systems.

- **Incident response:** Detecting, containing, and eradicating incidents is complicated without an accurate picture of your assets. Conversely, a full asset inventory prevents oversights in the incident response process.

■ **Risk assessment:** You can't measure risk for hardware or software you aren't aware of. Asset inventories can expedite the identification and prioritization of risks.

Program Deployment

Installing and updating software on endpoints can be accomplished using manual or automated mechanisms. In a manual approach, software installers are downloaded and run one system at a time. Windows users click through installation wizards, Apple macOS users open the App Store, and Linux users employ package managers. Manually installing and updating software can quickly become unwieldy, depending on the number of systems, the variety of platforms, and the software itself. Imagine manually deploying an application on 200 Windows computers—or, worse, a mixed environment of Windows, Linux, and macOS devices. And what happens when the program is updated in a month?

Automated deployment is advantageous because program deployment can be done through platform-specific and cross-platform tools:

■ **Platform-specific tools:** These tools are designed to manage software for specific operating systems. For uniform environments, such as purely Windows offices, these are adequate. A simple example of platform-specific deployment is the use of group policy objects (GPOs) to install applications on domain-joined Windows computers.

■ **Platform-agnostic tools:** These tools can be used for various operating systems. Such a tool can provide a single interface to manage software in a mixed environment. The following management solutions enable cross-platform application deployment (among other things, as we will discuss):

  ■ **Mobile device management (MDM)** solutions include Intune, ManageEngine, MaaS360, and Citrix Endpoint Management. MDM enables administration of mobile devices such as tablets, phones, and laptops but can also be used to manage desktop systems.

  ■ **Remote monitoring and management (RMM)** tools include ConnectWise and Datto RMM. RMM allows IT service providers to configure, update, monitor, and connect to endpoints.

The ability to automatically deploy programs is a significant win for IT workers, but outside of security tools, cybersecurity professionals won't regularly push out new programs. Where MDM, RMM, and related tools shine is in their ability to track and update software. Most management tools inventory software and hardware by default. Therefore, if a vulnerability is discovered in your organization's software, you can quickly determine which systems are affected and run updates on them.

Backups

Backups are alternate copies of data, generally stored on different media and in different locations. If storage devices or data are damaged, having an additional copy of data allows you to recover files. Two considerations when selecting a backup strategy are the backup location and the backup method. Backups can be stored locally or remotely (or both), using full, differential, or incremental methods. You can mix and match backup locations and methods to suit your needs.

10

Local and Remote Backups

Backups can be categorized by whether they're stored locally or remotely:

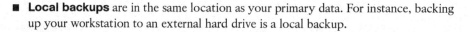

- **Local backups** are in the same location as your primary data. For instance, backing up your workstation to an external hard drive is a local backup.

- **Remote backups** (off-site backups) are stored far away from your primary data. They may be on a server in another geographic region or in cloud data centers.

It's generally best practice to maintain both local and remote backups of your workstations. Table 10-2 shows the strengths and weaknesses of each backup type.

Table 10-2   Local and Remote Backups

Strength or Weakness	Local Backups	Remote Backups
Location	The backup is stored near the primary data.	The backup is stored far away from the primary data.
Speed	You can quickly create and restore from local backups.	It takes more time to create and restore from remote backups.
Disaster resistance	Low: A disaster may destroy both the primary data and the local backup.	High: A disaster that destroys the primary data is unlikely to destroy the remote backup.
Internet dependence	Internet access is not required to create or restore from backups.	Internet access is required to create or restore from most remote backups.

Full, Differential, and Incremental Backups

The precise workings of full, differential, and incremental backups are covered in Chapter 14, "Disaster Recovery and Business Continuity," and this section introduces them in broad strokes. These backup methods differ in their degree of deduplication (avoidance of duplicate data). Full backups perform no deduplication; all data is copied with every backup. In the context of endpoints, where we may need to back up hundreds of devices, full backups aren't always feasible. Keeping seven days of full backups for 100 computers, each with 100 gigabytes of data, requires 70 terabytes of space! A large fraction of that 70 terabytes is duplicate data because many files are rarely modified.

To save space, differential and incremental backups can be created. Both methods use a periodic full backup followed by a series of partial backups. The contents of the partial backups are where differential and incremental backups differ. A differential backup copies any new data since the last full backup. An incremental backup copies any new data since the last full or incremental backup. The logic is shown in Table 10-3.

Table 10-3   Data Copied in Differential and Incremental Backups

Type of Backup	Day 0	Day 1	Day 2	Day 3
Differential	Full	Changes since day 0	Changes since day 0	Changes since day 0
Incremental	Full	Changes since day 0	Changes since day 1	Changes since day 2

Due to their deduplication strategies, differential and incremental backups consume storage at different rates. Differential backups require more space because their reference point is always the last full backup. For instance, data changed on day 1 will be copied in every differential backup until the next full backup. Incremental backups require less space because their reference point is always the previous backup (full or incremental). Data changed on day 1 will not be copied on subsequent days unless it is changed again.

To summarize, full backups require the most space, and incremental backups require the least. When selecting a backup strategy, remember that differential or incremental backups consume less space, require lower network utilization (if used), and tend to complete faster.

Bring Your Own Device (BYOD)

Key Topic

Bring your own device (BYOD) is a policy that allows employees to use their personal devices for work activities. Properly implemented BYOD policies can be beneficial for both employers and employees. Employees can use the devices they're comfortable with, increasing satisfaction and reducing training requirements. Employers benefit from reduced expenses on computer and mobile devices. Improperly implemented BYOD can be a mess, though, and we'll discuss some pitfalls in the "Pros and Cons of BYOD" section.

For now, let's focus on the fundamental facets of BYOD implementation. Three common components are well-defined security policies, mobile device management tools, and ongoing employee training:

- **Well-defined security policies:** Security policies and standards should be defined for BYOD devices. These policies and standards may provide details and guidance about the following controls:

  - Acceptable device access controls (such as PIN, pattern, fingerprint, or Face ID)

  - Storage encryption requirements (for example, some, but not all, devices may have encryption enabled by default)

  - Network encryption requirements (such as IPsec or SSL VPN)

  - Acceptable and unacceptable applications

  - Patching requirements for a mobile OS and applications

  - How personal and professional data is separated

  - Geolocation and remote wipe capabilities

- **Mobile device management (MDM) tools:** MDM software streamlines the management of employees' personal devices. BYOD doesn't require MDM tools, but these tools are beneficial for managing and securing BYOD devices. MDM provides many capabilities:

  - Enforcing security policies and standards (listed previously)

  - Automated deployment of company applications

  - Restrictions on which applications can be installed

10

- Data containerization—the separation of private and company data on the same device, which facilitates remotely wiping of sensitive data if an employee is terminated or their device is lost

- Device geolocation

- **Ongoing employee training:** Employees should be continuously trained to ensure that they maintain proper digital hygiene and protect their BYOD devices. Training can include

  - Security policy awareness training

  - Phishing and social engineering training

  - Password selection training

  - Using VPNs or avoiding use of public Wi-Fi

  - Handling lost and stolen devices

Pros and Cons of BYOD

We've listed some benefits of adopting BYOD, such as employee comfort and satisfaction and employer cost savings. In addition, BYOD can lead to improved productivity (due to user familiarity) and less downtime from jumping between personal and business devices. It also allows employees to use newer technologies. Whereas employers can't justify purchasing the latest laptop or iPhone each year, many employees will. This brings new features and better performance for workers who fork over the money.

BYOD also has downsides. It can be a security risk, particularly without strong security policies and MDM solutions. Employees may choose weak PINs, use public Wi-Fi without VPNs, or install questionable apps. Another concern is device support and compatibility. BYOD devices use different hardware, operating systems, and OS versions. This makes support more complex because IT staff must assist with many different device types. The device variety can also introduce compatibility issues for certain applications. Maintaining compatibility across platforms and OS versions can be difficult for in-house applications. Table 10-4 summarizes some of the benefits and drawbacks of BYOD.

Table 10-4   Benefits and Drawbacks of BYOD

Benefits	Drawbacks
Employee familiarity and satisfaction	Wider variety of devices to support
Improved flexibility and mobility	Compatibility issues
Cost savings for employer	Generally less control over devices
Potentially newer technologies	Legal and privacy concerns

Device and Configuration Management

Cross-platform MDM solutions greatly simplify your life when managing BYOD devices. MDM tools typically involve an agent on endpoints that receives and applies configurations and an on-premises (or cloud) server where configurations are centrally managed and deployed (see Figure 10-1). In order to benefit from MDM, devices must have the appropriate agent and configurations applied to communicate with MDM servers.

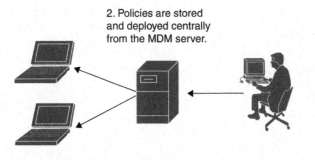

2. Policies are stored and deployed centrally from the MDM server.

3. MDM agents on computers, smartphones, and tablets receive and apply configurations.

1. The administrator defines MDM policies via the server's web interface.

Figure 10-1   *Generic MDM Architecture*

Many features of MDM have already been listed in prior discussions, including the following:

- Asset inventorying and management

- Operating system patch deployment

- Application installation and updates

- Application allow and deny lists

- Access control configuration

- Containerization of data (that is, separation of personal and work data)

- Remote wiping of data for lost or stolen device

- Device geolocation

While MDM is the most familiar management technology for mobile devices, you'll run into several other acronyms, such as MAM, MCM, MEM, and EMM (see Figure 10-2):

- **Mobile application management (MAM)** focuses on configuring and distributing enterprise applications on mobile devices.

- **Mobile content management (MCM)** provides secure access to enterprise data. Data can be distributed, password protected, or remotely wiped.

- **Mobile email management (MEM)** manages the setup and security of email clients.

- **Enterprise mobility management (EMM)** includes MAM, MCM, MDM, and MEM features.

Each of these is analogous to MDM, although their features vary. It's important to note that these categories are ill defined, feature sets are vendor specific, and there's overlap in some functionalities of MDM, MCM, and MEM.

10

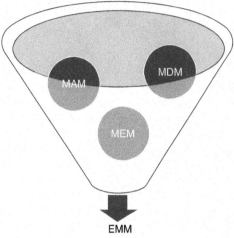

Figure 10-2 *EMM Can Be Seen as Inclusive of MAM, MCM, MDM, and MEM*

Data Encryption

Data encryption can be enforced in two forms on mobile devices: encryption of data at rest and encryption of data in motion. Android, macOS, iOS, and some editions of Windows have built-in data-at-rest (storage) encryption mechanisms. Depending on the operating system and its version, encryption may or may not be enabled by default. One way to encrypt stored data is via built-in configuration and settings utilities. Alternatively, MDM and related utilities can be used to enforce storage encryption for enrolled devices. This route tends to be more efficient and scalable.

Importantly, we must also protect the availability of data. In certain situations, such as with forgotten passwords or corrupted encryption keys, recovering the data on a device may be impossible. It's therefore advised to pair device encryption with regular backups. This ensures that the loss of a key doesn't guarantee the loss of data. Naturally, backups should be shielded with encryption as well!

Data in motion—data traversing a network—can also be encrypted. A large percentage of Internet traffic is already encrypted (such as web traffic over SSL/TLS), but many unencrypted protocols still exist. Mobile devices can be configured to use virtual private networks (VPNs) to prevent eavesdropping and traffic tampering. Like storage encryption, this can be applied manually or by using mobile device management technologies.

Two VPN technologies are in everyday use: IPsec and SSL VPNs. Both of them provide a secure, encrypted tunnel through which traffic is routed. But there are some differences. Most operating systems support IPsec without a VPN client, but IPsec occasionally has issues traversing NAT. SSL VPNs are the inverse: They may require a VPN client like OpenVPN but face fewer connectivity issues.

When employing VPN technologies, employees must be familiar with the "how," "why," and "when" of their use. In other words, workers should be instructed on how to successfully connect to VPNs (if only to reduce the number of help-desk tickets). They should also be taught the benefits of VPNs and when they should be used. Depending on your policies, VPNs may be required when connecting to untrusted networks or mandatory whenever workers aren't on the company LAN.

App Distribution

In a BYOD model, there are a few ways to distribute and control mobile applications. Depending on your management tool, distribution can follow a push model, a pull model, or both. In the push model, selected devices receive and install selected applications without user interaction. This can be useful for widely used applications, such as your company's internal email or VoIP apps. Alternatively, some management tools support a "pull" model, in which a portal containing corporate applications is established for users. When an application is needed, the users can select and install it via the portal.

You also might want to restrict which applications users can install. This can be accomplished with an allow list that specifies permitted applications (all others are denied) or a deny list that lists blocked applications (all others are allowed). Application restrictions can improve the security of devices, but be wary of enforcing them on BYOD devices. Any application restrictions should be clearly communicated in policy and before device enrollment.

Key Topic Regulatory Compliance

In the context of endpoints, certain security controls should be present for regulatory compliance. PCI-DSS, HIPAA, and GDPR arc three standards and regulations with security requirements. You'll notice a wide range of granularity in their clauses as we move through them. For example, PCI-DSS sets forth precise requirements, whereas GDPR defines nebulous security principles.

PCI-DSS

The Payment Card Industry Data Security Standards (PCI-DSS) is an industry standard for working with and securing cardholder data. It comprises 12 broad requirements, several of which apply to endpoint security. PCI-DSS controls go far beyond the scope of CCST Cybersecurity but contain many best practices. Some relevant examples include the following:

- Protect stored cardholder data:

  - Minimize data retention and purge unnecessary data.

  - Encrypt cardholder data.

  - Protect all encryptions keys.

- Protect all systems from malicious software:

  - Use antimalware.

  - Keep the antimalware agent updated.

  - Ensure that the antimalware agent cannot be disabled.

- Identify and authenticate users:

  - Ensure that all users have unique (not shared) usernames.

  - Require authentication for all users.

  - Protect administrative access with two-factor authentication.

- Log and monitor access to systems and cardholder data:

  - Log and audit all access to cardholder data.

  - Synchronize the time on all systems.

  - Ensure that logs cannot be altered.

  - Retain an audit trail for one year.

HIPAA

The Health Insurance Portability and Accountability Act (HIPAA) is a U.S. government regulation that protects the privacy and security of protected health information (PHI). A section of HIPAA, the Security Rule, dictates the applicable controls for systems that store or process sensitive data. HIPAA's requirements are far less concrete than the PCI-DSS requirements. The technical security clauses can be summarized as follows:

- **Access control requirements:** Access to systems containing PHI should be controlled.

  - Unique user accounts (no generic or shared accounts)

  - A mechanism for emergency access to PHI

  - Automatic logoff after periods of inactivity

  - Encryption of PHI

- **Audit controls:** Access to PHI should be logged and monitored.

- **Integrity:** The integrity of PHI should be protected.

- **Authentication:** Systems should require user authentication.

- **Transmission security:** It is important to ensure the confidentiality and integrity of PHI transmitted over networks.

GDPR

The General Data Protection Regulation (GDPR) is a European regulation primarily concerned with protecting the privacy of EU citizens. GDPR does not define specific security controls to implement. Instead, it dictates a series of principles that should be followed when working with personally identifiable information (PII). Its clauses include

- Data should only be collected and stored if needed.

- Data should be kept no longer than is necessary.

- Data should be protected with appropriate technical controls.

GDPR's security requirements are intended to be abstract. By not dictating particular security controls, the regulation is less likely to bog organizations down with legacy security controls. Instead, it defines the principle of "data protection by design and by default," which should consider current knowledge, risk, and people's rights when choosing safeguards. Organizations may pursue GDPR certification to ensure that their security controls are GDPR compliant.

Summary

Modern environments often have an eclectic mix of hardware, software, and personal and company devices. Asset inventories, management and automation tools, and clear policies all help manage complexity—and awareness of regulations helps you make solid management decisions. This chapter covers the following topics related to endpoint policies and standards:

- **Endpoints,** which are devices connected to and communicating over a network, may be workstations, servers, or mobile devices.

- Hardware and software inventories (and asset management more generally) benefit cybersecurity professionals in several ways.

- Programs can be deployed manually or automatically. Automated deployment stream-lines the installation and updating of software.

- **Backups** can be classified according to two dimensions:

  - Local or remote backups

  - Full, differential, and incremental backups

- A **bring your own device (BYOD)** policy enables employees to use their personal devices for work activities. BYOD has numerous advantages and disadvantages, and it requires special security considerations. Several categories of management tools assist in wrangling BYOD devices. These management tools help enforce security controls and distribute corporate applications.

- Three regulations are relevant to endpoint security:

  - **PCI-DSS** is aimed at protecting cardholder data.

  - **HIPAA** protects the privacy and security of protected health information (PHI).

  - **GDPR** defines security principles to protect the rights and privacy of EU citizens.

Exam Preparation Tasks

As mentioned in the Introduction, you can customize your strategy for exam preparation. Suggested tasks include the exercises here, Chapter 16, "Final Preparation," and the exam simulation questions on the companion website.

Review All Key Topics

Review the most important topics in this chapter, noted with the Key Topics icon in the outer margin of the page. Table 10-5 lists these key topics and the page number on which each is found.

10

Table 10-5   Key Topics for Chapter 10

Key Topic Element	Description	Page Number
Paragraph	Asset management	198
List	Local and remote backups	200
Section	Bring Your Own Device (BYOD)	201
Paragraph	Mobile device management (MDM)	202
Section	Data Encryption	204
Section	Regulatory Compliance	205

Complete Tables and Lists from Memory

There are no memory tables for this chapter.

Define Key Terms

Define the following key terms from this chapter and check your answers in the glossary:

endpoint, asset management, mobile device management (MDM), remote monitoring and management (RMM), backup, local backup, remote backup, bring your own device (BYOD), mobile application management (MAM), mobile content management (MCM), mobile email management (MEM), enterprise mobility management (EMM)

Review Questions

1. Which of the following is the most accurate definition of an asset?

   a. A tangible object a company owns

   b. Something with monetary value

   c. Anything of value to an organization

   d. None of the above

2. Which of the following allows remote access, monitoring, configuration, and updating of endpoints?

   a. MAM

   b. RMM

   c. REM

   d. MEM

3. Which of the following backup mechanisms uses the least storage capacity?

   a. Full backup

   b. Differential backup

   c. Incremental backup

   d. Remote backup

4. While implementing BYOD, you want to ensure that personal and company data is strictly separated on BYOD devices. What is the term for this capability?

    a. Firewalling

    b. Containerization

    c. FileVault

    d. None of the above

5. Which of the following regulations or standards contains the most specific and detailed security requirements?

    a. PCI-DSS

    b. HIPAA

    c. GDPR

    d. BYOD

CHAPTER 11

Network and Endpoint Malware Detection and Remediation

This chapter covers the following topics:

- **Monitoring and Detection:** An introduction to malware signatures, scanning methods, Cisco AMP, and reading scan logs.

- **Malware Remediation Best Practices:** The general malware removal process: containment, inoculation, quarantine, and treatment.

Beyond understanding malware, you need to know how it is detected and responded to. Numerous strategies exist for generating malware signatures (unique identifiers), and anti-malware tools employ signatures in different ways. This chapter helps you develop a fundamental understanding of how malware is caught and the best practices for eliminating it from endpoints.

This chapter covers information related to the following Cisco Certified Support Technician (CCST) Cybersecurity exam objective:

3.6. Demonstrate familiarity with malware removal.

"Do I Know This Already?" Quiz

The "Do I Know This Already?" quiz allows you to assess whether you should read this entire chapter thoroughly or jump to the "Exam Preparation Tasks" section. If you are in doubt about your answers to these questions or your own assessment of your knowledge of the topics, read the entire chapter. Table 11-1 lists the major headings in this chapter and their corresponding "Do I Know This Already?" quiz questions. You can find the answers in Appendix A, "Answers to the 'Do I Know This Already?' Quizzes and Review Questions."

Table 11-1 "Do I Know This Already?" Section-to-Question Mapping

Foundation Topics Section	Questions
Monitoring and Detection	1–3
Malware Remediation Best Practices	4–5

CAUTION The goal of self-assessment is to gauge your mastery of the topics in this chapter. If you do not know the answer to a question or are only partially sure of the answer, you should mark that question incorrect for purposes of self-assessment. Giving yourself credit for an answer you correctly guess skews your self-assessment results and might provide you with a false sense of security.

1. Which of the following signature or rule types is most susceptible to evasion by making small changes to malware?
   a. Fuzzy hash
   b. Cryptographic hash
   c. Import hash
   d. YARA rule
2. Which of the following scan types recursively searches through all filesystem contents?
   a. On-demand scan
   b. Quick scan
   c. Full scan
   d. Real-time detection
3. What term refers to testing malware in a segmented environment?
   a. Brick-yarding
   b. File retrospection
   c. Incubating
   d. Sandboxing
4. What is the first step in responding to malware infections?
   a. Containment
   b. Inoculation
   c. Quarantine
   d. Treatment
5. Two weeks after removing malware from a system, the infection suddenly resumes. What was probably overlooked?
   a. Running antivirus
   b. Encrypting the drive
   c. A persistence mechanism
   d. A data exfiltration

Foundation Topics

Monitoring and Detection

Malware is incredibly diverse. It comprises many variants (viruses, worms, Trojans, and so on) with diverse mechanisms and goals. Within each variant, there are tens of thousands of unique implementations—and more are unleashed daily. To identify and respond to malware, you must first know what to look for. The most fundamental approach to recognizing malware is using **malware signatures**—unique fingerprints of malicious payloads. Malware signatures follow a predictable lifecycle (see Figure 11-1):

1. Malware is first discovered "in the wild."
2. The vendors of antimalware technologies acquire a sample of the malware and generate signatures that can be checked against files.

3. New signatures are regularly published and downloaded to antimalware tools (often software agents).

4. The antimalware tools monitor for files or data that match the signature and block any detected malware.

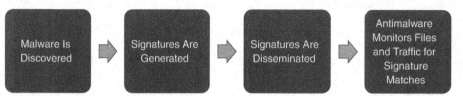

Figure 11-1   *The Lifecycle of Malware Signatures*

There are different approaches to generating signatures. Some are rigid and detect malware only if it's identical to the original samples. Others are "fuzzier" and can detect malware even if it has been modified. The following section introduces some common types of malware signatures.

Signature Types

Using cryptographic hashes such as MD5 and SHA-256 is one way to fingerprint malware. Once a malicious package is identified, its hash is calculated and added to an ever-growing list of malware hashes. Antimalware tools then receive the hash and append it to their local database. The antimalware agent dutifully calculates the hashes of files as they're downloaded or opened (or during scheduled filesystem scans) and blocks any files whose hashes are in its database.

Conventional hashing algorithms are performant and straightforward: Either a file hash matches, or it doesn't. However, there are drawbacks. Chief among them is that cryptographic hashing is very sensitive to changes. Flipping a single bit in a file results in a completely different hash. Malware developers can utilize this weakness to their advantage. They can, for instance, program malware to make tiny changes to itself over time. This ensures that its hash continuously changes so it can avoid detection. This evasion technique can be addressed with "fuzzier" matching techniques.

Fuzzy hashes are also fingerprints of files, but they're designed to be less sensitive to small changes. If malware flips a few bits, fuzzy hashes can still recognize it as the same file. To illustrate this, imagine that a single letter is changed in this book. According to a cryptographic hashing algorithm, it's now a totally different book! But with fuzzy hashes, the two texts are recognized as the same. In Figure 11-2, two copies of Chapter 12—with a single character changed—are compared with SHA-256 and a fuzzy hash called ssdeep. SHA-256 (top) produces two different hashes, and ssdeep correctly identifies the two files as matching.

An example of a fuzzy hashing tool is ssdeep. **ssdeep** divides files into several sections and calculates each section's hash. Under-the-hood details aren't necessary, but remember that ssdeep can detect structural similarities (called homologies). The degree of similarity is reported as a score between 0 (no resemblance) and 100 (identical). In Figure 11-2, the two copies of Chapter 12 have a similarity of 86. When used for malware detection, algorithms like ssdeep can identify malware even if it has numerous small changes from the original sample. A secondary benefit of this approach is that match sensitivity can be adjusted on a sliding scale. To maximize detection, the minimum similarity score can be kept low. Conversely, to minimize false positives, minimum similarity scores can be set much higher.

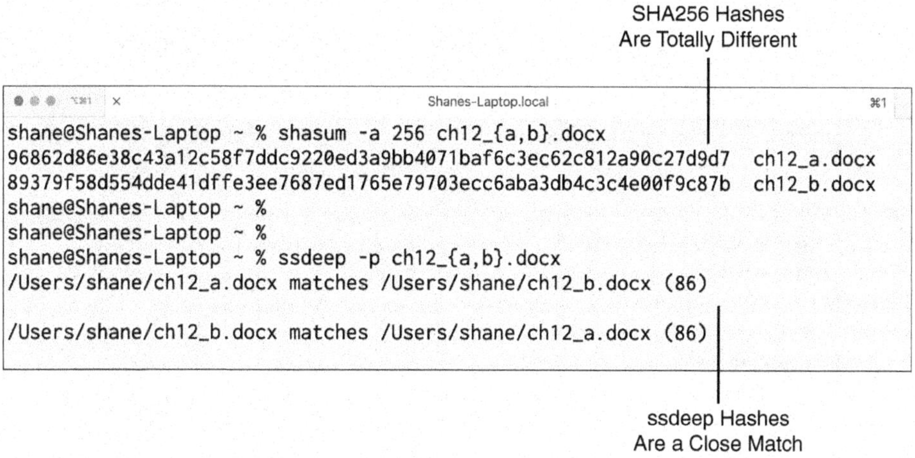

SHA256 Hashes
Are Totally Different

```
shane@Shanes-Laptop ~ % shasum -a 256 ch12_{a,b}.docx
96862d86e38c43a12c58f7ddc9220ed3a9bb4071baf6c3ec62c812a90c27d9d7   ch12_a.docx
89379f58d554dde41dffe3ee7687ed1765e79703ecc6aba3db4c3c4e00f9c87b   ch12_b.docx
shane@Shanes-Laptop ~ %
shane@Shanes-Laptop ~ %
shane@Shanes-Laptop ~ % ssdeep -p ch12_{a,b}.docx
/Users/shane/ch12_a.docx matches /Users/shane/ch12_b.docx (86)

/Users/shane/ch12_b.docx matches /Users/shane/ch12_a.docx (86)
```

ssdeep Hashes
Are a Close Match

Figure 11-2 *SHA-256 Versus ssdeep*

Another strategy for malware identification is import hashing. In **import hashing**, the functions and libraries a binary uses (and the order of their appearance) are gathered and fed into a hashing algorithm to generate a fingerprint. This approach is crafty. While malware can sometimes self-modify, it usually can't change the fundamental logic of its code. Its imports and their relative order, artifacts of software logic, can therefore be used to identify mutated malware.

Our final example of malware definitions is YARA: Another Recursive Acronym, or just YARA. Beyond being an acronym that includes itself, **YARA** allows us to write complex rules to match malware. It uses a simple, C-like syntax to define matching criteria for malware. Among other things, YARA rules can search for text strings, regular expressions, and other facets of malicious binaries. Example 11-1 shows a trivial example of YARA that matches occurrences of the textual or hexadecimal representation of 192.168.10.1. In the real world, you might use this rule to detect malware with hard-coded command-and-control (C2) server addresses.

Example 11-1 *A YARA Rule Matching on the Textual and Hexadecimal Representation of 192.168.10.1*

```
rule CommandAndControl
{
    strings:
        $ip_textual = "192.168.10.1"
        $ip_hexadecimal = { C0 A8 0A 01 }

    condition:
        $ip_textual or $ip_hexadecimal
}
```

Cryptographic hashes, ssdeep, import hashing, and YARA are typical malware signature techniques. None of them is perfect, but they form a set of complementary tools you can wield for malware detection. Many in-house, proprietary variations of these strategies are used by antimalware vendors seeking to maximize detection accuracy.

11

Scanning Systems

Once created, malware signatures and rules need to be employed. Different methods are used to match signatures to malicious files. Scanning may be scheduled or performed on demand, and system activity may be continuously monitored. Antimalware tools offer multiple scanning and detection approaches to enhance flexibility and protection. Three such approaches are filesystem scanning, real-time system monitoring, and network monitoring.

Filesystem scanning is straightforward. An antimalware agent searches through the contents of the filesystem, reading each file and generating its signature. The file signature is then compared against the agent's database of malware signatures. If a match occurs, the file may be malware. Depending on its configuration, the agent may respond in different ways:

- Generate an alert and take no action.

- Attempt to clean the file (for example, removing viral components from an otherwise benign file).

- Quarantine the malware. Quarantining involves moving malicious files to a safe location and blocking access to them.

- Permanently delete the file.

Most antimalware utilities offer both scheduled filesystem scans and on-demand scans. Scheduled scans ensure that systems are regularly evaluated for malware. On-demand scans are helpful if you're concerned about possible infections. For instance, if you accidentally open a seedy PDF, you might trigger an on-demand scan to rule out infections.

Just as most agents offer scheduled and on-demand scans, most have "full" and "quick" scans in some form. A **full malware scan** recursively searches through the entire filesystem. This type of scan tends to have high detection rates but also tends to consume a lot of time and resources. A **quick malware scan** looks through the directories where malware most commonly occurs. This type of scan offers a balance between speed and detection.

In addition to searching through the contents of a filesystem, antimalware agents also offer **real-time antimalware** mechanisms. These mechanisms evaluate files when triggered by different actions, such as the following:

- Downloading files

- Opening files

- Expanding archives

- Receiving an email

When events like these occur, antimalware agents act like a bouncer. After a download completes, or before you can open the file, the agent calculates its signature and consults its local database. If a match is found, the operation is blocked. The antimalware utility may generate a scary alert about the potentially malicious file. If you want to test your antimalware, you can download an EICAR test file. EICAR files contain benign text strings. By convention, they are classified as malicious by most antimalware agents (see Figure 11-3). EICAR test files can be downloaded from www.eicar.org.

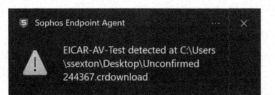

Figure 11-3 *An Antimalware Agent Detecting an EICAR Test File*

Another form of real-time detection is **network-based antimalware.** This software monitors traffic as it is received, sent, or traversing a device. Data is extracted from the network
flows and analyzed for signature matches. Depending on the location and configuration of
the sensor, it may generate alerts or proactively block the malware's transmission. Technologies like Cisco's Advanced Malware Protection (AMP) can interrupt malware simply by
withholding the last packet in a stream and causing downloads to fail (see Figure 11-4).

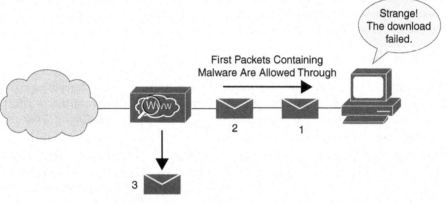

Figure 11-4 *A Cisco Security Appliance Holding Up the Final Packet Containing
Malware, Causing the Download to Fail and Preventing Infection*

Cisco AMP

The Cisco **Advanced Malware Protection (AMP)** is a multiplatform antimalware solution
that can be deployed throughout your infrastructure. Its various components reside on
endpoints, on network devices, and in the cloud. They work together to provide excellent
visibility of an environment in a single pane of glass.

AMP for Endpoints is the Cisco endpoint antimalware agent. It is compatible with Windows, macOS, Android, and Linux operating systems. AMP for Endpoints has numerous preventive and detective controls. Its preventive controls include exploit mitigations, protections
against malicious scripts and user behaviors, and the ability to control removable devices.
Meanwhile, its detective controls continuously monitor for vulnerabilities and indicators of
compromise (IoCs).

AMP for Networks integrates AMP's detection mechanisms into Cisco's portfolio of
network security appliances. Cisco Firepower, Email Security Appliances (ESA) and Web
Security Appliance (WSA), and Meraki all feature AMP integration. AMP integration

11

enables continuous monitoring and blocking of malware. Security appliances can be configured to take several actions for potentially malicious files:

- Calculate the file hashes and check them against **ThreatGrid**, Cisco's threat intelligence platform.

- Upload the file to a ThreatGrid sandbox, allow it to execute, and monitor its behavior.

- Hold files in "escrow," pending further checks.

- Block or reset connections.

Beyond visibility, a significant benefit of combining endpoint- and network-based antimalware is that it offers multiple layers of defense. The first layer, network-based protection, prevents much of the malware from ever reaching systems. It simply terminates connections before endpoints can fully download them. Then, any malware that sneaks through still needs to contend with the antimalware agent on the host itself. The overall AMP ecosystem provides many complementary detection and prevention controls, but three commonly highlighted items are file reputation, sandboxing, and file retrospection:

Key Topic

- **File reputation** information is generated by Cisco's Talos Intelligence. Talos draws telemetry from a vast array of sensors worldwide, performs analytics, and identifies emerging threats, vulnerabilities, and attacks. One of their outputs is file reputation intelligence (see Figure 11-5), a numeric score representing files' trustworthiness. AMP checks file reputation by calculating the SHA-256 hash, sending it to Cisco's cloud infrastructure, and receiving a verdict.

- Cisco provides **sandboxing** in the form of ThreatGrid. AMP utilizes ThreatGrid sandboxes by sending unknown files to Cisco's cloud servers. These servers create sandboxes, open files within them, and monitor their behavior. A verdict is returned based on the behavior of the sample. For highly sensitive environments, Cisco even offers on-premises ThreatGrid options.

- **File retrospection** provides a backward-looking view of malware that snuck through. If malware goes undetected by AMP for Networks and Endpoints and is deemed malicious days later, AMP generates an alert and details where the malware was seen.

Reviewing Logs

In a business environment, you usually use an antimalware solution that provides centralized logging from all installed agents. It's important to periodically review these logs to detect emerging patterns and failed remediations—and to ensure that scans are running!

When reviewing scan logs, you might keep in mind the following questions:

- Did the scans occur on schedule? Missing scans could indicate a disabled or faulty agent.

- Are their signatures (or patterns) current? If the agent is dutifully scanning, but its signatures are from last year, it won't detect the latest malware.

- How many instances of malware were detected? Naturally, the goal is zero. Any malware detections should be investigated.

- Did the configured action (quarantine, clean, delete, and so on) complete successfully? Even if it did, it's worthwhile to investigate manually.

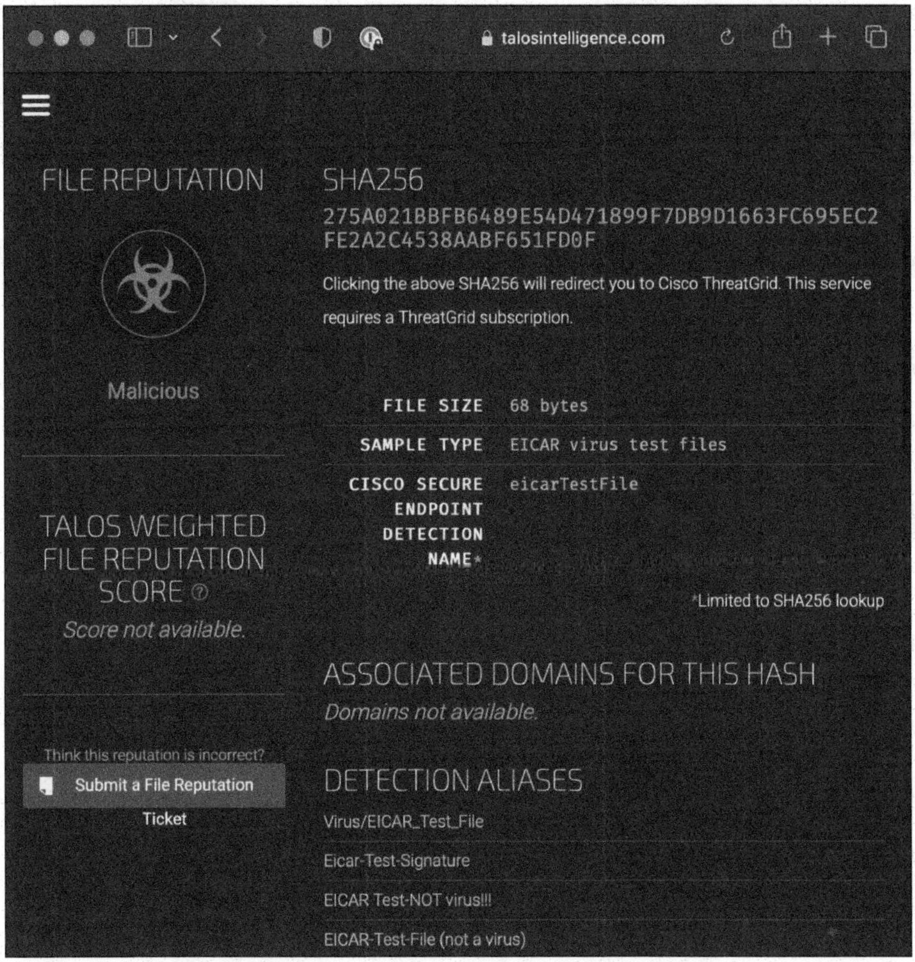

Figure 11-5   *The File Reputation Verdict for an EICAR Test File*

When reviewing events in detection logs, the information available depends on the vendor. Some solutions provide very rudimentary details (the malware that it detected, where it was, and how it responded). Others offer details such as what opened the malware and what the malware interacted with. Assuming that you have granular information, you might consider:

- What opened the malware, if relevant?

- What malware was detected, and does it make sense for this system (that is, is it a false positive)?

- What processes were created by the malware?

- What files and registry keys did the malware interact with?

Questions like these will help you determine which changes the malware made to your system. This information will be handy later, when you must remediate the affected computer.

Malware Remediation Best Practices

In a perfect world, we'd never "clean" systems of malware; rather, we'd completely reimage them. That's because, after infection, we can never be sure systems are trustworthy again. The malware may have installed persistence mechanisms or scattered other malicious payloads around. Generally, the simplest (and often easiest) response is to start from scratch. However, there are situations where you must remediate systems manually. Cisco defines four steps to malware response:

1. **Containment:** Containment involves taking immediate action to stop the spread of malware. Containment steps might include pulling the network cable, disconnecting Wi-Fi, or shutting down affected systems.

2. **Inoculation:** After containing the incident, you perform inoculation. Inoculation involves patching and configuring all unaffected systems so they aren't vulnerable to the malware. This is analogous to vaccinating healthy people so they're resistant to pathogens.

3. **Quarantine:** Quarantine (isolation) follows inoculation. Many of the steps undertaken during containment overlap with quarantine; the goal is system sequestration. During quarantine, you may go further and place infected systems on a separate, inaccessible network segment. This allows you to investigate their behavior if needed.

4. **Treatment:** Treatment is the final phase. In this phase, all traces of malware are removed, and affected systems are patched to prevent future infections. If you choose to manually treat an infected system, ensure that you check for common persistence mechanisms, which are often created to reinfect the system or grant attackers remote access (see Table 11-2). The most radical—and recommended—treatment is reimaging systems.

Table 11-2 Malware Persistence Mechanisms in Windows

Persistence Mechanism	Description
New users	Malware may create extra user accounts on a system to grant attackers access.
New services	Attackers may create new services that run automatically.
Scheduled tasks	Scheduled tasks may be used to execute programs on a regular basis and can be abused to periodically reinstall malware or grant attackers access.
Registry keys	The Windows Registry can be modified to run malicious programs when users log in or when the system boots.
File associations	Windows can be configured to associate certain file types with malicious software.
Shortcut hijacking	An attacker may point a shortcut at malware instead of its original (benign) target.

Summary

Detecting and responding to malware is a common task for cybersecurity professionals. To be effective in this realm, you must understand how antimalware utilities work and their strengths and weaknesses. Likewise, you must know how to respond to malware infections when they occur. This chapter covers the following topics related to network and endpoint malware detection and remediation:

- **Malware signatures** are used to identify files as malicious. Different signature types are used:

    - Cryptographic hashes

    - Fuzzy hashes

    - Import hashes

    - Definition languages (for example, YARA)

- Different methods are used for malware detection:

    - **Filesystem scanning:** Searching the contents of stored data for malware signatures

    - **Real-time detection mechanisms:** Monitoring for malware signatures in data as it is read, written, transmitted, or stored in memory

    - **Network detection:** Inspecting network communications for evidence of malware

- Cisco **Advanced Malware Protection (AMP)** is a robust antimalware ecosystem. It has three primary components:

    - **AMP for Endpoints:** A software agent installed on workstations, servers, and mobile devices

    - **AMP for Networks:** Antimalware woven into security appliances like Firepower, ESA, and WSA appliances

    - **AMP Cloud:** Cisco infrastructure for threat intelligence and sandbox analysis

- AMP has three defining features:

    - **File reputation intelligence:** Actionable information about the trustworthiness of files

    - **Sandbox malware analysis:** Running malware in a segmented environment to observe its characteristics

    - **File retrospection:** Retroactive alerting about files that were identified as malicious after being detected in an environment

- By regularly reviewing scan logs, you can ensure that you don't miss festering problems and can respond effectively to malware incidents.

- Cisco defines four phases of malware remediation:

    - **Containment:** Immediate action to stop the spread of malware

    - **Inoculation:** Preventing unaffected systems from being infected

    - **Quarantine:** Ensuring infected and uninfected machines are strictly separated

    - **Treatment:** Removing all traces of malware infection

11

- If manually cleaning a system, ensure that you check for common persistence mechanisms:

  - New users

  - New services

  - Scheduled tasks

  - Registry keys

  - File associations

  - Shortcut hijacking

Exam Preparation Tasks

As mentioned in the Introduction, you can customize your strategy for exam preparation. Suggested tasks include the exercises here, Chapter 16, "Final Preparation," and the exam simulation questions on the companion website.

Review All Key Topics

Review the most important topics in this chapter, noted with the Key Topics icon in the outer margin of the page. Table 11-3 lists these key topics and the page number on which each is found.

Table 11-3   Key Topics for Chapter 11

Key Topic Element	Description	Page Number
Paragraph	Malware signatures	211
Paragraph	Cryptographic hash signatures	212
Paragraph	Fuzzy hash signatures	212
Paragraph	YARA	213
Paragraph	Filesystem scanning	214
Paragraph	Real-time protection	214
Paragraph	Network-based malware detection	215
Paragraph	Advanced Malware Protection (AMP)	215
List	Three benefits of Cisco AMP	216
List	Malware remediation steps	218

Complete Tables and Lists from Memory

There are no memory tables for this chapter.

Define Key Terms

Define the following key terms from this chapter and check your answers in the glossary:

malware signature, fuzzy hash, ssdeep, import hashing, YARA, filesystem scanning, full malware scan, quick malware scan, real-time antimalware, network-based antimalware,

Advanced Malware Protection (AMP), AMP for Endpoints, AMP for Networks, ThreatGrid, file reputation, sandboxing, file retrospection, containment, inoculation, quarantine, treatment

Review Questions

1. Which of the following is a fuzzy hashing algorithm?

   a. MD5

   b. SHA-256

   c. YARA

   d. ssdeep

2. What technique does AMP for Networks use to interrupt the transmission of malicious payloads?

   a. Withholds the first packet

   b. Withholds the last packet

   c. Inserts random data into the packet payload

   d. None of the above

3. Which of the following items are features of Cisco AMP? (Choose two.)

   a. File reputation

   b. Sandboxing

   c. Port scanning

   d. HTTP proxying

4. What kind of file signature depends on an application's libraries and functions?

   a. Fuzzy hash

   b. Import hash

   c. Dependency graph

   d. YARA

5. Which malware remediation step does reimaging a computer fall into?

   a. Containment

   b. Inoculation

   c. Quarantine

   d. Treatment

11

CHAPTER 12

Risk and Vulnerability Management

This chapter covers the following topics:

■ **The Vocabulary of Risk:** This section discusses risk and its three prerequisites: assets, threats, and vulnerabilities.

■ **Vulnerabilities:** This section discusses vulnerabilities, vulnerability management, and scanning.

■ **Risk:** This section discusses risk prioritization, management, and response.

For cybersecurity professionals, it can be easy to see security as an end unto itself. Our infrastructure must be secure. When a major attack occurs, anyone who pushed back will rue the day they didn't heed our warning! But cybersecurity doesn't exist for its own sake: It serves to reduce organizational risk. Understanding risk, its components, and its management is crucial to making sensible decisions for your business.

This chapter covers information related to the following Cisco Certified Support Technician (CCST) Cybersecurity exam objective:

4.1. Explain vulnerability management.

4.3. Explain risk management.

"Do I Know This Already?" Quiz

The "Do I Know This Already?" quiz allows you to assess whether you should read this entire chapter thoroughly or jump to the "Exam Preparation Tasks" section. If you are in doubt about your answers to these questions or your own assessment of your knowledge of the topics, read the entire chapter. Table 12-1 lists the major headings in this chapter and their corresponding "Do I Know This Already?" quiz questions. You can find the answers in Appendix A, "Answers to the 'Do I Know This Already?' Quizzes and Review Questions."

Table 12-1 "Do I Know This Already?" Section-to-Question Mapping

Foundation Topics Section	Questions
The Vocabulary of Risk	1
Vulnerabilities	2, 3
Risk	4, 5

1. Which of the following items are prerequisites for risk to exist? (Choose three.)

   a. A vulnerability

   b. A threat

   c. A person

   d. An asset

2. Which of the following can be vulnerabilities? (Choose three.)

   a. The location of a building

   b. Misconfigured systems

   c. Unpatched systems

   d. Disgruntled former employees

3. Which steps are generally conducted in preparation for vulnerability assessments? (Choose two.)

   a. Applying remediations

   b. Prioritization of assets

   c. Discovery of the devices on our networks

   d. Verification that remediations are working properly

4. Which two inputs does qualitative risk analysis use? (Choose two.)

   a. Asset value

   b. Likelihood

   c. Exposure factor

   d. Impact

5. Which of the following controls protects data in motion?

   a. File system permissions

   b. Full disk encryption

   c. Protocol encryption

   d. Process isolation

Foundation Topics

The Vocabulary of Risk

Risk is the potential loss of systems' or data's confidentiality, integrity, or availability. The ensuing negative consequences can take many forms (for example, financial, reputational, or legal). Risk exists at the intersection of an asset, a vulnerability, and a threat (see Figure 12-1). It requires an **asset**—something of value—that the risk may damage. Risk also requires a **vulnerability**—an exploitable weakness—because you can't (by definition) exploit an invulnerable system. It also requires **threats**, which exploit vulnerabilities. Table 12-2 summarizes these components and provides examples. Unfortunately, these risk ingredients—assets, vulnerabilities, and threats—frequently come together and mingle. It is important to methodically assess and prioritize risks to minimize the potential for adverse events.

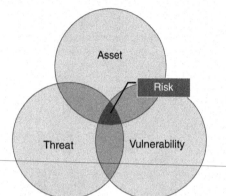

Figure 12-1 *The Ingredients of Risk*

Table 12-2 The Components of Risk

Component	Definition	Example
Asset	Something of value	An up-and-coming payment processing application
Vulnerability	An exploitable weakness	Lack of input validation and sanitization
Threat	Something that exploits a vulnerability	An attacker performing a SQL injection
Risk	Possible negative outcome	Loss of confidentiality, integrity, or availability for databases

Assets, threats, and vulnerabilities aren't optional. All three are needed for a risk to exist, so removing one will address the risk. Of the three, you have little control over threats. Attackers, natural disasters, and other threats are here to stay. While you can choose between more- and less-secure assets, you can rarely eliminate them completely. A business needs assets such as workstations, servers, data, and employees in order to continue functioning as a business. You have more control over vulnerabilities. Therefore, vulnerability management is an important component of risk management.

Vulnerabilities

Vulnerabilities take many forms. They may exist in hardware, software, network protocols, processes, procedures, or even the physical location of a facility. By themselves, vulnerabilities cause no harm. A vulnerability must meet with a threat—something that exploits a vulnerability—in order for a risk to be actualized. Vulnerabilities may be technical, physical, or administrative:

- Technical vulnerabilities occur in information systems (hardware or software). They can include misconfigurations, missing security controls, and exploitable bugs.

- Physical vulnerabilities occur in the physical environment. They can include unlocked doors, unsecured devices, or a lack of alarm systems.

- Administrative vulnerabilities occur due to employee behavior. They can include a lack of awareness training, absent or unenforced security policies, or insufficient auditing of employee compliance.

Consider each of the following scenarios and identify the vulnerability, its type, and the threat:

- A disgruntled employee wreaks havoc on important data due to lax permissions.

- A script kiddie exploits the lack of input validation in a web application to deface the website.

- A hurricane floods a branch office located in Hurricane Alley.

- A self-encrypting drive (SED) with improperly implemented encryption allows attackers to steal the decryption key and access data.

- An attacker sniffs your traffic with Wireshark and extracts sensitive information that is unencrypted.

- An employee falls for a phishing email and buys $500 worth of cards, supposedly on the CEO's order.

Each vulnerability in an organization contributes incrementally to its net risk. Therefore, it is essential to continuously assess which vulnerabilities are present, prioritize the response to them, and address them. This eternal game of whack-a-mole is vulnerability management.

The Vulnerability Management Lifecycle

Managing vulnerabilities is a continuous activity called the vulnerability management lifecycle that involves six steps. New vulnerabilities are constantly discovered, so the lifecycle is a cycle of evaluation and response. Figure 12-2 summarizes the vulnerability management lifecycle.

The first phase, your springboard into vulnerability management, is discovery. During this phase, you aren't discovering vulnerabilities yet; rather, the discovery phase involves determining what assets (or unexpected devices) are on your networks. Which hosts are present? What are their operating systems, services, and configurations? Are there unapproved devices on your network? You need to have a clear and detailed picture of your infrastructure before progressing to the next phase.

Having gleaned a detailed view of your environment during discovery, you can prioritize assets. How critical are they to your business? If a threat exploits a domain controller or database server, the company might grind to a halt. The Wi-Fi-enabled intelligent coffee maker is probably less essential (depending on who you ask). During the prioritization phase, you classify all assets according to their criticality and how destructive their loss would be.

Knowing the relative importance of your systems optimizes your ability to triage vulnerabilities. It ensures that you patch your domain controller before your Keurig. In addition, asset prioritization helps you decide how closely to monitor systems. You can tune the frequency and rigorousness of vulnerability assessments according to each system's importance.

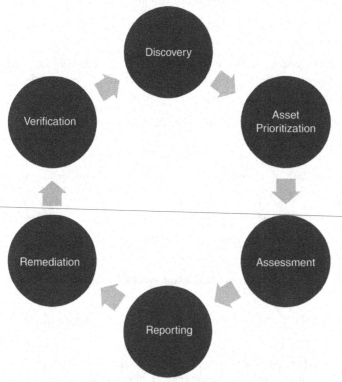

Figure 12-2 *The Vulnerability Management Lifecycle*

Armed with knowledge from the prior two phases—the systems on your network and their relative importance—you enter the assessment phase. Here, you generally employ vulnerability scanners to discover any weaknesses in your networks. **Vulnerability scanners**, like Nessus or OpenVAS, are automated tools that probe for vulnerabilities. In broad strokes, you give a scanner a target (for example, an IP address range) and define how the scan behaves. Is it exhaustive and aggressive, or more conservative? Is it restricted to evaluating systems externally, or does it have credentials to log in to targets? There's a balancing act here: Invasive scans are more accurate but likelier to cause problems such as server crashes. With the targets and scan parameters configured, you trigger the scan and wait for the results. The output is often expansive and enumerates missing patches, misconfigurations, or improper security controls. Each discovered vulnerability is assigned a **Common Vulnerability Scoring System (CVSS)** score, if available. CVSS scores provide a rough indication of the severity of vulnerabilities. The higher the CVSS score, the riskier the vulnerability. It isn't a perfect system, but CVSS can be quite helpful with prioritization. You might use this information, asset priority, and other contextual information to analyze and respond to the vulnerabilities. An example of the output of Nessus Essentials is provided in Figure 12-3.

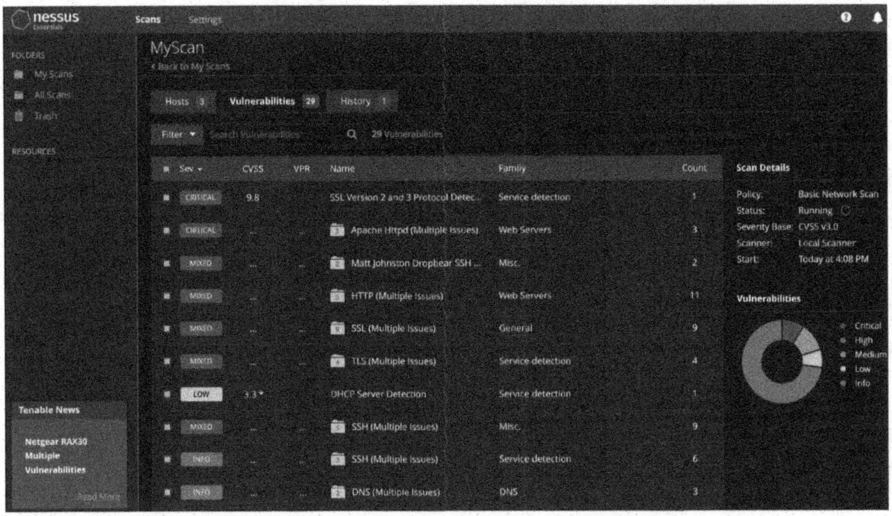

Figure 12-3 *Results in Nessus Essentials, a Free Vulnerability Scanner*

During a vulnerability assessment, you should consider whether each result is valid. Like intrusion detection systems, vulnerability scanners are not infallible. They may find vulnerabilities that don't exist or miss those that do. There are four categories you can sort scan results into: **true positives**, **true negatives**, **false positives**, and **false negatives**. Table 12-3 provides an example for each type. False positives are frustrating, but false negatives are downright dangerous; you can't fix vulnerabilities you don't know about.

Table 12-3 Categorizing Vulnerability Scan Results

	Positive	Negative
True	**True positive:** A vulnerability does exist and is detected by the scanner.	**True negative:** A vulnerability doesn't exist and therefore wasn't detected.
False	**False positive:** A vulnerability doesn't exist, but the scanner mistakenly detects one.	**False negative:** A vulnerability does exist, but the scanner overlooks it.

It's tempting to start patching systems immediately, but you shouldn't jump right in. Blindly remediating vulnerabilities can cause problems such as system downtime or degraded functionality. Rather, it's important to spend time in the reporting phase, where you collate, analyze, and disseminate information to stakeholders. Stakeholders may be IT workers, developers, security personnel, managers, and executives. Reports should be appropriate for each party's level of technical understanding and provide sufficient details for informed decisions. Depending on the audience, reports may be precise, down to individual vulnerabilities, or very broad, looking at overall trends. Having notified stakeholders and (if necessary) received authorization to fix vulnerabilities, you can, at long last, address them.

In the remediation phase, the rubber meets the road. Here, you implement technical responses to discovered vulnerabilities. You may patch systems, reconfigure them, segment them, decommission them, or apply other controls. In selecting an approach, you must weigh the vulnerability's severity, the affected system's criticality, the complexity or difficulty of the change, and how effectively the change mitigates the vulnerability. Many vulnerabilities can't be cured with a simple patch. Many have no patch at all. In these instances, you might apply compensating controls to reduce risk, such as introducing network segmentation, restricting traffic rules on the network or host firewalls, or expanding your monitoring of affected systems. Compensating controls reduce, but don't eliminate, the risk associated with a vulnerability.

Applying remediations isn't helpful if they don't work. Relying on the placebo effect isn't best practice in cybersecurity. Risks aren't thwarted by firmly held beliefs alone. This brings us to the verification phase. If you applied a patch, did it remove the vulnerability? If you reconfigured a system, did you do so appropriately? Are your compensating controls having the intended effect? Did your changes expose other vulnerabilities? You need to ensure that you've fixed the issue without introducing new ones. Completing the verification phase ends one revolution of the vulnerability management lifecycle, but the process never ends. Instead, you return to the discovery phase and begin the cycle anew. The sands are constantly shifting in cybersecurity: New vulnerabilities appear, threats evolve, and systems come and go. Vulnerability management, therefore, must be implemented methodically and continuously.

Active and Passive Scanning

You can use active or passive techniques to gather information about vulnerabilities. **Active scanners** send traffic to targets and identify vulnerabilities by inspecting return traffic and the targets' behavior. These scanners are considered active because they directly engage other systems. Unless otherwise specified, vulnerability scanners are usually active scanners. Because they interact directly with systems, active scanners can be configured to authenticate to the systems (credentialed scans) for more accuracy. They also perform many tests in quick succession. However, active scanners aren't perfect. They generate a flood of traffic, which can negatively affect systems' performance. Furthermore, an active scanner provides only a snapshot of a target system at a point in time. Active scanners are noisy, intrusive, and resource-intensive, and so they are not suited to running continuously. It is common to schedule them to run at regular intervals (preferably outside business hours).

Passive scanning is a different and complementary approach. **Passive scanners** generate no traffic. Instead, they monitor regular network traffic for evidence of vulnerable systems. Passive scanners serenely watch packets go by and don't have the same capabilities as active scanners. Without sending traffic, they can't authenticate to systems for credentialed inspection. Likewise, they can't prod target systems' ports and services to generate response traffic. They are limited to monitoring the traffic that systems produce in their "natural state." The benefit of passive scanners is that they can run continuously and provide ongoing network visibility with no performance impacts. Table 12-4 summarizes active and passive vulnerability scanning. The accuracy of active scanning pairs well with the continuous monitoring of passive scanning.

Key Topic

Table 12-4 Comparing Active and Passive Scanning

Factor	Active	Passive
Generates traffic	Yes	No
Stresses systems and network	Yes	No
Detections and accuracy	Higher	Lower
Continuous detection	No	Yes

Port Scanning

Active vulnerability scanners generally perform port scanning of their targets. **Port scanning** involves sending traffic to different TCP and UDP ports on a target system to determine their state. Open ports indicate the presence of a service on a system. If a system is open on TCP port 80, it is probably (but not conclusively) hosting a web server. Vulnerability scanners scan ports but go beyond simple port states by testing for vulnerabilities in the relevant services.

Port scanning is not just a function of vulnerability scanning, however. It is helpful on its own for both defenders and attackers. Tools like **nmap** can enumerate the hosts on a network, their port states (and, by extension, their services), and firewalls, to name a few. Defenders can use port scanners to detect unauthorized systems and services on a network. Conversely, attackers use them during reconnaissance to find exploitable targets. Figure 12-4 shows the output of an **nmap** scan. You're unlikely to encounter **nmap** questions in the CCST Cybersecurity exam but, as it's a ubiquitous tool, examples of **nmap** commands are provided in Table 12-5.

```
● ● ●   ⌥⌘1                         student@rhel1                        ⌘1   +

[student@rhel1 ~]$ sudo nmap -sS 192.168.0.53
[sudo] password for student:
Starting Nmap 7.91 ( https://nmap.org ) at 2023-04-16 14:21 MST
Nmap scan report for 192.168.0.53
Host is up (0.0020s latency).
Not shown: 997 closed ports
PORT    STATE SERVICE
22/tcp open   ssh
53/tcp open   domain
80/tcp open   http

Nmap done: 1 IP address (1 host up) scanned in 0.19 seconds

[student@rhel1 ~]$
```

Figure 12-4 *nmap Scan of a DNS Server*

Table 12-5 Example **nmap** Scan Commands

Command	Description
nmap -sS 10.0.0.1-5	Scans 10.0.0.1–10.0.0.5 with TCP SYN segments.
nmap 10.0.0.0/24 -p 22	Looks for systems in 10.0.0.0/24 with port 22.
nmap -sV 10.0.0.7	Tries to determine services' versions on 10.0.07.
nmap -O 10.0.0.22	Attempts to determine the operating system at 10.0.0.22.

Risk

Risk occurs when a threat meets a vulnerability. Depending on a risk's nature, it may have financial, reputational, or even legal consequences. Until now, we've focused on reducing risk through vulnerability management. Vulnerability management is a noble endeavor, but it's only a component of risk management. There may be vulnerabilities that cannot be fixed or that are too expensive to fix. An organization may face a multitude of potential risks that need prioritization. How do you soberly and effectively manage risk in the messy real world? The following sections address these questions.

Risk Prioritization

Identifying risks is important. You can't respond to what you don't know about. Organizations are exposed to risk in countless ways. Some risks require immediate action, while others are comparatively unimportant. Risk prioritization helps you respond to the greatest risks first. It is also important because there are far more risks than there are resources to deal with them. There are a few tools you can use to compare risks, including qualitative and quantitative analysis.

Risk Ranks and Levels

In **qualitative risk analysis**, each risk is assigned a numeric score. The score doesn't correspond to a dollar value. It's just an approximation of each risk relative to others. Two factors are used to calculate qualitative risk: **likelihood** and **impact**. The scale isn't important; here, we'll use 1 (low) to 5 (high). We might assign a likelihood of 1 and an impact of 5 to an unlikely but potentially devastating risk. Its risk score is then calculated by multiplying the likelihood and impact numbers: $1 \times 5 = 5$. On the other hand, a risk with medium likelihood and impact might be assigned 3 for each, resulting in a risk score of 9. Table 12-6 provides an example of a risk matrix using this scale.

Table 12-6   A Risk Matrix

Impact					
Likelihood		**1**	**2**	**3**	**4**	**5**
	5	5	10	15	20	25
	4	4	8	12	16	20
	3	3	6	9	12	15
	2	1	4	6	8	10
	1	1	2	3	4	5

Qualitative risk analysis is easy. Pick a scale, choose a rough value for likelihood and impact, and multiply them together. When you've done this for multiple risks, you have a rough metric to prioritize the risks. As you've probably noticed, this process has the downside of being subjective, based in part on intuition. We'll now turn to a more rigorous approach.

In **quantitative risk analysis**, you look at the expected yearly cost of a risk. Here too you multiply two numbers, but this time, the products are dollar amounts. The inputs are single loss expectancy (SLE) and annualized rate of occurrence (ARO):

- **Single loss expectancy (SLE)** is the anticipated financial loss due to a single risk being realized. For example, the SLE of a lost laptop might be $1000.

- **Annualized rate of occurrence (ARO)** is how many losses are expected per year, and this number is often determined based on previous years' trends. If you estimate that three laptops are lost per year, the ARO is—you guessed it—three.

Multiplying the SLE by ARO gives you the **annualized loss expectancy (ALE)**, or the financial impact over a year (see Figure 12-5). In our example, three lost laptops at $1000 each result in an ALE of $3000. Quantitative risk analysis helps you approximate the costs of risk to our tangible assets. It is more complex when pointed at intangible assets. What is the value of your secret sauce, employees, or corporate reputation? There are ways to determine such values, but they are far more nebulous for assets lacking a sticker price. Table 12-7 compares qualitative and quantitative risk analysis.

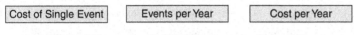

$$\text{SLE} \times \text{ARO} = \text{ALE}$$

Figure 12-5 *Basic Quantitative Analysis*

Table 12-7 Qualitative and Quantitative Risk Analysis

Factor	Qualitative	Quantitative
Calculations	Based on arbitrary likelihood and impact scales	Based on actual dollar values and estimated frequencies
Components	Likelihood and impact	SLE and ARO
Speed	Quick	Slower
Data	More subjective	More objective

Data Types and Classification

Not all data is created equal. Most businesses work with data of varying sensitivities. One end of the range includes public whitepapers, email chains about a Halloween party, or the background image you set on your workstation. Data like this is inconsequential: It doesn't matter who sees it. The opposite end of the range includes customers' financial information, medical records, or your secret recipe. If data like this is exposed, your company may face financial, legal, and reputational damage. To manage data risks, you need to know how sensitive data is. In other words, you need to classify it. **Data classification** is the analysis, categorization, and labeling of data according to its importance or sensitivity. Data classification dictates which security controls are applied.

You're probably familiar with government classification levels, such as confidential, secret, and top secret (summarized in Table 12-8). These classifications are assigned based on how damaging the release of documents would be. Companies use a similar approach, although the names of the classifications are different. An example classification scheme is shown in Table 12-9. Note that definitions are not standardized and may vary between companies.

Table 12-8 Government Classification Levels

Classification	Impact if Exposed
Confidential	Damage to national security
Secret	Serious damage to national security
Top Secret	Exceptionally grave damage to national security

Table 12-9 Example of an Information Classification Scheme

Classification	Sensitivity	Accessibility	Example
Public	None	Anyone	An advertisement
Internal	Limited	Employees	A Teams chat
Confidential	Significant	Authorized employees	Customer addresses
Restricted	Serious	Need-to-know	Protected health information (PHI)

The classification assigned to data determines what security controls you apply to it. Non-sensitive data may require few (if any) additional security controls. Conversely, highly sensitive data is often wrapped in many extra security controls. For instance, your policies may require rigorous auditing, restrictive file system permissions, encryption, data loss prevention (DLP) tools, or multifactor authentication (MFA).

Data classification is one factor in choosing security controls; another is data state. **Data state** refers to where data is. There are three states of data:

- **Data at rest:** Data stored on nonvolatile media (for example, hard drives or solid-state drives) and not currently in use

- **Data in motion:** Also referred to as "data in transit," data being transferred between systems, usually across a network

- **Data in use:** Data being actively used, generally in CPU caches or RAM

These states aren't mutually exclusive, and any data may exist in all three states simultaneously. For instance, a pharmacy's web application may store prescription information in a database (data at rest), load it into RAM when the patient logs in (data in use), and transfer it to the patient's system (data in motion). Table 12-10 lists security controls for the three data states.

Table 12-10 State-Specific Security Controls

State	Controls
Data at rest	■ Full-disk encryption (FDE) ■ File- or directory-based encryption ■ File system permissions ■ Mandatory access control (MAC) policies ■ Logging and auditing of user activities
Data in motion	■ Protocol encryption (for example, SSL/TLS, IPsec, SSH) ■ Strong peer authentication ■ Limits on which data can be transferred ■ Data loss prevention (DLP) inspection ■ Restrictive firewall rules
Data in use	■ Memory encryption ■ Kernel security mechanisms ■ Process isolation ■ Control of access to the broader system

It's important to consider each state when selecting security controls. Consider our example of the pharmacy's web application. The pharmacy might protect its database with all possible security controls but, if it uses plaintext HTTP, protecting data at rest amounts to little. Without protocol encryption, it would be trivial to intercept and eavesdrop on patients' medical information.

Security Assessments

Security assessments help impose structure on risk management activities. Risk prioritization and data classification are excellent tools, but organizations are complex and dynamic. Many things change within companies, including systems, data, security controls, policies, and procedures. Externally, vulnerabilities, attacks, and attackers are constantly churning. A methodical, repeatable, and well-defined assessment process assists in managing these complexities.

The National Institute of Standards and Technology (NIST) publication "Guide for Conducting Risk Assessments" is a great resource to lean on. The document defines four phases of cybersecurity risk assessments: preparation, implementation, communication, and maintenance. These aren't necessarily sequential because the communication and maintenance steps can co-occur.

The first step is preparation. We've established that security assessment is complex and doesn't lend itself to an ad hoc approach. A clear picture of goals, capabilities, and philosophy is necessary. During preparation, you answer questions like these:

- Why are we performing this assessment?

- Where will we gather our assessment information?

- What limitations and assumptions are there?

- How do we think about risk (for example, in terms of models or frameworks)?

Next, you conduct the assessment. With the context developed during preparation, you consider a new set of questions. Here are a few examples:

- What threats and threat actors apply to our specific organization?

- What vulnerabilities (technical, managerial, or otherwise) might these threats exploit?

- What are the likelihood and impact of each threat and vulnerability colliding?

- How certain or uncertain is our analysis? Are we using a qualitative risk assessment based on intuition or a quantitative risk assessment based on historical trends?

Having conducted the assessment, you then communicate and maintain it. The communication phase involves disseminating results to decision makers and stakeholders. Even a brilliant security assessment is useless if it languishes on SharePoint without being reviewed and acted on. All appropriate parties should receive the results so they make rational risk management decisions. Assessments must also be maintained—that is, kept current with internal and external changes. Treat your security assessment as a living document and update it accordingly. NIST lists three things to monitor during maintenance:

- **Effectiveness:** Are the risk responses having the intended effect?

- **Changes:** What changes have occurred, and is risk impacted?

■ **Compliance:** Are internal policies and procedures being followed? If subject to regulations, is the organization compliant?

Regular assessments and ongoing monitoring help support other policies and processes in the organizational risk-reduction portfolio. Systems' and employees' compliance with information security policies can be evaluated. Likewise, detecting and investigating changes is helpful in enforcing change management processes. **Change management** involves planning, requesting, approving (or denying), and documenting changes. Change management reduces risk in several ways. It ensures that another person evaluates changes, thereby reducing the likelihood of downtime, errors, and even malicious changes by disgruntled employees. It also ensures that an accurate picture of systems is maintained. If employees can make changes on their own authority—without necessarily informing anyone—the environment may diverge significantly from your mental model of it. This may result in "safe" changes unexpectedly breaking things, troubleshooting being more difficult, and security holes slipping through.

Risk Management

Risk management is an ongoing business process that involves identifying, analyzing, prioritizing, and responding to risk. Organizations use risk management to avoid events that might have negative financial, legal, or reputational impacts. The information gleaned during risk management has additional benefits, such as enabling leaders to make more informed strategic decisions. Every topic in this chapter falls under the risk management umbrella, but how can we tie everything together into a coherent process? Thankfully, we don't have to start from scratch.

NIST has published a useful framework that organizes and adds structure to many of the topics introduced in this chapter. Its Risk Management Framework (RMF) is a freely available document that defines seven risk management phases. The RMF is recommended reading for any cybersecurity professional, but it's not a thrilling read, so we'll summarize the seven phases:

■ **Prepare:** Define roles and responsibilities, create a risk management strategy, and perform a risk assessment.

■ **Categorize:** Categorize systems and data according to their risk levels.

■ **Select:** Choose controls, tailor them to requirements, and document them.

■ **Implement:** Deploy the controls and document deviations from the deployment plan.

■ **Assess:** Verify that the controls are functioning and address any issues.

■ **Authorize:** A designated person evaluates the residual risk (after controls are applied) and permits or denies its operation.

■ **Monitor:** Changes to information systems are monitored, and ongoing risk assessments and risk responses are conducted.

Risk Management Strategies

"Risk responses" have been mentioned a few times, but how exactly is risk responded to? What are the options? The vocabulary may differ, but risk management strategies generally fall into four categories: mitigation, avoidance, transference, and acceptance. Table 12-11 summarizes these approaches.

Table 12-11   Risk Management Strategies

Strategy	Description	Example
Mitigation	Reducing (but doesn't eliminate) risk by modifying or adding security controls	Placing a firewall in front of the accounting subnet to protect against network attacks
Avoidance	Removing risk by eschewing anything that may introduce it	Responding to a print spooler vulnerability by disabling the spooler service on all systems
Transference	Moving risk to another party	Purchasing cybersecurity insurance
Acceptance	Choosing not to respond to a risk	Taking no action because other responses are more costly than the risk's realization

Risk mitigation approaches involve using security controls to reduce (but not eliminate) risks. For example, you can improve network security with firewalls and intrusion prevention systems, but these tools can't block every possible attack. Likewise, employee training reduces the risk of phishing attacks, but one person always clicks the link. The goal of risk mitigation is to reduce risk to an acceptable level but leave some remaining (residual) risk. It can be classified according to the controls it uses to mitigate risk:

- **Preventive controls** (such as firewalls or intrusion prevention systems) make attacks more difficult.

- **Detective controls** (such as intrusion detection systems, syslog, or SIEM systems) speed up the detection of incidents.

- **Corrective controls** (such as backups) help in repairing damage due to incidents.

- **Deterrent controls** (such as signs or banners) dissuade attackers.

NIST has published a far more expansive and granular treatment of mitigating security controls. In "Security and Privacy Controls for Information Systems and Organizations," NIST defines 20 families of security controls, each organized into subcategories. The document, currently containing 500 pages of dense information, is worth skimming and keeping as a reference. Table 12-12 lists the security control families and provides an example control for each.

Table 12-12   NIST 800-53 Revision 5 Security Control Families

Code	Name	Example
AC	Access Control	AC-6: Least Privilege
AT	Awareness and Training	AT-3: Role-Based Training
AU	Audit and Accountability	AU-2: Event Logging
CA	Assessment, Authorization, and Monitoring	CA-8: Penetration Testing
CM	Configuration Management	CM-2: Baseline Configuration

Code	Name	Example
CP	Contingency Planning	CP-3: Contingency Testing
IA	Identification and Authorization	IA-12: Identity Proofing
IR	Incident Response	IR-6: Incident Monitoring
MA	Maintenance	MA-6: Timely Maintenance
MP	Media Protection	MP-6: Media Sanitization
PE	Physical and Environmental Protection	PE-13: Fire Protection
PL	Planning	PL-9: Centralized Management
PM	Program Management	PM-5: System Inventory
PS	Personnel Security	PS-3: Personnel Screening
PT	PII Processing and Transparency	PT-4: Consent
RA	Risk Assessment	RA-5: Vulnerability Scanning
SA	System and Service Acquisition	SA-5: System Documentation
SC	System and Communication Protection	SC-7: Boundary Protection
SI	System and Information Integrity	SI-16: Memory Protection
SR	Supply Chain Risk Management	SR-11: Component Authenticity

Skim Table 12-12 or, better yet, get the document itself from NIST's website and take a look. What are the benefits of using it (or similar options, like ISO/IEC 27001)? Are security controls less likely to be overlooked? Does the common language reduce ambiguities and misunderstandings? Would an exhaustive and rigid structure help in meeting and maintaining regulatory compliance? The answer is "Yes!" Zooming back out to risk management strategies, notice that these are all mitigations: They reduce risk but don't eliminate it. The remaining risk management strategies are far less expansive.

Risk avoidance involves eliminating risk by avoiding whatever that risk stems from. You might prevent website defacement by not having a website, for example, or cure network attacks by tearing out your network. Risk avoidance isn't always an option, but for unimportant systems and assets, it can be an excellent option. For instance, you might remove the smart coffee maker from your network if it's deemed a potential risk.

Risk transference involves moving risk to another party. Cybersecurity insurance is the obvious example because the insurance company assumes some financial risk in exchange for a recurring fee. In the event of a qualifying incident, the insurance company assists with the financial repercussions. Risk may also be transferred in other ways, such as via contracts with third parties.

Finally, there is the least satisfying strategy: **risk acceptance**. With risk acceptance, you evaluate risk and decide against responding to it. Acceptance is sensible when other approaches are more damaging than the risk they address. Imagine that your company has a simple website that is backed up nightly. You evaluate the risk of website defacement and determine that the cost of restoring from backups is $200 yearly. Deploying your cloud provider's web application firewall (WAF) would cost $100 yearly. In this situation, deploying the WAF reduces the risk of website defacements, but the mitigation costs more than the risk!

Summary

Risk and vulnerability are closely related concepts, and the activities and processes used to manage them overlap. For a cybersecurity professional, it's imperative to understand these topics. After all, beneath all the technical work, your fundamental deliverable to companies is reduced risk. To summarize:

- **Risk** is a potentially negative event. It has three required ingredients:
  - **Assets:** Tangible or intangible items with value
  - **Vulnerabilities:** Exploitable weaknesses
  - **Threats:** People, things, or events that exploit vulnerabilities
- **Vulnerabilities** (just like security controls) can take different forms:
  - Technical
  - Physical
  - Administrative
- **Vulnerability management** is an ongoing process of addressing vulnerabilities in an organization. It is common to employ automated vulnerability scanners to detect vulnerabilities.
- Organizations have limited resources to manage risk, so they need to rank risks and prioritize their responses. Different techniques and inputs may inform risk prioritization:
  - **Qualitative risk analysis** provides a relative risk score based on perceived likelihood and impact.
  - **Quantitative risk analysis** determines a risk's estimated financial impact.
  - **Data classifications** categorize data by sensitivity.
  - **Security assessments** provide updated pictures of an organization's security posture and risk exposure.
- **Risk management** is a business process that involves identifying, prioritizing, and responding to risks.
- There are four potential responses to risk:
  - **Mitigation:** Take action to reduce a risk to an acceptable level.
  - **Avoidance:** Eliminate a risk by avoiding the activity, asset, or system that introduces it.
  - **Transference:** Share the risk with another party.
  - **Acceptance:** Take no action to address a risk.

Exam Preparation Tasks

As mentioned in the Introduction, you can customize your strategy for exam preparation. Suggested tasks include the exercises here, Chapter 16, "Final Preparation," and the exam simulation questions on the companion website.

Review All Key Topics

Review the most important topics in this chapter, noted with the Key Topics icon in the outer margin of the page. Table 12-13 lists these key topics and the page number on which each is found.

Table 12-13   Key Topics for Chapter 12

Key Topic Element	Description	Page Number
Table 12-2	The Components of Risk	224
Table 12-3	Categorizing Vulnerability Scan Results	227
Table 12-4	Comparing Active and Passive Scanning	228
Paragraph	Qualitative risk analysis	230
Paragraph	Data states	232
Table 12-11	Risk Management Strategies	235
Paragraph	Risk mitigations	235

Complete Tables and Lists from Memory

Print a copy of Appendix B, "Memory Tables," found on the companion website, or at least the section for this chapter, and complete the tables and lists from memory. Appendix C, "Memory Tables Answer Key," includes completed tables and lists you can use to check your work.

Define Key Terms

Define the following key terms from this chapter and check your answers in the glossary:

risk, asset, vulnerability, threat, vulnerability scanner, Common Vulnerability Scoring System (CVSS), true positive, true negative, false positive, false negative, active scanner, passive scanner, port scanning, qualitative risk analysis, likelihood, impact, quantitative risk analysis, single loss expectancy (SLE), annualized rate of occurrence (ARO), annualized loss expectancy (ALE), data classification, data state, change management, risk management, risk mitigation, preventive control, detective control, corrective control, deterrent control, risk avoidance, risk transference, risk acceptance

Review Questions

1. Which of the following are examples of detective controls? (Choose two.)
   a. Security camera
   b. Firewall
   c. IDS
   d. Disk encryption

2. Which two components are multiplied in quantitative risk analysis? (Choose two.)
   a. Likelihood
   b. Single loss expectancy (SLE)
   c. Impact
   d. Annualized rate of occurrence (ARO)
3. Which of the following items can be considered assets? (Choose all that apply.)
   a. Intellectual property
   b. Brand and reputation
   c. Employees
   d. Supporting IT infrastructure
4. You schedule your vulnerability scanner to run at 11 p.m. each day to ensure that employees aren't affected by its significant network utilization. What type of scanner are you using?
   a. Generation 1
   b. Generation 2
   c. Active
   d. Passive
5. Which of the following options are examples of threats? (Choose two.)
   a. Natural disaster
   b. Ransomware gang
   c. Lack of input validation
   d. Unencrypted network traffic

CHAPTER 13

Threat Intelligence

This chapter covers the following topics:

- **Threat Intelligence:** This section covers threat intelligence, which is information about threat actors that has been processed and analyzed to produce richer context and insights.

- **Vulnerability Databases and Feeds:** This section discusses vulnerability databases and feeds, CVE, CVSS, and vulnerability assessment tools.

- **Additional Sources of Threat Intelligence:** This section discusses reports, news, and threat intelligence categories such as collective, ad hoc, and automated intelligence.

- **How and Why to Proactively Share Threat Intelligence:** This section discusses the importance and benefits of maintaining open lines of communication—internally and externally—about threat actors.

Threat intelligence—understanding of threat actors—helps you move from a reactive security stance to a proactive one. Investigating threats and their characteristics enables you to make informed security decisions. Understanding bad actors, their tactics, and their targets helps you gauge risk. You can then minimize risk by preemptively adopting security controls and obstructing attacks before they occur. Many sources and forms of threat intelligence exist, and this chapter introduces several of them.

This chapter covers information related to the following Cisco Certified Support Technician (CCST) Cybersecurity exam objective:

4.2. Use threat intelligence techniques to identify potential network vulnerabilities.

"Do I Know This Already?" Quiz

The "Do I Know This Already?" quiz allows you to assess whether you should read this entire chapter thoroughly or jump to the "Exam Preparation Tasks" section. If you are in doubt about your answers to these questions or your own assessment of your knowledge of the topics, read the entire chapter. Table 13-1 lists the major headings in this chapter and their corresponding "Do I Know This Already?" quiz questions. You can find the answers in Appendix A, "Answers to the 'Do I Know This Already?' Quizzes and Review Questions."

Table 13-1 "Do I Know This Already?" Section-to-Question Mapping

Foundation Topics Section	Questions
Threat Intelligence	1
Vulnerabilities Databases and Feeds	2
Additional Sources of Threat Intelligence	3, 4
How and Why to Proactively Share Threat Intelligence	5

1. Which of the following are commonly used categories of threat intelligence? (Choose three.)
   a. Operational
   b. Tactical
   c. Strategic
   d. Statistical

2. Which of the following uniquely identifies vulnerabilities?
   a. CVSS
   b. STIX
   c. CVE
   d. CPE

3. Which of the following is defined by the collaborative sharing of intelligence across organizations or industries?
   a. Ad hoc threat intelligence
   b. Collective threat intelligence
   c. Automated threat intelligence
   d. Verification that remediations are working properly

4. Which of the following statements is true? (Choose two.)
   a. The current version of STIX uses XML.
   b. The current version of STIX uses JSON.
   c. TAXII connections are protected by IPsec.
   d. TAXII connections are protected by HTTPS.

5. Which of the following is a group focused on information and intelligence sharing within an industry?
   a. ISAC
   b. NVD
   c. SCAP
   d. TAXII

Foundation Topics

Threat Intelligence

In our discussion of risk in Chapter 12, "Risk and Vulnerability Management," we defined its three essential components: assets, vulnerabilities, and threats. Most of our focus was on vulnerabilities (weaknesses that threats exploit). We now focus on threats and, specifically, threat actors. **Threat actors** are individuals or groups that seek to do harm. Unlike with vulnerabilities, which you can respond to in numerous ways, you have little control over threat actors. Nevertheless, it's important to understand them. An accurate picture of threat actors informs risk management decisions, security controls, and what you monitor for. The Internet is replete with information and analyses about threat actors, commonly called **threat intelligence**.

Threat intelligence is more than just raw data about threat actors. Further processing—such as data analysis, aggregation, and correlation—transforms plain data into insights and context. This richer information, or threat intelligence, helps us understand threat actors and respond appropriately. Threat intelligence falls into one of three categories, depending on the scope of its insights:

- **Tactical intelligence** is technical and specific. Its scope may be limited to a particular attack. For example, it may describe malicious IP addresses or domains, hashes of files, and other indicators of compromise (IOCs).

- **Operational intelligence** extends beyond technical identifiers to describe threat actors themselves. It may include their tactics, techniques, procedures (TTPs), or their motivations or targets.

- **Strategic intelligence** provides a broad understanding of the threat landscape. For instance, it may identify attack trends across an entire industry, emerging attack methods, or geopolitical concerns.

A staggering amount of threat intelligence is generated each day—far more than any person or team can ingest by reading reports or news articles. The written word can convey threat intelligence well, but it isn't scalable. Therefore, it's beneficial to use other intelligence sources and types. Numerous databases, tools, and standards exist to streamline the exchange of this information. Some emerging standards represent data or intelligence in machine-readable formats. They allow systems to send, receive, and respond to threat intelligence programmatically. This chapter looks at some forms and sources of threat intelligence. The first section covers threat actors' favorite things: vulnerabilities.

Vulnerabilities Databases and Feeds

Placing vulnerabilities under the threat intelligence umbrella may seem strange. We've already established that vulnerabilities and threats are distinct, so why muddy the waters? Following that logic, many refer to "vulnerability intelligence" as a discrete category. Others view vulnerability information as a component of threat intelligence, perhaps because vulnerabilities are what threat actors target. The CCST Cybersecurity objectives follow the latter approach. However you decide to classify vulnerability information, you should know where to gather it.

There are several freely available vulnerability databases, with **Common Vulnerabilities and Exposures (CVE)** and the **National Vulnerability Database (NVD)** being the most widely used. CVE is maintained by the MITRE Corporation and provides a unique identifier and brief description for each vulnerability. The NVD is provided by the U.S. government and enhances CVE data with severity scores, remediation information, and more (see Figure 13-1). The NVD is a superset of what CVE provides.

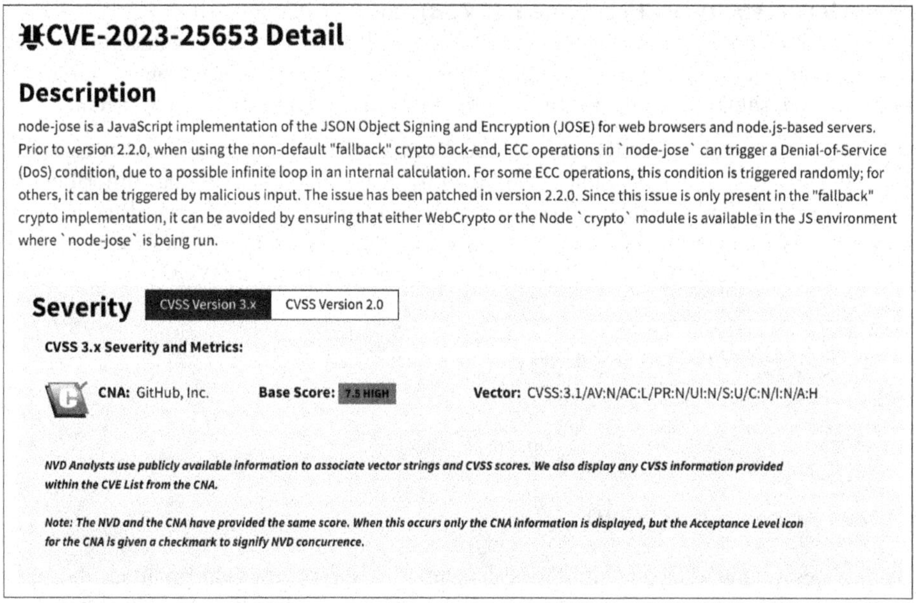

13

※CVE-2023-25653 Detail

Description

node-jose is a JavaScript implementation of the JSON Object Signing and Encryption (JOSE) for web browsers and node.js-based servers. Prior to version 2.2.0, when using the non-default "fallback" crypto back-end, ECC operations in `node-jose` can trigger a Denial-of-Service (DoS) condition, due to a possible infinite loop in an internal calculation. For some ECC operations, this condition is triggered randomly; for others, it can be triggered by malicious input. The issue has been patched in version 2.2.0. Since this issue is only present in the "fallback" crypto implementation, it can be avoided by ensuring that either WebCrypto or the Node `crypto` module is available in the JS environment where `node-jose` is being run.

Severity   CVSS Version 3.x   CVSS Version 2.0

CVSS 3.x Severity and Metrics:

CNA: GitHub, Inc.   **Base Score:** 7.5 HIGH   **Vector:** CVSS:3.1/AV:N/AC:L/PR:N/UI:N/S:U/C:N/I:N/A:H

NVD Analysts use publicly available information to associate vector strings and CVSS scores. We also display any CVSS information provided within the CVE List from the CNA.

Note: The NVD and the CNA have provided the same score. When this occurs only the CNA information is displayed, but the Acceptance Level icon for the CNA is given a checkmark to signify NVD concurrence.

Figure 13-1   *Part of an NVD Record*

Pros and Cons of Vulnerability Databases

Vulnerability databases such as CVE and NVD confer many benefits, including the following:

- They maintain consistency in the reporting, confirmation, and dissemination of vulnerability information.

- They are available in standardized, machine-readable formats and can be ingested via feeds or API calls.

- Unique identifiers improve clarity when communicating about (or responding to) vulnerabilities.

- Because they are public, they encourage vendors to address known vulnerabilities in their products.

Additional advantages exist, but you get the picture. Interestingly, there are some arguments against public vulnerability databases. The chief criticism targets their timeliness. Creating a new CVE is often a slow and difficult process for security researchers. Likewise, the NVD has several days of latency between a CVE being published and its NVD counterpart being created. Slowness isn't inherently bad: Vulnerability details are commonly withheld until a CVE's publication. However, vulnerabilities are also sometimes announced irresponsibly, with no warning. This may give threat actors extra time to exploit them before they become widely understood.

CVE and CVSS

In gathering intelligence about vulnerabilities, you'll constantly encounter CVE IDs and **Common Vulnerability Scoring System (CVSS)** scores. As Figure 13-1 shows, CVE and CVSS information are front-and-center in the NVD. You'll also see them in vulnerability scanning reports, news articles, and vendor security announcements. Given how common they are (and the similarity of the acronyms), it's worth discussing them in more detail.

CVE is, foremost, a registrar of IDs for individual vulnerabilities. It provides a process for requesting and receiving unique vulnerability identifiers from CVE numbering authorities (CNAs). CVE IDs follow a simple, standard format (see Figure 13-2). CVE records contain additional information (such as a brief descriptions and links to references) but are often sparse. Other sources, such as the NVD, provide more information for CVEs.

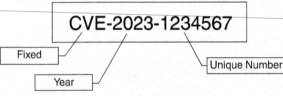

Figure 13-2 *Anatomy of a CVE ID*

CVSS provides a standardized method for calculating the severity of vulnerabilities. Its primary inputs are measures of ease of exploitation and potential impact. Its output is a score between 0 and 10, with 10 being the most severe. CVSS has been criticized for being complicated and potentially misleading. Indeed, CVSS scores are not infallible and should always be considered in the context of a particular organization. Tables 13-2 and 13-3 explain the exploitability and impact metrics used by CVSS. Newer CVSS revisions also add a "scope" metric concerning whether exploitation can affect other systems or components.

Table 13-2 CVSS Exploitability Metrics

Name	Description
Attack Vector	Where attacker must be in relation to system
Attack Complexity	Difficulty of successfully executing the attack
Privileges Required	Level of access attacker must gain to exploit a vulnerability
User Interaction	Whether or not user(s) must take some action for exploitation

Table 13-3 CVSS Impact Metrics

Name	Description
Confidentiality	Potential data disclosure following exploitation
Integrity	Potential data alteration following exploitation
Availability	Potential downtime or data lost following exploitation

Vulnerability Scanning and Assessment Tools

We've already discussed vulnerability scanners, which test systems for the presence of vulnerabilities. But how exactly do they find vulnerabilities? CVE records are minimal by design and don't define tests or signatures for vulnerability detection. In fact, vendors of vulnerability scanners need to create rulesets that are used to detect individual vulnerabilities. These go by different names—for example, Nessus calls them plugins, and OpenVAS calls them vulnerability tests—but they fundamentally do the same thing: Define the actions and conditions by which vulnerabilities are found. The need to create detection rulesets for new CVEs introduces delays. As a result, scanners often take multiple days to detect newly published vulnerabilities.

Beyond vulnerability scanners, there are other tools for vulnerability assessment. One example is the **Security Content Automation Protocol (SCAP)**, maintained by the NVD, which draws on several standards to evaluate systems' vulnerabilities and configurations. SCAP uses the CVE and CVSS information we've already discussed, along with several other standards. For instance, it also uses the Common Platform Enumeration (CPE), which defines specific software and hardware classes. In this context, a CVE is bound to the CPE identifiers of any vulnerability-affected products. Table 13-4 describes some components used by SCAP. As an open project, numerous security tools are SCAP compliant. One free assessment tool is OpenSCAP.

Table 13-4   Common Components of SCAP

Name	Description
Common Configuration Enumeration (CCE)	Uniquely identifies system configuration options.
Common Platform Enumeration (CPE)	Identifies and classifies software and hardware.
Common Vulnerabilities and Exposures (CVE)	Provides unique identifiers for system vulnerabilities.
Common Vulnerability Scoring System (CVSS)	Provides a vulnerability's severity score, based on ease and impact of exploitation.

These components and others make SCAP an excellent option for evaluating system vulnerabilities and compliance. SCAP checklists—which define what state systems should be in—are published by multiple entities. The Department of Defense (DoD), National Security Agency (NSA), and NIST are a few maintainers of SCAP checklists.

Additional Sources of Threat Intelligence

Vulnerability feeds are one source of intelligence, but other mediums and mechanisms exist. Written threat intelligence, such as reports and news articles, is one form. There are also threat intelligence automation standards. Sources can be further categorized as collective, ad hoc, or automated, depending on how intelligence is gathered and distributed.

Reports and News

Some threat intelligence is too novel or nuanced to fit cleanly into simple signatures, scoring systems, or feeds. It may describe broad industry trends, geopolitical developments, or future trends. As beneficial as standardization is, reality resists simplification. Even where standardization is used, it often strips context from intelligence. For instance, threat actors may target two vulnerabilities with CVSS base scores of 10. One vulnerability might affect Internet backbone routers, and the other might affect smart toasters. Numerically, the vulnerabilities are equally severe—but are they really equally severe? Some intelligence is best conveyed by more flexible vehicles like the written word.

Before discussing reports and news, though, we should address how to evaluate intelligence critically. A common technique used by the U.S. military is to rate a source's reliability and the credibility of its information. Sources are rated from A to F, based on their historical performance. A source with an A rating is completely reliable, and trustworthiness decreases from there. Likewise, information credibility is rated between 1 and 6. Information is rated 1 when it makes sense, aligns with known facts, and is confirmed elsewhere. As the number increases, credibility goes down. Reliability and credibility are paired to create scores like B2 or D3. Table 13-5 summarizes the levels in this system.

Table 13-5   Intelligence Evaluation Table from NATO Standard AJP-2.1

	Source Reliability		Information Credibility
A	Completely reliable	1	Completely credible
B	Usually reliable	2	Probably true
C	Fairly reliable	3	Possibly true
D	Not usually reliable	4	Doubtful
E	Unreliable	5	Improbable
F	Reliability unknown	6	Credibility unknown

We don't evaluate reports or news articles and assign them discrete scores. Still, it's beneficial to consider the dimensions of source reliability and information credibility. If the source is a news site, how accurate has it been historically? How long has it been around? Is it objective or oozing with clickbait? Similarly, does the news article make logical sense? Does it align with what you already know? Have other sources corroborated its information? There are many threat intelligence sources, and approaching them critically reduces the signal-to-noise ratio.

Reports

Intelligence reports are published by individuals, companies, and government agencies. Academic institutions also generate research, though it's commonly printed in prohibitively expensive journals. White papers and blog posts can both qualify as reports, with the latter being less formal. White papers are research essays: The authors gather data, analyze it, and report their findings. Typical subjects are yearly threat trends and the threat landscapes facing technologies and industries. We probably don't need to define blog posts, but they can be lengthy and detailed or shorter and targeted.

Companies often create white papers as thinly veiled marketing releases. Others produce insightful and truly helpful analyses (maybe they're still marketing, at least a little). Don't write off corporate threat reports—they're working in the trenches—but note a document's quality and primary motivation. Cisco Talos's blog is a good source of blog posts and white papers. It provides excellent analysis and reporting on varied topics. While it refers to downloadable PDFs as its "white papers," you'll find its standard blog posts equally helpful. Recorded Future, which specializes in intelligence, has some of the best threat intelligence white papers. Full access to Recorded Future's intelligence costs a hefty sum, but some stellar white papers are free in the Research section at www.recordedfuture.com.

Government bodies such as the Cybersecurity and Infrastructure Security Agency (CISA), the NSA, and NIST also release valuable reports. These reports are often prescriptive—that is, geared at what should be done—rather than being intelligence. However, the Cybersecurity Advisories available from the NSA have some juicy intel. The European Union Agency for Cybersecurity (ENISA) also regularly releases reports about threat actors, the threat landscape, and emerging trends. These are freely available at enisa.europa.eu, in the Publications section.

The corporate and government sources listed in Table 13-6 are only examples (and suggestions), and many other sources exist. I encourage you to review them.

Table 13-6   Publishers of Threat Intelligence Reports

Publisher	URL	Type
Cisco Talos	blog.talosintelligence.com	Commercial
Recorded Future	recordedfuture.com/research/intelligence-reports	Commercial
NSA	nsa.gov/Press-Room/Cybersecurity-Advisories-Guidance/	Governmental
ENISA	enisa.europa.eu/publications	Governmental

News

There's no clear dividing line between news and reports. Both are written documents that (ideally) provide good analysis. For some people, "news" has the connotation of being less technical, but, as we'll see, that isn't universal. Generally, news focuses on—surprise—new things. It puts a premium on recency. Last month's big hack may be discussed in an annual report, but it won't still be plastered all over news sites. Keeping abreast of the news helps you understand and respond to the threat landscape more quickly. Naturally, news written for casual readers may lack technicality or detail, but many security-savvy sources are available. Some examples are provided in Table 13-7.

Table 13-7   Sources of Threat Intelligence News

Outlet	URL
The Hacker News	thehackernews.com
The Register (Security)	www.theregister.com/security/
Krebs on Security	krebsonsecurity.com

Collective, Ad Hoc, and Automated Intelligence

Threat intelligence can take many forms beyond the feeds, reports, and news we've introduced. There are other written and verbal threat intelligence mediums, such as advisories, newsletters, and podcasts. Also, additional mechanisms exist for representing and disseminating threat intelligence. The upcoming section "STIX and TAXII" discusses some of them. In any case, threat intelligence is categorized based on how it is collected, represented, and disseminated. Cisco enumerates three threat intelligence categories, which are not necessarily mutually exclusive: collective, ad hoc, and automated threat intelligence.

Collective threat intelligence involves many entities (people or organizations) collaboratively gathering and sharing intelligence among themselves. Rather than a company being an island unto itself, it shares its intelligence with others. Conversely, the company benefits from the intelligence shared with it. A collective approach to threat intelligence confers many advantages, including:

- All participants in collective intelligence have a broader picture of the threat landscape. Companies can learn from others' experiences before encountering threat actors themselves.

- Enhanced understanding of threat actors facilitates incident detection (by providing indicators of attacks) and incident response (because attack methodologies are better understood).

- Companies that engage in collective intelligence can benefit from the aggregate skill and work of the group. They can tap a deep well of expertise at a lower cost than by using alternatives. Maintaining a purely in-house capability or subscribing to threat intelligence feeds is far more expensive.

Collective and other forms of threat intelligence can be further characterized by how intelligence is gathered, analyzed, and disseminated. Ad hoc and automated threat intelligence are opposite, but complementary, approaches to this process.

"Ad hoc" translates to "for this," and **ad hoc threat intelligence** implies intelligence that is generated for a specific reason. It is created and distributed "for this," whether "this" is a threat actor, an attack pattern, or a group of malicious domains. Ad hoc intelligence requires a person to gather information manually, analyze it to produce intelligence, and then distribute their findings. As you can imagine, this approach can be labor intensive, slow, and far from scalable. Still, ad hoc intelligence can be specific and highly relevant among similar environments. Used correctly, it can be very actionable.

On the other hand, **automated threat intelligence** is created, disseminated, and ingested programmatically. By employing machine-readable formats, information can be continuously gathered and analyzed. Standards like STIX and TAXII ensure that two systems can share intelligence without human interaction. Unsurprisingly, automated threat intelligence is faster and more scalable than manual approaches. Collective and automated threat intelligence pair nicely. The automation of intelligence sharing makes large-scale (collective) intelligence sharing feasible. Our next topic, STIX and TAXII, expands on threat intelligence automation.

STIX and TAXII

STIX and TAXII are complementary standards maintained by the OASIS Cyber Threat Intelligence Committee. They allow threat intelligence to be defined (STIX) and exchanged (TAXII) without human interaction. Together, STIX and TAXII are related and complementary standards that have seen growing adoption in recent years.

STIX

Key Topic

Structured Threat Information Expression (STIX) provides a way of representing threat intelligence using machine-readable JSON. It includes two kinds of objects: STIX domain objects (SDOs) and STIX relationship objects (SROs). SDOs can be various data points, such as attack patterns, identities, locations, and vulnerabilities. SROs tie SDOs together by explaining how they relate. There are two SRO types: relationships ("this is how these SDOs are related") and sightings ("these were seen"). Table 13-8 lists 8 of the 18 currently defined SDOs.

Table 13-8   A Sampling of STIX Domain Objects (SDOs)

Name	Description
Attack pattern	Methods used by attackers (tactics, techniques, and procedures)
Identity	Individuals or organizations
Indicator	A pattern or signature of malicious behavior
Location	A physical (geographic) location
Malware	An instance of malicious code
Threat actor	Malicious individuals or groups
Tool	Software (not malware) that may be used in attacks
Vulnerability	An exploitable bug in software

SDOs like these are then related using SROs. Example 13-1 shows a simplified example to help you see how STIX works. This example strips out most of the metadata that would otherwise be included. It also doesn't include all possible information that SDOs and SROs can convey.

Example 13-1   *Simplified Example of STIX*

```
objects": [
        {
            "type": "threat-actor",
            "id": "threat-actor-A"
            "name": "Kitten Surprise",
            "threat_actor_types": ["hacker"],
        },
        {
            "type": "tool",
            "id": "tool-A",
            "name": "nmap",
            "tool_types": ["information-gathering"]
        },
        {
            "type": "relationship",
            "relationship_type": "uses",
            "source_ref": "threat-actor-A"
            "target_ref": "tool-A"
                    }
]
```

This STIX document contains two SDOs (a threat actor and a tool) related by an SRO ("uses"). JSON is an acquired taste, so let's put it in English: The threat actor "Kitten Surprise" is a hacker uniquely identified as "threat-actor-A." The information-gathering tool Nmap is uniquely identified as "tool-A." They are related as follows: The threat-actor-A object (Kitten Surprise) uses tool-A (Nmap).

Unabridged STIX documents can be impressively granular, conveying a great deal of valuable information. For instance, our "Kitten Surprise" threat actors could also have fields denoting their goals, expertise, resources, and more. Both the threat-actor and tool objects can include textual descriptions for additional context.

TAXII

Trusted Automated Exchange of Intelligence Information (TAXII) is the mechanism used to transfer STIX information. TAXII establishes secure connections over HTTPS and offers two mechanisms for exchanging data: collections and channels. They work as follows:

- Collections use standard request/response (client/server) exchanges. A client requests information, and TAXII manages the delivery of the requested material (if available).

- Channels use a "pub/sub" (that is, publisher/subscriber) model. Rather than wait for client requests, TAXII channels push updated information to clients. The published information is disseminated to any clients who subscribe.

There's a lot more to TAXII, but the nitty-gritty details are beyond the scope of the CCST Cybersecurity exam. The main thing to remember is that TAXII manages the exchange of STIX data, and the relationship between the two is much like that of HTTP and HTML.

How and Why to Proactively Share Threat Intelligence

In preparing for and responding to threats, all stakeholders should be provided with the information necessary to work effectively. This includes intelligence about threat actors, actions taken to preempt them, and changes made when responding to attacks. Sharing information intelligence (both internally and externally) confers several benefits.

Inside an organization, looping in stakeholders enables appropriate responses to threats. Imagine a new phishing technique targeting finance departments. Looping in stakeholders might look like this:

- IT and security personnel can use the knowledge to mitigate the attack by applying security controls.

- Leadership may update awareness and training policies.

- Workers in the finance department are less likely to be tricked simply because they're aware of the threat.

Quickly and consistently updating documentation is also essential. Changes—whether proactive or reactive—introduce risk if not properly communicated. Blocking a port or deploying an IPS may prevent an attack, but doing these things can also break legitimate services. Maintaining documentation and communicating changes can prevent issues before they happen and make troubleshooting more efficient. At a minimum, documentation should be centralized, version controlled, and subject to an approval process. Otherwise, when responding to threats, you might introduce risk.

As we've touched on already, there are advantages to sharing information and intelligence externally. If your industry has an **information sharing and analysis center (ISAC)**, sharing what you know can protect other companies from any threats you've encountered. Helping potential competitors may seem strange, but they'll also share their knowledge.

The net effect is that members of an industry—even competitors—can cooperate to protect against threats. There are ISACs for numerous industries. Table 13-9 lists some examples. A more extensive list is available at nationalisacs.org.

Table 13-9 Examples of ISACs

Name	Link
Automotive ISAC	www.automotiveisac.com
Electricity ISAC	www.eisac.com
Information technology ISAC	www.it-isac.org
Oil and natural gas ISAC	www.ongisac.org
Water ISAC	www.waterisac.org

Summary

Knowledge is power. The more you know about threat actors and their activities, the better you can proactively protect your infrastructure. This chapter introduces the following concepts:

- **Threat intelligence** is threat information after analysis, processing, and interpretation. It provides the context needed to make sound decisions. There are three categories of threat intelligence:

  - **Tactical intelligence** is technical and specific. An example is a signature indicating a network attack.

  - **Operational intelligence** is broader. For instance, a threat actor's overall attack patterns fall into this category.

  - **Strategic intelligence** is the broadest category. Threat trends for a particular industry are strategic in scope.

- Vulnerability intelligence is commonly grouped with threat intelligence (since it describes weaknesses that threat actors seek to exploit). Standard tools and sources used for vulnerability intelligence are

  - **CVE:** Assigns unique identifiers and brief descriptions for vulnerabilities.

  - **NVD:** Expands on and enriches CVE information.

  - **CVSS:** Scores vulnerabilities based on their difficulty, impact, and other metrics.

- Reports, news articles, and other written threat intelligence can be rich in detail and nuance. When reading, consider the source's reliability and the information's credibility.

- Threat intelligence can be categorized based on how it is collected, distributed, and ingested:

  - **Collective threat intelligence** involves many entities collaboratively producing and exchanging intelligence.

  - **Ad hoc threat intelligence** is created and consumed on a case-by-case basis.

■ **Automated threat intelligence** uses standards such as STIX and TAXII to enable the programmatic exchange of intelligence.

■ **STIX** and **TAXII** are used to represent threat intelligence and disseminate it, respectively.

■ There are several benefits to sharing threat intelligence both internally and externally. It is also important to ensure that documentation is consistently maintained and communicated.

Exam Preparation Tasks

As mentioned in the Introduction, you can customize your strategy for exam preparation. Suggested tasks include the exercises here, Chapter 16, "Final Preparation," and the exam simulation questions on the companion website.

Review All Key Topics

Review the most important topics in this chapter, noted with the Key Topics icon in the outer margin of the page. Table 13-10 lists these key topics and the page number on which each is found.

Key Topic

Table 13-10   Key Topics for Chapter 13

Key Topic Element	Description	Page Number
Paragraph	Threat intelligence	242
Paragraph	CVE	244
Paragraph	CVSS	244
Section	Collective, Ad Hoc, and Automated Intelligence	247
Section	STIX	248
Section	TAXII	250

Complete Tables and Lists from Memory

There are no memory tables for this chapter.

Define Key Terms

Define the following key terms from this chapter and check your answers in the glossary:

threat actor, threat intelligence, tactical intelligence, operational intelligence, strategic intelligence, Common Vulnerabilities and Exposures (CVE), National Vulnerability Database (NVD), Common Vulnerability Scoring System (CVSS), Security Content Automation Protocol (SCAP), collective threat intelligence, ad hoc threat intelligence, automated threat intelligence, Structured Threat Information Expression (STIX), Trusted Automated Exchange of Intelligence Information (TAXII), information sharing and analysis center (ISAC)

Review Questions

1. Which kind of threat intelligence includes specific identifiers such as IP addresses or indicators of compromise?

    a. Strategic

    b. Operational

    c. Tactical

    d. None of the above

2. Which of the following are components that CVSS uses to measure impact? (Choose two.)

    a. Authentication

    b. Availability

    c. Authorization

    d. Integrity

3. What characteristics should be evaluated when consuming threat intelligence? (Choose two.)

    a. Source reliability

    b. Writing style

    c. Source likability

    d. Information credibility

4. Which of the following are STIX domain objects (SDOs)? (Choose three.)

    a. Indicator

    b. Malware

    c. Relationship

    d. Threat actor

5. Which of the following are models that TAXII uses to distribute threat information? (Choose two.)

    a. Mailing lists

    b. Channels

    c. Collections

    d. Broadcast

CHAPTER 14

Disaster Recovery and Business Continuity

This chapter covers the following topics:

- **Disaster Recovery Plans:** This section discusses procedures for responding to specific disasters, including recovering IT capabilities at alternate sites.

- **Business Impact Analyses (BIAs):** This section helps in determining critical business functions, their dependencies, and the consequences of their disruption.

- **Business Continuity Plans:** This section covers ensuring that business functions can endure in the face of disruptions or disasters.

- **Disaster Recovery Versus Business Continuity:** This section helps you distinguish between these two often-confused concepts.

It can be easy to fixate on attacks and threat actors, but cybersecurity professionals aren't restricted to adversarial activities. They're also responsible for protecting the confidentiality, integrity, and availability of systems from other threats. This chapter mainly focuses on availability. Disaster recovery and business continuity are two related business processes that aim to preserve the availability and continuity of critical systems and business processes.

This chapter covers information related to the following Cisco Certified Support Technician (CCST) Cybersecurity exam objective:

4.4. Explain the importance of disaster recovery and business continuity planning.

"Do I Know This Already?" Quiz

The "Do I Know This Already?" quiz allows you to assess whether you should read this entire chapter thoroughly or jump to the "Exam Preparation Tasks" section. If you are in doubt about your answers to these questions or your own assessment of your knowledge of the topics, read the entire chapter. Table 14-1 lists the major headings in this chapter and their corresponding "Do I Know This Already?" quiz questions. You can find the answers in Appendix A, "Answers to the 'Do I Know This Already?' Quizzes and Review Questions."

Table 14-1 "Do I Know This Already?" Section-to-Question Mapping

Foundation Topics Section	Questions
Disaster Recovery Plans	1, 2
Business Impact Analyses (BIAs)	3
Business Continuity Plans	4
Disaster Recover Versus Business Continuity	5

1. Transitioning to which of the following alternate sites requires the least downtime?

   a. Cold

   b. Warm

   c. Hot

   d. None

2. Which of the following backup types is most resistant to natural disasters?

   a. On-site

   b. Off-site

   c. Full

   d. Differential

3. Which metrics are commonly used when performing a business impact analysis (BIA)? (Choose two.)

   a. ROI

   b. CVSS

   c. RTO

   d. RPO

4. Which of these are standard inputs used when forming a business continuity plan (BCP)? (Choose two.)

   a. Market analysis

   b. Risk assessment

   c. Acceptable use policy (AUP)

   d. Business impact analysis

5. Which of the following statements are true of disaster recovery (as opposed to business continuity)? (Choose two.)

   a. Focuses on data and information systems

   b. Focuses on business functions

   c. Has a broader scope

   d. Has a more specific scope

Foundation Topics

Key Topic

Disaster Recovery Plans

Security isn't limited to preventing or responding to attacks and malicious activity. Cybersecurity professionals are also tasked with maintaining or restoring the availability of critical resources following catastrophic events. The destruction of systems and data cannot always be avoided, but by implementing disaster recovery procedures and controls, you can ensure that a disaster isn't an existential threat to your organization. A **disaster recovery plan (DRP)** defines detailed response procedures for a specific disaster. DRPs are often focused on recovering IT capabilities at alternate sites. Well-formed DRPs minimize the downtime, damage, and cost of disasters. They also contain provisions for returning to normal operations after disasters.

The first step in establishing a DRP is establishing the team responsible for its creation, execution, testing, and maintenance. As with incident response teams, roles and responsibilities must be well defined, and contact information must be closely maintained. The disaster recovery team should likewise be multidisciplinary and representative of all stakeholders in the organization.

Once formed, the team must gather all the information needed to generate a DRP. Which disaster scenarios are possible? For instance, we face different natural disasters based on our geographic regions, but nearly all of us are at risk of disastrous cyberattacks. Any disaster with a reasonable likelihood of occurring should be noted and planned for. In addition to answering "What are the risks?" we must answer "What is at risk?" In other words, what assets are critical to the company? Assets are anything of value. They can include hardware, software, data, and employees. Thoroughly documenting and prioritizing assets ensures that DRPs focus on recovering the most important things.

With a clear picture of risks and assets, the disaster recovery team then creates plans for disaster scenarios. DRPs should include all the information that may be needed to mount effective responses, including the following:

- Procedures for failing over to alternate sites

- Procedures for failing back to primary sites

- Backup requirements and restoration procedures

- Evacuation plans

- Communication requirements and contact information

- Infrastructure documentation and vendor lists

- Training and testing expectations

Plans should be specific to potential disasters; the response to a hurricane wouldn't necessarily work well for a cyberattack. Let's take a closer look at different categories of disasters.

Key Topic

Disasters

A **disaster** is any occurrence of significant degradation, damage, or destruction of critical assets. Any disaster with a reasonable likelihood of occurring should be planned for, so it's worth discussing common disaster scenarios. There are two categories of disasters: natural disasters and human-caused disasters.

Natural disasters (sometimes called "acts of God") are natural events that humans do not cause and cannot control. They are generally caused by weather or tectonic events, and their likelihood is always dictated by geographic region. For example, an organization in Florida doesn't need to plan for avalanches, but it might need to plan for hurricanes. Figure 14-1 provides a rough view of common natural disasters in different regions of the contiguous United States. Natural disasters include the following:

- Hydrological disasters, such as mudflows, avalanches, and floods

- Geophysical disasters, such as landslides, earthquakes, and volcanoes

- Meteorological disasters, such as hurricanes, tornadoes, and cyclones

- Climatological disasters, such as droughts and wildfires

- Biological disasters, such as bacterial and viral pandemics

- Space-based disasters, such as solar storms and, less commonly, solar impacts

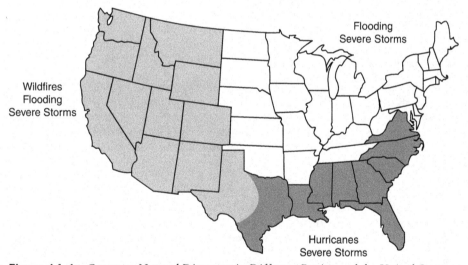

Figure 14-1   *Common Natural Disasters in Different Regions of the United States*

Human-caused disasters are caused or controlled by human activity. Like natural disasters, they are usually location dependent. Certain regions experience war or terrorism at a higher rate than others. On the other hand, cyberattacks can occur regardless of location. Human-caused disasters include the following:

- Terrorist attacks

- Hazardous material leaks

- Infrastructure failures (for example, dams, electrical grids, or gas lines)

■ Transportation accidents (for example, plane crashes and train derailments)

■ Cyberattacks

After determining what natural and human-caused disasters have a reasonable likelihood of occurring for your organization, you need to choose which disaster recovery controls to implement.

Disaster Recovery Controls

The CCST Cybersecurity exam objectives specify three categories of disaster recovery controls: detective, preventive, and corrective. **Detective controls** help alert you when disasters occur. In the context of cyberattacks, detective controls can be any detection mechanisms we've already discussed (IDSs, SIEMs, antimalware, and so on). Detective controls are perhaps less relevant to natural disasters—which are usually hard to miss—but they do exist. For instance, periodic pings to sites and systems can be detective controls; if the target goes offline, you know something is wrong—perhaps an earthquake at a remote branch.

Preventive controls aim to stop disasters from causing damage. High-availability mechanisms, dynamic routing protocols, and redundant power sources are preventive controls. Because they allow systems to continue functioning after major failures, these techniques can stop IT issues from blossoming into actual disasters. For example, Internet exchange points (IXPs) are places where major ISPs and content distribution networks (CDNs) connect their networks. If an IXP goes down, it's certainly a disaster for anyone who works there, but it's probably not an Internet-wide disaster. That's because routers detect outages and respond by sending traffic down alternate routes.

Finally, **corrective controls** react to incidents that have already occurred. One corrective control is maintaining and failing over to alternative sites (usually in different regions). When your primary site is flooded, you certainly haven't prevented the disaster, but you can quickly address its effects by failing over. Alternate sites come in a few flavors, depending on their level of readiness (and cost). In Special Publication 800-34, NIST defines five categories (see Table 14-2):

Key Topic

■ Cold sites: A **cold site** has the necessary space, infrastructure, and utilities; however, it is not stocked with servers, workstations, networking equipment, or other assets. To move to a cold site, a business must acquire hardware and set it up. Cold sites are the least expensive option but take the longest to get up and running.

■ Warm sites: A **warm site** is stocked with most or all of the necessary equipment. It isn't fully configured and may require some setup before the organization can transition.

■ Hot sites: A **hot site** has all the necessary hardware, infrastructure, and support staff. Businesses can very quickly switch to hot sites, but they are expensive.

■ Mobile sites: A **mobile site** is a preconfigured, transportable failover site. Mobile sites are commonly housed in trailers or shipping containers.

■ Mirrored sites: A **mirrored site** is identical to the primary site. It has all the necessary equipment and maintains identical, synchronized copies of data and systems.

Table 14-2   Cold, Warm, Hot, Mobile, and Mirrored Sites

Type of Site	Features Provided	Transition Speed	Cost
Cold site	Space and infrastructure	Slow	Low
Warm site	Space, most hardware, and infrastructure	Moderate	Moderate
Hot site	All systems and personnel needed for operations	Fast	High
Mobile site	Variable	Variable	High
Mirrored site	Identical, fully synchronized backup environment	Instantaneous	Very high

In addition to moving to (and back from) alternate sites, another major corrective control is recovering from data backups. By storing copies of data elsewhere, you can recover files even if the original system has been destroyed. There are several backup strategies, as we'll discuss next.

Backups

A **backup** is a copy of data stored on alternate media or in another location. Backups can be categorized by where the data is stored (on-site or off-site backups) and how they are created (full, incremental, and differential backups). Ideal backup locations and methods vary depending on company requirements and the disasters deemed possible.

On-site backups are created and stored locally within a single building or campus. The benefit of on-site backups is their speed. LAN access is generally much quicker than Internet access, so creating and recovering from backups takes less time. The downside of on-site backups is that, because they're near the systems they protect, certain disasters can destroy all the data at once. If your backup server is 50 feet away from the systems it protects and a tornado destroys the building, you aren't recovering your data.

Off-site backups are stored further away from the protected systems, perhaps in other geographic regions or cloud data centers. Their pros and cons are the inverses of on-site backups. Whereas on-site backups are fast, off-site backups are limited to the speed of the Internet connection. However, maintaining off-site backups reduces the chances of a single disaster destroying all your data. In a perfect world, both on-site and off-site backups would be maintained: on-site for speedy recovery and off-site to ensure that the data is truly safe.

For both on- and off-site backups, it's vital to protect the data as if it's the primary copy. This includes encrypting any data in transit or at rest (as backups are sent to on-site or off-site locations and stored) and implementing appropriate access controls. Without encryption and access controls, your information is more likely to be exposed, tampered with, or destroyed.

Another consideration with backups is the specific method used to copy data. There are three commonly used backup mechanisms: full, incremental, and differential backups. They differ in terms of what data is copied when a backup is performed:

- The **full backup** strategy is straightforward: A copy of all the data is created with each backup. The downside of full backups is their size. All data, changed or unchanged, is copied every time. This consumes more storage on the backup solution and causes higher network utilization.

- **Incremental backups** are one approach to deduplicating data and being more space efficient. In an incremental backup, a full backup is taken, and subsequent backups only copy data that has changed since the previous (full or incremental) backup.

- A **differential backup** is similar to an incremental backup but copies any data that has changed since the last full backup.

Figure 14-2 provides a graphical representation of full, incremental, and differential backups, and Table 14-3 summarizes these backup methods.

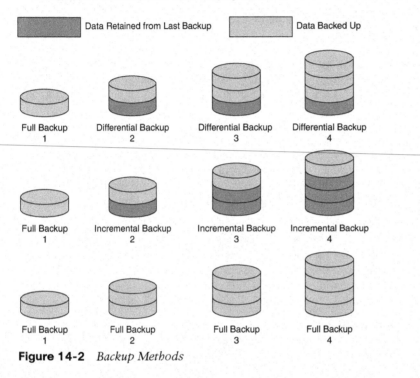

Figure 14-2 *Backup Methods*

Table 14-3 Summary of Backup Methods

Backup Method	Data Copied	Backup Speed	Space Consumed
Full	All data, always	Slow	Highest
Incremental	Changes since last full or incremental backup	Fast	Lowest
Differential	Changes since last full backups	Moderate	Moderate

We'll conclude this section by introducing a common mantra in backup design: the **3-2-1 rule** (see Figure 14-3). Initially created by photographer Peter Krogh, the 3-2-1 rule has since been adopted and promulgated by bodies like the Cybersecurity and Infrastructure Security Agency (CISA). It consists of three simple rules to follow:

- Keep three copies of data (the primary and two backups). This reduces the risk that a single disaster will destroy all data.

- Use at least two different types of media. These can be hard drives, solid-state drives, optical media, cloud storage, or even magnetic tape. Storing data on at least two media types helps protect against different hazards. For instance, a power surge may damage connected mass storage drives, but it's less likely to corrupt optical media disks. Similarly, maintaining at least one **offline backup** that is not network connected can prevent ransomware from encrypting all your primary and backup copies. A related option is to use **immutable media**, which is written to only once. Examples include CD-R and DVD-R discs, which cannot be modified after data is written to them.

- Ensure that one copy is stored offsite, away from your home or business. The importance of this has already been covered: If all your data is in the same place, a natural disaster may ruin all copies.

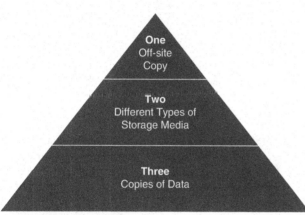

Figure 14-3   *The 3-2-1 Rule*

Business Impact Analyses (BIAs)

A process that is related to disaster recovery is **business impact analysis (BIA)**. BIA is a methodical process of discovering and analyzing the business impact of losing critical assets or business functions. It assists in risk management decisions by rating the importance of assets, acceptable downtime, or maximum data loss. NIST divides BIAs into three discrete phases:

1. Identify critical business processes and the IT resources they rely on. Critical processes are often identified and cataloged using stakeholder interviews. After input is gathered from personnel across all functional areas, the supporting IT resources are determined.

2. For each critical resource, determine its impact and the maximum acceptable disruption. There are many kinds of impacts, both quantitative and qualitative, including the following:

   a. Financial impact (through decreased revenue or increased expenses)

   b. Strategic impact (slowed, degraded, or stopped long-term plans)

   c. Reputational impact (harm to customer satisfaction or brand)

   d. Legal impact (lawsuits, breaches of contract, or compliance issues)

3. Based on the impact of outages, prioritize the recovery order.

BIAs can function as inputs to disaster recovery plans or business continuity plans (BCPs), which we will discuss shortly. Two metrics used in BIAs are recovery time objectives (RTOs) and recovery point objectives (RPOs).

Recovery Time Objectives

Recovery time objectives (RTOs) define the maximum time systems or business processes can be disrupted. If a server has a 1-hour RTO, the business can tolerate an hour of downtime before there are unacceptable consequences. Determining an RTO for each critical function helps prioritize mitigations and recovery efforts. The RTO will also impact decisions about whether an organization uses hot, warm, or cold alternate sites.

Imagine two different servers at a popular financial institution: The first handles high-speed payment transactions, and the other sends out billing reminders to customers. The transaction server may process several real-time payments per second and have an RTO of 60 seconds. Conversely, the billing reminder server might go down for hours and happily pick up where it left off. Its RTO could be 12 hours. Looking at the RTO of each server, it's obvious which should be prioritized. You would put more effort into preventing downtime on the transaction server (redundant NICs, power supplies, RAID arrays, load balancing, and so on). If both systems were to go down simultaneously, the billing reminder server wouldn't even be on your radar!

Recovery Point Objectives

Recovery point objectives (RPOs) are distinct from RTOs. Whereas RTOs define how long systems or processes can be down, RPOs dictate the acceptable data loss. In other words, what is the earliest point in time to which data can be restored without unacceptable consequences? If we can feasibly restore from a week-old backup (therefore losing the last week's data), our RPO is said to be a week,

The RPO for a retail transaction database might be 10 minutes; that is, the retailer would be willing to lose up to 10 minutes' worth of data when recovering from a loss. Conversely, a workstation may have an RPO of 12 hours. When the RPO is very short, you need to implement additional controls to protect data (for example, more frequent backups, RAID, high-availability clustering, database mirroring). For higher RPOs, periodic backups may suffice. Table 14-4 summarizes RTO and RPO.

Table 14-4   RTO and RPO

Metric	Description	Applies To
Recovery time objective (RTO)	Maximum downtime of systems or processes	Hardware, software, business processes
Recovery point objective (RPO)	The maximum acceptable amount of data loss following an incident or disaster	Data

Business Continuity Plans

The final acronym we'll look at in this chapter is BCP. An organization creates a **business continuity plan (BCP)** to ensure that it can continue functioning in the face of disruption, It is easy to confuse BCPs with DRPs, but BCPs emphasize different things. A BCP assesses the critical functions identified in a BIA—not necessarily technical—and develops plans for keeping the company running. A BCP can define how operations are continued in the face of disaster, how different departments can be quickly reconstituted, and other organizational concerns. A business continuity plan typically includes these elements:

- An accounting of critical business functions, risks, and business impact analysis
- Maintenance of a multidisciplinary business continuity team and clearly defining roles and responsibilities
- Communication requirements and contact information
- Provisions for testing the BCP
- Training and awareness needs

The business continuity planning process can generally be described in three phases:

1. Perform a business impact analysis to gauge the consequences of business function disruptions and perform a risk assessment to estimate overall risk.

2. Evaluate available business continuity strategies and create a business continuity plan. Strategies employed may include the following:

    a. Mitigating or preventive techniques to reduce or avoid negative scenarios.

    b. Implementing recovery and restoration strategies to minimize the disruption of critical systems and business functions.

    c. Implementing emergency, crisis, and incident response strategies detailing immediate actions to take in these situations. These are often defined in separate documents (emergency response plans, incident response plans, and so on). Naturally, these specific plans should align with the broader BCP.

3. Regularly review, test, and maintain the BCP.

Disaster Recovery Versus Business Continuity

Disaster recovery and business continuity planning are conceptually similar, but they aren't the same. In disaster recovery, the focus is on systems and data. A business continuity plan often includes a disaster recovery plan but is broader in scope and concerned with critical business functions and other non-technical items. Table 14-5 compares the two.

Table 14-5 Disaster Recovery Versus Business Continuity

Factor	Disaster Recovery	Business Continuity
Focus	Data and systems	Business processes
Goal(s)	Reduce downtime and data loss	Maintain continuity of operations during disruptions
Scope	Technical response	Includes and expands on disaster recovery concerns

One commonality between disaster recovery and business continuity is the need for regular testing and improvement. There are several approaches to testing a DRP and a BCP. Regularly employing varied test mechanisms helps reduce omissions or outdated components in DRPs and BCPs. In order of cost, these tests are checklist scenarios, tabletop exercises, and partial or full simulations:

- In a **checklist exercise**, leaders go through a plan point-by-point, ensuring that its contents are current and there are no glaring omissions. These exercises are quick, cheap, and require the least preparation. However, they are unlikely to be sufficient alone.

- In a **tabletop exercise**, team members are presented with a fictional scenario, and they discuss how they would handle it. These exercises are useful for concretizing team members' roles, honing teamwork, and evaluating the plan.

- A **partial simulation** is a fictional scenario involving a subset of an organization's systems and personnel. A partial simulation can provide a nice balance between realism and cost when stress-testing recovery and continuity plans.

- A **full simulation** involves nearly all systems and personnel and is the most realistic way to test plans. It is a great way to identify subtle deficiencies in DRPs and BCPs but requires the most time and money.

Summary

Disaster recovery plans, business impact analyses, and business continuity plans are complementary, overlapping documents. They ensure that organizations can recover from—and continue operating in the wake of—disruptions to critical systems and business functions. This chapter introduces the following concepts:

- **Disaster recovery plans (DRPs)** define detailed response procedures for specific disasters. Steps to creating DRPs include:

  - Defining a disaster recovery team

  - Finding and prioritizing assets

  - Determining which threats are relevant

  - Developing specific disaster recovery plans

- Disasters can be natural or caused by humans:

  - **Natural disasters** include earthquakes, hurricanes, and flooding.

  - **Human-caused disasters** include terrorism, war, and cyberattacks.

- Different controls can be implemented as part of disaster recovery plans:

  - **Detective controls** identify imminent or ongoing disasters.

  - **Preventive controls** aim to avoid disasters or their consequences.

  - **Corrective controls** fix systems in the wake of disasters.

- A **business impact analysis (BIA)** catalogs critical business functions, their dependencies, and the ramifications of disruptions. Two important BIA metrics are

  - **Recovery time objective (RTO)** defines the maximum acceptable downtime for systems or processes

- **Recovery point objective (RPO)** defines the maximum acceptable loss of data

- A **business continuity plan (BCP)** defines how a business continues to function in the face of disruptions. In broad strokes, BCPs are created as follows:

  - Review business impact analysis and risk assessment.

  - Select continuity strategies and form a plan.

  - Regularly review, test, and maintain the BCP.

- DRPs are data- and system-centric, whereas BCPs are broader and inclusive of business functions.

- Both DRPs and BCPs should be regularly tested. Testing options include the following:

  - Checklist exercises

  - Tabletop exercises

  - Partial simulations

  - Full simulations

Exam Preparation Tasks

As mentioned in the Introduction, you can customize your strategy for exam preparation. Suggested tasks include the exercises here, Chapter 16, "Final Preparation," and the exam simulation questions on the companion website.

Review All Key Topics

Review the most important topics in this chapter, noted with the Key Topics icon in the outer margin of the page. Table 14-6 lists these key topics and the page number on which each is found.

Table 14-6   Key Topics for Chapter 14

Key Topic Element	Description	Page Number
Section	Disaster Recovery Plans	256
Section	Disasters	256
List	Cold, warm, and hot sites	258
Table 14-2	Cold, Warm, Hot, Mobile, and Mirrored Sites	259
Section	Backups	259
Table 14-3	Summary of Backup Methods	260
Paragraph	BIAs	261
Paragraph	RTO	262
Paragraph	RPO	262
Paragraph	Business continuity plans	262
Table 14-5	Disaster Recovery Versus Business Continuity	263
List	DRP and BCP testing strategies	264

Complete Tables and Lists from Memory

Print a copy of Appendix B, "Memory Tables," found on the companion website, or at least the section for this chapter, and complete the tables and lists from memory. Appendix C, "Memory Tables Answer Key," includes completed tables and lists you can use to check your work.

Define Key Terms

Define the following key terms from this chapter and check your answers in the glossary:

disaster recovery plan (DRP), disaster, natural disaster, human-caused disaster, detective control, preventive control, corrective control, cold site, warm site, hot site, mobile site, mirrored site, backup, on-site backup, off-site backup, full backup, incremental backup, differential backup, 3-2-1 rule, offline backup, immutable media, business impact analysis (BIA), recovery time objective (RTO), recovery point objective (RPO), business continuity plan (BCP), checklist exercise, tabletop exercise, partial simulation, full simulation

Review Questions

1. Which of the following disaster scenarios are natural disasters? (Choose three.)

    a. Hurricane

    b. Pandemic

    c. Flooding

    d. Terrorism

2. Which of the following backup methods uses the least storage capacity?

    a. On-site

    b. Incremental

    c. Differential

    d. Full

3. What recovery metric defines the maximum acceptable downtime of a system?

    a. ROI

    b. ROE

    c. RPO

    d. RTO

4. Which of the following is a key goal of BCPs?

    a. Maintaining business functions during disruptions

    b. Responding to incidents effectively

    c. Recovering from backups quickly

    d. Monitoring for policy violations

5. Which of the following DRP or BCP testing methods requires the least preparation?

    a. Tabletop exercise

    b. Checklist exercise

    c. Partial simulation

    d. Full simulation

CHAPTER 15

Incident Handling

This chapter covers the following topics:

- **Events and Incidents:** This section discusses benign and malicious observables.

- **Incident Response:** This section discusses the four phases of incident response, as defined in NIST SP 800-61.

- **Attack Frameworks and Concepts:** This section covers conceptual tools that help in analyzing attacks and attackers.

- **Evidence and Artifacts:** This section discusses how to understand and protect forensic information.

- **Compliance Frameworks:** This section discusses common regulations, their purposes, and notification requirements.

Computer security incidents range from being relatively minor, such as policy noncompliance, to catastrophic cyberattacks. As much as we strive to prevent incidents, they happen in every company. Organizations that develop incident response capabilities reduce their risk because quick, effective action limits the impact of incidents. On the other hand, unprepared companies swiftly discover that the worst time to plan is during an incident! This chapter introduces incident handling and several related topics.

This chapter covers information related to the following Cisco Certified Support Technician (CCST) Cybersecurity exam objective:

5.1. Monitor security events and know when escalation is required.

5.2. Explain digital forensics and attack attribution processes.

5.3. Explain the impact of compliance frameworks on incident handling.

5.4. Describe the elements of cybersecurity incident response.

"Do I Know This Already?" Quiz

The "Do I Know This Already?" quiz allows you to assess whether you should read this entire chapter thoroughly or jump to the "Exam Preparation Tasks" section. If you are in doubt about your answers to these questions or your own assessment of your knowledge of the topics, read the entire chapter. Table 15-1 lists the major headings in this chapter and their corresponding "Do I Know This Already?" quiz questions. You can find the answers in Appendix A, "Answers to the 'Do I Know This Already?' Quizzes and Review Questions."

Table 15-1 "Do I Know This Already?" Section-to-Question Mapping

Foundation Topics Section	Questions
Events and Incidents	1
Incident Reponses	2
Attack Frameworks and Concepts	3
Evidence and Artifacts	4
Compliance Frameworks	5

CAUTION The goal of self-assessment is to gauge your mastery of the topics in this chapter. If you do not know the answer to a question or are only partially sure of the answer, you should mark that question incorrect for purposes of self-assessment. Giving yourself credit for an answer you correctly guess skews your self-assessment results and might provide you with a false sense of security.

1. Which of the following is the most appropriate category for a server crash?

    a. Incident

    b. Adverse event

    c. Event

    d. Artifact

2. Which of the following are signs of an incident? (Choose two.)

    a. Precursors

    b. Correlations

    c. Indicators

    d. Causations

3. What is the first phase of the Cyber Kill Chain?

    a. Pretexting

    b. Staging

    c. Weaponization

    d. Reconnaissance

4. Which of the following is most volatile?

    a. CD-ROM

    b. Hard drive

    c. RAM

    d. Solid-state drive

5. What regulation seeks to protect the privacy and security of healthcare information?

    a. FERPA

    b. HIPAA

    c. FISMA

    d. GDPR

Foundation Topics

Events and Incidents

Events and incidents are core concepts in incident response. NIST defines an **event** as almost any positive or negative occurrence that can be observed. Events include successful logons, programs executing, and files being opened—each of which can be good or bad, depending on context. **Adverse events** are events with negative consequences. They can result from accidents (such as mistakenly rebooting a domain controller), natural disasters, or malicious activity. Adverse events stemming from malicious activity are often called **incidents**. NIST describes incidents as adverse events in which security policies and practices are violated. Figure 15-1 shows the relationship between events, adverse events, and incidents.

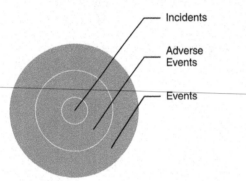

Figure 15-1   *Events, Adverse Events, and Incidents*

Incident Response

Incident response is the systematic process of identifying, responding to, and recovering from incidents. A methodical, well-defined approach to incidents is hugely beneficial to organizations. The sooner you discover security breaches, the sooner you can intervene. And, if you intervene effectively, the scope and impact of incidents is lessened. In other words, a solid incident response capability reduces organizational risk. NIST's Special Publication 800-61 defines four phases of incident response:

1. Preparation
2. Detection and analysis
3. Containment, eradication, and recovery
4. Post-incident activity

Preparation

Preparation is crucial. Without it, you're less equipped to detect incidents, respond to them efficiently, or learn and improve. The preparation phase lays the groundwork for all later activities.

The preparation phase encompasses all activities you perform before an incident response. Common elements include assembling an incident response team, gathering needed tools, ongoing training, and developing standard operating procedures (SOPs). The more effort you put into these activities, the more likely you are to mount effective incident responses.

Team

An **incident response team (IRT)** is typically multidisciplinary and includes technical and non-technical members. Typical roles in incident response teams include the following:

- Leadership that coordinates team members and has the authority to approve emergency changes

- Security analysts who watch for and respond to attacks

- Subject matter experts (SMEs) who understand how important systems work and how changes can affect them

- Communications staff who manage how employees, customers, and other stakeholders are informed

- Human resources officers for managing policy violations and insider threats

- Legal experts who interpret regulations, analyze legal risks (such as the risk of fines or lawsuits), and liaise with law enforcement

Imagine the potential pitfalls of omitting some of these roles. Without leadership, the incident response team may lack the authority to make urgent changes. Without SMEs, the team might make changes that break critical systems. Without communications experts, even well-intentioned announcements could exacerbate problems. Not all roles are needed in every situation—the database administrator can't help much during a DDoS—but it's worth considering who should be involved when different incidents arise.

Beyond divvying up roles and responsibilities, the team must determine how it interacts and communicates. Is contact information readily available? Has an alternate method of communication been agreed upon? If your usual systems are under attack, you will need to be able to communicate some other way. Finally, is there a schedule for who is on call? If the alarms go off at 3 a.m. and there is no on-call schedule, everyone might roll over and fall back asleep.

Tools

Incident response tools—both hardware and software—should be gathered and maintained. NIST provides a great list of incident response tools in SP 800-61. Examples include the following:

- Laptops, which allow team members to perform their duties regardless of location. They should be prepared with any needed software, such as SSH clients, protocol analyzers, and cryptographic utilities.

- Storage devices (USB thumb drives, external hard drives, optical media, and so on) to store forensic disk images, software installers, and other data.

- Spare equipment (servers, workstations, switches, and so forth) to replace anything that has been infected or damaged.

15

Many of these tools may be stowed away and used primarily when incidents occur. Another set of tools is deployed and used consistently before things go haywire. These tools, which include the following, are primarily detective in nature:

- Vulnerability scanners automatically search for and report on vulnerable systems in an environment.

- Intrusion detection systems (IDSs) look for signatures of malicious activity and alert on detections. Intrusion prevention systems (IPSs) go further and block potential attacks.

- Security information and event management (SIEM) systems aggregate log data from disparate sources and help find correlations between events.

- **Security orchestration, automation, and response (SOAR)** tools enable rapid, programmatic responses to security incidents.

Training and SOPs

Another aspect of the preparation phase is training the team and developing standard operating procedures (SOPs). Training often covers several domains. First, an incident response team should be taught the roles and responsibilities of its members. This ensures that certain activities aren't duplicated or outright missed. Next, team members should be taught how to use their tools effectively; learning during an emergency is less ideal. Other training may cover general cybersecurity, emerging threats, internal policies, or regulatory concerns. Incident response teams can also be trained and tested in tabletop exercises. In the context of incident response, tabletop exercises are simulated attacks in which team members discuss which actions they'll take. Conducting these exercises ensures that everyone knows their roles and responsibilities, established procedures, and other facets of incident response.

Responding to actual incidents can be stressful, and even well-trained teams are liable to make mistakes. To ensure consistent and quick action, SOPs define sequences of steps to take when faced with specific situations. SOPs may be created for countless scenarios, from minor account breaches to devastating ransomware attacks. Unlike ad hoc approaches, clearly defined procedures ensure that steps aren't missed, ensure that the team isn't paralyzed while determining what to do, and ensure that incident response continually improves. SOPs are frequently revised with lessons learned during tabletop exercises or actual cybersecurity incidents.

Reporting and Notification Requirements

A final consideration during the preparation phase is reporting and notification requirements. Reporting may be required internally—such as to company leadership. It may also be mandatory for external parties. Depending on the industry or jurisdiction, a company may be legally required to inform governmental bodies, customers, or other stakeholders. Examples include the following:

- The Cyber Incident Reporting for Critical Infrastructure Act (CIRCIA) compels critical infrastructure companies to report certain incidents within 72 hours.

- The Health Insurance Portability and Accountability Act (HIPAA) requires that affected individuals are notified of data breaches within 60 days of their discovery.

- The Gramm–Leach–Bliley Act (GLBA) mandates that regulators are informed if sensitive customer information is exposed.

- Certain states, such as California, have their own data breach reporting obligations.

Such regulations and requirements should be considered during preparation and folded into incident response procedures. Failure to comply with reporting requirements can result in reputational, financial, and legal repercussions. This chapter concludes with a more detailed discussion of common regulations.

Detection and Analysis

Having prepared for incident response, the next phase is to detect and analyze possible incidents. Detection can be difficult. How do you distinguish between events, adverse events, and bona fide incidents? Incident detection often involves using several data sources to correlate signs, and practice and knowledge are required to do this well. Potential incidents must then be accurately analyzed. Is the data accurate? Does it signify a real incident? If it is an incident, what is its priority? These complexities highlight the importance of solid training during the preparation phase.

Given the volume of log data that systems generate, using dedicated systems for storage, analysis, and review can be beneficial. A security information and event management (SIEM) platform is one such system. A SIEM system aggregates log data from many sources, searches for correlations between events, and provides a centralized platform for alerting and analysis. A related technology—security orchestration, automation, and response (SOAR) platforms—can programmatically detect and respond to incidents. Whereas a SIEM system focuses on detection, a SOAR platform is more geared toward response.

Data—whether ingested by a SIEM system or manually inspected—comes from any number of places. Collecting logs from varied sources provides a more comprehensive view of your infrastructure. Common examples enumerated by NIST include the following:

- IDS and IPS platforms, which can log potential network or host intrusions

- Antimalware agents, which detect malicious software using signatures and other techniques

- Host logs, which record events on workstations and servers

- Network device logs, which record network events such as dropped packets

Imagine a scenario where these varied log sources are fused to paint a complete picture. Malware is detected on a workstation; soon after, the operating system records a series of successful privilege escalations. Your network IDS and firewall then record scanning activity and dropped packets almost simultaneously. Combined, these sources are more than the sum of their parts. They clearly show malware triggering privilege escalations, followed by reconnaissance activity.

After detecting a potential incident, you must move to analysis and prioritization. What signs are you seeing? NIST defines two kinds of signs to be on alert for:

- **Precursors** signal that an incident may happen. A port scan or a vulnerability scan of a server may be a precursor of a forthcoming attack.

■ **Indicators** point to an ongoing (or finished) incident. Excessive outbound DNS traffic to an unknown server—a characteristic of data exfiltration or DDoS attacks—is an indicator.

You must then drill down into the available information. Do events deviate from expected behavior on the network? Are some events correlated with others (as in the malware scenario)? How certain are you that it's an incident at all? During analysis, you get a better handle on the nature and scope of the incident. If your analysis suggests that an incident has occurred, you must prioritize it. NIST delineates three factors to use for prioritization:

■ **Functional impact:** The downtime or degradation of systems caused by an incident

■ **Information impact:** The loss of data confidentiality, integrity, and availability

■ **Recoverability:** The difficulty of restoring systems and data

Containment, Eradication, and Recovery

After the detection and initial analysis of an incident, you respond to it. NIST groups three response activities into this phase: containment, eradication, and recovery. The most immediate goal is the containment of the incident—that is, slowing down and stopping ongoing damage. Examples of containment strategies include disconnecting affected systems from the network, quarantining and monitoring them on a separate network, and shutting them off. The overriding concern during containment is to buy time to prepare a more thorough response.

After initial containment actions, steps are chosen and followed to terminate incidents. If applicable, you now work on eradicating the incident, perhaps by cleaning malware-infected systems, addressing vulnerabilities, blocking compromised accounts, or using security systems to obstruct certain activities. The idea is to identify and remove any facets of the incident you can. After containing and eradicating an incident, you proceed to recovering from it. Recovery includes restoring systems' functionality and averting similar incidents in the future. You might roll back actions taken during containment and eradication (for instance, bringing systems back online) or prevent reoccurrences by patching systems and expanding security controls. Containment, eradication, and recovery conclude incidents, but there's one final phase to incident response: post-incident activities.

Post-Incident Activities

In the final incident response phase, post-incident activities, NIST emphasizes **lessons learned**. During lessons learned, the entire incident response process is reviewed. Team members critically evaluate how well they were prepared, how efficiently the incident was detected and analyzed, and the effectiveness of the response. Where deficiencies are identified, improvements are implemented. No incident response is perfect, and each one is an opportunity to learn and improve.

Another component of post-incident activities is creating and disseminating incident reports. An incident report contains a detailed summary of the whole incident response sequence and is beneficial for a few reasons. First, documenting incidents can assist with similar occurrences in the future. Also, reports can be provided to stakeholders (internal or external) to ensure that everyone is in the loop. Table 15-2 summarizes the incident response lifecycle.

Key Topic

Table 15-2   The Incident Response Lifecycle

Phase	Description
Preparation	Building and training the incident response team; gathering and maintaining tools
Detection and analysis	**Detection:** Finding signs (precursors or indicators) of an incident **Analysis:** Evaluating signs, determining whether an incident occurred, and gauging its priority
Containment, eradication, and recovery	**Containment:** Immediate actions to slow or stop ongoing incidents **Eradication:** Specific steps to wipe out all facets of an incident **Recovery:** Restoring functionality and preventing reoccurrences of similar incidents
Post-incident activities	Steps taken to learn from and document incidents

15

Digital Forensics and Incident Response

Digital forensics and incident response (DFIR) is a superset of the incident response process we've introduced. Compared to traditional incident response—which is focused on quickly and effectively ending incidents—DFIR folds in forensic analysis and investigation. Specifically, DFIR adds the collection, preservation, and dissection of evidence. It can therefore answer questions that incident response isn't typically concerned with. For instance, adding forensic investigation answers the questions "What was the precise sequence of events?" and "Who was the source of the incident?" A huge concern in DFIR is gathering evidence without tainting it. It is important to zealously guard the integrity of evidence because it may end up in court. Later in this chapter, in the section "Evidence and Artifacts," we discuss evidence gathering and handling.

Attack Frameworks and Concepts

Incidents and attacks are often complex. Bad actors proceed through numerous steps to achieve their goals, and your visibility into their activities is usually incomplete. The frameworks and concepts in this section help you handle complexity by teasing out patterns in attackers' behaviors, relating different components of attacks, or simply providing an exhaustive accounting of attack techniques. Like Newtonian physics, they aren't perfect models, but they are often accurate enough. This section discusses three frameworks: the Cyber Kill Chain, the ATT&CK framework, and the Diamond Model. It concludes with tactics, techniques, and procedures (TTPs), a concept common to each framework.

Lockheed Martin Cyber Kill Chain

The Lockheed Martin **Cyber Kill Chain** describes seven discrete steps that attacks often follow. These steps tend to occur serially, with each phase relying on those preceding it. Like all other attack models, the Cyber Kill Chain doesn't fit every situation perfectly. Nonetheless, it is a valuable lens throughout which to view attacks and incidents. Table 15-3 provides a description and example of each phase in the Cyber Kill Chain.

Table 15-3   The Cyber Kill Chain

Phase	Description	Example
Reconnaissance	Gathering information about a target	An attacker scans a web server and discovers a vulnerability.
Weaponization	Developing an attack (such as an exploit) that targets an identified weakness	The attacker writes code to exploit the web server vulnerability.
Delivery	Getting the weapon to the victim	The attacker uploads the payload by exploiting a misconfigured web application.
Exploitation	Exploiting the system by using the delivered weapon	The attacker executes the code by sending a GET request for its URL.
Installation	Installing additional software, such as malware or persistence mechanisms, on the target	The payload downloads and deploys persistence mechanisms.
Command and control (C2)	Establishing a channel through which to remotely control target	The attacker establishes interactive shell access.
Actions on objectives	Executing the end goal of the attack	The attacker extracts a database table containing payment information.

MITRE ATT&CK

MITRE's Adversarial Tactics, Techniques, and Common Knowledge (**ATT&CK**) framework provides another lens through which to view threat actors and attacks. It is structured as matrixes of observed tactics and techniques, arranged into various attack phases. MITRE provides several matrixes, including a wide-ranging enterprise matrix and numerous platform-specific matrixes. ATT&CK is expansive: It covers 14 attack phases, many comprising dozens of techniques and subtechniques. MITRE's ATT&CK matrixes are freely available at attack.mitre.org. While a detailed treatment of ATT&CK is beyond the scope of the CCST Cybersecurity certification, it is well worth perusing the matrixes. Each technique enumerated in the ATT&CK matrixes is a link you can click to read an explanation, review real-world examples, and find relevant mitigations and detection mechanisms.

Diamond Model of Intrusion Analysis

The **Diamond Model of Intrusion Analysis** (often shortened to "Diamond Model") relates four components of attacks: adversaries, infrastructure, capabilities, and victims. Its name stems from the distinctive, four-cornered diagram used to relate these items (see Figure 15-2). Each component (or corner) is a distinct element of the attack:

- Adversaries are the attackers who carry out intrusions.

- Infrastructure includes any resources attackers use to further the intrusion. Examples are servers and public services such as DNS.

- Capabilities are developed by adversaries to perform attacks. They include tactics, techniques, and procedures (TTPs), exploits, and attack tools.

- Victims are the people or groups targeted by adversaries.

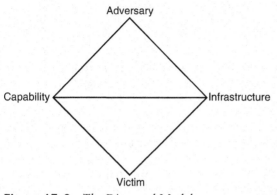

Figure 15-2 *The Diamond Model*

15

Imagine a family member installing a malicious browser toolbar that records keystrokes and uploads the credentials and other data collected to a cloud-hosted server. In this case, the adversary is whoever created the toolbar, the victim is your family member, the capability is the malicious toolbar, and the infrastructure is the server used to collect keystrokes. This (admittedly simplified) example is shown in Figure 15-3.

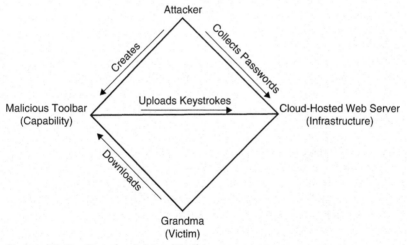

Figure 15-3 *Grandma's New Toolbar*

Tactics, Techniques, and Procedures

Tactics, techniques, and procedures (TTPs) are methods both attackers and defenders use to achieve their goals. Understanding adversarial TTPs is a core aim of the Cyber Kill Chain, ATT&CK framework, and Diamond Model. Notice that each of these conceptual lenses tends to focus on the actions used by threat actors. The acronym TTP seems redundant as tactics, techniques, and procedures are nearly synonyms, but NIST distinguishes between them as follows:

- Tactics are the broadest descriptions of attacker behaviors. For instance, a threat actor may adopt the tactic of stealing financial information by hacking websites.

- Techniques are more specific behaviors that occur while pursuing a tactic. The threat actor may use SQL injection techniques to pursue their broader tactic (of stealing data from websites).

- Procedures are highly granular descriptions of what is done within a technique. Our threat actor's procedure could be to send a predictable sequence of SQL injection strings as part of their SQL injection technique.

This example is illustrated in Figure 15-4. Actual attacks may use multiple techniques as part of their tactics, and they may use multiple procedures within a technique.

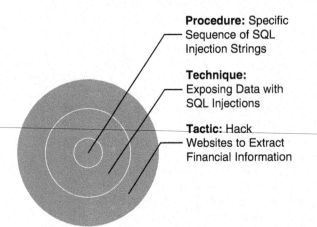

Procedure: Specific Sequence of SQL Injection Strings

Technique: Exposing Data with SQL Injections

Tactic: Hack Websites to Extract Financial Information

Figure 15-4   *Tactics, Techniques, and Procedures (TTPs)*

Evidence and Artifacts

Identifying, collecting, and maintaining relevant information is challenging during both incident response and forensic investigation. There are countless **artifacts**, or data points, generated as the result of activity. Artifacts include log entries, timestamps, command histories, registry entries, caches, and deleted files. Some artifacts expose what occurred during an incident, and many are irrelevant. When artifacts are pertinent and illustrate what transpired (or a sliver of what transpired), they're referred to as **evidence**.

Sources and Volatility

To gather evidence and artifacts effectively, you must consider the differing volatilities of data types. **Volatility** refers to how quickly data degrades or disappears on a system. Highly volatile data, such as the contents of RAM, may be quickly overwritten or evaporate when power is removed. Nonvolatile data, such as data burned to DVDs, tends to persist for long periods, regardless of power. As you have likely gathered, data volatility influences the order in which evidence is gathered. Figure 15-5 shows the relative volatilities of different data storage mechanisms.

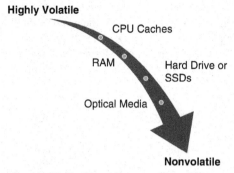

Figure 15-5 *Data Storage Volatilities*

Preservation and Chain of Custody

In addition to gathering evidence in the proper order, you must also maintain the evidence correctly. Evidence could end up in court, and it needs to be protected so that it retains its integrity. It is possible to verify the integrity of evidence by using techniques like forensic imaging and chains of custody. **Forensic imaging** involves using tools to make perfect copies of data—identical down to individual bits! The idea is to have exact copies of data that can be dissected without affecting the original evidence. A forensic imaging process could use built-in utilities, as in this example:

1. Mount a partition (the original evidence) in read-only mode. This ensures that the operating system can read, but not alter, the storage device's contents. If you don't trust your OS, you may also use hardware devices called "write blockers" to guarantee that write operations are blocked.

2. Use a command such as **dd** to copy the entire partition, bit by bit, to an image file.

3. You now have the original storage device and a file containing a copy of it. But is it genuinely identical? To confirm, you can run a hashing command like **sha256sum** against the original and against the copy. If the hashes match, the data is identical.

4. Unmount the original and store it safely.

5. Mount the image file as a partition for forensic analysis. This, too, should be mounted in read-only mode so that its data isn't inadvertently altered.

Forensic imaging yields a provably identical copy of the evidence that can be analyzed. Even if you have a copy, you must zealously protect the integrity of the primary evidence. This is commonly done by maintaining a strict chain of custody. A **chain of custody** document records how evidence is handled from collection until it (potentially) ends up in court. It is often a form filled out with detailed custody information. Chain of custody documents include information such as the following:

- Who collected the evidence

- How the evidence was collected

- Each person who handled the evidence (and when it was handled)

- Where and how the evidence was stored

Ideally, a chain of custody should be an unbroken record detailing everything between evidence collection and presentation in court. Imagine an hour-long gap in the chain of custody because an analyst forgot to log some activity. Particularly in legal contexts, such an error could lead to evidence being thrown out. After all, what happened during that hour? What was done with the evidence A chain of custody must be a chain with no missing links.

Compliance Frameworks

While introducing the incident response process, we mentioned the importance of understanding any regulations your organization is subject to. Numerous industry- or region-specific regulations influence how incidents should be handled. The CCST Cybersecurity objectives list five frameworks (more accurately called regulations and standards) you need to know: GDPR, HIPAA, PCI-DSS, FERPA, and FISMA. This section briefly introduces each framework and its impact on incident handling. It focuses on the notification requirements these frameworks impose (summarized in Table 15-4).

GDPR

The **General Data Protection Regulation (GDPR)** is a European Union law enacted in 2018. Its goals are to expand European citizens' control over personal data and strengthen privacy controls. GDPR is multifaceted and affects many areas of business and technology. For instance, the ubiquity of cookie consent banners on the Internet stems from GDPR compliance. GDPR generally requires security breaches to be reported to authorities within 72 hours of their detection.

HIPAA

The **Health Insurance Portability and Accountability Acts (HIPAA)** is a U.S. regulation implemented in 1996 that aims to strengthen the privacy and security of protected health information (PHI). In fact, two major components of HIPAA are the Privacy Rule and the Security Rule. Unsurprisingly, the Privacy Rule covers the sharing of healthcare data. The Security Rule dictates the technical and organizational security controls needed to protect healthcare data. In the event of a data breach, HIPAA requires a notification letter to be sent to affected parties within 60 days.

PCI-DSS

The **Payment Card Industry Data Security Standard (PCI-DSS)**, which was developed and adopted jointly by all major credit card processors, applies to any organization that works with cardholder data. PCI-DSS has stringent security control requirements and mandates regular audits and reports. Interestingly, PCI-DSS doesn't directly address notification requirements, but it is implied and expected in supporting documentation published by the standards body.

FERPA

The **Family Educational Rights and Privacy Act (FERPA)** is a U.S. law initially enacted in the 1970s. Its goal is to protect educational records and give students more control over how their information is disseminated. FERPA's approach to notifications is particularly bizarre. It does not require students to be informed when their information is exposed. Instead, schools only need to note breaches in academic records. (A student would need to request and review their records to find out.) The U.S. Department of Education advocates a more proactive approach!

FISMA

The **Federal Information Security Management Act (FISMA)** is another U.S. regulation geared toward federal government information systems. FISMA requires security controls, the development of incident response capabilities, and compliance with NIST security standards and guidelines. It contains stringent notification requirements: Proper authorities must be notified within an hour after detecting a major incident.

Comparing Regulatory Frameworks

If you're new to these regulations, their acronyms and summaries presented may make your eyes glaze over. Thankfully, you won't need to be a legal expert to take the CCST Cybersecurity. The broad strokes, such as each regulation's purpose and notification requirements, are the most important things to remember. Table 15-4 provides a concise comparison of all five items.

Key Topic

Table 15-4   Regulations and Their Notification Requirements

Name	Brief Description	Notification Requirements
GDPR	European Union privacy law	Authorities notified within 72 hours
HIPAA	U.S. health care privacy law	Patients sent letter within 60 days
PCI-DSS	Payment card security standard	Nebulous (but encouraged)
FERPA	U.S. educational records privacy law	Noted in student record
FISMA	U.S. federal agency security law	Authorities notified in 1 hour (major incidents)

15

Summary

A solid incident response process allows businesses to respond to attacks and other occurrences quickly and effectively. Given the complexity of incidents and attacks, numerous frameworks exist to facilitate our understanding. Furthermore, incident response has interrelationships with forensics, regulations, and threat intelligence. This chapter introduces the following concepts:

- **Incident response** is a process of identifying, responding to, and recovering from incidents. NIST defines four phases of incident response:

  - Preparation

  - Detection and analysis

  - Containment, eradication, and recovery

  - Post-incident activities

- The **Lockheed Martin Cyber Kill Chain** lists seven distinct phases of cyberattacks:

  - Reconnaissance

  - Weaponization

  - Delivery

  - Exploitation

- Installation

- Command and control (C2)

- Actions on objectives

- MITRE's **ATT&CK framework** is a rich collection of attacker techniques with corresponding mitigations and examples.

- The **Diamond Model** looks at the relationships between four elements of attacks:

  - Adversary

  - Victim

  - Infrastructure

  - Capabilities

- The Cyber Kill Chain, ATT&CK framework, and Diamond Model all focus heavily on adversaries' tactics, techniques, and procedures (TTPs).

- It is vital to consider data volatility during incident response and forensic investigation. Gathering information in the wrong order can result in crucial information being lost.

- Forensics should never be performed on original evidence (lest it be inadvertently altered). Analysis should instead be conducted on forensic copies whenever possible.

- **Chain of custody** should be obsessively maintained if the integrity of evidence is important (for example, if it will end up in court).

- Maintaining compliance with regulations and standards is important. Some prominent examples include the following:

  - GDPR

  - HIPAA

  - PCI-DSS

  - FERPA

  - FISMA

Exam Preparation Tasks

As mentioned in the Introduction, you can customize your strategy for exam preparation. Suggested tasks include the exercises here, Chapter 16, "Final Preparation," and the exam simulation questions on the companion website.

Review All Key Topics

Review the most important topics in this chapter, noted with the Key Topics icon in the outer margin of the page. Table 15-5 lists these key topics and the page number on which each is found.

Table 15-5   Key Topics for Chapter 15

Key Topic Element	Description	Page Number
Paragraph	Incident response	270
Table 15-2	The Incident Response Lifecycle	275
Table 15-3	The Cyber Kill Chain	276
Paragraph	The MITRE ATT&CK framework	276
Paragraph	The Diamond Model of Intrusion Analysis	276
Paragraph	Tactics, techniques, and procedures	277
Paragraph	Sources of evidence and their volatility	278
Paragraph	Evidence preservation and forensic imaging	279
Paragraph	Chain of custody	279
Table 15-4	Regulations and Their Notification Requirements	281

Complete Tables and Lists from Memory

There are no memory tables for this chapter.

Define Key Terms

Define the following key terms from this chapter and check your answers in the glossary:

event; adverse event; incident; incident response; incident response team (IRT); security orchestration, automation, and response (SOAR); precursor; indicator; lessons learned; digital forensics and incident response (DFIR); Cyber Kill Chain; ATT&CK; Diamond Model of Intrusion Analysis; tactics, techniques, and procedures (TTP); artifact; evidence; volatility; forensic imaging; chain of custody; General Data Protection Regulation (GDPR); Health Insurance Portability and Accountability Act (HIPAA), Payment Card Industry Data Security Standard (PCI-DSS); Family Educational Rights and Privacy Act (FERPA); Federal Information Security Management Act (FISMA)

Review Questions

1. A user accidentally enters the wrong password and then successfully logs in to their account. How are these occurrences best categorized?

    a. Events

    b. Adverse events

    c. Incidents

    d. None of the above

2. What tool can collect log data from different sources, aggregate it, and correlate events?

    a. IDS

    b. SIEM system

    c. Firewall

    d. Protocol analyzer

3. Which of the following are core components of the Diamond Model of Intrusion Analysis? (Choose two.)

  a. Infrastructure

  b. Motivation

  c. Expertise

  d. Victim

4. What document is maintained to track evidence and attest to its integrity?

  a. Risk register

  b. Chain of custody

  c. SOP

  d. None of the above

5. Which regulation protects educational data?

  a. FISMA

  b. HIPAA

  c. FERPA

  d. GDPR

CHAPTER 16

Final Preparation

The prior chapters introduce the security concepts you need to understand to pass the Cisco Certified Support Technician (CCST) Cybersecurity exam. Among other things, we introduce security principles, network and endpoint security, risk management, and incident handling. If you have a photographic memory, you may now be ready to take the exam. However, if not, it's highly recommended that you spend more time studying. Reviewing the exam material will help you identify where you have room for improvement, fill in those gaps, and ultimately pass the exam with flying colors. This chapter provides recommendations for infusing variety and rigor into your exam preparation.

Tools and Resources

One way to concretize your knowledge and deepen your understanding is to get hands-on with the tools and resources this book mentions. While the CCST Cybersecurity exam doesn't have many applied cybersecurity questions, getting hands-on helps make abstract concepts more concrete. It also lends some variety to the exam preparation journey. Some examples of activities include the following:

- Review the security and configuration options for your small office/home office (SOHO) wireless router.

- Practice interacting with the command-line interfaces of Windows or Linux.

- Familiarize yourself with the **netstat**, **nslookup**, and **tcpdump** commands.

- Look through system logs such as Event Viewer in Windows.

You can also supplement this book by perusing free online resources. Such resources often go into more detail and can be quite interesting. While the contents of this book cover everything necessary to pass the exam, doing "extra credit" can only help as you pursue future certifications and jobs. Some worthwhile resources include the following:

- **The CVE database:** cve.mitre.org

- **The CVSS standard:** first.org/cvss

- **STIX and TAXII standards:** oasis-open.github.io/cti-documentation

- **The ATT&CK matrices:** attack.mitre.org

- **The NIST Incident Handling Guide:** doi.org/10.6028/NIST.SP.800-61r2

Study Tips

This book is constructed to streamline your study and review. Nothing is required, and you are encouraged to study in whatever way suits you but consider using the following strategies to gauge your readiness for the CCST Cybersecurity exam:

- Review the key topics listed at the end of each chapter. Ensure that you understand each concept and that nothing seems to come out of left field.

- Check the key terms listed at the end of each chapter. Can you explain each term in a sentence or two? Knowing the vocabulary is often half the battle.

- Quiz yourself with the "Do I Know This Already" and review questions. If any knowledge gaps are exposed, emphasize studying them.

- Where memory tables are available, fill in the blank cells to test your memory of the material.

- Take practice tests with the Pearson Test Prep software. They provide realistic approximations of the CCST Cybersecurity exam and provide excellent preparation for the real thing.

- Go through the CCST Cybersecurity Exam Blueprint at learningnetwork.cisco.com/s/ccst-cybersecurity-exam-topics. A point-by-point review will ensure that you haven't missed a topic and further reinforce concepts in your long-term memory.

One final note: Part of studying is knowing when to stop! Don't cram late into the evening only to start the exam tired and irritable. The night before your scheduled exam, get a good night's sleep, arrive at the testing center early (if taking the exam in person), and avoid having to rush and stress out. Beginning the exam with a clear, calm mind will benefit your exam score and the test-taking experience itself.

Summary

The tools and suggestions in this chapter have been designed with one goal in mind: to help you develop the skills required to pass the CCST Cybersecurity exam. This book has been developed from the beginning to teach you both the concepts and how they're applied. No matter your experience level, we hope the many preparation tools, and even the book's structure, will help you breeze through the exam. Cybersecurity is a dynamic and engaging field, and we want the CCST Cybersecurity certification to be your stepping stone to a career that never gets old. Good luck with the exam and all your future endeavors!

CHAPTER 17

Cisco Certified Support Technician (CCST) Cybersecurity 100-160 Official Cert Guide Exam Updates

The Purpose of This Chapter

For all the other chapters of this book, the content should remain unchanged throughout this edition of the book. However, this chapter will change over time, and an updated PDF will be posted online so you can see the latest version of the chapter even after you purchase this book.

Why do we need a chapter that gets updated over time? For two reasons:

- To add more technical content to the book before it is time to replace the current book edition with the next edition. This chapter will include additional technology content and possibly additional PDFs containing more content.

- To communicate detail about the next version of the exam, to tell you about our publishing plans for that edition, and to help you understand what it all means for you.

After the initial publication of this book, Cisco Press will provide supplemental updates as digital downloads for minor exam updates. If an exam has major changes or accumulates enough minor changes, we will then announce a new edition. We will do our best to provide any updates to you free of charge before we release a new edition. However, if the updates are significant enough in between editions, we may release the updates as a low-priced standalone eBook.

If we do produce a free updated version of this chapter, you can access it on the book's companion website. Simply go to the companion website page and go to the Exam Updates Chapter section of the page.

If you have not yet accessed the companion website, follow this process:

Step 1. Browse to **www.ciscopress.com/register**.

Step 2. Enter the print book ISBN (even if you are using an eBook): **9780138203924**.

Step 3. After registering the book, go to your account page and select the **Registered Products** tab.

Step 4. Click on the **Access Bonus Content** link to access the companion website. Select the **Exam Updates Chapter** link or scroll down to that section to check for updates.

About Possible Exam Updates

Cisco introduced CCNA and CCNP in 1998. For the first 25 years of those certification tracks, Cisco updated the exams on average every 3 to 4 years. However, Cisco did not pre-announce the exam changes, and those changes felt very sudden. Usually, a new exam would be announced, with new exam topics, suddenly, giving students 3 to 6 months before the only option was to take the new exam. As a result, a student could be studying with no idea about Cisco's plans, and the next day, they had a 3- to 6-month timeline to either pass the old exam or pivot to prepare for the new exam.

Thankfully, Cisco changed its exam release approach in 2023. Called the Cisco Certification Roadmap (https://cisco.com/go/certroadmap), the current plan includes these features:

- Cisco considers changes to all exam tracks (CCNA, CCNP Enterprise, CCNP Security, and so on) annually.

- Cisco uses a predefined annual schedule for each track, so even before any announcements, you know the timing of possible changes to the exam you are studying for.

- The schedule moves in a quarterly sequence:

  - Privately review the exam to consider what to change.

  - Publicly announce if an exam is changing, and if so, announce details like exam topics and release date.

  - Release the new exam.

- Exam changes might not occur each year. When changes occur, Cisco characterizes them as minor (less than 20% change) or major (more than 20% change).

The specific dates for a given certification track can be confusing because Cisco organizes the work by fiscal year quarters. Figure 17-1 spells out the quarters, using an example showing the 2024 fiscal year. Cisco's fiscal year begins in August, so, for example, the first quarter (Q1) of fiscal year (FY) 2024 begins in August 2023.

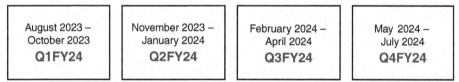

| August 2023 – October 2023 **Q1FY24** | November 2023 – January 2024 **Q2FY24** | February 2024 – April 2024 **Q3FY24** | May 2024 – July 2024 **Q4FY24** |

Figure 17-1 *Cisco Fiscal Year and Months Example (FY2024)*

Focus on the sequence of the quarters to understand the plan. Over time, Cisco may make no changes in some years and minor changes in others.

Impact on You and Your Study Plan

Cisco's new policy helps you plan, but it also means that the exam might change before you pass the current exam. That impacts you and affects how we deliver this book to you. This chapter gives us a way to communicate in detail about any changes as they occur. But you should watch other spaces as well. In particular, bookmark and check these sites for news:

■ **Cisco:** Check their Certification Roadmaps page, at https://cisco.com/go/certroadmap. Make sure to sign up for automatic notifications from Cisco on that page.

■ **Publisher:** Visit our page about new certification products, offers, discounts, and free downloads related to the more frequent exam updates: https://www.ciscopress.com/newcert.

■ **Cisco Learning Network:** Subscribe to the CCNA Community at http://cs.co/9780138203924, where I expect ongoing discussions about exam changes over time. If you have questions, search for "roadmap" in the CCNA community, and if you do not find an answer to your question, ask it!

As changes arise, we will update this chapter with more detail about exam and book content. At that point, we will publish an updated version of this chapter, listing our content plans. The details will likely include the following:

■ Content removed, so if you plan to take the new exam version, you can ignore this information when studying

■ New content planned per new exam topics so you know what's coming

The remainder of this chapter shows the new content that may change over time.

News About the Next Exam Release

This statement was last updated in November 2023, before the publication of the *Cisco Certified Support Technician (CCST) Cybersecurity 100-160 Official Cert Guide*.

This version of this chapter has no news to share about the next exam release.

At the most recent version this chapter, the CCST 100-160 exam version number was Version 1.

Updated Technical Content

The current version of this chapter has no additional technical content.

Answers to the "Do I Know This Already?" Quizzes and Review Questions

Chapter 1

Do I Know This Already?

1. D
2. C
3. C
4. B

Review Questions

1. A. Encrypting data is all about confidentiality, hashing is all about integrity, and redundancy is all about availability. Therefore, hashing data at rest is an example of integrity. Hashing allows you to verify that the data has not been altered by comparing the hash value generated on receipt of the data to the original hash value from when the data was originally put at rest or before it was transmitted. When the hash values match, you know the data has not changed at rest or in transit.

2. C. Fixing vulnerabilities in an environment to eliminate or reduce the risk associated with a threat that could exploit a vulnerability is known as hardening. Attack vector refers to methods cybercriminals use for their attacks to exploit vulnerabilities. Defense-in-depth is a strategy that uses a multitude of layered measures to defend against various threats. Risk is the probability or chance that anyone or anything could exploit a vulnerability in an environment.

3. D. A hacktivist is a person or group that is attacking for social or political purposes. They have some type of social or political agenda—a cause—and they attack to achieve that cause. A hacktivist fights for justice and uses digital disobedience to do so. A recreational cybersecurity attacker is someone who attacks computer systems or networks for fun or curiosity rather than for financial gain or malice. A script kiddie is someone who takes advantage of already existing tools and scripts that are available on the Internet and Dark Web. A cybercriminal is a person or group that attacks for financial gain. Regardless of how they are attacking you or what they are attacking, they are motivated by the money they will receive. An insider is a person or group within an organization that poses a threat to the CIA of that environment. A cyberterrorist is a person or group that works for their country to attack other countries. They typically have access to unlimited resources and can launch highly sophisticated attacks.

4. D. A code of ethics is a set of rules you follow when you are a cybersecurity professional, and without a code of ethics, it would be very hard to make the consistent, repeatable decisions that need to be made every day to uphold the CIA in your organization.

Chapter 2

Do I Know This Already?

1. A
2. C
3. C
4. C
5. C
6. A
7. A, D
8. C

Review Questions

1. D. A backdoor is malicious software that is designed to allow an attacker to remotely access and control the system it has been installed on. A logic bomb is malicious software that is designed to execute on its own at a specific time and date. A worm is malicious software that is standalone and self-replicating, does not need its code to be injected into other programs or files, and does not need human interaction to spread. A Trojan horse is malicious software disguised as a legitimate program or file that executes when the user attempts to access the software.

2. A, B. One very common vulnerability is default accounts with passwords that are weak, guessable, posted to the Internet, or hardcoded in the device. If you don't change the passwords or create different accounts with stronger passwords, you will be at risk. Updates are also a vulnerability for IoT devices. Updates are almost nonexistent for many IoT devices. It seems like manufacturers build an IoT device but forget about or ignore the need to support it. Although IoT devices are easy to purchase and rely on the cloud, those are not in and of themselves vulnerabilities, although they could absolutely lead to other vulnerabilities.

3. A, B, C. Malware being installed on a system and shutting down the system, a server being flooded with useless traffic that overwhelms the server's resources and crashes it, and a user tripping on a power cable and cutting power to various systems are all examples of DoS attacks. A user exfiltrating data from a database would not result in a DoS attack because the system and the data would still be available.

4. B, D. DHCP spoofing and ARP cache poisoning are examples of on-path attacks. Trojan horses and logic bombs are types of malware.

5. A, B, C. The three correct options all have to do with employees accidentally or purposely causing harm or damage to systems or data. They are all examples of insider threats. A cybercrime organization brute-forcing a password for a system they have remote access to is not an insider threat because the attackers are external to the organization.

6. A. Phishing attacks are email-based social engineering attacks that target as many people as possible. An email-based social engineering attack that targets a very specific group of people is a spear phishing attack. An email-based social engineering attack that targets the CEO or CFO of an organization is a whaling attack. An email-based social engineering attack that targets as many systems as possible is not correct because social engineering attacks are human based, not systems based.

7. A, C. Cloning badges and cable cutting are both physical attacks. A logic bomb is an example of malware, and whaling is an example of social engineering.

8. A. Although all these options will help defend against APTs, they are single, individual solutions that you would need to consider as part of a larger solution. The best way to defend against an APT is with a defense-in-depth strategy.

Chapter 3

Do I Know This Already?

1. C
2. D
3. B
4. D
5. D

Review Questions

1. C. AAA stand for Authentication, Authorization, and Accounting.

2. B, E. A bank card and a memorized PIN is MFA because the bank card is something you have, and the memorized PIN is something you know. A username/password and a notification sent to your phone where you must click yes or no is MFA because the username/password is something you know, and the notification sent to your phone where you must click yes or no is something you have. A USB authentication key that needs to be connected to the USB port on the system and then a notification displayed on your phone that needs to be accepted or rejected is not MFA because these factors are both something you have. A fingerprint scan followed by a facial scan is not MFA because these factors are both something you are. A username/password and a four-digit PIN that you have memorized is not MFA because these factors are both something you know.

3. B, C, D. The least-privilege principle (giving users only the minimum permissions they need to do their job), the need-to-know principle (only giving users access to what they need to know to do their job), and the implicit-deny principle (denying

implicitly unless explicitly allowed) are all authorization principles. Enabling MFA is an authentication principle, and recording all activity is an accounting principle.

4. A. A SIEM (security information and event management) solution helps you collect logs, consolidate logs, correlate logs, get notified about abnormalities and threats in logs that are in breach of established policies. A SOAR tool helps you automate responses and reduce the amount of human intervention when an abnormality/threat has been detected. A RADIUS server is a system that helps you implement AAA. MFA (multifactor authentication) is a method of securing authentication by requiring two or more factors to be used when authenticating.

5. C. Port numbers 1812 and 1813 are the default port numbers typically used for RADIUS. Ports 20 and 21 are for FTP, port 22 is for SSH, port 23 is for Telnet, port 3388 is for RPC method calls, and 3389 is for RDP.

Chapter 4

Do I Know This Already?

1. C, D
2. A
3. D
4. A, C
5. B, E
6. A
7. A, B, C
8. A, B
9. D

Review Questions

1. C. Data at rest is data that is being stored in any type of storage. Data in transit is any data that is being transmitted over a wired or wireless network. Data in use refers to any data that is being processed by a CPU. Data that is being exfiltrated is data that is being stolen from a network.

2. A. Symmetric cryptography is also known as private key cryptography because both parties need a copy of the same secret key. So, in this case, Alice sending Bob a message that has been encrypted using a private key that has been shared with Bob so they can both encrypt and decrypt information they have exchanged with each other would be an example of symmetric cryptography. Options B and C are examples of asymmetric cryptography. Option D would never be done and is not an example of symmetric or asymmetric cryptography.

3. A, D. With asymmetric cryptography, if you encrypt with a public key, only the corresponding private key can decrypt it, and if you encrypt with a private key, only the corresponding public key can decrypt it. The other options are not correct examples of asymmetric cryptography.

4. B, D. You can use asymmetric cryptography to generate and exchange symmetric cryptographic keys as well as prove that the data exchanged is from an authentic source. Symmetric cryptography would be used to encrypt data at rest on a server and securely transfer data over a VPN.

5. A, C, D. DH, RSA, and DSA are all examples of asymmetric ciphers. AES and 3DES are symmetric ciphers.

6. C. A CRL is a list of all the digital certificates that have been revoked by the certificate authority (CA) that issued them. OSCP is an Internet protocol defined in RFC 6960 that can be used to get the current revocation status of a single X.509 certificate. SCEP is a protocol for authenticating a CA server, generating a public/private key pair, requesting an identity certificate, and then verifying and implementing the identity certificate. PKI is a set of identities, roles, policies, and actions for the creation, use, management, distribution, and revocation of digital certificates.

7. A, B. MD5 and SHA are both hashing algorithms. AES is a symmetric algorithm, and RSA and DH are asymmetric algorithms.

8. A, B. During web browsing, symmetric cryptography is used to conceal the data traffic as it moves from an end user's device to a web server, and asymmetric cryptography is used to verify that the web server an end user device is connecting to is in fact the correct device.

9. A, C. The following are Cisco next-generation cryptography recommendations:

    AES-GCM-256 for authenticated encryption

    SHA-256, SHA-384, or SHA-512 for integrity (with SHA-384 or SHA-512 preferred over SHA-256)

    HMAC-SHA-256 for integrity

    ECDH-384 for key exchange

    ECDSA-384 for authentication

Chapter 5

Do I Know This Already?

1. C

2. A, B, C

3. B, D, F

Review Questions

1. D. The Link layer for TCP/IP is responsible for the transmission of data frames between adjacent network nodes over a physical medium and the addressing of those frames. It provides mechanisms for error detection, flow control, and data framing. Ethernet is a commonly used protocol in this layer, and therefore MAC addressing is used to address the source and destination of the frames. It is the layer switches use to forward frames within a subnet/VLAN/broadcast domain.

Appendix A: Answers to the "Do I Know This Already?" Quizzes and Review Questions   297

A

2. D. With an on-path attack, attackers intercept HTTP traffic to eavesdrop on or modify data exchanged between a client and a server. To mitigate this, you would implement secure HTTP (HTTPS) with Transport Layer Security (TLS) to encrypt communication between clients and servers so that any communication captured would not be readable by the attacker.

3. E. VLANs are a form of network segmentation that operates at the data link layer (Layer 2) of the OSI model. VLANs allow logical grouping of devices across different physical LAN segments, regardless of their physical location. VLANs are created by configuring network switches to assign specific ports to a particular VLAN. Devices within the same VLAN can communicate with each other as if they were connected to the same physical LAN, and devices in different VLANs are isolated from each other and can only communicate with each other if the traffic is routed using a router. VLANs provide enhanced security by segregating sensitive systems and restricting network access between VLANs.

Chapter 6

Do I Know This Already?

1. B, D, E, G
2. C
3. C
4. C
5. C

Review Questions

1. B, D, F. Secure domains are the security concepts that you need to consider in order to protect the PINs. Management, security intelligence, compliance, segmentation, threat defense, and secure services are all critical domains. PINs are places in a network that you need to secure, such as a data center, a branch office or small office/home office (SOHO), the campus, the WAN, the cloud, and the Internet edge.

2. B, D. There are many benefits associated with virtualization, including the ability to create virtual sandboxes for testing and analyzing potentially malicious software or suspicious network traffic as well as the ability to create isolated virtual networks within a single physical network infrastructure.

3. D. The Cisco Web Security Appliance (WSA) is a hardware or virtual appliance offered by Cisco Systems that provides web security and content filtering capabilities. It is designed to protect organizations from web-based threats, enforce acceptable use policies, and ensure secure and compliant web browsing for users within the network.

4. C. A honeypot is a security mechanism used to detect, deflect, or study unauthorized access attempts or malicious activity within a network or system. It is essentially a decoy or trap designed to attract and deceive attackers, providing valuable insights into their methods, motives, and techniques.

5. B. An IDS/IPS that is configured for behavioral-based detection analyzes normal patterns of network traffic or system behavior and detects deviations from those patterns. It establishes a baseline of normal activity and can then alert you and block traffic when anomalies or suspicious behavior are detected. Behavioral-based detection is useful for identifying unknown or zero-day attacks but may have a higher rate of false positives.

Chapter 7

Do I Know This Already?

1. B, D
2. C
3. A
4. C, D

Review Questions

1. A, B, E. A site-to-site VPN allows two or more separate networks in different physical locations to securely communicate with each other over the Internet. A remote-access VPN allows remote users to establish a secure connection to a corporate network or any private network as if they were directly connected to it. Cisco AnyConnect is a secure remote-access software application developed by Cisco Systems. It is commonly used by organizations to provide secure and encrypted remote access to their networks for employees or authorized users. It is not an automation feature that allows for the dynamic creation and termination of site-to-site VPN connections. The IPsec ESP (not AH) protocol is best suited for remote-access and site-to-site VPN connections. IPsec tunnel mode encapsulates an entire IP packet, including the original IP header.

2. D. Cisco Firepower NGFW integrates with Cisco Advanced Malware Protection (AMP), a cloud-based threat intelligence platform. This integration enables the detection and blocking of advanced malware, zero-day threats, and fileless attacks. The NGFW can leverage file reputation analysis, sandboxing, and retrospective security analysis to identify and mitigate threats.

3. B, C, D, E. With an extended ACL, you can filter traffic based on the source and destination IP address, the Layer 4 protocol, the source and destination application port numbers, and QoS markings, among other things. You can't filter based on application layer header information or the ingress interface of the packet. To do either of those, you would need to use an NGFW that supports those features.

4. C, D. NAC verifies the identity and security posture of devices attempting to connect to the network. It ensures that only authorized devices, such as laptops, desktops, smartphones, or IoT devices with valid credentials, digital certificates, or other authentication mechanisms are granted access. NAC solutions typically offer centralized management consoles or platforms that allow administrators to configure policies, monitor network activity, and generate reports. This centralized approach simplifies policy enforcement, provides visibility into network access activities, and

Appendix A: Answers to the "Do I Know This Already?" Quizzes and Review Questions   299

A

helps with compliance requirements. NAC solutions often include health assessment or posture assessment capabilities. This involves checking the security posture of devices, such as the presence of up-to-date antivirus software, the installation of security patches, and compliance with organizational security policies. Devices that fail the health assessment can be placed in a restricted network segment or denied access until they meet the security requirements.

A NAC is not needed to gain access to a SIEM or SOAR system or to provide an intrusion prevention system and AMP solution.

Chapter 8

Do I Know This Already?

1. C, D
2. C, D
3. A, D
4. C
5. A

Review Questions

1. C, E. By default, wireless SOHO routers and access points are not as safe and secure as they need to be. They have flaws that emerge as time passes that, if left unchanged, could easily jeopardize confidentiality, integrity, and availability. In addition, cybersecurity threats and attack techniques are constantly evolving, so keeping firmware up to date is essential for maintaining the security, performance, and compatibility of wireless devices. Finally, in certain industries or environments, compliance regulations may mandate regular firmware updates as part of security best practices. Adhering to these requirements helps maintain compliance and demonstrate a commitment to security.

2. C, F, I. WPA3 is the recommended wireless encryption standard. It use the AES encryption algorithm, has a maximum key length of 256 bits, and supports both Personal and Enterprise modes.

3. A, C, E. Enterprise mode uses 802.1X with EAP and RADIUS. A RADIUS server is a centralized user management and authentication server that can provide fine-grained control over user access and policies. Enterprise mode also provides detailed logs and accountability for each user, making it easy to trace specific user actions.

4. C. MAC address filtering is a security feature used on wireless networks to control access based on the unique Media Access Control (MAC) addresses (hardware addresses) of devices. It involves creating a whitelist or blacklist of MAC addresses that are either allowed or denied access to the network. When MAC address filtering is enabled, only devices with MAC addresses listed in the whitelist are permitted to connect, while those in the blacklist are blocked.

5. D. War driving is a technique used to discover and map wireless networks by driving around in a vehicle equipped with a Wi-Fi-enabled device, such as a laptop or smartphone. The purpose of war driving is to identify vulnerable or unsecured wireless networks for potential exploitation or unauthorized access.

Chapter 9

Do I Know This Already?

1. D
2. C
3. D
4. C
5. D
6. A
7. B
8. D
9. C
10. B

Review Questions

1. B. **netstat** lists network connections, listening ports, and protocol statistics. **nslookup** is used to generate DNS requests. **tcpdump** and Wireshark capture network traffic but don't necessarily expose listeners that have no traffic.

2. C. BitLocker, FileVault, and LUKS all encrypt whole volumes, so they are examples of full-disk encryption (FDE). Host-based firewalls are software that filters traffic to and from individual hosts. Protocol encryption protects network traffic, not stored data. File system permissions protect stored data but do not use encryption like FDE.

3. B. An error indicates that the system is up but in a degraded state. A warning indicates a possible future issue. A complete outage is an emergency, so neither C nor D can be correct.

4. D. **nslookup** tests DNS. **tcpdump** captures network traffic. **dnf** is a package manager for Linux. **name** is not a command.

5. A. **sudo** enables you to elevate privileges for a single command. **su** enables you to become root for a period of time (not for single commands). **dnf** is a package manager, and **root** is not a command.

6. A, B, D. The major log categories in Event Viewer are Application, Security, Setup, System, and Forwarded Events.

7. C. The first position is a dash, meaning this is a file (a d indicates a directory). The next three positions, rwx, are the owner, indicating that the owner has read, write, and execute permissions. The next three positions, r---, are the group's, so the group

has read permissions. The final three positions, ---, indicate that others have no permissions.

8. B, D. Packet capture (PCAP) files contain captured network traffic, usually generated by either **tcpdump** or Wireshark. **ezcappr** and **deeptap** aren't real programs.

9. C. Automatic updates may accidentally break production systems, so it's wise to test updates before deploying them. Automatic updates are likely to be applied more quickly and are less likely to be missed, so A and B aren't correct. Updates can slow down systems, but automatic updates can be scheduled, so D isn't a huge concern.

10. B. Linux package managers often handle all OS and application updates in one place. Windows and macOS generally have more varied update mechanisms for different types of software.

Chapter 10

Do I Know This Already?

1. A, D
2. B
3. B
4. A, B, C
5. C

Review Questions

1. C. An asset is anything of value to an organization. It can be hardware, software, data, a process, an employee, and so forth. Assets do not need to be tangible, nor do they need to have monetary value (although they often do).

2. B. Remote management and monitoring (RMM) tools, often used by IT service providers, allow remote access and management of endpoints. They often include built-in monitoring, scripting, and inventorying capabilities.

3. C. Full backups copy all data with each backup, so they consume the most space. Differential and incremental backups both employ deduplication strategies to save space, and the strategy employed by incremental backups is the most space efficient. Remote backups have no bearing on size: They can be full, differential, or incremental.

4. B. Containerization enforces the separation of personal and company data. It enables organizations to enforce data protection policies and perform remote wipes without affecting users' personal data.

5. A. PCI-DSS contains very specific security requirements. HIPAA and GDPR have far more general requirements. BYOD isn't directly related to security requirements.

Chapter 11

Do I Know This Already?

1. B
2. C
3. D
4. A
5. C

Review Questions

1. D. MD5 and SHA-256 are cryptographic hashing algorithms. One of their defining characteristics is sensitivity to small changes. YARA is a language used to define the characteristics of malware payloads (for example, text strings or file size). ssdeep is a fuzzy hash because it generates fingerprints that are relatively indifferent to minor changes.

2. B. To calculate the signature of data being transferred, AMP for Networks must first see the entire file. As the last packet traverses the network device, a signature of the fully reconstructed file is generated and checked against known-malicious signatures. If it is deemed malicious, the last packet is withheld.

3. A, B. AMP has many features, but three are commonly highlighted: file reputation, sandboxing, and file retrospection.

4. B. Fuzzy hashing is a general term for file fingerprints that are not very susceptible to minor changes. Dependency graphs are used in computer science but aren't relevant in this context. YARA is a language used to define the characteristics of malware.

5. D. Treatment is the step where malware is removed from systems. It can be carefully resected from an existing operating system or eradicated by reinstalling the operating system completely.

Chapter 12

Do I Know This Already?

1. A, B, D
2. A, B, C
3. B, C
4. B, D
5. C

Review Questions

1. A, C. Security cameras monitor physical environments to detect potentially concerning activities. Intrusion detection systems look for patterns associated with intrusions. Both detect issues. Firewalls attempt to prevent attacks by filtering traffic. Disk encryption protects data by wrapping volumes in strong encryption.

Appendix A: Answers to the "Do I Know This Already?" Quizzes and Review Questions   303

A

2. B, D. Quantitative analysis multiples the SLE (cost of a single risk event) by the ARO (number of events per year) to estimate the ALE (cost per year). Qualitative analysis uses likelihood and impact as inputs.

3. A, B, C, and D. An asset is anything of value, so all these options can be considered assets.

4. C. Active scanners find vulnerabilities by generating network traffic and interpreting host responses. They can get very noisy. Passive scanners listen for indicators of vulnerabilities but do not generate traffic. Generations 1 and 2 are made up.

5. A, B. Natural disasters and ransomware gangs are threats that may exploit vulnerabilities. Lack of input validation and unencrypted network traffic are weaknesses that may be exploited.

Chapter 13

Do I Know This Already?

1. A, B, C
2. C
3. B
4. B, D
5. A

Review Questions

1. C. Tactical threat intelligence tends to be highly specific and can include IP addresses, indicators of compromise (IOCs), and file hashes. Operational intelligence is more general and may describe threat groups and their activities. Strategic intelligence is the most general and can describe overall trends in threat groups, attacks, and industries.

2. B, D. CVSS measures impact using the CIA triad: confidentiality, integrity, and availability.

3. A, D. Source reliability and information credibility need to be evaluated when consuming intelligence.

4. A, B, and D. Indicators, malware, and threat actors are examples of STIX domain objects (SDOs). STIX relationship objects (SRO) are used to relate SDOs.

5. B, C. TAXII supports collections (request/response) and channels (publisher/subscriber) for distributing STIX-formatted information and intelligence.

Chapter 14

Do I Know This Already?

1. C
2. B
3. C, D

4. B, D

5. A, D

Review Questions

1. A, B, C. Natural disasters are occurrences that humans do not directly cause or directly control. Hurricanes, pandemics, and flooding are natural occurrences because humans have little or no ability to prevent them.

2. B. On-site and off-site backups have no bearing on capacity; they may be full, differential, or incremental. A full backup copies all data with each backup, and a differential backup copies all new data since the last full backup. An incremental backup—which copies only data that changed since the last full or incremental backup—copies the least data overall.

3. D. Return on investment (ROI) is a business term, and rules of engagement (ROE) are commonly used in penetration testing. The recovery point objective (RPO) is the maximum acceptable amount of data loss. The recovery time objective (RTO), which stipulates the upper limit on downtime, is the correct metric.

4. A. Monitoring for policy violations and responding to incidents are more closely related to incident response plans (IRPs), discussed in Chapter 15, "Incident Handling." Recovering from backups quickly is associated with disaster recovery. While IRPs are indirectly related to business continuity plans, BCPs are most concerned with maintaining business functions during disruptions, emergencies, or disasters.

5. B. A checklist exercise involves going through plans line-by-line, looking for errors or omissions. At a minimum, tabletop and simulation exercises require a fictional scenario to be prepared.

Chapter 15

Do I Know This Already?

1. B

2. A, C

3. D

4. C

5. B

Review Questions

1. A. These are events—because they occurred. They aren't adverse events because there were no negative consequences. Furthermore, they weren't incidents because security policies and practices weren't violated.

2. B. A security information and event management (SIEM) platform collects data from different sources, normalizes the different formats, and helps with analysis and correlation. Intrusion detection systems (IDSs) monitor for signatures of intrusion. Firewalls allow or deny network traffic based on traffic rules. Finally, protocol analyzers, such as Wireshark, are used to drill down through the different layers of network traffic.

3. A, D. The four corners of the Diamond Model are adversary, victim, infrastructure, and capability. Motivation and expertise are important characteristics for attackers, but they aren't part of this model.

4. B. Chain of custody documents list the who, how, what, and where of evidence handling. A risk register is used to document and track risks. Standard operating procedures (SOPs) are repeatable procedures for regular tasks.

5. C. The Family Educational Rights and Privacy Act (FERPA) was enacted to protect student records. FISMA pertains to federal organizations, HIPAA to healthcare information, and GDPR to European citizens' privacy.

3-2-1 rule   A rule which says that data should be stored in three places (one primary, two backups), on two types of storage media, and with one copy off site.

3DES   *See* Triple Data Encryption Standard (3DES).

802.1X   A framework used for network access control that operates in conjunction with EAP. It defines the process for authenticating devices attempting to connect to a network and enforcing access policies.

A

AAA   A framework that helps you build the controls needed to access computing resources, enforce policies, and audit usage.

access control entry (ACE)   A rule within an ACL that consists of criteria used to determine if traffic matches the entry.

access control list (ACL)   A set of rules or filters commonly used on routers and firewalls to define the permissions and restrictions applied to network traffic. It acts as a security mechanism, allowing or denying access to network resources based on specific criteria, such as source/destination IP addresses, port numbers, protocols, and other factors.

accounting   The process of keeping track of who, what, where, when, why, and how by monitoring, recording, and auditing everything in an organization.

ACE   *See* access control entry (ACE).

ACL   *See* access control list (ACL).

active scanner   A vulnerability scanner that generates traffic and interacts directly with systems.

ad hoc threat intelligence   Intelligence that is manually generated and distributed for a particular topic.

Address Resolution Protocol (ARP)   A protocol that is used to map IP addresses to MAC addresses in a local network. It enables devices to determine the MAC address associated with an IP address for direct communication in a subnet/VLAN/broadcast domain. ARP is a data link layer protocol.

Advanced Encryption Standard (AES)   The most common symmetric key encryption algorithm in use today.

Advanced Malware Protection (AMP)   The Cisco antimalware ecosystem, which consists of endpoint, network, and cloud components.

advanced persistent threat (APT)   A highly sophisticated threat that is designed to go undetected for a prolonged period of time so that the attacker can slowly exfiltrate as much data as they can and spy for as long as they can without being noticed.

adverse event   An event with negative consequences.

AES   *See* Advanced Encryption Standard (AES).

AH   *See* Authentication Header (AH).

ALE   *See* annualized loss expectancy (ALE).

AMP   *See* Advanced Malware Protection (AMP).

AMP for Endpoints   The AMP component installed on endpoints (for example, computers, servers, and mobile devices).

AMP for Networks   The AMP component that detects malware in traffic flows. AMP for Networks is integrated into many Cisco security appliances.

annualized loss expectancy (ALE)   The expected cost of a particular risk over one year.

annualized rate of occurrence (ARO)   The number of expected risk occurrences per year.

anti-replay protection   A VPN protection feature that sequences the packets that flow over a tunnel, ensuring that if someone or something hijacks the VPN tunnel and tries to use existing packets to take over one of your sessions, they can't.

application layer   The topmost layer of the TCP/IP stack and the OSI model, which provides a means for applications to communicate with each other over the network.

APT   *See* advanced persistent threat (APT).

ARO   *See* annualized rate of occurrence (ARO).

ARP   *See* Address Resolution Protocol (ARP).

artifact   Any data point generated by activity on a system.

asset   Anything of value. Examples include hardware, software, data, employees, and reputation.

asset management   The process of deploying, tracking, maintaining, upgrading, and decommissioning assets.

asymmetric cryptography   A type of cryptography that requires the use of two different keys that are related to each other. Together, these keys are known as a public/private key pair.

ATT&CK   MITRE's Adversarial Tactics, Techniques, and Common Knowledge framework, which is a repository of attacker tactics and techniques.

Attack vector   The method a cybercriminal uses for an attack to exploit vulnerabilities.

authentication   The process of proving the identity of someone or something. Verification that someone or something is in fact truly who they say they are.

Authentication Header (AH)   An IPsec protocol that provides integrity, authentication, and protection against replay attacks.

authorization   The process of granting and controlling what an authenticated user is able to do.

automated threat intelligence   Intelligence that is created, disseminated, and ingested programmatically.

availability   A component of the CIA triad that focuses on ensuring that data is accessible when and where it is needed, in a safe and secure manner.

B

backdoor   A type of malicious software that allows an attacker to remotely access and control a system that it has been installed on.

backup   An extra copy of data that is stored to protect against the loss of the primary copy.

BCP   *See* business continuity plan (BCP).

BIA   *See* business impact analysis (BIA).

BitLocker   Microsoft's implementation of full-disk encryption (FDE) for the Windows operating system.

bot   A system (computer/server) under the control of a C2 server.

botnet   A large group of bots.

bring your own device (BYOD)   A policy that allows employees to use their personally owned work devices for work activities.

brute-force attack   An attack that involves systematically trying every possible combination of characters until the correct password is found. Brute-force attacks can be time-consuming but are effective against weak or short passwords.

business continuity plan (BCP)   A plan that seeks to ensure continued business operations in the face of disruption or disaster.

business impact analysis (BIA)   An examination of critical business functions and the consequences of their disruption.

BYOD   *See* bring your own device (BYOD).

C

C2 server   *See* command and control server.

C&C server   *See* command and control server.

CA   *See* certificate authority (CA).

cable cutting   Physically cutting any type of cable to cause an outage that affects availability.

certificate authority (CA)   An entity that creates and issues digital certificates.

certificate revocation list (CRL)   A list of all the digital certificates that have been revoked by the certificate authority (CA) that issued them so that the validity and trustworthiness of the certificates can be verified.

chain of custody   A document that records the entire path taken by evidence, from collection to court.

change management   A business activity that reduces risk by defining how changes are planned, requested, approved, and documented.

checklist exercise   A test for DRPs and BCPs in which leaders evaluate plans line-by-line to ensure that they're current and complete.

CIA triad   A model that represents the foundational principles behind security.

CIDR   *See* classless interdomain routing (CIDR).

Cisco AnyConnect   A secure remote-access software application developed by Cisco Systems that organizations commonly use to provide secure and encrypted remote access to their networks for employees or authorized users.

Cisco Firepower Next-Generation Firewall   Cisco's very own next-generation firewall.

Cisco next-generation cryptography   A Cisco best-practice guidance and approach that is meant to keep everyone up to date with the ever-changing security landscape and ensure that there is a widely accepted and consistent set of cryptographic algorithms that provide strong security and good performance for everyone.

Cisco SAFE (Security Access for Everyone) Security Reference Architecture   A security reference architecture developed by Cisco that helps you design a secure infrastructure for the edge, branch, data center, campus, cloud, and WAN by creating layered defenses and enforcing security policies to safeguard the network infrastructure and data from potential risks.

Cisco Web Security Appliance (WSA)   A hardware or virtual appliance offered by Cisco Systems that provides web security and content filtering capabilities. It is designed to protect organizations from web-based threats, enforce acceptable use policies, and ensure secure and compliant web browsing for users within the network. It is Cisco's version of a proxy server.

Cisco WSA   *See* Cisco Web Security Appliance (WSA).

classless interdomain routing (CIDR)   A method used to represent IP addresses and their associated network prefixes (for example, 192.168.0.0/24).

cloning badges   Taking existing authorized users' badges and cloning them so unauthorized users can use them to gain access to areas and systems.

CMD   An older command-line interface (CLI) used for managing Windows.

CnC server   *See* command and control server.

code of ethics   A set of rules a cybersecurity professional follows.

cold site   An alternate site with space, utilities, and little else.

collective threat intelligence   Intelligence that involves many entities (people or organizations) collaboratively gathering and sharing intelligence between themselves.

command and control server   A server that an attacker sends instructions to that then relays those instructions to multiple bots that are being controlled by the server.

Common Vulnerabilities and Exposures (CVE)   A catalog of publicly known vulnerabilities.

Common Vulnerability Scoring System (CVSS)   A tool used to score vulnerabilities based on their difficulty and impact.

confidentiality   A component of the CIA triad that focuses on ensuring that the privacy of data is maintained and making sure that only individuals who should be able to access systems and view data are able to do so.

containment   Immediate steps taken to control the spread of malware.

corrective control   A security control that addresses the consequences of attacks, incidents, or disasters.

CRL   *See* certificate revocation list (CRL).

cryptography   The process of using mathematical techniques to transform data and prevent it from being read or tampered with by unauthorized parties.

CVE   *See* Common Vulnerabilities and Exposures (CVE).

CVSS   *See* Common Vulnerability Scoring System (CVSS).

Cyber Kill Chain   A seven-stage model of attacker behavior created by Lockheed Martin.

cybercriminal   A person or group that attacks for financial gain.

cyberterrorist   A person or group that works for their country to attack other countries.

D

data at rest   Data that is being stored in any type of storage.

data classification   Categorization of data according to its sensitivity, which often determines the level of security controls for a given data set.

Data Encryption Standard (DES)   A symmetric key encryption algorithm.

data in transit   Data that is being transmitted over a wired or wireless network, whether that network is a private trusted network or a public untrusted network.

data in use   Data that is being processed by the CPU.

data link layer   The layer of the OSI model that is responsible for the transmission of data frames between adjacent network nodes over a physical medium and the addressing of those frames. It provides mechanisms for error detection, flow control, and data framing.

data state   Data's location, including stored data (data at rest), data being transmitted (data in motion), and data being worked on (data in use).

DDoS   *See* distributed denial of service (DDoS).

decryption   The act of turning unreadable ciphertext back into its original plaintext message.

Defender   A suite of security features included in Microsoft Windows (for example, firewall, antimalware, and reputation-based protection).

defense-in-depth   A strategy that uses a multitude of layered measures to defend against various threats.

demilitarized zone   *See* screened subnet (DMZ).

denial of service (DoS)   A type of attack against availability in which the attacker does something to make a service unavailable.

DES   *See* Data Encryption Standard (DES).

detective control   A security control that identifies (and often alerts on) attacks and incidents.

deterrent controls   A control that is used to make attacks less appealing (for example, an ominous warning message when connecting to a server).

DFIR   *See* digital forensics and incident response (DFIR).

DH   *See* Diffie-Hellman (DH).

DHCP   *See* Dynamic Host Configuration Protocol (DHCP).

Diamond Model of Intrusion Analysis   A model that relates four components of attacks: adversary, victim, infrastructure, and capabilities.

dictionary attack   An attack in which the attacker uses pre-generated lists of common passwords or words from dictionaries and systematically tries each one against the target network. This method is faster than a brute-force attack and relies on users' tendencies to choose easily guessable passwords.

differential backup   A partial backup of data that has changed since the last full backup.

Diffie-Hellman (DH)   An asymmetric algorithm that is used to securely generate and exchange symmetric keys between two parties over an untrusted network.

digital certificate   Also known as a public key certificate, a certificate that is used to cryptographically link ownership of a public key with the entity that owns it.

digital forensics and incident response (DFIR)   A combination of forensic investigation and the incident response process.

Digital Signature Algorithm (DSA)   An asymmetric algorithm that is typically used to generate digital signatures today.

disaster   Any occurrence of major degradation, damage, or destruction of critical assets.

disaster recovery plan (DRP)   Detailed procedures for responding to a specific disaster.

distributed denial of service (DDoS)   A more aggressive DoS attack in which many bots being controlled by a C2 server perform an attack against a victim to make it unavailable.

DMZ   *See* screened subnet (DMZ).

DNS   *See* Domain Name System (DNS).

Domain Name System (DNS)   A protocol that translates domain names (such as www.example.com) into IP addresses (such as 203.0.113.10), facilitating the use of easy-to-remember names when referring to resources. It is an application layer protocol.

DoS   *See* denial of service (DoS).

downloader   Malicious software that is designed to download other malicious software.

DRP   *See* Disaster Recovery Plan (DRP).

DSA   *See* Digital Signature Algorithm (DSA).

Dumpster diving   A physical attack that involves looking through the garbage of a victim to find information that could help with an additional attack.

Dynamic Host Configuration Protocol (DHCP)   A protocol used for dynamically assigning IP addresses and network configuration parameters to devices on a network. It simplifies network management and reduces manual configuration. DHCP is an application layer protocol.

E

EAP   *See* Extensible Authentication Protocol (EAP).

ECC   *See* elliptic-curve cryptography (ECC).

elliptic-curve cryptography (ECC)   Newer, modern, asymmetric algorithms that are faster, smaller, and more efficient than RSA and DSA because they are based on the algebraic structure of elliptic curves over finite fields.

EMM   *See* enterprise mobility management (EMM).

Encapsulating Security Payload (ESP)   An IPsec protocol that provides confidentiality, integrity, authentication, and protection against replay attacks.

encryption   The act of turning a plaintext message into ciphertext so it is unreadable.

endpoint   A device that connects to a network and exchanges data with other devices. Examples of endpoints are workstations, servers, smartphones, tablets, and IoT devices.

enterprise mobility management (EMM)   A combination of processes and tools (MDM, MAM, MCM, and MEM) to provide wide-ranging management capabilities for mobile devices.

Enterprise mode   A method of authenticating individual users or devices accessing a network by using 802.1x, EAP, and RADIUS.

ESP   *See* Encapsulating Security Payload (ESP).

ethical hacker   A hacker who uses their skills for good, in a just and lawful manner.

event   Any occurrence that can be observed.

Event Viewer   A graphical utility in Windows for reviewing, analyzing, and filtering log events.

evidence   Artifacts that are pertinent and indicate that some event transpired.

evil twin attack   A type of wireless network attack in which an attacker creates a fake wireless access point (AP) that appears identical to a legitimate one. This is 100% malicious.

exploit   Anything that can take advantage of a vulnerability.

extended ACL   A type of IPv4 ACL that can match the source and/or destination address of a packet, the source and/or destination port of a packet, the protocol of a packet, the QoS markings of a packet, and more.

Extensible Authentication Protocol (EAP)   An authentication framework that enables multiple authentication methods within an enterprise environment.

F

false negative   An event isn't detected, but it did occur.

false positive   An event is detected, but it did not occur.

Family Educational Rights and Privacy Act (FERPA)   A law that aims to protect students' educational records.

FDE   *See* full-disk encryption (FDE).

Federal Information Security Management Act (FISMA)   A regulation that defines how federal agencies should protect their information systems.

FERPA   *See* Family Educational Rights and Privacy Act (FERPA).

file reputation   A score assigned to a file based on its calculated trustworthiness. Talos Intelligence and Microsoft SmartScreen employ file reputation techniques.

file retrospection   A Cisco AMP feature that detects when permitted files are later determined to be malicious. If brand-new malware gets into your network and is deemed malicious days later, file retrospection generates an alert.

file system permissions   Rules defined on file system objects (files and directories) that define who can do what.

File Transfer Protocol (FTP)   A protocol that is used to facilitate the transfer of files between computers on a network. It provides a standard set of commands and protocols for uploading, downloading, and managing files on remote servers.

filesystem scanning   Searching through the contents of storage media for files that match malware signatures.

FileVault   Apple's implementation of full-disk encryption (FDE) for macOS.

fire damage   Any type of damage that is caused by a fire.

firewall   A network security device that acts as a barrier between an internal network and external networks, such as the Internet. It monitors and controls incoming and outgoing network traffic based on predefined security rules and policies. Firewalls play a critical role in network security by protecting the network from unauthorized access, malicious activities, and potential threats.

firmware   Software code embedded in electronic devices that provides instructions for their operation.

FISMA   *See* Federal Information Security Management Act (FISMA).

forensic imaging   An identical, bit-for-bit copy of data.

forward proxy server   A server that acts as an intermediary between client devices and the Internet. When a client device, such as a computer or mobile device, requests access to a resource on the Internet, it sends the request to the forward proxy instead of directly connecting to the target server. The forward proxy then forwards the request to the target server on behalf of the client and returns the response back to the client.

FTP   *See* File Transfer Protocol (FTP).

full backup   A complete backup of all data, regardless of what data has or hasn't changed.

full-disk encryption (FDE)   A confidentiality control that protects stored data by encrypting everything written to disk.

full malware scan   A scan that exhaustively searches through the contents of a filesystem. Full scans tend to be slower but more accurate than quick scans.

full simulation   A test for DRPs and BCPs in which all (or most) personnel and systems are involved in testing plans against a fictional scenario.

fuzzy hash   A file fingerprint that is less change-sensitive than a cryptographic hash and that can detect similarities in file contents.

G–H

GDPR   *See* General Data Protection Regulation (GDPR).

General Data Protection Regulation (GDPR)   A European regulation that seeks to protect the rights of EU citizens.

gray hat hacker   A hacker who uses their skills for good and/or bad, depending on how you look at it.

hacker   Someone who has the skills needed to breach systems and steal data by exploiting any number of vulnerabilities that exist.

hacktivist   A person or group that attacks for social or political purposes.

hardening   The act of fixing vulnerabilities in an environment to eliminate or reduce the risk associated with a threat that could exploit a vulnerability.

hashing   A one-way process in which a hash is generated from data and can be used for confidentiality purposes or integrity purposes.

Health Insurance Portability and Accountability Act (HIPAA)   A U.S. regulation that aims to protect the privacy and security of patient information.

HIPAA   *See* Health Insurance Portability and Accountability Act (HIPAA).

honeypot   A security mechanism used to detect, deflect, or study unauthorized access attempts or malicious activity within a network or system. It is essentially a decoy or trap that is designed to attract and deceive attackers and that provides valuable insights into attackers' methods, motives, and techniques.

host-based firewall   Software installed on individual systems to restrict incoming and outgoing network traffic.

hot site   An alternate site with all hardware, infrastructure, and personnel needed to resume operation immediately.

HTTP   *See* Hypertext Transfer Protocol (HTTP).

human-caused disaster   Disruptive event caused or controlled by human activity.

Hypertext Transfer Protocol (HTTP)   An application-layer protocol used for transmitting and receiving web-based content. It enables communication between web clients (such as web browsers) and web servers. HTTP operates at the application layer of the TCP/IP stack.

I

ICMP   *See* Internet Control Message Protocol (ICMP).

Identity Services Engine (ISE)   A comprehensive Cisco NAC solution that provides centralized policy management, authentication, and access control for network devices.

IDS   *See* intrusion detection system (IDS).

immutable media   Storage media, such as CD-R and DVD-R disks, that can be written to only once. Data on immutable media cannot be encrypted or destroyed by malware.

impact   In qualitative risk analysis, the estimated damage of a risk occurring.

implicit-deny principle   A principle that says to implicitly deny access to everyone and everything unless they are explicitly allowed.

import hashing   A signature generation technique that hashes an application's imported libraries and functions to generate a fingerprint.

incident   A violation (or potential violation) of security policies or practices.

incident response   The process of identifying, analyzing, and responding to incidents.

incident response team (IRT)   A group of people (often interdisciplinary) charged with preparing for and responding to incidents.

incremental backup A partial backup of data that has changed since the last full or incremental backup.

indicator A sign that an incident is occurring or has occurred.

information sharing and analysis center (ISAC) An organization that facilitates information sharing between members of the same industry.

inoculation Patching of uninfected systems to ensure that they aren't affected by a malware outbreak.

insider A person or group within an organization that poses a threat to the CIA of that environment.

insider threat Any accidental or malicious threat that an organization could face from an insider.

integrity A component of the CIA triad that focuses on ensuring that data is accurate, authentic, and in the state it should be in.

Internet Control Message Protocol (ICMP) A protocol that is primarily used for diagnostics and error reporting in IP networks. It allows network devices to send control messages, such as echo requests (pings) and error notifications, and even trace the path through a network (traceroute). ICMP is an Internet layer protocol.

Internet Protocol Security *See* IPsec.

Internet Protocol version 4 (IPv4) The fourth version of the Internet Protocol, which is responsible for addressing and routing packets with routers across networks. It uses 32-bit addresses, allowing for approximately 4.3 billion unique addresses for devices around the world. It operates at the Internet layer of the TCP/IP stack, and it is the foundation of Internet communication.

Internet Protocol version 6 (IPv6) The successor to IPv4, which is designed to overcome the limitations of address exhaustion in IPv4. It uses 128-bit addresses, allowing for a significantly larger number of unique addresses. It is responsible for addressing and routing packets across networks, and it operates at the Internet layer of the TCP/IP stack.

Internet of Things (IoT) The generic name that has been given to all Internet-enabled devices.

intrusion detection system (IDS) A device that passively monitors network traffic, looking for suspicious patterns or indicators of malicious activity. It analyzes network packets, system logs, and other data sources to identify potential security incidents. When an IDS detects an anomaly or a known attack signature, it generates an alert to notify administrators or security personnel.

intrusion prevention system (IPS) A device that actively prevents and blocks malicious activities. This can involve blocking network traffic, dropping malicious packets, or reconfiguring network devices to protect against the identified threats.

IoT *See* Internet of Things (IoT).

IPS *See* intrusion prevention system (IPS).

IPsec A framework that helps provide secure communication over IP networks. It is widely used for establishing virtual private networks to ensure confidentiality, integrity, and authentication of all network traffic.

IPv4 *See* Internet Protocol version 4 (IPv4).

IPv6 *See* Internet Protocol version 6 (IPv6).

IRT *See* incident response team (IRT).

ISAC *See* information sharing and analysis center (ISAC).

ISE *See* Identity Services Engine (ISE).

J–K–L

jumping fences Scaling fences to gain access to areas.

key logger Malware designed to capture the user's keystrokes.

least-privilege principle A principle that says to give users the minimum permissions they need to accomplish their objectives.

lessons learned A review of a process (such as incident response) after the fact to learn and continually improve.

likelihood In qualitative risk analysis, the estimated probability of a risk occurring.

local backup A backup that is kept in physical proximity to the primary data. Compared to remote backups, local backups are typically faster but offer less protection against disaster scenarios.

lock breaking Breaking a lock to gain access to an unauthorized area.

lock bumping Bumping lock pins in a lock to gain access to an unauthorized area.

lock picking Picking a lock to gain access to an unauthorized area.

logic bomb A type of malware that is designed to trigger/execute at a specific time or based on a specific condition.

M

MAC address A unique identifier assigned to a network interface card (NIC) at the data link layer to facilitate the identification of devices within a local network. Switches use the destination MAC address listed in a frame to make forwarding decisions.

MAC address filtering A security feature used on wireless networks to control access based on the unique Media Access Control (MAC) addresses (hardware addresses) of devices.

malvertising A type of social engineering attack that is also a physical attack that takes advantage of people's curiosity or need to get a great deal.

malware Any type of software that is malicious.

malware signature   The fingerprint of a malware sample that is used to identify the presence of that malware on other systems.

MAM   *See* mobile application management (MAM).

MCM   *See* mobile content management (MCM).

MD5   *See* Message Digest 5 (MD5).

MDM   *See* mobile device management (MDM).

Media Access Control address   *See* MAC address.

MEM   *See* mobile email management (MEM).

Message Digest 5 (MD5)   The Message Digest version 5 hashing algorithm.

MFA   *See* multifactor authentication (MFA).

mirrored site   An identical, fully synchronized copy of the primary site; mirrored sites are highly expensive but allow for instantaneous failover.

mobile application management (MAM)   Software that enables IT professionals to deploy, manage, and secure mobile applications.

mobile content management (MCM)   Software that provides secure, easy sharing of data to and from mobile devices.

mobile device management (MDM)   Software that enables IT professionals to control, configure, and monitor mobile devices.

mobile email management (MEM)   Software that allows administrators to manage and secure emails and apply security controls to email applications.

mobile site   A preconfigured, transportable alternate site typically housed in a trailer or shipping container.

multifactor authentication (MFA)   A type of authentication that involves using two or more authentication factors in order to authenticate.

N

NAC   *See* network access control (NAC).

NAT   *See* Network Address Translation (NAT).

nation-state attacker   *See* cyberterrorist.

National Vulnerability Database (NVD)   A database of vulnerabilities and vulnerability management information maintained by the U.S. government.

natural disaster   Natural disruptive events that humans do not cause and cannot control.

need-to-know principle   A principle that says to give users access to what they absolutely need to do their jobs and perform their roles.

netstat   A command-line tool that displays open connections, listeners, and protocol statistics.

network access control (NAC)   A security framework that ensures only authorized and compliant devices gain access to a network infrastructure. It helps organizations enforce security policies, mitigate risks, and protect against unauthorized access and threats. NAC typically involves a combination of hardware and software components that work together to establish and enforce access control policies.

Network Address Translation (NAT)   A service that can convert a private RFC 1918 address that is routable only on private networks into a public IP address that is routable on the Internet.

network-based antimalware   Antimalware that scans network traffic for malicious files.

network layer   The layer of the OSI model where Internet Protocol (IP) operates. This layer also handles the routing and forwarding of data packets across interconnected networks.

next-generation firewall (NGFW)   A network security device that builds on the capabilities of a traditional firewall by incorporating additional features and technologies to provide enhanced security and advanced threat protection by offering several key advancements over a traditional firewall.

NGFW   *See* next-generation firewall (NGFW).

nslookup   A command-line tool for testing DNS queries and responses.

NVD   *See* National Vulnerability Database (NVD).

O

offline backup   A backup that is not network connected, which protects against ransomware and other threats that often target mounted backups.

off-site backup   A backup that isn't stored in proximity to the systems it protects; it is stored in another state or geographic region.

Online Certificate Status Protocol (OSCP)   An Internet protocol defined in RFC 6960 that can be used to get the current revocation status of a single X.509 certificate.

on-path attack   An attack in which the attacker intercepts communications by placing themself between two communicating devices.

on-site backup   A backup that is stored in proximity to the systems it protects—in the same building or locality.

operational intelligence   Intelligence with a moderate scope, such as a threat actor's tactics, techniques, and procedures (TTPs).

OSCP   *See* Online Certificate Status Protocol (OSCP).

OSI (Open Systems Interconnection) reference model   A conceptual framework that standardizes and describes the functions and interactions of a communication system.

P

packet capture (PCAP)   A file that contains captured network traffic (often generated by tcpdump or Wireshark).

partial simulation   A test for DRPs and BCPs in which a subset of personnel and systems are used to test plans against a fictional scenario.

passive scanner   A vulnerability scanner that relies on monitoring normal traffic and does not generate traffic.

Payment Card Industry Data Security Standard (PCI-DSS)   An industry standard enforced by all major credit card companies.

PCAP   *See* packet capture (PCAP).

PCI-DSS   *See* Payment Card Industry Data Security Standard (PCI-DSS).

Personal mode   A method of authenticating individual users or devices accessing a network by using pre-shared keys.

phishing   An email-based attack that attempts to convince the receiver to click a link and provide confidential or personally identifiable information or open an attachment so that malware is installed on the system.

physical layer   This layer of the OSI model that deals with the physical transmission of data through network cables, wireless signals, or other media. It defines the electrical, mechanical, and functional specifications for transmitting raw bits across the network.

piggybacking   A type of social engineering attack that involves an unauthorized person—the attacker—gaining access to an authorized area by using an authorized person(s)—the victim(s). The victim thinks they are helping someone who has a legitimate need to enter the area.

PKI   *See* public key infrastructure (PKI).

port scanning   Scanning that enumerates available hosts, which ports they have open, and (commonly) version information.

PowerShell   A newer and more feature-filled command-line interface (CLI) used for managing Windows.

precursor   A sign that an incident may occur in the future.

presentation layer   The layer of the OSI model that is responsible for data representation, encryption, and compression. It ensures that data exchanged between applications is in a format that both applications can understand.

pre-shared key (PSK)   A password or passphrase shared among all users and devices that is used to authenticate to a wireless network.

preventive control   A control that tries to block risk events from happening (for example, a firewall blocking many potential attacks).

privilege escalation   The process of gaining privileges one is not entitled to. It is a technique that attackers use to expand their control over systems.

PSK *See* pre-shared key (PSK).

public key infrastructure (PKI) A set of identities, roles, policies, and actions for the creation, use, management, distribution, and revocation of digital certificates.

public/private key pair Two related keys that are used for asymmetric cryptography.

Q

qualitative risk analysis A type of analysis that involves generating a relative risk score based on likelihood and impact. (*See* likelihood, impact)

quantitative risk analysis A type of analysis that involves generating an estimated annual cost, called the annualized loss expectancy (ALE). ALE is calculated by multiplying the single-loss expectancy (SLE) by the annualized rate of occurrence (ARO). (*See* annualized loss expectancy, annualized rate of occurrence, and single loss expectancy)

quarantine Steps taken to keep infected and uninfected systems separate.

quick malware scan A scan that searches through areas where malware is commonly found. Quick scans tend to be faster than full malware scans.

R

RADIUS *See* Remote Access Dial-In User Service (RADIUS).

RADIUS server A device that acts as a central authority responsible for authenticating and authorizing users attempting to connect to a wireless network.

rainbow table attack An attack in which the attacker uses rainbow tables, which are pre-computed sets of hash values for different possible passwords. The attacker compares captured password hashes with entries in the rainbow table to quickly determine the password corresponding to a specific hash.

ransomware Malware that is designed to hold systems and data for ransom.

RAT *See* remote access Trojan.

real-time antimalware Antimalware functions that scan data as it is interacted with (such as after it is downloaded or when it is opened).

recovery point objective (RPO) The maximum data loss a business can accept (that is, the earliest acceptable point in time at which data can be recovered).

recovery time objective (RTO) The maximum acceptable amount of time a system or business function can be disrupted.

recreational attacker Someone who attacks computer systems or networks for fun or curiosity rather than for financial gain or malice.

Remote Access Dial-In User Service (RADIUS) A client/server protocol used for incorporating authentication, authorization, and accounting into an environment.

remote access Trojan   A type of Trojan (*see* Trojan horse) that creates a backdoor into a system once it is executed.

remote-access VPN   A type of VPN connection that enables individual users or devices to securely access a private network from a remote location over the Internet.

remote backup   A backup that is kept away from the primary data (such as in another state or region). Remote backups are generally slower than local backups because they must be transferred over the Internet. However, they offer better protection against disasters.

remote monitoring and management (RMM)   A tool commonly used by IT service providers that provides monitoring, configuration, patching, inventorying, and other features for enrolled assets.

reverse proxy server   A server that sits between client devices on the Internet and web servers in a data center, acting as an intermediary for inbound Internet traffic. Unlike a forward proxy, which handles outbound traffic, a reverse proxy manages incoming requests from Internet clients and forwards them to the appropriate backend servers. The reverse proxy receives the requests on behalf of the servers and sends back the responses to the clients.

risk   The probability or chance that anyone or anything could exploit a vulnerability in an environment.

risk acceptance   A risk management strategy that involves accepting the presence of a risk and doing nothing. Often chosen when responses are more costly than the risk itself.

risk avoidance   A risk management strategy that involves eliminating a risk by avoiding the asset or system associated with it (for example, avoiding web server attacks by not maintaining a website).

risk management   A business activity that aims to identify, prioritize, and respond to risks.

risk mitigation   A response to risk that involves reducing (but not eliminating) risk; any steps taken to reduce the potential impact of a risk.

risk transference   A risk management strategy that involves transferring some risk to another party (for example, cyber insurance).

Rivest, Shamir, and Adleman (RSA)   An asymmetric algorithm used primarily for authentication.

RMM   *See* remote monitoring and management (RMM).

rogue access point   An unauthorized wireless access point (AP) that has been deployed within a network without proper authorization or knowledge, for either malicious or non-malicious purposes.

rootkit   Malware designed to provide an attacker with administrative-level access to a system and potentially gain access to parts of the system that only the operating system would normally have access to.

RPO   *See* recovery point objective (RPO).

RSA   *See* Rivest, Shamir, and Adleman (RSA).

RTO   *See* recovery time objective (RTO).

S

salting   The process of adding random characters on the fly as part of the hashing process to ensure unique hashes.

sandboxing   The process of creating a segmented environment for safely testing software (for instance, to observe malware behavior).

SCAP   *See* Security Content Automation Protocol (SCAP).

screened subnet (DMZ)   A separate network segment that acts as a buffer zone between an internal trusted network and an external untrusted network, such as the Internet.

script kiddie   Someone who takes advantage of already existing tools and scripts that are available on the Internet and Dark Web and has limited knowledge or skills to create their own tools or scripts.

Secure Hash Algorithm (SHA)   A family of hashing algorithms with different bit lengths.

Secure Shell (SSH)   A protocol that provides secure encrypted communication and secure remote administration of network devices and systems. It allows users to establish secure command-line, file transfer (SFTP), and tunneling sessions over an unsecured network.

security automation, orchestration, and response (SOAR)   Tools that help streamline and automate security operations.

Security Content Automation Protocol (SCAP)   A constellation of complementary standards used to evaluate system vulnerabilities and compliance.

security information and event management (SIEM)   A system that helps collect logs, consolidate logs, correlate logs, and get notified about abnormalities/threats in logs that are in breach of established policies.

security orchestration, automation, and response (SOAR)   A tool that helps you automate responses and reduce the amount of human intervention when an abnormality/threat has been detected.

service set identifier (SSID)   A unique name assigned to a wireless network to identify it among other nearby networks. It acts as the wireless network's name.

session layer   The layer of the OSI model that establishes, manages, and terminates communication sessions between applications. It enables processes running on different devices to establish a dialogue and coordinate their communication.

SHA   *See* Secure Hash Algorithm (SHA).

shared secret key   A password, passphrase, or random characters that all parties know.

SIEM   *See* security information and event management (SIEM).

single loss expectancy (SLE)   The expected cost of a single risk occurrence.

site-to-site VPN   A type of VPN connection that allows two or more separate networks in different physical locations to securely communicate with each other over the Internet.

SLE   *See* single loss expectancy (SLE).

small office/home office (SOHO)   A type of network setup in which individuals or businesses operate from their residences or small office spaces.

smishing   A social engineering attack in which an attacker texts a victim and attempts to compromise them via text.

SOAR   *See* security orchestration, automation, and response (SOAR).

social engineering   An attack that is accomplished through human interaction, taking advantage of people's tendency to be kind and helpful and tricking them.

SOHO   *See* small office/home office (SOHO).

something you are   An authentication factor based on unique aspects of yourself that relies on biometrics.

something you do   An authentication factor based on habits and characteristics.

something you have   An authentication factor based on possession.

something you know   An authentication factor based on knowledge.

somewhere you are   An authentication factor based on location.

spammer   Malware software that is designed to send unsolicited messages to as many people as it can by using tools like email, instant messaging, and newsgroups.

spear phishing   A more targeted type of phishing attack in which the attacker researches their intended victims ahead of time and targets them more directly.

ssdeep   A fuzzy hashing algorithm that divides files into smaller sections and calculates their hashes piece-by-piece.

SSH   *See* Secure Shell (SSH).

SSID   *See* service set identifier (SSID).

standard ACL   A type of IPv4 ACL that only matches the source address of a packet.

state-sponsored attacker   *See* cyberterrorist.

STIX   *See* Structured Threat Information Expression (STIX).

strategic intelligence   Intelligence with an expansive scope, such as trends across many threat actors.

Structured Threat Information Expression (STIX)   A standard that allows threat intelligence to be expressed using machine-readable JSON.

symmetric cryptography   A type of cryptography that requires a single key for both encryption and decryption.

syslog   A format used to arrange log information, as well as a protocol used to transmit it to other devices (such as syslog servers).

T

tabletop exercise   A test for DRPs and BCPs in which team members gather, are presented with a scenario, and talk through how they would respond to a fictional scenario.

tactical intelligence   Intelligence with a tight scope, such as specific attack identifiers.

tactics, techniques, and procedures (TTP)   The behaviors of attackers.

tailgating   A type of social engineering attack that involves an unauthorized person—the attacker—gaining access to an authorized area by using an authorized person(s)—the victim(s). The victim does not know that the attacker has slipped in behind them.

TAXII   *See* Trusted Automated Exchange of Intelligence Information (TAXII).

TCP   *See* Transmission Control Protocol (TCP).

TCP/IP stack   Also known as the Internet Protocol suite, a set of communication protocols that form the foundation of the Internet and many other computer networks.

tcpdump   A command-line tool used to capture and analyze network traffic.

Telnet   A protocol that is used to establish a remote terminal connection between a client and a server over a network. It allows users to log into a remote host and access its command-line interface.

theft   The act of stealing an asset from an organization.

threat   Anyone or anything that could exploit vulnerabilities in an environment.

threat actor   A person or group that intends to cause harm.

threat intelligence   Information about threats that has been enriched through analysis, aggregation, or correlation.

ThreatGrid   The Cisco threat intelligence and malware analysis platform. ThreatGrid has cloud and on-premises deployment options.

Transmission Control Protocol (TCP)   A reliable and connection-oriented transport protocol that operates at the transport layer of the TCP/IP stack. It ensures that data sent over the network reaches the intended destination accurately and in the correct order.

transport layer   The layer of the OSI model and TCP/IP stack that ensures reliable and efficient end-to-end data delivery between applications running on different devices. The most widely used transport protocol in the TCP/IP stack and OSI model is Transmission Control Protocol (TCP), which provides features such as error correction, flow control, and congestion control. Another transport protocol is User Datagram Protocol (UDP), which is a connectionless and lightweight alternative.

transport mode   An IPsec mode that encapsulates only the payload of the IP packet.

treatment   Removal of malware from a system. This may involve manually deleting malware components or simply wiping the affected system.

Triple Data Encryption Standard (3DES)   A symmetric key encryption algorithm that is an extension of DES and uses three keys instead of one.

Trojan horse   A malicious program or file disguised as a legitimate program or file that tricks the victim into executing the Trojan, thinking it is legitimate. Trojans typically do not replicate like viruses and worms do.

true negative   An event isn't detected, and it did not occur.

true positive   An event is detected, and it occurred.

Trusted Automated Exchange of Intelligence Information (TAXII)   A transport mechanism for STIX-formatted threat intelligence that supports collections (request/response architecture) and channels (publisher/subscriber architecture).

TTP   *See* tactics, techniques, and procedures (TTP).

tunnel mode   An IPsec mode that encapsulates the entire original IP packet, including the original IP header.

two-step authentication   An authentication concept that involves using two or more steps in order to authenticate.

U–V

UDP   *See* User Datagram Protocol (UDP).

unethical hacker   A hacker who uses their skills for bad, in an unlawful and unjust manner.

User Datagram Protocol (UDP)   A connectionless and lightweight transport protocol that operates at the transport layer of the TCP/IP stack. It provides for faster transmission of data between communicating devices compared to TCP but does not offer the reliability and error-correction mechanisms of TCP. Therefore, UDP is commonly used for real-time streaming, VoIP, and DNS.

vehicle ramming   Driving a vehicle into a building to gain access to an unauthorized area.

virtual private network (VPN)   A technology that allows you to create a secure and encrypted connection over a less secure network, such as the Internet. It essentially extends a private network across a public network, enabling users to send and receive data as if their devices were directly connected to the private network.

virus   Malware that is designed to insert its code (payload) into a system's programs and files and lives within a document or an executable file, and remaining dormant, until some type of human interaction occurs to launch its attack and cause it to spread to other systems.

vishing   A social engineering attack in which an attacker calls a victim and attempts to compromise them over the phone.

volatility   How quickly data degrades and disappears on a system.

VPN   *See* virtual private network (VPN).

vulnerability   A weakness in any part of an enterprise that, if exploited, could jeopardize the confidentiality, integrity, or availability of the systems and the data.

vulnerability scanner   An automated tool that performs tests against defined hosts or network ranges, looking for signs of vulnerabilities.

W–X–Y–Z

war driving   A technique used to discover and map wireless networks by driving around in a vehicle equipped with a Wi-Fi-enabled device, such as a laptop or smartphone. The purpose of war driving is to identify vulnerable or unsecured wireless networks for potential exploitation or unauthorized access.

warm site   An alternate site with most hardware and systems available but that requires some setup and configuration during disaster recovery.

water damage   Any type of damage that is caused by water.

WEP   *See* Wired Equivalent Privacy (WEP).

whaling   A phishing attack that targets a high-profile person, such as a CEO, CFO, CTO, or CISO.

Wi-Fi Protected Access (WPA)   A wireless security protocol designed to be the successor to WEP. WPA introduced stronger encryption and security mechanisms, such as Temporal Key Integrity Protocol (TKIP).

Wi-Fi Protected Access 2 (WPA2)   A current standard for wireless network security. It is an improvement over WPA and offers stronger encryption and authentication methods. WPA2 uses Advanced Encryption Standard (AES).

Wi-Fi Protected Access 3 (WPA3)   The latest generation wireless security protocol. It uses AES and provides enhanced security features compared to its predecessors, WPA and WPA2.

Wi-Fi Protected Setup (WPS)   A network security standard designed to simplify the process of connecting devices to a Wi-Fi network.

Wired Equivalent Privacy (WEP)   An encryption protocol used to secure wireless networks. It was introduced as the first standard encryption method for Wi-Fi networks.

worm   Standalone, self-replicating, malicious software that wreaks havoc and spreads without human intervention through vulnerabilities in other software.

WPA   *See* Wi-Fi Protected Access (WPA).

WPA2   *See* Wi-Fi Protected Access 2 (WPA2).

WPA3   *See* Wi-Fi Protected Access 3 (WPA3).

WPA3 Enhanced Open   A method of providing encryption and privacy on open, non-password-protected networks.

WPS *See* Wi-Fi Protected Setup (WPS).

WPS PIN attack An attack in which the attacker tries different PIN combinations until they discover the correct one when the Wi-Fi network uses Wi-Fi Protected Setup (WPS).

YARA A language that can define various file characteristics of malware samples.

Index

Numerics

A

G

H

I

J-K

L

Q

R